MALTA'S GREATER SIEGE

&

ADRIAN WARBURTON

DSO* DFC** DFC (USA)

This book is dedicated to all of the men, women and children who gave their lives in Malta – or in its support – during its Greater Siege. Especially remembered are the 2,301 Commonwealth airmen who were lost, flying from bases in the Mediterranean theatre during the Second World War, and who have no known grave. They are commemorated on the Malta Memorial in Floriana.

PROPOSITI INSULA TENAX TENACES VIROS COMMEMORAT
An island resolute of purpose remembers resolute men.

Also remembered is Jack Vowles (28 June 1921–15 January 2015)

MALTA'S GREATER SIEGE

&

ADRIAN WARBURTON

DSO* DFC** DFC (USA)

'The Most Valuable Pilot in the RAF'

Paul McDonald

Pen & Sword
AVIATION

First published in Great Britain in 2015
and reprinted in this format in 2021 by
Pen & Sword Aviation
an imprint of
Pen & Sword Books Ltd
47 Church Street
Barnsley
South Yorkshire
S70 2AS

ISBN 978 1 52679 683 7

A CIP catalogue record for this book is available from the British Library

Typeset in Ehrhardt by
Mac Style Ltd, Bridlington, East Yorkshire
Printed and bound in the UK by CPI Group (UK) Ltd,
Croydon, CR0 4YY

Pen & Sword Books Ltd incorporates the imprints of Pen & Sword
Archaeology, Atlas, Aviation, Battleground, Discovery, Family History,
History, Maritime, Military, Naval, Politics, Railways, Select, Transport,
True Crime, and Fiction, Frontline Books, Leo Cooper, Praetorian Press,
Seaforth Publishing and Wharncliffe.

For a complete list of Pen & Sword titles please contact
PEN & SWORD BOOKS LIMITED
47 Church Street, Barnsley, South Yorkshire, S70 2AS, England
E-mail: enquiries@pen-and-sword.co.uk
Website: www.pen-and-sword.co.uk

Contents

Plates

E very effort has been made to trace copyright owners and obtain permission for photographs used; however, the provenance of some is uncertain. If there have been any errors or omissions we apologise and will be pleased to make appropriate acknowledgements in any future editions.

Some photographs are UK MOD Crown Copyright and have been released under the Open Government License (OGL). Their publication in this book does not imply any endorsement or official sanction for the book.

Photographs not credited are from the author's own collection.

Acknowledgements

Via Frederick Galea: 10, 19–21, 26–37, 44
UK MOD: 1, 12–14, 48–9, 52, 58–60, 67
Lynda Studdert-Kennedy: 22–5, 42–3, 46–7
Ordnance Survey: 53–4
RAF Museum: 17–18, 41, 45
Keith Bastard: 15–16
Ivan Berryman: 55–6
Tim Callaway: 51, 57
Alan Bovingdon Cox: 50
Brian Crook: 80
Fiona Vella: 69

Maps

Acknowledgements

The first to write about Adrian Warburton was the journalist Roy Nash, in the 1950s. Tony Spooner then went on to produce *Warburton's War* some thirty years later. But for Tony's efforts, Adrian Warburton would probably have been long forgotten. I fully acknowledge the value of Roy and Tony's work.

I am especially grateful to my good friends in Malta, Frederick and Valerie Galea. Frederick is a well-known Second World War historian and writer, and he very kindly gave me permission to quote from his books. He also made many photographs available. As Honorary Secretary of the National War Museum Association of Malta and a founder member of the Malta Aviation Museum, Frederick has done a great deal to ensure stories of Malta's war made it into print. His books and other collaborative projects, together with the work of his colleagues in Malta, make a valuable contribution to Maltese and British history. Both Frederick and Valerie are also important characters in their own right in this story.

Thanks are also due to Michael Longyear for permission to quote from his childhood reminiscences of growing up on an island at war. Peter Elliot, Head of Archives at the RAF Museum, has also been of great help in allowing me access to unpublished material, photographs and scrapbooks. Some documents quoted in this work are contained within official British Government records held at the National Archives in Kew. These are Crown Copyright and their use is in accordance with the Open Government Licence.

Three airmen of the period offered first-hand recollections: an Englishman, a Canadian and an American. I met Jack Vowles in 2013. He was 92-years-old and living in a nursing home in Gloucestershire. I spent hours with Jack. His memories of wartime Malta and of Adrian Warburton were vivid and I very much looked forward to our discussions, and to going through his notes and sketch-maps, painstakingly prepared despite failing eyesight. Jack and I became firm friends. He was one of a number who paid tribute to Adrian at Durnbach in 2003 and at the Berinsfield Memorial dedication in 2004. I am most grateful to Lynda Studdert-Kennedy, Jack's eldest daughter, and to Nigel her husband, for spending so much time with me going through Jack's photographs and allowing me to use them.

Lieutenant General (Ret'd) William Keir 'Bill' Carr, CMM, DFC, OStJ, CD, RCAF was also ninety-two when we came into contact. His memory of Adrian and his views on leadership, and Warburton himself, are hugely important even today and

I am grateful for his permission to quote from his written work. My son Matthew, in Los Angeles, put me in touch with Scott Blyth, son of Lieutenant Colonel (Ret'd) John Blyth USAF, the pilot of *Spitfire 944*, portrayed in the acclaimed American short film of the same name. Through Scott I learnt of John's friendship with Adrian during the weeks he spent at Mount Farm before his final flight.

Two Maltese ladies who knew Christina personally have also been most helpful. As a child Miriam Farrugia was befriended by Christina, whose summer house in Bugibba was next door. Thank you Miriam for your moving words about the vibrant and vivacious lady you remember so well. Ingrid Scerri very kindly allowed me access to the roof of her Floriana apartment to see for myself the views Christina described so well in 1940. Thank you Ingrid and also for your memories of the English lady who lived around the corner when you were growing up.

Thanks also to Keith Bastard for making his late father's logbook extracts and photographs available. I am also grateful to Peter Woods for allowing me to look at his late father's logbook, and the photographs and scrapbook so carefully maintained by his late mother.

To Eman Bonnici, archivist at *Santa Maria Addolorata* cemetery, a special thank you; our meeting was accidental, but proved invaluable. Thank you for responding to my many questions and for your contacts. Sincere thanks also to Major Joseph Borg of the Malta Police Force and to the journalist Fiona Vella.

Many who attended Adrian's funeral in 2003 have been extremely helpful: Tim Callaway, Editor of *Aviation Classics*, Heidi Burton, née Cox, was the RAF photographer, Glyn Strong from the Veterans' Agency, and Sue Raftree from the Joint Compassionate and Casualty Centre at Innsworth. Sue very kindly forwarded my requests for information to Adrian's nephew, Charles Gethen, and to Shelia Hunt, daughter of Betty Westcott, née Warburton. Thanks also to Martin Ratcliffe, Christina's nephew, for sharing his memories of his aunt. I am also grateful to Alan Bovingdon Cox, President of the Ridgeway Military and Aviation Research Group, for sharing photographs and information, and for the time he spent with me at what was RAF Mount Farm. Thanks also to Dr Chris Joy, archivist at Manchester High School for Girls, for making available extracts from school records and magazines.

I am especially grateful to Anne Dowie for her support and for engaging the help of so many of her relatives and friends: in Malta, Lora Dimech, Tess Gatt, and the Buhagiar families; in the UK, Ruth Johnston and the Rose family. Thank you all very much. Nothing was too much trouble for Anne trying to put me in touch with others; it was through her that I was able to gain contact with Christina's friend, Miriam. Also through Anne, I was able to get in touch once more with a former colleague from XIII Squadron: Brian Crook. Thank you Brian, and Francesca, for your support and for the many photographs you took for me while you were both on holiday in Malta.

To John Miles, meteorological forecaster at RAF Linton-on-Ouse for over twenty years, I offer my special thanks for liaising with Mark Beswick, the Archive Information Officer at the National Meteorological Archive. Having obtained the actual weather and forecasts, both British and German, for Taranto on the days on either side of the Fleet Air Arm's attack, and also for Europe on the day Adrian was killed, it was John who spent time going through the charts, figures and symbols so I could come up with an accurate picture of the weather on those days.

To three good friends, all experienced and able former RAF flying instructors still teaching like me at RAF Linton-on-Ouse, I offer grateful thanks. John Houlton and Steve Pepper shared my enthusiasm for this project from the start and were of great help with the first draft. Brian Russell later spent many, many hours going through the final draft in fine detail. I would also like to thank my cousin, Juliet Foster, for her editorial advice and help in finding the real 'Warby and Chris'.

I owe a special thank you to Ivan Berryman for his permission to use two of his excellent paintings – *Tribute to Wing Commander Adrian Warburton* and *Prelude to Taranto* – to illustrate this work (www.ivanberrymandirect.com). I am also grateful for the help and support I received from Laura Hirst, Pen and Sword's Aviation commissioning editor, Ken Patterson, my editor, and designer Jon Wilkinson and all at Pen and Sword.

Very special thanks go to my wife Jackie for her support while living through yet another obsession, and to our children Matthew and Hannah for their encouragement. Matthew combined a broad perspective with a meticulous eye for detail. He designed the original jacket and collated and enhanced many of the images. Ever the perfectionist, his work on the maps was painstaking and most effective.

I was pleased Jack Vowles was able to read an early draft of this work, but sadly he was unable to see it through to its conclusion. He died after a short illness on 15 January 2015. *Sahha* Jack, and thank you.

York
August 2015

Author's Note: The spelling of place names in Malta can be problematic, with the letters 'k' and 'q' commonly used as alternatives. Ta' Qali and Takali, Qrendi and Krendi are often used, although neither captures the Maltese pronunciation. Some place names such as Hal Far and Ta' Qali are often presented as one word or two. Throughout this work Ta' Qali, Qrendi and Hal Far have been used.

Foreword

Bill Carr was 20-years-old when he flew a Spitfire PR Mark XI to Malta in 1943 to join 683 Squadron. His new commanding officer was Wing Commander Adrian Warburton. Bill first came across his new boss at the squadron dispersal, stretched out on a table drinking tea with the airmen, who quite obviously worshipped their 25-year-old boss. Bill soon realised the extraordinary tales about a man they called Warby were true.

Bill served on eleven squadrons and commanded two of them, but his memory of the extraordinary squadron commander he met in Malta never faded. By 1973, Lieutenant General William Keir 'Bill' Carr was Canada's Deputy Chief of Defence Staff. Following retirement in 1978, he was often referred to as the father of the modern Canadian Air Force. Twice he wrote articles about leadership in which he portrayed Adrian Warburton as an exemplary leader:

'Leadership is simply the ability to inspire others to achieve goals. The leader may establish the goals, but often the achievements of others are not in his or her hands. Yet, in the exercise of leadership, the leader perhaps *manages* how they are achieved. This is an over-simplification of a complex process, and usually the view of leadership by those being led is based on many factors, not the least of which is peer pressure.

'Humans need "recognition" and it is little different in peace or war. A person needs to be seen by his contemporaries as well as his superiors and subordinates to be carrying their fair share of the load. A member must feel that their contribution is what is expected of them and is up to the level of those around them involved in similar pursuits. For the warriors specifically, they need their fellow fighters to see that they too are a worthy comrade-in-arms.

'In my thirty-nine years of military service in peace and war, I saw good leaders and bad ones. The good ones inspired me. The bad ones confused and dispirited me. Indeed, some disgusted me. I do not profess to have a profound understanding of leadership, but I do believe that certain factors identify what the elusive subject involves. And I am firmly of the view that leaders are developed, not trained. Managers are trained.... Only one squadron commander ... stands out as the ideal, because:

- 'He inspired people to fly to their limits (not *his*) and to achieve objectives with zeal even though they might be killed.
- 'He had courage and wisdom. His wisdom was demonstrated continuously by the manner in which he survived, and if you listened to him, caused others to survive by making them *think*.
- 'He was a superb pilot but he didn't flaunt it, and he didn't in all humility, think he was as good technically as many of the squadron members.... .
- 'He demonstrated loyalty to his superiors and subordinates through being concerned about others, not himself.
- 'He was sensitive to people, their foibles and their differences.
- 'He demanded, expected, and got the best you could give – and then thanked you.
- 'He *did* have charisma, but he was not aware of it.
- 'He was an innovator but tried the new idea himself, whether he invented it or not, before accepting it. If it worked, he thanked the originator in front of his peers. If it did not, he thanked them privately and told them *why* it did not.
- 'He always put his service and his people before himself.... .
- 'He was not *outwardly* ambitious, nor, do I think *inwardly* selfishly ambitious.
- 'He fought for and got the best for his guys, and he knew all of us individually by our first names. We respected him as an airman, a commander, and as a man.
- 'He would not suffer fools, and he did not condone carelessness.
- 'He saved many "weak sisters" lives.... .
- 'He had the marks of greatness in his appearance, his approach, his "hell-raising", his stamina, his common sense, and his moral guts.'

Bill Carr
March 2015

Bill saw peace and war, and served at the very highest levels of command. He knew what attributes were needed in a squadron commander and he judged Adrian Warburton, whom he knew well, as exceptional. Adrian Warburton's attributes have stood the test of time. In March 2015, seventy-one years after Warburton's death, Bill's article about leadership, and a man they called Warby, was published once again in the *Canadian Military Journal*.

Paul McDonald
July 2015

Prologue: A Selfless Act

14 October 1942

How many more times was he going have to do this? He was stretching even his famed 'luck'. Couldn't they see he was sending them a message, asking them to follow him? Yet all they wanted to do was blast him out of the sky. He jinked left and right, changing his height to avoid the flak, yet trying to maintain a recognisable orbit. The tracer appeared to rise slowly at first, arcing gently upwards before accelerating rapidly, missing his cockpit by what seemed like inches. 'Flaming onions' René called them. Poor gallant René, those onions did for him and for young Jacques and George. Had it really been nearly two years ago? They were the first 69 Squadron crew to go in; so many had bought it since.

Here and now those 'flaming onions' were getting damnably close! The Eyetie gunners seemed more accurate each time he came back. He realised there were many more machine-gun bullets heading his way he couldn't see. There were also shell bursts from heavier guns. Where would the next dirty white and grey smudge appear, he wondered? From a distance they looked like harmless white puffs, almost like a cluster of mini-cumulus clouds. Up close and personal he could feel their force trying to pitch and roll his aircraft violently before his right hand teased the elevators and ailerons to calm his steed. Given his constant jinks, he hoped his flight path was proving difficult for the gunners to predict. He didn't want to get any closer to those 'harmless' puffs.

He had no real choice; he needed to circle the warship two or three times to make them realise he was sending them a message – a life or death message. After the third orbit he flew a straight course in the fervent hope they would follow him. So far they hadn't. Why had those damned Eyeties not cottoned on? They had of course, but it was a while before Adrian Warburton realised. He could hardly blame them for trying to shoot him down. After all, he was flying a Spitfire, a variant known as the PR IV, and he was circling a large Italian motor torpedo boat acting as escort to an armed Italian merchant ship. And Italy and Britain had been at war since June 1940.

Adrian rolled his aircraft's wings level once more. The well-harmonised controls responded crisply. They were beautifully balanced. No matter how often he flew the Spitfire he always got enormous pleasure from such a thoroughbred, a world-beater. He loved flying single-seat aircraft, although at one stage it looked as if his career as a pilot would be over before it began. He was a disaster in those days, and not just in the air. Was it only two years ago? It seemed like a lifetime, so much had happened since. Thank goodness for dear old Tich from 'down-under'. He had sorted him out. Without him, Adrian's piloting days would have ended long ago. He loved the freedom being a recce pilot gave him, a role perfectly designed for him, the loner. A lonely warrior; he smiled at the thought. At least in a single-seat aircraft, he no longer had to worry about his crew. Yet he realised things would have to change now he was in command of 69 Squadron: he would have to change. He also knew he would have to move out of the flat in Valletta – her flat. How would she react he wondered, although he knew she would understand when he explained that his crews were to be accommodated together in Sliema.

He still yearned every day to be airborne and often took aircraft assigned to others at very short notice. Some, like Harry, thought Adrian totally selfish. Few knew the real reason why he acted as he did. Malta's recce pilots, a tiny clique, were all highly intelligent men. When they compared notes it wouldn't take them long to realise, as he had done, that when they stumbled on enemy ships there was sometimes more to it than luck; of being in the right place at the right time. And, having found the enemy, why were they sometimes required to transmit details in clear? It wasn't always the case, and it certainly hadn't been like that in 1941, but it was now happening more often. Adrian knew he must limit his pilots' chat about this as best he could, try and preserve a secret even he was not privy to; a number of their missions were intelligence-led, designed to disguise a very different intelligence source. He often wondered what it was. For the moment though, the others could continue to call him selfish, or 'Lucky Warby', when he took trips allocated to others. He could live with that.

He headed north-west again. 'Please, please follow me,' he thought. After a couple of miles, Adrian looked back; they still seemed to be ignoring him, still following in the wake of the cargo ship heading at full steam for Tripoli. Rommel would be pleased. But the Italians weren't ignoring him.

Adrian had no choice; he had to try again – it was ingrained in his nature not to give up. He also knew he was their only hope. They were definitely alive, but they had no hope of rescue without his help. They were too far from land to be spotted before nightfall. They would last a few days but would eventually succumb to the inevitable: thirst which would slowly, but surely, become intolerable, and then exposure. It would not be a pleasant death. That was his greatest fear, to come down into a sunless sea and die slowly. Even his prowess as a swimmer would count for little if rescue was not near at hand. That was why he simply had to keep trying. Trying until he was down to his very last reserves of fuel before heading back home to Malta and to his battered base of Luqa on an equally battered island.

Adrian moved his left hand gently forward on the red-engraved throttle with the ivory handle. The response was instantaneous and immensely satisfying as the Rolls-Royce Merlin 45 engine, with its de Havilland metal three-bladed constant-speed propeller, wound up. It still made the hairs on the back of his neck stand up whenever he heard the unique sound of a Merlin engine. He hauled his aircraft into a high wing-over through 180 degrees and then back he went to the Italians. Maybe this time they would get the message, realise what he was trying to do. Yet, as he approached once again, it seemed they had not, as both ships' guns opened up on him once more. He was beginning to get a little irritated with this. Oh, come on you lot, do sharpen up! What do you think I'm doing? Offering some target practice in the middle of the Med?

He found himself thanking Supermarine for fitting leading edge fuel tanks – from wing roots toward the wing tips – to the recce Spitfire. He needed the extra fuel now, the extra endurance.

The day had begun like many others. The mission was routine. A routine war mission, was there such a thing? Three Beaufighters from 227 Squadron at Luqa were tasked against an Axis 2,000-ton merchant ship being escorted by a single Italian warship. They were somewhere off the coast of Tripolitania, one of three provinces in Mussolini's Italian Libya, his so-called new Roman Empire. Even old Benito might be having second thoughts about his empire these days, having lost so many ships crossing the *Mare Nostrum*, 'Our Sea', as he described it. The cargo ship was carrying supplies destined for Rommel's Afrika Korps. The ship must be sunk. That was Malta's primary role: attack, strike at Rommel's tenuous supply lines so the British 8th Army, now under Montgomery, could succeed in Egypt. 'When would Monty's attack begin?' everyone asked. 'Who would strike first?' Even a single Axis supply ship could make a difference. So they had to sink it.

It was a strange game. The RAF and the RN were doing their utmost to strangle Rommel's lifeline while Field Marshal Kesselring – 'Smiling Albert' – and the might of the Luftwaffe and the Regia Aeronautica were doing their utmost to do the same to Malta. If Allied convoys were stopped, Malta could not survive. Without Malta, the Allied campaign in North Africa was doomed. Sink their ships! That was Hugh Lloyd's directive from the moment he took over and now his successor Park had taken up the same cry. Warburton liked Lloyd, Hugh Pughe everyone called him, but not to his face; he was an individualist just like Adrian and gave Adrian a lot of slack; the New Zealander, Keith Park, was more of a team man.

The Beaufighter was a great attack and recce aircraft and a good fighter too, as Adrian knew from personal experience, but he loved his PR Spitfire, its solitude and its majesty. He could outrun any aircraft the Axis could throw against him, providing he saw them coming of course! That's why many of his colleagues wore scarves and silk cravats; it was not an affectation, but essential, given how you needed to keep your head moving, constantly scanning the sky for trouble, for the 'Hun in the Sun' as the posters put it. See the enemy was the requirement, and know where to look. In that lay the true art of the fighter pilot. It was not a gentlemanly dual of eagles, but a sneaky game using every conceivable tactic, all of your skill and guile, to strike fast and from on high, unnoticed by your enemy for just as long as it takes to blast him from the sky before he can react. Then get the hell out of it, as fast as you can.

They all hoped death, when it came, would be sudden, but often it was not. Sometimes it was slow and painful; you might see it coming yet be powerless to do anything about it. Adrian hoped when his end came, as he knew it would, he would not fall into the wide blue yonder, far from shore and out of sight of friends. As a recce pilot operating on his own, he suspected he would most likely die alone and unnoticed, far from friendly eyes. Chris would mourn his passing but he couldn't let himself dwell on the thought. It wasn't going to happen on this flight. Yet he knew it would, one day.

The Beaufighter was so much better than its predecessor, the Blenheim, whose crews were slaughtered. But they carried on undaunted; theirs was a conscious courage. The three 227 Squadron crews were experienced and able, confident in their aircraft and each other. The pilot of the lead aircraft was a squadron leader; a very capable operator decorated for bravery only a few days earlier. All would be well. All Adrian needed to do was record a successful strike with his cameras and they could all head home for tea and medals.

It hadn't quite worked out that way. The Italian crews saw them coming in the clear blue sky and their well-trained gunners were ready. As the Beaufighters performed their graceful, insanely low, coordinated attack the anti-aircraft fire was intense and deadly accurate. Whether the lead Beaufighter, with the tail letter 'Q' for Queen, was hit was unclear. Having attacked the merchant vessel with cannon fire, its bombs hung up. It may have hit a mast as it lifted above the ship's superstructure. What was very clear was what happened next. It exploded in the air only yards past the ship, and toppled into the sea in a great ball of flame, vividly red, horribly black, and terminal. The crew would have known for a second or two they were about to die. Their friends saw it all. Maybe the shocking loss of their leader put them off. The second aircraft – 'Y' for Yorker – straddled the ship's deck with cannon fire, but its bombs overshot. It departed to the north-west trailing smoke. 'H' for Hotel also attacked with cannon fire and Adrian observed hits on the ship's deck amidships. No bombs were dropped. Hotel made a second run but the bombs undershot. It could do little except exit stage right at speed and make its escape. Maybe theirs would be another day. The mission was an abject failure. There was little left for Adrian to record on his cameras except a merchant ship turning for Tripoli with its valuable cargo intact, destined for the Afrika Korps.

Adrian turned away, saddened by the deaths of friends. He gradually overtook poor Yorker trailing smoke, thickening smoke as the mortally wounded Beaufighter got lower and lower with every mile. They had no hope, they weren't going to make it back home, or to any other airfield for that matter. Nor would they make landfall. By now they were also too low to bale out. Ditching was their only option, a hazardous manoeuvre at best. The Beaufighter pilot did very well getting his dying aircraft down onto the water in one piece. As Adrian flew overhead he saw the crew of two, apparently unharmed, clambering into their small dinghy before their faithful Yorker slipped beneath the waves. Within seconds she was gone and they were on their own bobbing about in a tiny two-man dinghy, with a lone PR Spitfire circling helplessly above and little hope of rescue. Now what? They were much too far away from Malta and there was no possibility of any friendly ship passing nearby. Apart from the Axis ships just out of sight over the horizon, there was nothing on the wide expanse of the Mediterranean to offer any hope of salvation. The Beaufighter crew's deaths would be long and lingering. Unless... .

Surely life in an Italian prisoner-of-war camp was preferable to death at sea. Could he somehow get the Italians, so recently fighting for their own lives, to follow him and save the lives of their former assailants? How were the Italians likely to react to an attacker returning? Perhaps they would assume he had come back to guide others in for the kill? They gave Adrian their answer in no uncertain terms. He had circled the motor torpedo boat three times before setting course for the dinghy and then he flew round the dinghy three times, slightly higher and in sight of the Italians, before returning to the torpedo boat to do the whole thing again. So far his efforts were to no avail, except the Italian gunners seemed to be getting more proficient. His fuel was now becoming critical. Thank goodness for his aircraft's extra endurance, but even so this had to be his last throw of the dice. The Beaufighter crew deserved whatever chance he could give them.

Three times more he circled, ducking and weaving before setting course for the Beaufighter crew. After a mile or so he looked back. Hurrah! The Italians were at last following him! He flew low over the dinghy for the final time, waggling his wings and saw them waving. They knew he had found help. He just hoped they would not be too disappointed when they recognised the shape of their rescuer. The Italians would treat them well: they were honourable captors. Adrian pulled up into a wide orbit as the Italians got closer. He hung around for a little longer until he saw the Beaufighter crew hauled safely aboard the Italian vessel. At least the Eyeties had stopped shooting at him! There was a reason for that as Adrian was about to discover and it wasn't because they were busy rescuing the downed crew.

Now at last Adrian could set course for home. He had spent twenty minutes messing about since the failed strike. Or could he? Suddenly, out of nowhere, or so it seemed, six Italian Macchi fighters swooped towards him. Adrian had misjudged the game. He had not given the Italian captain enough credit. He had played a wily game, knowing all along what Adrian was doing, simply trying to keep Adrian loitering until he summoned the cream of the Regia Aeronautica from the Italian airbase at Homs on the coast east of Tripoli.

The Italian fighters approached fast from the south. They would have done better to have swung wide around him out of sight, to get between him and Malta.

Maybe their numbers made them overconfident, but with six they were definitely a threat. The Macchi was the best fighter the Italians had, but it was no match in combat against a Spitfire: a normal Spitfire. Alas he wasn't flying a normal Spitfire. The price his PR Spitfire paid for its extra speed, very high ceiling and extended endurance, was to have no guns, no armament of any kind. Not even any armour-plating. It relied wholly on speed and agility, and a good pair of hands. He would need all of these qualities in full measure, and especially the latter, if he was to make good his escape. Four of the enemy fighters got onto his tail, but they struggled to close the range to fire their guns and his powerful Merlin engine soon accelerated him out of trouble. Once clear he began a cruise climb, throttling back gently as he didn't have a great deal of fuel. He kept a wary eye on his six o'clock.

Adrian then lit a cigarette. It was his way of unwinding and he often smoked in the cockpit even though it was against the rules. He always made sure the oxygen was switched off first though! The lads who serviced his aircraft didn't seem to mind when they found his cigarette butts stuffed under his parachute. He reassured them he made sure they were 'out' before putting them down there. That usually made them laugh; he had always got on well with his ground crew. He well remembered the look on Jack's face when he met Adrian's Maryland and found Adrian sitting on his parachute balanced on a tin helmet. It was for, 'protection down there!' Adrian said. That was over a year ago. The airmen were a brilliant bunch. Not for them a posting to Egypt for a rest. When they arrived in Malta they were there for the duration and for much of their time it was hell on earth. Adrian missed Air Marshal Tedder's visit to the island in May when he had described the ground personnel as the spirit of Malta. Tedder was a good judge.

He finished his cigarette, carefully stubbed it out and pushed it easily beneath his parachute. He rarely did up the straps of his parachute anyway; there never seemed to be much point on a low-level mission. But perhaps he should ask for an ashtray to be fitted. He smiled at the thought.

He was going to be late. Chris would be worried. It was her watch on duty at Lascaris: D Watch. She had been captain of D Watch for ten long months. Like everyone else in 'the hole', she would be well aware he was overdue and two of the three Beaufighters had bought it. He knew she often worried about him. There was not a lot he could do about that. He often said to her he was safer in the air while everyone 'copped it' on the ground. He didn't know how the Maltese population had coped for so long on starvation rations under incessant bombing, but they had. They were a remarkable people.

He often worried about Chris; she was desperately thin when he got back from Egypt in August. Soon he was within range of Malta and in answer to his call he heard the deep, resonant and reassuring voice of Bill Farnes, the senior controller. He would soon be home; Chris would now relax as she moved his marker across the plot. Home for tea and medals. Would there be any tea, he wondered?

Chapter One

A Quest

I was at my desk in the NATO HQ at Ramstein in Germany one quiet April morning in 2003, when I received a call to say the remains of a wartime Royal Air Force (RAF) pilot had been found in the wreckage of his aircraft in Bavaria. The discovery brought to an end a fifty-nine year old mystery. The pilot was Wing Commander Adrian Warburton. I had never heard of him.

A military funeral was arranged with an interment at Durnbach, south of Munich. Warburton was evidently held in high regard as Air Marshal Sir Roderick 'Rocky' Goodall, my UK superior at Ramstein, represented the RAF's Chief of the Air Staff (CAS). The service on 14 May 2003 was taken by Squadron Leader the Reverend Alan Coates, Ramstein's RAF chaplain, and members of the Queen's Colour Squadron of the RAF Regiment were pallbearers. US military personnel formed an Honour Guard. I made a note to find out more about Warburton but, at the time, I never did.

A year later, when driving to Salzburg, I passed a sign to Durnbach. It rang a bell and I felt compelled to stop. Like similar cemeteries the world over, Durnbach is well looked after by the Commonwealth War Graves Commission. It was quiet, tranquil and quite beautiful, despite the poignancy and air of sadness. The majority of the 2,934 graves are of British and Commonwealth airmen. The ages of those who lay there gave me pause. I soon found the grave I sought:

WING COMMANDER
A WARBURTON
DSO & BAR DFC & 2 BARS
ROYAL AIR FORCE
12TH APRIL 1944 AGE 26
FOND MEMORIES OF
OUR SHORT TIME TOGETHER

Warburton's age was sadly not unusual – he was in good company. Neither was his rank at such a young age, given the circumstance of wartime service. His decorations, though, make him truly outstanding. What story could he tell, I wondered? Once again, at the time, I did nothing to find out about the man named on the headstone, the man behind the medals.

Five years later I read *Warburton's War* by Tony Spooner. I was struck by Warburton and our mutual associations with Malta and photo reconnaissance from Luqa, albeit over thirty years apart. I felt slightly unnerved, as I could relate to Adrian's struggle to become an operational pilot too. Like him, I taught ship recognition to colleagues which helped us each establish a reputation within our respective squadrons. After that the similarities between us faded rapidly. Adrian's experience was almost entirely of a service at war; my experience was one of a service largely at peace. I also felt slightly embarrassed. Despite my photo-reconnaissance background and being well read about RAF history, to my regret I had never heard of Adrian Warburton until that chance telephone call in 2003.

He was involved with an English dancer called Christina who became an aircraft plotter. She appeared to fill an important role in his life. I began to wonder about her too. What story could she tell? The link between a recce pilot in Malta and a plotter reminded me of a post-war film called *Malta Story*. My interest was further aroused when I read three short stories under the title *Carve Malta on my heart and other wartime stories*. Published by the Maltese writer and researcher on the air battle, Frederick Galea, the opening story is about Christina. It left me with many questions. Increasingly I reflected on my own association with the island.

I first saw Malta through the small windows of an RAF VC10. The tiny walled fields and the rocky, waterless landscape made an immediate impression. The sun's brightness and the heat hit us like a wave as we exited the aircraft. It was Wednesday, 27 August 1975, and a blisteringly hot day, such a change from the mild summer weather we had left behind at RAF Brize Norton. There was a lot to take in. Luqa was Malta's international airport and nothing like the RAF airfields with which I was familiar. Everything was light brown; even the uniforms of the airmen were stone in colour, matching the many walls. The countryside was sun-baked, dry and dusty, with no signs of crops or greenery except for clumps of prickly pear. Many of the villages dotted around had high-domed churches.

Luqa opened in 1940. It was difficult to imagine it as one of the most heavily bombed airfields anywhere in the Second World War. The control tower, not the wartime original, was south-east of Runway 24/06, Luqa's single useable runway at the time. Behind the tower was a low flat-roofed building with a second storey in the middle. This was the HQ of my new squadron: XIII Squadron. I was a 26-year-old married flying officer, a pilot, and about to embark on my second tour. The dispersals contained the unmistakeable shape of my new aircraft, reconnaissance Canberras. Each was fitted with an array of cameras developed in the Second World War when the RAF gained a deserved reputation for photo-recce and photographic interpretation, a reputation it has never lost.

To the north of my new HQ, and across a long-disused runway, was the main airport terminal. The village to its left gave the airfield the name Luqa, one of a number of surviving Arabic names. Left of the village, the ground sloped toward

Grand Harbour and further left, near Runway 24's threshold, was the original air traffic control building. The whole area was dominated by a high hill to the north-west. On its summit, Rabat adjoined the battlements of the ancient so-called silent city of Mdina.

Our first home, in Birkirkara, was a great vantage point to watch the regular and loud firework displays as nearby villages celebrated their *festa*, the feast of their patron saint. There was always a special one in August, although it was some time before I grasped its significance.

Over the next three years, I spent many hours over Sicily and southern Italy taking photographs of ports and harbours like Augusta and Palermo, Taranto and Naples, all of them photographed many times in the past, but in rather testing circumstances. Italian airfields like Trapani and Sigonella were practice targets and again, like my predecessors, I always received a very warm welcome there, only in a very different sense. The Regia Aeronautica's successors were very hospitable, a spirited and professional lot, not unlike their own predecessors, who often earned the professional respect of those posed by their politicians as Italy's enemy. Years later, I served on a Tornado squadron commanded by an Italian *tenente colonelo* and my navigator was a *leutnant* in the Luftwaffe. I developed the utmost respect for both air forces. When returning to Luqa from Italy, I often coasted out from Sicily at Gela before heading for Gozo. A left turn brought me to Grand Harbour with Luqa soon in my sights. It took no time at all.

Our son was born in the Royal Navy (RN) Hospital at Mtarfa. Mtarfa is due north of Mdina and the valley between leads to a dried-up lake on which the RAF airfield Ta' Qali was built. Long disused in 1975, it was home to small, flourishing craft industries operating from wartime Nissen huts. Nearby are the small, pretty towns of Attard and Balzan and only a short distance north is Mosta with its famed, some say miraculous, church, visible from much of the island. On 9 April 1942, a bomb crashed through the dome in the middle of a service, rolling past the congregation without exploding, hence the church's reputation.

Our Maltese babysitter was evacuated in 1940 from the Three Cities to Birkirkara following heavy bombing. When she told us her story it seemed odd, given how close Birkirkara was to the main residential areas. Bombing was often localised around the docks and the airfields but, on such a small island, nowhere was immune. The Three Cities – Vittoriosa, Senglea and Cospicua – are close-knit communities that grew around two fishing villages: Birgu, now Vittoriosa, and L-Isla, now Senglea. They prospered around the dockyards, which ultimately led to their destruction under some of the most intensive bombing the world has ever known. Since then they have become a rare and unexpected find: history, thriving communities and welcoming warmth, all hidden in the open and only visited by the more inquisitive of Malta's tourists.

Balzan was the location of our second home. It overlooked San Anton Palace, the official residence of Malta's president and the former residence of Malta's wartime governors. It was in nearby Attard, at St Catherine's Nursing Home, that our daughter was born in our final summer on the island.

At the end of September 1978 there was an air display at Luqa to mark the end of RAF operations from Malta. I was proud to take part, flying in the second element of a nine-ship Canberra formation. As I came in to land I flew over the Officers' Mess and smiled when I saw once more the message left after HMS *Ark Royal*'s farewell visit to Malta: Fleet Air Arm crews had painted FLY NAVY in large white letters on the flat roof. My squadron flew out en masse on 4 October 1978, relocating to RAF Wyton in Huntingdonshire, my final flight before posting. No. XIII Squadron was the very last RAF squadron to be based in Malta. Its withdrawal ended a tradition of RAF photo reconnaissance which began in 1940 with a few American aircraft, built for the French, but delivered to Britain and brought to the island by an Australian. They created a legend.

On 31 March 1979, the last RAF personnel left the island, ending Britain's 179-year association with Malta. There is so much that links the two nations and bears testament to the sacrifice of many in two world wars; testament that will last regardless of politics and politicians who come and go. Some personal links can never be broken and we now had two rather important ones that would draw us back to the island twelve years later, each wishing to visit where they were born.

In the summer of 1990, we landed on the 11,500 foot long main runway which was under construction the last time I'd seen it. It was built partially on top of what was the main wartime runway, orientated north-west to south-east, which had been disused in my day. The terminal appeared unchanged and my old squadron's dispersals and buildings were still visible, though there was no activity nearby. The former administrative site was now an industrial estate but, across the road from the main gate, the old Officers' Mess seemed much as it was, with the 'bull-ring', the scene of many a Summer Ball, still visible. The Mess was now occupied by a Maltese Government department. Did the Maltese officials know of the light-hearted legacy left by the Fleet Air Arm?

Our former homes in Birkirkara and Balzan were now hotels, but San Anton Gardens was unchanged, its walls cutting out the noise and bustle of the nearby streets. Mdina, with its narrow atmospheric streets, is a magical place, described as a hauntingly beautiful city dreaming quietly behind impenetrable walls. Whoever offered that image must only have visited as dusk approaches, or in the evening when the tourists had gone. As we left Malta, just like in 1978, we gave little thought to the possibility of returning. We were drawn back twenty-two years later.

In 2010, while researching my memoirs, I contacted Frederick Galea to check one or two facts about Malta. He was most helpful. This reawakened my interest in Adrian Warburton and Christina Ratcliffe. In 2012, my wife and I visited the island once more and inevitably I began to delve deeper into their Malta story. I found it intriguing. What happened on Adrian's final mission? How important was Christina to the man who became known as 'Six-Medal Warburton'?

Christina was living in Floriana when we lived in Malta in the 1970s. We were frequent visitors to the NAAFI and the Medical Centre in the former St Francis Barracks, which was overlooked by the house in which Christina lived in 1937 and to which she returned in 1940. She was living there when the Italians declared war in June 1940 and described what she saw from her balcony in the aftermath of the bombing raids on the first day of Malta's war. Later, Christina moved to an apartment in Floriana, which we often drove past going to and from Valletta, or driving down to Malta's quayside. How I wished I had known about Adrian and Christina when I was based on the island. Yet even if I had, it was most unlikely I'd have been able to learn more. By then she was a very private lady. Yet on my short visit in 2012, almost everywhere I turned there were links with Christina and Adrian. I again felt unnerved, disconcerted. Did she want their story told?

A talented writer, Christina wrote quite extensively, yet said little about her relationship with Adrian and nothing about her feelings towards him until shortly before she died. Why was that? As I started reading more, I realised Frederick Galea knew far more about Malta's air war than I realised. After a chance meeting with Frederick at the entrance to the Malta Aviation Museum at Ta' Qali, I began to delve deeper. I'm not sure I would have pursued the story but for that brief encounter. When I returned from Malta, I was hooked. From then onwards Frederick and I began to exchange notes and photographs, and we became good friends. Later, I was privileged to meet and spend many hours with the late Jack Vowles, a former airman who had been hooked since he met and served with Adrian in Malta in 1941.

What was it about Malta? Was there something there which 'hooked' Adrian and Christina, sparked something between them? Was it the island's history that captured their imagination and allowed them to shine? Or was it simply the circumstances of life on an isolated island at war and under siege, the excitement of the times that brought these two people together, a shy loner who didn't fit in and an outgoing, vivacious dancer? And what was it about their story that drew me in, sending me back to Malta on a quest to find out the truth about the man Marshal of the Royal Air Force, Lord Tedder, described as, 'the most valuable pilot in the RAF'?

Chapter Two

A Place in History

I began by looking at just what makes Malta unique. What is so enchanting about the place and what events conspired to give it such spellbinding qualities? The answer is not a simple one. Some I knew from our time there, but, as I began to unravel a Maltese tragedy, there was much more to discover, more that makes Malta what, perhaps even who it is.

The island has its own language and alphabet, and its people have roots in every country from Portugal to Palestine. The main island stretches fourteen miles north-west to south-east and is seven miles wide at its broadest point. Its ninety-five square miles put it at a similar size to the Isle of Wight, yet its population, triple that of its English cousin at 450,000, makes Malta one of the more densely populated countries in the world. Gozo, to the north-west, measures less than eight miles west to east, by three miles north to south. Some 30,000 people live on those twenty-six square miles. Between the two main islands is tiny Comino whose one square mile supports a handful of farmers.

Retreating glaciers left outcrops of pale yellow limestone in a rolling landscape. The stone is easy to quarry and to cut. There are few trees and, for most of the year, little greenery to soften the sun-bleached landscape. There is almost a total lack of rain throughout the long summer, which adds to the pale-yellow aura, contrasting sharply with the bright azure summer sky and the deeper blue sea of the Mediterranean. In autumn and spring, Malta is visited by the *Sirocco:* a dry, hot and dusty wind originating in the Sahara. It can last half a day or several days, reaching hurricane force. It is little wonder the land often has a dry and bleached-out quality. Thin soil led to extensive terracing, still a striking feature of the terrain, which, combined with the absence of any permanent rivers, makes farming doubly difficult. Life for the early inhabitants can never have been easy.

Human settlement dates back to at least 5200 BC. Little is known about the earliest inhabitants, except they built great temples around 3600 BC and were moving fifty-ton megaliths and creating buildings aligned to the winter solstice sunrise a thousand years before the first pyramid in Egypt. Near the village of Mgarr, the temples are the oldest free-standing stone structures in the world. The temple period came to an end between 1800 BC and 2500 BC; no one is sure why. What directly followed is uncertain but, in what became a pattern marking good times and bad, the islands were invaded and occupied in around 800 BC.

Sixty nautical miles south of Sicily and one hundred and eighty north of Libya, the islands are physically European, lying on Europe's continental shelf, but they also have North African overtones. This situation determined Malta's destiny, while its relative isolation shaped the inhabitants. As travel and trade developed, the part-way position of the islands attracted commercial and military strategists alike. Invasion, or attempted invasion and occupation, became a feature of Malta's history – another aspect of the islands that gives them commonality with Britain. It most certainly contributed to the development of the character and psyche of both nations.

The first recorded occupation was by the Phoenicians, a maritime people from the eastern Mediterranean. They seized Malta, having recognised the importance of the natural harbours on either side of a peninsula known as Mount Sciber-Ras, the 'light on the point'. Much that came with the Phoenicians survives today as part of Malta's character. Their Semitic language, based on Hebrew, was the beginning of Maltese and the only Semitic tongue to use the Latin alphabet. Indeed, Malta's name may have come from the Phoenician word for harbour. Also still part of Maltese culture, they brought their rowing boats and sailing galleys. Even now the colourful Maltese fishing boats, the *luzzu*, *dghajsa* and *kajjik*, with watchful eyes painted on their bows, are little changed from Phoenician vessels. The Phoenicians held on to Malta until defeated by the Romans in 218 BC.

When the Romans arrived they came in friendship, treating Malta in a very different manner to other occupied nations. Malta and Gozo were made free towns, or *municipiums*, with liberty to control their own affairs, mint their own coins and send an ambassador to Rome. Paul the Apostle, a Roman citizen, was shipwrecked on Malta in February 60 AD. He was on his way with other prisoners to Rome to be tried for his life. The site of his shipwreck is said to be the tiny, uninhabited St Paul's Island, at the northern entrance to St Paul's Bay. In Acts 28:2 Paul wrote, 'And the barbarous people showed us no little kindness; for they kindled a fire, and received us every one, because of the present rain, and the cold.' The word barbarous simply meant the islanders did not speak Latin or Greek. Paul stayed in Malta for three months as the guest of the Roman Governor, Publius, and they became firm friends.

The villa of Publius was in the former Phoenician settlement of Malet, by now a large Roman town, Melita. It spread over an area three times the size of the later medieval citadel. Legend suggests Rabat Cathedral now stands on the site of the villa. Publius allowed Paul to preach, giving rise to some of the first Christian converts in the village of Naxxar. Pronounced 'nassar', it means, 'made into a Christian'. Publius was baptised and went on to become the first Bishop of Malta. Paul went on to Rome and martyrdom. Malta prospered under Roman rule and became the first country in Europe outside Italy to convert to Christianity, beginning the country's long history of religious devotion. This played an important part in the development of the Maltese character and the island's history.

The Byzantines were next, ruling Malta until their defeat by the Arabs in 870 AD. The new Arab rulers treated the islanders largely with respect. At a time when there was bloody conflict between the Crescent and the Cross – the infamous Crusades – the Arabs seemed to tolerate Christianity in Malta. It nevertheless declined as the Saracen rulers taxed Christians but not Moslems. The Saracens did bring irrigation to Malta, a sun-baked rock for six months a year. Their influence on the language is also clear. Many Arab place names still exist, such as Hamrun, Mdina (*imdeena*), Mtarfa (*imtarfa*), Luqa (pronounced loo-ah), and Qormi ('*ormy*). They also made Mdina, the Arabic word for 'walled city', the capital, reducing its size, building strong walls and a deep moat. They left the Roman villa of Publius outside its walls in the suburbs; a suburb is known as *rabat* in Arabic.

The Normans arrived in 1090 and theirs was a brief but pleasant era. Legend has it Roger Guiscard, Count Roger I of Sicily, ripped a piece from his red, personal standard and gave it to the Maltese, who added the white section to make the fragment up to a suitable size for a flag. The motif on the left-hand side of the current flag didn't appear until 852 years later. Ousting the Arabs, Count Roger was welcomed and Christianity was formally restored, along with the cathedral in Mdina. The Maltese enjoyed relative independence while Count Roger, ruling from Sicily, repaired decaying churches and rescued a desolate country. Although his rule lasted only eleven years, a mass for his soul was still being offered in Mdina on 4 November, some 800 years later.

In 1194, Malta's fortunes changed again and control passed to the German dynasty of Hohenstaufen. Then Charles of Anjou seized Sicily, only to be defeated by King Pedro I of Aragon in a naval battle at Grand Harbour in 1282. From then on, the Maltese found themselves exploited from Aragon – modern Spain – and harassed by marauding Turks and Barbary corsairs. Mdina, known by then as *Citta Notabile*, or the Noble City, became the favoured residence of the Maltese aristocracy and the seat of their governing council, the *Universita*. Although the Aragonese crown pledged never to give Malta to any other power, the Holy Roman Emperor Charles V of Spain broke the agreement. In 1530 he gave Malta to the Knights of the Order of St John of Jerusalem, who, for the past eight years, had wandered the Mediterranean after expulsion from Rhodes by the Ottoman Empire. Charles V hoped the knights, also known as the Hospitallers, might help contain Turkish ambition.

The arrival of the Knights of St John, under Grand Master Philippe de L'Isle Adam, marked a significant point in Malta's history. It was not long before the Turks, under Sultan Suleiman the Magnificent, recognised Malta's location made it a crucial strategic gateway between east and west. With Malta's much-coveted natural harbour such a draw to any strategist, the scene was set for the Great Siege of 1565, a test of courage and endurance few could ever imagine.

The knights were unimpressed with the barren, waterless and poorly defended islands. They settled in Birgu (now Vittoriosa) and set about fortifying the harbour, the key to their existence and strategy. Originating from various European countries, the majority from France and Spain, others from Italy, Germany and England, they formed divisions, called *langues*, based on a common language. Each *langue* had its own small palace or *auberge*. De L'Isle Adam was like the king of a small nation in status and, as did those he sought to emulate, failed to consult the 15,000 or so local inhabitants, also excluding the local aristocracy.

By 1565, a new Grand Master, Jean Parisot de la Valette, had turned Malta into a fortified naval base. Fort St Angelo, on the tip of Birgu, was rebuilt and strengthened, augmenting Fort St Michael on the tip of Isla (Senglea, built by la Valette's predecessor Claude de Sengle). A third fort, Fort St Elmo, was built at the end of the uninhabited Sciberras peninsula. The knights knew what was coming and these three forts were vital, as was the ancient capital. They, perhaps wisely, and to prevent panic, did not forewarn the Maltese, who must still have suspected as they toiled to strengthen the forts.

Suleiman the Magnificent had spent thirty years building and strengthening his vast fleet. The potential of Malta and its harbour to become part of his growing empire and expansionist ambitions was a major temptation. That it was in the hands of the Order of St John of Jerusalem, a relic of the Crusaders and their holy war against Allah, made Malta all the more irresistible.

Admiral Piali Pasha commanded the Ottoman fleet of close to 200 vessels. It took a month to travel from Constantinople, arriving on 19 May 1565. Rough seas prevented the fleet from reaching the preferred anchorage of Marsaxlokk in the south-east. Instead, they proceeded to Gnejna and Ghajn Tuffieha Bays in the north. They returned to Marsaxlokk the following day, landing in force, and set up their main camp in present-day Marsa. Within twenty-four hours the southern half of the island was occupied. The Maltese population took refuge behind the walls of Birgu, Senglea and Mdina. Many of them, taken by surprise, had not gathered their grain harvest or secured their animals. This seems to confirm that the knights did not inform many locals of the imminent invasion. Had they done so, however, would focus have been on harvest rather than on constructing fortifications?

In the first two days, the Turks suffered many casualties from harassing cavalry attacks. The Turks also tortured and executed two captured knights who gave false information. Estimates of the size of the Turkish army, under General Mustapha Pasha, vary widely, from 22,000 to over 40,000. The defenders were outnumbered by between three and five to one.

La Valette's strategy was simple: defend the three mutually-supporting forts controlling access to Grand Harbour whilst retaining a stronghold inland at Mdina to the west, and importantly, to the rear of the Turks.

Suleiman's strategy was not so straightforward. The Ottoman war council favoured naval priorities and directed General Mustapha to safeguard the fleet. The battle on land was not to compromise that. The sultan did not intend to see his armada squandered against a barren island at the very edge of his empire, despite its useful location. His war council wanted Marsamxett Harbour accessible to the whole fleet; therefore Fort St Elmo must be captured. General Mustapha offered a sound alternative of occupying most of Malta, picking off the blockaded strong points one by one. The admiral, twenty years younger than the general, had greater influence within the council because of his relationship with the sultan's favourite son. His view prevailed. The strategy certainly fulfilled the sultan's overall wish to protect the fleet, but it was seriously flawed. The shared power and uneasy 'jointery' offered great advantage to La Valette.

With the Turks focusing on St Elmo, the defenders had time to strengthen St Michael and St Angelo. La Valette knew only too well the loss of St Elmo, along with its defenders, was inevitable. He did not expect quarter, nor would he offer it. The Turks built a dyke across the ridge of Mount Sciberras from which to mount their assault on St Elmo and the siege began in earnest on 27 May 1565.

Fort St Elmo held out for a month, its final days terrible for the maimed and half-starved defenders. The Turks' concentration on the fort cost them at least 6,000 men. None of the 600 defenders survived. When Mustapha Pasha mourned his dead he could only wonder, 'if the daughter meant so much loss to us in dead and wounded, what is the mother going to cost us?' The mother was Fort St Angelo.

Soon after the fall of Fort St Elmo, General Mustapha employed gruesome intimidation tactics, ordering several captured knights beheaded. The heads were nailed to stakes looking out toward Birgu's defenders and the bodies fixed to crucifixes, then floated across the harbour. In response, La Valette decapitated all Turkish prisoners and used their heads as cannonballs fired back at the Turks. Such was medieval warfare.

General Mustapha urged Mdina and Senglea to surrender, promising to respect privileges, give freedom from the knights and grant trading rights with the Turks. The Maltese answer was a resounding 'No'.

With Fort St Elmo captured, Marsamxett Harbour was now open to the Turkish fleet. They could enter Grand Harbour, but were still unable to row past Fort St Angelo. Instead, they dragged their vessels overland from the head of Marsamxett Harbour to the head of Grand Harbour. The knights countered, driving wooden stakes into what is now Frenchman's Creek. Turkish swimmers were sent to destroy them, but were defeated by their Maltese counterparts. Despite further fierce assaults, things were going badly for the Turks. They suffered an epidemic of dysentery when the local population poisoned wells and cisterns, throwing dead animals into the water. Throughout this, the knights lived, ate, slept and died in their heavy suits of armour, coping on strict and unpalatable rations.

General Mustapha, aware things were going badly, ordered a five-day barrage, breaching the walls of Fort St Angelo. The Turks surged in. Of the Maltese, everyone joined the fight. Women and children hurled stones and poured burning oil onto their assailants. Now the commander of Mdina launched a counter-attack with cavalry, surprising the Turks, creating havoc and destruction. Even though victory for the Turks was at hand, General Mustapha ordered a retreat, fearing the appearance of cavalry heralded much talked about reinforcements from Europe.

When he realised his error, Mustapha renewed the siege, turning to tunnels and mines. These also failed. A huge siege engine achieved some success until the defenders tunnelled beneath their own walls, captured the tower and turned it against the Turks. Turkish morale plummeted, drained by a long hot summer and increasing casualties. The defenders too were exhausted.

Within the Ottoman war council, General Mustapha pressed for the army to stay until spring. The weak Turkish strategy now became decisive. As the Mediterranean sailing season ended traditionally with the storms of late September, Admiral Piali insisted the fleet depart at the first sign of winter.

On 7 September, reinforcements for the defenders arrived from Sicily. General Mustapha was again fooled, believing them a much larger force and withdrew. The relief landed at Mellieha Bay, occupying the high ground at Naxxar. Realising the ruse, Mustapha ordered his men to disembark at St Paul's Bay. Many of the tired and dispirited Turkish soldiers were slaughtered.

On 8 September 1565, Malta's defenders woke to find they had won the four-month siege in that long hot summer. In the Great Siege of Malta, they had endured bombardment by 130,000 cannon balls, one of the bloodiest and most fiercely contested sieges in history. Estimates of Turkish casualties vary as widely as those of the original number: it is likely they lost over 20,000 men. At least 7,000 defenders died, perhaps as many as 9,000. At the end of hostilities it was said only 600 islanders were capable of bearing arms. Malta had lost one third of her people, both Birgu and Senglea levelled. But the Turks never came back.

That date, 8 September – *Il Bambina*, or the Feast of the Birth of the Virgin Mary – is a day especially celebrated in the Maltese calendar and still commemorated as the Victory Day public holiday.

Such was the gratitude of Europe for the heroic defence that money poured in to the island. Jean de la Valette was thereby able to construct the fortified city of Valletta on Mount Sciberras, denying the position to any future enemies. The city, called *Humillima Civitas Vallettae*, the 'most humble city of Valletta', was built in less than two and a half years. La Valette died of a heart attack in 1568, aged seventy-three, and did not live to see its completion. His legacy, and the city he left behind though, are magnificent. Valletta was the first planned city in Europe, a regular grid of streets, underground sewers and massive fortifications packed into an area of about 1,000 metres by 600 metres.

The Knights of St John, the oldest Order of Chivalry in existence and the third oldest religious order in Christendom, became so famous they are known throughout the world as The Knights of Malta. Although the accolades are well deserved, it must be acknowledged the Knights may have achieved less without the grimly resolute efforts and sacrifice of the Maltese. It was largely Maltese women and children who repaired the walls, brought food and ammunition to the soldiers, and tended the wounded. Inevitably, the effect of the siege on the people was near catastrophic and it took decades to recover from the loss of such a vast proportion of so small a population.

Many of the Grand Masters who followed left their mark, or their names, on different parts of Malta. The period following 1565 saw building, not only of massive new fortifications and watchtowers, but also of churches, palaces and *auberge*. Birgu was renamed Vittoriosa, or Victorious, after the siege. Jean de la Cassiere oversaw the construction of the magnificent St John's Church, which became a co-Cathedral, and Alof de Wignacourt provided funding for a new aqueduct from Mdina to Valetta. The decadent Antoine de Paule built San Anton Palace and used it for hedonistic parties, hardly in keeping with the knights' image, but a lifestyle that was becoming ever popular. The infamously dour Jean de Lascaris Castellar gave rise to the Maltese phrase meaning 'face of Lascaris' to describe someone with a sour facial expression. He also gave his name to a bastion.

Generally, the knights had little to do with the local population, which faced extreme famine and severe outbreaks of plague, with precious little reward from the knights. The exception was Antoine Manoel de Vilhena, who did most to improve the lives of the Maltese and achieved great popularity. He built Manoel Theatre in Valletta and Fort Manoel in Marsamxett Harbour. He also built Floriana and a terrace bears his name.

In the mid-eighteenth century, Manuel Pinto de Fonseca embellished many of the restrained Renaissance buildings. He also epitomised the change that came over the Order which had moved far beyond its vows of chastity, obedience and poverty. Members concerned themselves less with militarism and monasticism and more with drinking and duelling, with some commerce and piracy. To many of the Maltese, the knights were simply affluent foreigners living off the labours of a downtrodden peasantry.

Over 200 years, the power and influence of the order declined greatly. By the late eighteenth century, around three quarters of their income came from the knights of the French *langue*. After the French Revolution and confiscation of the Order's properties and estates in France, it found itself in dire financial straits. The new French leader, Napoleon Bonaparte, had designs on Malta, stating the fortress could be seized easily, and the starving Maltese were friendly toward the French and much estranged from the knights. Bonaparte thought with Malta, Sardinia and Corfu in his hands, the French could make themselves masters of the Mediterranean. A British sailor by the name of Nelson thought differently.

The end for the knights came in 1798, when Bonaparte's fleet stopped in Malta on its way to Egypt. They sought permission to take on water, a pretext. With Grand Master Ferdinand von Hompesch dithering, the French landed. On 11 June the Grand Master capitulated without a shot fired and control of the islands was handed to the French Republic. Napoleon himself landed at Customs House steps and stayed at the Parisio Palace on what became Merchants Street.

To begin with, Malta welcomed the French as liberators, but these new masters proved no better than the old. Napoleon imposed taxes on an already poor people to pay for the French garrison and seized treasure before heading for Egypt on 19 June 1798, and to defeat at Nelson's hands in the Battle of the Nile. The seized treasures met the fate of the French ship-of-the-line *Orient*, catching fire and sinking.

Back in Malta, the French closed convents and seized church treasures. When they tried to auction those from the Church of Our Lady of Mount Carmel in Mdina, the Maltese rebelled, lynched the Mdina garrison and drove the remainder of the French back into the stronghold of Valletta. Once more the capital was under siege, but this time the locals were on the outside. They asked Britain for assistance and Nelson imposed a blockade lasting two years and two days. On 4 September 1800, the French garrison surrendered and French rule came to an end. So began an association between Malta and Britain which lasted 179 years.

The Maltese people wanted to be part of the growing British Empire and why not? With their experience of invasion and occupation, what other great power at the beginning of the nineteenth century could protect their homeland from further subjugation? There could also be significant economic benefits for the islanders. As Napoleon went into exile on another small island, the 1814 Treaty of Paris declared: 'The island of Malta and its dependencies shall belong in full right and sovereignty to his Britannic Majesty'. British rule began.

Britain was, of course, a colonial power at the very height of its strength and followed the colonial trend. An Anglican Cathedral was built on the site of the German *auberge* in Valletta. The *Auberge de Provence* became the Union Club, for 'officers only'. Maybe some Maltese were disappointed at their new rulers' more strategic than altruistic attitude, but Britain had much to gain by possessing Grand Harbour and its docking facilities. The Suez Canal opened in 1869, adding further confirmation of the vital importance of Malta in maintaining Britain's territorial interests. Malta grew wealthy as an important refuelling and staging post for British steamships. The docks of Senglea and Vittoriosa grew and ships of many nations helped build Malta's economy. Malta's only railway was built running between Valletta and Rabat. Although it never flourished, it left a legacy in the form of a tunnel cut through Valletta's ramparts.

But soon economic depression hit Malta. As the island lacked a sound economy and had a rapidly rising population, inevitably there were tensions between the Maltese and the British. Nonetheless, the Maltese workforce put its grievances to one side as it worked for victory in the First World War. Malta served as a military hospital and became known as the Nurse of the Mediterranean, providing 25,000 beds for the disastrous Gallipoli campaign against Turkey.

Colonial rule though was not without tensions. Not long after the First World War, prices and taxes rose and the economy slumped. Riots broke out and four Maltese citizens were shot dead when British soldiers panicked. The government responded by giving the Maltese a greater say in the running of their country and, in 1921, they had a taste of self-government, maybe their first since Roman times. A thirty-two strong Legislative Assembly looked after everything but defence, foreign policy and immigration. This collapsed after six years because of local issues and arguments over the official language. Italian, the language of polite conversation and the judiciary, was spoken by only 15 per cent of the population, yet the upper classes would have it spoken as the official language in many institutions. Part of the language issue was that street names, especially in Valletta and Floriana, were in Italian. Mussolini had already made the ridiculous claim Maltese was merely a dialect of Italian and said the Maltese Islands rightly belonged within his 'New Roman Empire'. By 1936, Malta was a British colony once more, but with a new constitution banning Italian as an official language. Any thoughts about self-government for Malta went on hold as tension increased throughout Europe with the rise and ever-growing threat of fascism.

Thus Malta survived many great upheavals, outlived many a master and grew strong. Its people understood courage and sacrifice, knowing these traits would carry them through. Galvanised by turbulent times throughout the centuries, Malta braced itself for yet another war. The Second World War put every citizen on the front line and tested every ounce of their spirit. The fortifications created by the knights endured; the ancient forts important to the islands' survival yet again. Malta's strategic importance was also the key to success for either the Axis or the Allies in North Africa.

So, with such a turbulent but determined history surrounding them and such a glorious nation spirit, one can hardly be surprised two equally spirited young individuals would fall for one another as 'the light on the point' shone around them. And so begins the story of a man she called 'Warby' and a girl he called 'Chris'.

Chapter Three

Stepping Stones & Flying Lessons

Mary Christina Ratcliffe was born on 1 July 1914, in Dukinfield, a small industrial town on the eastern outskirts of Manchester. She had two brothers. Her father, Henry Marsland Ratcliffe, originated from Glossop in Derbyshire and her mother, Jeanie King Ratcliffe, née Downs, was Scottish.

Historically part of Cheshire, Dukinfield was a product of the Industrial Revolution. The cotton trade in particular shaped the town, which at the beginning of the nineteenth century had two cotton mills. By the century's end there were fourteen, but the industries that sustained Dukinfield were soon dying as the twentieth century progressed and the cotton industry declined. This was the landscape in which Christina, known as Mary as a child, grew up. She wanted something different. With her outgoing nature and sense of adventure she wasn't content with the routine and the prospect of what she saw as a dreary existence in an industrial town in the shadow of the Pennines in no way appealed.

She grew into a tall, slim, attractive girl, with brown eyes and blonde hair. Intelligent and confident, her independent nature was apparent from an early age. Like many other girls, Christina began ballet lessons at the age of eight and it was her dancing shoes that shaped her future. Few could have imagined just where her determination and search for excitement would take her, least of all her ballet mistress, who told Christina's mother her little girl, 'will never get anywhere with her dancing. She's far too wooden.'[1] For any child, such criticism was stinging, but coming at the end of a matinee given by pupils at her dancing academy, it was particularly hurtful. However, Christina was not put off by the devastating comment. Indeed, it served to strengthen her yearning to pursue her dream.

She attended the private Ashton High School. At thirteen she moved on to Manchester High School for Girls, a leading independent fee-paying school, travelling each day by train. The Ratcliffes were well placed in depression-hit Britain. Her father was a cotton manufacturer and the family's standing is confirmed by Christina's reference to his cotton factory as 'our mill'. At school, she took additional lessons in gymnastics and was a member of the dramatic society. She proved particularly adept at French and was awarded her School Certificate in 1931 in five subjects.

---

1. *Carve Malta on my heart and other wartime stories*, by Frederick Galea, page 6.

After leaving school having just turned seventeen, Christina worked in her father's mill, but it did not hold her for long: she longed to go on stage and to travel, despite her parents' hopes she would become a nurse. At some stage she appeared on the same billing as George Formby at the old Manchester Hippodrome. Then, having won the grand total of £40 in a crossword competition, she set off for the bright lights of London. Her prize could hardly have financed her for long, so she must have had support from her parents. In 1933, Christina was 19-years-old and she soon found work and danced in the film *Charing Cross Road*, starring John Mills. She then joined an English dancing troupe, *Miss Frances Mackenzie's Young Ladies* and the lavish show, complete with nudes, was produced in Paris. It was called *Jusqu aux Etoiles* and toured France, Italy, Switzerland and North Africa.

Fascism was on the rise at the time and there was growing concern about Hitler and Mussolini's territorial ambitions. In an effort to create a 'New Roman Empire', as his supporters called it, Mussolini ordered the invasion of Abyssinia in 1935. His far superior forces were soon victorious. Although many European nations were colonial powers, their expansionist programmes had ended decades earlier. With the international mood being against colonialist expansion, Italy's actions were roundly condemned, particularly by Britain. Unfortunately, these events coincided with the appearance of *Jusqu aux Etoiles* in Genoa. Italian theatre-goers, well known for displaying their emotions, reacted badly, when, in the troupe's final number, the backdrop was revealed to include the Union Jack. *Miss Frances Mackenzie's Young Ladies* were booed off the stage.

Christina then joined the *Rodney Hudson Girls* for a six-month contract at the Tivoli Theatre in Barcelona. The overland, overnight, train journey was uneventful until they were stopped, twelve miles short of Barcelona. The date was 17 July 1936, the first day of the Spanish Civil War. By the time news reached the passengers, Barcelona had been bombed in the opening round of what became a vicious, terrifying conflict. The train's passengers remained stranded for three days, sustained by local villagers. Eventually they made their way to Barcelona, having waited with fearful anticipation through the sound of bombing, shellfire and gunfire. Their eyes were opened to the reality of war when they came across evidence of executed rebels. There were dead animals and shattered houses with street barricades manned by machine-gun armed defenders.

The war between the Republican Government, and the Nationalists, a rebel group led by the fascist, General Franco, lasted for close on three years. With Britain and France anxious to appease Hitler, there was no prospect of an anti-fascist alliance with the elected Spanish Government. There were atrocities on both sides with tens of thousands of civilians killed for their political or religious views. Estimates vary widely, but probably not less than 200,000 died. Franco emerged victorious, but there was no reconciliation, with thousands of Republicans sent into exile. Nor did the executions end. For Italy and Germany's military, the Spanish Civil War was a perfect proving ground for their tanks and aircraft. Italy provided 50,000 volunteers, as well as aircraft, tanks, artillery and munitions; some 16,000 Germans were also involved in support of Franco.

Thankfully for Christina and the other stranded British nationals, after one terrifying night in Barcelona the RN came to their rescue. They were taken on board HMS *London,* the only rescue ship to berth inside Barcelona Harbour. The crew organised the ship as a reception centre accommodating 900 people in the first three days of the war; they were then sent in smaller groups to destroyers which took them to Marseilles. Christina's group spent two days on *London* before the destroyer, HMS *Gallant,* took them to Marseilles and safety.

Within a week, Christina was considering another engagement in India, but opted instead for one in Stockholm. Coming so soon after such a traumatic experience, Christina's resilience and enthusiasm for travel indicates something of the steel within her character and her thirst for further adventure. She had only just turned twenty-two years of age. The work in Sweden came to an end after only a month, and she returned to London, appearing as a guinea-a-day extra in *Dark Journey* starring Vivien Leigh. Next, she worked as an extra in *The Mill on the Floss* with Geraldine Fitzgerald.

Christina's next film opportunity was as a dancer in the Hollywood-style musical crime film *Premiere,* made in Vienna at the end of 1936. Christina eventually saw the finished product in the Regent Cinema in Valletta. The work was more than balanced by a very active social life, dining in style in their hotel, the Heitzinger Hof, and waltzing to the music of Strauss. A highlight was listening to Richard Tauber sing in the opera *Tiefland* at the Vienna Opera House. While Christina was in Vienna there was widespread evidence of Austrian Nazi Party activity within the capital, which led to *Wehrmacht* troops entering the country soon afterwards. Nazi Germany then annexed Austria in the *Anschluss.* There were a few voices of protest, but little else to what amounted to Hitler's first major move toward the creation of a Greater German Reich. Czechoslovakia was next, then Poland.

Adrian Warburton was born in Middlesbrough on 10 March 1918, the only son of Commander Geoffrey Warburton, a highly respected RN submariner, and Muriel Warburton, née Davidson. Awarded the Distinguished Service Order (DSO) for gallantry in a world war which still had eight months to run, Geoffrey was not done with courageous acts or awards. For his next, though, he would have to wait for the war that followed the war to end all wars. Gallantry and military service were something of a Warburton tradition: an uncle of Adrian's earned the DSO in the trenches, a cousin was the first officer awarded the Victoria Cross in the Second World War and a great uncle was equerry to King Edward VII.

Geoffrey remained in the RN after the Armistice and saw much service overseas. A strong-willed and dominant individual, he arranged for Adrian to be christened in a submarine. With the ceremony taking place in Grand Harbour Valletta, a link was perhaps established that would in time draw Adrian back. He may have grown up slightly in awe of his highly-disciplined, traditional father whom he saw infrequently. Winning his father's approval may also have been difficult when he was young, but over time they became close. Adrian's mother Muriel was an attractive lady, the daughter of a distinguished colonial police officer. With both parents often thousands of miles away, Adrian's relationship with them in those early years was distant, although his mother worshipped him.

In the 1920s, 'class' meant a great deal in British society. The Warburtons were upper-middle class and Adrian enjoyed the privileges of a good, if disjointed, upbringing and a comfortable lifestyle. In what was common practice for children of military officers, Adrian became a boarder at a preparatory school in Bournemouth. He and his sister, Alison, five years his senior, spent their holidays with their grandmother in her large house not far from the school, his grandfather having died when Adrian was four years old. The family was affluent and the house had numerous members of staff. To family members outside the immediate circle, Adrian was a normal friendly boy, but his character was influenced by the atmosphere at home. He became something of a loner and ran away from his first school at least once. According to his mother, Adrian didn't make many friends and never minded being by himself.

Defence cuts saw Geoffrey Warburton placed on the retired list in July 1927 at his own request and in the rank of commander. Finances must have taken a tumble and any boarding school allowance ended. Geoffrey became a cinema manager in Shepherd's Bush and the family moved to Enfield. The transition into commerce from an overseas military lifestyle to a suburban one would have come as a shock, particularly to Adrian's mother, whom he later referred to as 'the Lady Margaret'. Such a change of circumstance must have hit both parents hard, but Geoffrey was well capable of adapting, although he would have needed to be firmly focused, perhaps even single-minded, in carving out a new career and providing for a young family. Adrian did not get on well with his father at the time, maybe sensing some family tension as his mother struggled with the family's change of standing, smothering Adrian with the affection he may not have got from his father.

At the age of fourteen and a good average scholar, Adrian was sent to the private, fee-paying, public school of St Edward's in Oxford; the headmaster was a cousin of Adrian's mother. Adrian arrived in January 1932 at about the same time as another quiet boy who later became a household name: Guy Gibson. Curiously, Douglas Bader attended the same school some years earlier. At St Edward's, Adrian was seen as a loner who didn't fit in. He was often in trouble with authority, avoided team games and exercise, but was keen on swimming, and for his age, was by far the best swimmer in the school. Despite a reluctance to take part in other physical exercise, Adrian became a strong, fit young man. He left in early 1935, aged seventeen, somewhat earlier than normal. This was the end of his full-time education. He was certainly up to the mark academically and was particularly good at mathematics, so the reason for leaving may have been financial. No evidence exists he was asked to leave early.

Adrian's interest in aviation began early, the seed almost certainly being sown on one of his mother's regular visits when Adrian was at prep school. His first experience of flying was in what Muriel described as a 'ten-bob flip'. Asked by the pilot whether they 'wanted the works', Adrian was thrilled by the loops and rolls that followed; his mother was less amused.

This early experience made a major and lasting impression on a youngster who grew up on a diet of tales about heroes of ancient Greece. With a heroic father and a long line of such men in his family, Adrian probably dreamt of being a hero too. With few friends, he grew up enjoying his own company, although he was fun-loving with a great sense of adventure. He was also extremely fond of animals and often stayed up all night tending a sick dog or cat. He loved climbing trees, showing no fear at all. He became good at shooting, but it is doubtful whether that and his prowess in the pool would have been sufficient to satisfy his demanding father. Later, at St Edward's, Adrian's interest in aviation developed further and he joined an aeroplane group, shunning all other school societies.

From an early age, he showed an evident rebellious streak. For example, when he was two he visited Australia with his parents. The fashion in those days was for young boys up to the age of five to wear their hair long and Adrian's mother took great delight in her son's long, blonde, curly hair. One day, Adrian slipped away from his governess, went to the ship's barber and had all of his lovely locks cut off. This independence of spirit marked him out in future years, and it surfaced again and again. In a hair-raising, rather than hair-shedding, demonstration at age fifteen, Adrian built a canoe, strapped it to his back, and cycled off. The following day he was rescued off the Essex coast.

In Malta in adult life, one of Adrian's colleagues suggested he was boastful and eager to portray his actions in a positive light. This is at odds with his parents' and others' experience of Adrian; his father later said Adrian did not talk about his wartime achievements, even though they corresponded and met regularly. His mother only learnt about Adrian's awards from others, not from Adrian. There may have been more than a little jealousy beneath accusations of boastfulness.

By the age of seventeen, Adrian was bright and articulate, extremely strong and fit, and good-looking, with blonde hair and blue eyes. He was very much an individual, a non-conformist who liked to do things his way rather than as a member of a team or group. He was charming company, despite inheriting a slight sneer from his father which he often used at school. This would do nothing to endear him to future colleagues and, together with his privileged upbringing, it is easy to see why some might not warm to him. Adrian needed to soften aspects of his character to limit provoking those feelings of jealousy.

So, what was next for Adrian? How would his talents be put to best use? A career in the RAF certainly appealed but was firmly vetoed by his father, causing a significant clash between the two. Instead, Geoffrey arranged for Adrian to become an articled clerk, a daily commuter on the tube into Central London, to work with a traditional and well-established firm of accountants in Cheapside. It was a wholly unsuitable choice.

It is interesting to speculate about Adrian's likely future if his father had supported his ambition to join the RAF in 1935. Adrian would certainly have been commissioned: he was well-educated, fit, naturally confident, and imbued with those qualities engendered by public school education which were then considered necessary for service as an officer. His long-established service connections would also have worked in his favour. But he would have demonstrated no more piloting aptitude then than he did four years later. The RAF would also have been under less pressure to ensure Adrian qualified as a pilot. He could easily have found himself as an observer, as he had definite navigational skills. If that had been the case, 'Warby' might never have emerged.

Not surprisingly, Adrian and accountancy didn't hit it off, although he stuck with it for some time, maybe even as long as three years. It was never going to last and he made little positive impression on the firm's business partners. In a sign of things to come, he made a very positive impression on the mother of one his work colleagues who thought he was charming. Many ladies of all ages were charmed by this blue-eyed, blonde-haired Adonis, but he seemed unsure how to respond; he was thought to be inexperienced with girls.

In due course, Adrian's articles were terminated by mutual consent. Like many others who experienced the First World War, Geoffrey Warburton saw another war coming and encouraged Adrian to prepare for it. Adrian volunteered for the local Territorial Army unit and, on 1 November 1937, he became a part-time soldier as a private with 22nd London Armoured Car Company, part of the Royal Tank Corps. A year later, he was accepted by the RAF for pilot training.

The beginning of 1937 saw Christina out of work in London, living at the Theatre Girls' Club in Soho. There were no film jobs available and many shows and pantomimes were only at the beginning of long runs. Every morning she joined a dozen other girls staying at the Theatre Club trooping round agents' offices, all to no avail. With the winter weather worsening, and, despite the pleasant company,

Christina was getting bored and wanted to be seeing the world, not sitting around watching her savings dwindle. And then someone mentioned Malta.

The idea came from a girl called Sheila who accepted a contract there. Her 'good news' was greeted with cries of derision from many of the others, who, while lacking any direct experience of working in Malta, had heard lurid stories about appearing in cabaret in the many less salubrious establishments for which Valletta was renowned. Apparently it was a particular challenge for an attractive female in cabaret when the fleet was in, as Valletta's Grand Harbour was home to the RN's Mediterranean Fleet. Sheila hoped one or two of the other girls might join her, but no one seemed interested. Christina listened to everyone's comments but kept her own counsel. A cousin of her mother was married to a sailor once based in Malta and Christina recalled prints of, 'a city of narrow, stepped streets and tall buildings with tier upon tier of romantic-looking balconies … lovely old palaces and churches, horse-drawn cabs with curtains and little rowing boats with a hint of the gondola about them.'[2] Her impressions, however, revolved around a Malta of long ago, whereas her friends seemed to know all about modern Malta, 'infested with low-down taverns and bawdy music halls, a date that only the dregs of the theatrical profession would think of working.'[3]

There was one dissenting voice from an older girl who had previously worked in Malta. She said cabaret in Valletta was not for the faint-hearted, and any performer had to be capable of appearing in front of unruly crowds of servicemen. Working conditions were not perfect either. But there were advantages. The island was charming with wonderful weather and bathing. There was lots of sightseeing for those interested in exploring Malta's history. The pay could not be compared with that of the West End, but neither could the cost of living. What was needed most were guts, and a sense of humour.

Christina listened carefully: there was the prospect of work in the sun measured against no work in a dreary English winter. With rain lashing at the windows there was a rumble of thunder outside: her mind was made up. A week later, Sheila and Christina were ready to leave, despite the continuing efforts of their friends to dissuade them. They signed a three-month contract to perform a double act of song-and-dance numbers at a Valletta music hall called the Morning Star. Vera, a friend of Christina's from her French revue days, and a girl called Rosa, saw them off from London Victoria on their long, mostly overland, journey.

Following an exhausting four days, passing through Paris and Rome, they arrived in Syracuse, Sicily, where they boarded the SS *Knight of Malta* for the final leg of their journey. On the short voyage they were accosted by the wife of a naval officer serving on HMS *Barham*, a battleship stationed in Grand Harbour. This lady regaled Christina with her tales of Malta, but her demeanour changed instantly

---

2. *Carve Malta on my heart and other wartime stories*, by Frederick Galea, pages 11–15.
3. *Ibid.*

and for the worse when she realised she was talking to a pair of cabaret artistes who would soon be working in one of Valletta's music halls. Such were the attitudes of some in those days of empire and 'officers-only'. Those attitudes would count for little within a few years. Nor, sadly, would HMS *Barham*.

The girls had heard the view of Grand Harbour by night must not be missed, but they were not prepared, 'for the utter loveliness of the scene. Standing there on the deck of the slowly moving boat, it was as though we were passing through the portals of fairyland. The full moon illuminated the bastions and turrets of the ancient fortifications on either side of us and the entire harbour was aglow with thousands of twinkling lights. They were the lights, not of fairyland, but of a host of ships riding at anchor in their island base; ships of our Mediterranean Fleet, which in 1937 was in its heyday. It was an impressive, awe-inspiring sight.'[4]

In 1937, the Mediterranean Fleet was a showpiece of Britain's naval power and the pride of the RN. It was a prestigious command and appointments were highly sought after, not least because of its idyllic anchorage. With thousands of sailors, little wonder the bars and dance halls for which Valletta was renowned were often full to overflowing and there was a constant cry for entertainment. The pleasures of Strait Street, known to many a matelot as 'The Gut' were sampled. The fleet had a huge impact on both the social scene and the local economy. It provided employment and prosperity for many, from the *dghaisas*, one of the picturesque brightly coloured boats rowed by a man standing at the prow, which provided a water-taxi service, through to the laundries, shops and bars.

Malta has an old aristocracy with most titled families deriving their patents of nobility from the Grand Masters, although some titles are older. Others have Papal titles or British knighthoods. Maltese society was well-organised and structured, perhaps more so than British society in the 1930s. No one was allowed to enter the Malta Casino unless invited by a member, nor could anyone sit at the gambling or dinner tables without white tie and tails. With several dances each week aboard the many battleships or cruisers, 'there was many a young woman in Malta who thought ships were there merely for the dancing.'[5] No doubt there was a dance the very evening Christina and Sheila arrived. With ships bedecked with pennants and flags, their crews' 'whites' reflecting the lights, guests danced to music played by the Royal Marines; these were the good times. Two of the ships on display, unrecognised by Christina, were HMS *London* and HMS *Gallant*, her rescuers from Barcelona. As the girls stepped off the SS *Knight of Malta* on that idyllic spring evening they looked back in wonder at the many magnificent well-lit warships lying serenely at anchor. If they had any idea what was soon to befall those same ships, they would have wept.

---

4. *Ibid.*
5. *Soldier, Sailor & Airman Too*, by Woody Woodhall, pages 97–8.

Christina and Sheila were taken to the landing stage in front of the Customs House steps in a *dghaisa*. They soon met the owner of the Morning Star music hall, Gianni Fiteni, his charm and opulence as impressive as his large Daimler and uniformed chauffeur. 'Rolling back in the cushions, purring smoothly along in super-luxurious style, life seemed exceedingly good. There was moonlight. There were twinkling stars and a silvery sea. Yes, on a warm scented, Mediterranean evening such as this, life was exceedingly good. Sheila and I had done well to take the plunge. The poor girls back at the club would be huddled around the fire ... and the rain would still be beating ceaselessly on the window panes.'[6] Sheila suggested the first thing they should do was write and tell the other girls what they were missing. Their smug feeling was not to last.

Valletta in the 1930s catered very much for the sailor. Near the main entrance gate – *Porta Reale* – was the magnificent Royal Opera House, a showpiece on the *Strada Reale*. But the opera was most definitely not for Jolly Jack. Italian theatre companies performed there regularly and with its pomp, glitter and splendour, it would rarely see a matelot pass through its grand entrance. For Jolly Jack, apart from one small uncomfortable cinema which showed old, fifth-rate films, there were only the bars and music halls and to these, Jolly Jack turned by the thousand. The most popular haunts were on Strait Street – the Gut.

The Gut, a long, narrow avenue of cheap bars, dance halls and eating houses, was the name given to the lower part of *Strada Stretta*. Known to sailors the world over, it has an inconspicuous beginning off Ordnance Street and continues in a die-straight course to lower Valletta. The 1930s were the halcyon days of the Gut, the part of Strait Street extending beyond Old Theatre Street toward Fort St Elmo, but to capture its mood, to see the place as it really was, it had to be visited by night. In the hours of daylight, 'it put up its shutters and slept off the hangover in an atmosphere of peace and sobriety, a drab, dusty and sunless alley where, curiously enough, Dirty Dick's bar had the cleanest look of the lot. In the evenings the Gut leaped to life and opened its doors and its heart to teeming masses of servicemen on the lookout for an hour or so of vice and pleasure. Noise was the overriding feature of this alleyway and the later in the evening, the louder the racket, as the wine went in and the worst came out – raucous singing, yells, foul language, brawls in plenty. And, above it all, the din of the scores of jazz bands beating and sawing out their melodies on the rostrums of pocket-sized dance halls. At almost every door sat small groups of heavily made-up women, some young and pretty, others distinctly passé, but all adorned with gold earrings and bangles and all cajoling the passers-by to sample the delights of their particular establishment.'[7]

---

6. *Carve Malta on my heart and other wartime stories*, by Frederick Galea, page 16.
7. *Ibid.*

There were respectable establishments on *Strada Stretta*, such as the Rexford, the Moulin Rouge and Auntie's, but these were very strictly 'for officers and civilians only'. The Morning Star, shared with the Lancaster Ear, the John Bull and Charlie Palmer's, the distinction of not actually being on the Gut, escaping by a matter of yards being on *Strada San Nicola*, an adjacent street near Fort St Elmo.

As the Daimler wound its way into Valletta, the girls had little idea of their final destination. The car turned onto a narrow, dingy and ill-lit street which seemed grim even in the moonlight. They overtook a horse-drawn vehicle, the upper part of which resembled a sedan chair, drawn by a single horse. This was a *gharry*, for which Valletta was well known. They could see a lone sailor with his head slumped onto his chest and his cap tipped over his eyes. Soon they arrived at a brightly-lit building which illuminated a large patch of the gloomy street: 'we could hear the sound of loudly played jazz music and roar after roar of laughter.... . A feeling of apprehension came over me. This couldn't be the end of our few days journey. But instinctively I knew that it was and my instinct rarely plays me false.'[8] From Gianni's beaming expression it was clear he was immensely proud of his establishment.

There was no red carpet – just a one-man reception committee in the form of a bouncer by the name of Manwel. He was massive, with bulging muscles, a broken nose and a black eyepatch. Apparently the finest chucker-out on the island, his ferocious expression soon relaxed into a grin and he turned out to have a very high-pitched voice. Manwel's mission was not dedicated solely to chucking out. First he had to persuade passers-by to come in. The *gharry* they passed earlier arrived, complete with its single occupant who stumbled out hiccupping loudly. When Manwel caught sight of the sailor's hat-band he mounted a step higher, flexed his muscles and 'bellowed in a voice decidedly more in keeping with his Goliath-like physique: "Come right inside now *Queen Elizabeth*, all your ship's company inside." With killing wit he added: "All drunk"'.[9]

Once inside, the girls realised the term 'music hall' was somewhat misleading, but it was as good a term as any. 'After all there was music and there was a hall. The music was loud and lively, the hall long and narrow with mirrored walls and a tiled floor packed with dancing couples. The dancers were mainly sailors partnered by dark-haired, heavily made-up girls, and sailors partnered by sailors. Those of the clientele who were not dancing were seated on benches and stools around old-fashioned, marble-topped tables, smoking and drinking.

'Through the haze of blue smoke, I could see at the far end of the hall a set of orange and purple curtains, covering what was presumably the stage. Immediately beneath, in the orchestra pit, sat the band – a pianist and a drummer.

'"Nice place, eh, girls?" Gianni said, fairly bristling with pride.

---

8. *Ibid.*
9. *Ibid.*

'Before either of us could reply a great burst of cheering broke out and a chorus of wolf-whistles went up from a group of sailors at one of the tables.

'"Hi there, blondie".... "Come over here, blondie."

'I felt the blood mounting to my cheeks. Sheila caught hold of my hand and dug her fingernails into the palm. The wolf-whistles and yells grew louder. Soon the whole place was in uproar and Sheila and I found ourselves surrounded by a seething, ogling mob.'[10]

With some difficulty, Gianni extricated them into his restaurant next door. He was quite clearly delighted with their reception and certain he would get a good return on his investment in bringing the girls to Malta. He later gave them the unexpected news they were to be joined three days later by their friends Vera and Rosa, who had seen them off from Victoria. This was all the more surprising given their views on cabaret in Malta. Maybe the work situation in London had worsened. Nevertheless, it was good news, especially when they saw the standard of performance as well as audience reaction.

Gianni quietly referred to the first act as 'Budapest Bessie', who was due to return to Hungary the following week. Her 'ballet', to the music of the *Dying Swan*, was rewarded by catcalls, whistles and shouts. The second act was a song and dance routine by two attractive English girls who were first-class cabaret artistes. Disappointingly, their very polished performance got no better reaction. Christina and Shelia began to doubt the wisdom of their decision, but they were not lacking in guts, and they had a sense of humour so were determined to make the best of it.

Soon, with six talented English girls working together, the standard of entertainment rose to an unprecedented level. Catcalls and shouts of derision were a thing of the past, although little could be done about the long, low whistles, as the sailors registered their approval. Soon the Morning Star was a byword throughout the fleet with the well-dressed, well-presented girls putting on a popular revue. With British seamen rolling up in their hundreds, Manwel no longer had to persuade a passing sailor to enter the establishment. The dancehall enjoyed such popularity the British authorities opened the Vernon United Services Club in an attempt to break the monopoly of the Morning Star.

Gianni employed local dance hostesses, or 'sherry queens' as the sailors called them. 'Sherry' covered a multitude of innocuous, watered-down drinks bought by the clientele at sixpence a tot for their dance partner. The 'sherry queens' received a token, called *landi*, for each drink purchased and as they shared profits on a fifty-fifty basis, they were anxious to maximise their low income.

The cabaret artistes worked from 6.00 pm until 11.00 pm when the Morning Star closed, but the hostesses worked longer hours. By comparison, the girls were well

10. *Ibid.*

off; they were well paid, had free accommodation, light work and, if they wanted to make more money, could also earn *landi* by dancing with clients after their show. There was always keen competition to dance with the performers, who could rarely complete one dance before being whisked off for another with someone else. Of the six girls, only Rosa refused to come out of the microscopic dressing room beneath the stage, insisting there was nothing in her contract that required her to shake a leg with the rank and file of HM Forces. As the hostesses relied entirely on their tokens for their income, a number would move on to Cinderella's, a dancehall on *Strada Stretta* which stayed open until one in the morning. The Morning Star hostesses wore jumpers and skirts, whereas the girls in the up-market 'Officers and Civilians Only' establishments wore full evening dress. The trade was the same, but the 'sherries' were now 'cocktails'.

For the English girls, with only five hours work each evening, life was good. They lived in a large, well-furnished house in Floriana in which Christina shared a room with Sheila. From the roof they could see Grand Harbour and at the front it looked toward St Francis' Barracks. The house was near Queen's Store, owned by Felix Mallia, on *Strada San Tomaso*, where they obtained their groceries. These were delivered by the Mallia's niece, Connie, who enjoyed her daily visits to the house of the *Inglizi*. The cost of living was very low. Eggs were the equivalent of two and a half pence a dozen and the price of milk depended on the size of the jug. Although there were no cows on the island, there was an abundance of fresh goat's milk provided by herdsmen who drove their flocks through the streets and sold their produce direct from the animal's udder. Shopping at the many Indian bazaars was inexpensive, although no self-respecting customer would ever dream of paying the price originally asked. The girls never became infatuated with the Morning Star but they lived well. So did Gianni, who invoked an option to engage them for a further three months until September.

Adrian Warburton's first pilot training course was at RAF Prestwick, on the Ayrshire coast near Troon, south-west of Glasgow. It began on 31 October 1938 and lasted ten weeks. He was granted a Short Service Commission for four years and appointed as an acting pilot officer on probation. He was then posted to RAF Hullavington, in Wiltshire, for a seven-month course flying the Tiger Moth biplane, the standard RAF elementary trainer. He was no natural and struggled to achieve the minimum standard. Nevertheless he was awarded his pilot's brevet in May 1939, although his assessment of below average was the lowest possible. Anything less and his probationary commission could have been terminated; certainly his pilot training would have ended. He was probably lucky: with war imminent there was pressure to train pilots – little wonder Adrian, an obvious training risk, was retained for further training despite his lack of basic piloting skills. At any other time his fledgling career would have stalled.

Adrian continued advanced flying training at Hullavington on the Hawker Hart and Hawker Fury biplanes. He also undertook night flying in the Hawker Audax. Yet his struggles continued. In a sign of things to come he wrote off his aircraft's undercarriage in a botched landing. His landings, as well as his take-offs, were always problematic and these are rather fundamental. A colleague said Adrian took nothing seriously and verged on the eccentric. Nevertheless, he successfully completed the course and was posted to a torpedo training course at Gosport in Hampshire at the end of August.

The Gosport course lasted six weeks, during which Britain declared war on Germany. Paddy Devine was on the same course and later described Adrian as a dark horse and a loner; others thought him a line-shooter and egoist. He was not popular with either his colleagues or his superiors. He was probably very unsure of himself given his struggles in the air and may have resorted to flamboyance to either disguise his failings or attract attention. Attention he certainly got, as well as an early reputation for irresponsibility, although the height of his irresponsibility was never known until after the war was over. With the course complete, Adrian was posted to 22 Squadron, at nearby Thorney Island, on 12 October.

Young men in uniform were commonplace throughout Britain in the autumn of 1939. A young man of Adrian's looks wearing 'light-blue' and sporting pilot's 'wings' attracted admirers. Adrian attracted one in particular at a favourite haunt for junior officers, an upmarket public house called The Bush, in Southsea. She was a barmaid known as 'Betty of the Bush' and Adrian set off in eager pursuit. Her name was Eileen Adelaide Mitchell. She was a very good looking lady, some six years older than Adrian, who was twenty-one. Betty's background was very different; working-class, her father a shipwright in Portsmouth Dockyard. After the briefest of courtships, Adrian and Betty married in a hastily arranged registry office ceremony, on 28 October, which her father refused to attend. Adrian did not tell his parents then or later and, in a clear breach of regulations, he did not inform the RAF either. No one on Adrian's new squadron was aware of the marriage and at no stage did Adrian ever alter his next-of-kin forms, which named his father.

In 1943, Adrian said he married so someone could receive a widow's pension in the event of his death. For that to be the case the RAF needed to know he was married; in Adrian's lifetime the RAF never did, so Betty would not have been notified of his death. That she eventually found out was only because of his fame.

From the moment Adrian arrived at Thorney Island he virtually ignored his new bride. Although he rented a nearby bungalow for Betty, he lived in the Mess and visited rarely, making no attempt to maintain his new wife. She never received any form of marriage allowance to which she became entitled. In her later years she described the marriage as a wartime thing. Adrian was incredibly young and she was simply bowled over by him. She said, in a way they were never really married, as they didn't live together. He was a nice man, she said, but too young. Was marriage an escape from loneliness for Adrian? If so it was short-lasting. Betty too had a secret she kept hidden from Adrian. She never revealed to Adrian she married at seventeen, later divorced and had a 9-year-old daughter in her parents' care. Adrian may, of course, have found out from someone else and this may have impacted his future actions. Whatever the true situation, within days, it seems Adrian regretted his rash and thoughtless action.

At Thorney Island, 22 Squadron was equipped with ancient, single-engine Vickers Vildebeest biplanes, but these were being replaced by modern, twin-engine, Bristol Beaufort torpedo-bombers, the first of which arrived in mid-November 1939. The Beaufort was far in advance of anything the squadron or its pilots had experienced and accidents became commonplace. Adrian was sent on a month's course to RAF Thornaby, near Middlesbrough. On his return he continued to fly the Vildebeest, but also practiced circuit flying in a twin-engine Blenheim, his first experience flying a twin. His weaknesses were immediately apparent and this one flight may have been sufficient for his superiors to make up their minds. In mid-January, Adrian was posted supernumerary, as he was sick. He did not return to flying duties until April, but no attempt was ever made to convert Adrian onto the Beaufort. Given the pressure on the squadron commander to get as many of his pilots operational as possible, he must have had very serious reservations about Adrian's potential as a pilot: he simply did not appear to have any.

In April 1940, 22 Squadron moved to RAF North Coates in Lincolnshire, and was involved in mine-laying operations and night bombing of enemy ports. Within a month the squadron commander failed to return from a mission. The squadron was also involved in daylight raids in a vain attempt to stem the tide of the German Blitzkreig. Throughout these epic events, where was Adrian? He had still not flown the Beaufort and was not involved in any operational flying, simply flying a Hawker Audax biplane on target-towing duties. In the ten months since being posted to 22 Squadron, he achieved only forty-four flying hours, a very low amount for a first-tour pilot, mostly split between the two biplanes, the Vildebeest and the Audax. Had 22 Squadron given up on Adrian?

With the Battle of Britain raging in the skies above south-east England, Adrian was sent on yet another course, this time a navigation and reconnaissance course at Blackpool. This appeared to be a fairly clear statement from his superiors. Italy also declared war on Britain and France and war fell upon a small island in the Mediterranean with which Adrian's fate would become inextricably linked. By then Geoffrey Warburton had also been recalled and was posted to the RN base at Port Said in Egypt.

Adrian's course was at RAF Squire's Gate, later Blackpool Airport, and lasted until September. It covered navigation and photography and he flew in the twin-engine Anson, but not as a pilot. Betty, abandoned in the bungalow near Thorney

Island with no support, realised marrying Adrian was a huge mistake and began suing for divorce, not an easy matter in those days. Adrian must also have recognised his foolish action, but by then he had more pressing matters on his mind: he was in serious financial trouble. Betty, hearing Adrian was in Blackpool, travelled there to agree a divorce. She met Adrian, but divorce papers were never served. Betty never saw Adrian again.

By the time Adrian returned to North Coates his complicated personal life was unravelling. He was in serious debt and in trouble over bounced cheques, including those used to pay his Mess Bill. For an officer this was a heinous crime. There is some suggestion Adrian may have been under investigation by either the civil police or the RAF police, although this could have been because of bounced cheques. There were also rumours he had woman trouble. Could these have emanated from Betty's visit to Blackpool where at least one other member of 22 Squadron was attending the same course? Maybe the summer spent under Blackpool's bright lights was more than an immature Adrian could handle and it seemed as if the debt issues went far beyond unpaid Mess bills, although there is no record of any disciplinary action ever being taken against him.

Adrian had achieved his ambition of becoming an RAF pilot, but everything he touched subsequently seemed to have turned to dust. To others he may have appeared an abject failure beneath a veneer of charm and bravado. Sometimes personal failings can be overlooked if the individual is good in the air, but with Adrian this was not the case. All in all, the future for 22-year-old Acting Pilot Officer Adrian Warburton looked very bleak indeed.

From mid-June, 22 Squadron's commanding officer was Wing Commander Jos Braithwaite. No doubt well briefed about the officers under his command, he gave Adrian's future much thought. He may simply have been considering moving his problem child on, although he could equally have been looking to give the young misfit a fresh start. Years later, Braithwaite suggested there was a need to get Adrian out of the country quickly because of problems relating to women, money and the law. Despite this admission, it is inconceivable Braithwaite, a senior RAF officer with a bright future and a man of integrity, would simply arrange a posting overseas for someone being pursued by the police. Braithwaite was well aware of Adrian's debts and may have heard rumours of 'woman trouble', although he had no idea of the extent of Adrian's deception. Adrian had shown promise on his course and maybe Braithwaite was looking for an opportunity for Adrian to find his feet elsewhere. An unlikely solution soon presented itself. Originally destined for France, it came by ship across the Atlantic to Liverpool, then to RAF Burtonwood in Cheshire for assembly, before Braithwaite flew the first of them to Lincolnshire. It would take an Australian to show faith in Adrian, who would later pay it back many times over.

Chapter Four

Malta Unprepared

hroughout the 1920s and 1930s, Malta was only lightly garrisoned despite its importance as a naval base. In Grand Harbour, there were often seven battleships at anchor at the same time, with up to twenty cruisers, thirty destroyers and a dozen submarines moored in the triple inlets. There were also minesweepers, minelayers, supply ships, corvettes and launches, as well as a steady stream of ferries, tramp steamers and mail ships, along with troopships and passenger liners bringing service personnel and their families as well as holidaymakers to the island. A popular saying amongst sailors at the time was: 'You can't see the fleet for the funnels.'[1]

After years of neglect and under-funding, Britain's armed forces were unprepared for what was coming. As in 1914, it would be the ill-equipped peacetime servicemen who would buy time with their lives so Britain could again harness herself for war. With such naval power on display in Grand Harbour, few could have imagined the cost soon to be paid by these very same ships and their crews. The scale and majesty of the fleet disguised weaknesses. Many of the battleships and battle cruisers were leviathans, relics of a previous war, and they would struggle valiantly, yet ultimately fail against a new form of warfare. Battleships had perhaps had their day and only one of those at anchor would survive the coming war. Of the forty major warships riding at their moorings on the evening of Christina and Sheila's arrival, twenty-two, along with many thousands of sailors relaxing in Valletta that March evening, would not see their homes again. The *Knight of Malta*, built by Swan Hunter of Newcastle-upon-Tyne, would do her duty.

Was the potential of air power, and what was needed to defend against it, fully understood? There was very little time left to wake up to the future of warfare. The RN could tap into vast reserves of experience and ability, and was never short of courage and endurance, but it was about to be tested in the most severe of circumstances and air power would prove to be a determining factor.

Thankfully, the RN recognised the need for landing grounds in order to disembark carrier-based aircraft; this later paid dividends. A grass airfield was built at North Front Gibraltar and another in Malta on the cliffs not far from the RAF seaplane base of Kalafrana. This was Hal Far. Woody Woodhall was a Royal Marine pilot

---

1. Quoted in *Soldier, Sailor & Airman Too*, by Woody Woodhall, page 97.

who served there. The constraints of the Maltese terrain posed many problems for airmen and Woody experienced first-hand one that later concentrated the minds of many a Hurricane and Spitfire pilot: how to force-land successfully in one of those tiny fields between very solid stone walls. On his birthday, in 1928, his Blackburn Dart biplane's single engine failed after take-off from Hal Far about forty feet off the ground. He was lucky: his aircraft was not 'shot-up', nor was he being harried by enemy fighters at the time. He was able to walk away. Woody thought the aircraft carriers *Eagle* and *Courageous* were the navy's centrepieces, but readily admitted the Admiralty was very conservative in those days and classed aircraft carriers, along with submarines, as 'other vessels'. Alex Woods was a Fleet Air Arm Swordfish pilot who also served on both carriers. All too soon he became familiar with the threat posed by submarines within the narrow confines of the Mediterranean, experiencing first-hand the vulnerability of aircraft carriers.

With such an exotic and lively island on offer, postings to the Mediterranean Fleet were eagerly sought. The large, totally male service population resulted in the island being a desirable trawling ground for females looking for a husband. 'We called the numbers of young and not-so-young women from Britain who were in Malta's social arena "the Fishing Fleet" and the ladies' lounge of the Union Club in Valletta was the "Snake Pit".'[2] The Union Club, the former *Auberge de Provence*, was a favourite drinking haunt on a night out in Valletta. But, as an 'officers-only' establishment, woe betide any 'other rank' found there.

A new arrival in 1937 was 5-year-old Michael Longyear. His father was a Royal Engineer, accompanied by his wife and five of their six children; Michael's eldest brother was serving in the army in India. Michael's father developed peritonitis and was admitted to hospital on arrival. 'Visiting him gave me my first insight into a pre-war military hospital with the regimental line up of beds and blankets and the fearsome autocratic matron of the time. I believe the blankets were coloured either red or blue and the floor shone with polish. The uniform of the walking wounded and sick was the standard "Hospital Blues": blue trousers and jacket, white shirt and red tie.'[3] Michael would later see this uniform again; two of his brothers were wearing it.

The Longyears were housed at Msida Bastion, overlooking Marsamxett Harbour, with Michael's father based in Floriana Barracks. Life was comfortable with the population largely pro-British. For Michael it was fascinating and exciting with an endless round of beach parties, lunches, swimming, sight-seeing and picnic trips to Ghajn Tuffieha Bay by coach. He learnt to swim at the 'Horseshoe', a jetty in Marsamxett Harbour, and would often swim near Manoel Island, in use as a submarine depot. Further expeditions by *dghaisa* outside the harbour beyond Tigne

---

2. *Ibid.*
3. *Malta 1937–1942*, by Michael Longyear, pages 4–9.

Point allowed him to swim in the open sea. 'We boys were allowed to go on a tented camp with the troops when they were on exercise on Victoria Lines or on Marfa Ridge. I learned to load a Lewis gun pan magazine on the ranges at the age of seven and was even allowed to fire one with a rolled up sweater against my shoulder. The firing of grenades from a standard Lee Enfield rifle, with a cup fitted on the muzzle for the grenade, always fascinated me. They were good days in the open air, with something interesting happening and ample food for good appetites. We ate the same food as the troops; that is food produced in a field kitchen eaten out of mess tins. No one imagined they would soon be on the front line.

'More sedate entertainment was to lunch in Queen Street (now Republic Square) at the Savoy Hotel. I remember it well, with a white marble statue of Queen Victoria bang in the middle of the square. A luxury was to have an ice cream called "Eskimo Pie", which was in the shape of an igloo but embedded with glace cherries, angelica and nuts: all for six pence, which I suppose was a lot of money then. We also enjoyed the Maltese workers' lunch, which was a pennyworth of bread (*Hobz*) and a ha'porth of tomato paste. The chunk of bread, about half a loaf, had the middle scooped out and filled with the tomato paste which tasted of basil and rich tomato and a drizzle of oil: quite a feast.'[4] For a young boy, life was idyllic. Michael attended primary school within Floriana Barracks, not far from the parade ground below Floriana Gardens. But Britain was at last rearming. Michael's brother joined the Suffolk Regiment at the age of fourteen and was soon shipped back to England. His photograph appeared in the *Times of Malta* on embarkation. 'He looked such a small soldier in his big shorts and military topi.'[5]

There were many social events, including balls at the Vernon United Services Club in Valletta. With its large terrace overlooking Floriana and Grand Harbour, functions at the Vernon were always well attended by ladies in long dresses and men in their 'Blues'. In June 1938, the Vernon held a ball in honour of the Italian Navy, despite growing tension.

There were concerns in London that Malta might become untenable in the event of war involving Italy because of the island's proximity to Sicily and Italy's North African empire. Malta was vulnerable to Italian bombers and the island's lifeblood, seaborne supplies, could all too easily be halted. With Britain allied to France, which also had an immensely powerful Mediterranean fleet, there was some security of passage through the western Mediterranean, but if Britain was alone, many thought nothing could be done in Malta's defence. There were also concerns, though rarely expressed, about how the Maltese might react to war with Italy, its nearest neighbour, which had long been friendly toward the islanders.

---

4. *Ibid.*
5. *Ibid.*

Even if the Maltese were supportive of Britain, how would they react to bombing? Only sixty nautical miles from Sicily, the whole island was within minutes of Italian bombers. The impact of German and Italian bombing of Spanish cities, notably Guernica, in the Spanish Civil War, was also fresh in the minds of the military planners. A few heavy raids on Malta could reduce the island to rubble. How would the Maltese react then? And what would it cost to defend the island? It was probably this aspect which held sway in an unprepared and parsimonious London despite one or two voices to the contrary. One who argued Malta was the key to the Middle East was Winston Churchill, but, for most of the 1930s, he was in the wilderness. Britain would be at war for eight months before he became Prime Minister and even then he only got the job because someone else turned it down.

The Admiralty advocated strengthening Malta's defences as a deterrent, but the Air Ministry said the proximity of Italian airfields rendered the island unsafe as a major naval base. Admiral Sir Andrew Cunningham, soon to take command of the Mediterranean Fleet, felt Malta should be held, but he faced strong opposition; some opposition actually lasted into 1942. Many in London thought Malta a waste of resources better concentrated in North Africa. Churchill foresaw that in the event of war with Italy and Germany, the retention of Malta as an offensive base astride Axis routes to North Africa was the key to military success. Malta's loss would lead to Allied defeat in North Africa and the loss of Suez, giving the Axis all-important access to Middle Eastern oil.

Malta would always be reliant on resupply, as would any enemy army attempting to operate in North Africa. It was therefore essential to retain the island as a secure base from which to disrupt enemy supply routes. The advocates of defending Malta had to fight long and hard to convince the 'doubters'; by the late 1930s, it was still largely defenceless. There was a plan to reinforce, but that was all it was, a plan. A basic early-warning system was completed in 1935, but plans to extend it were cancelled. The building of submarine shelters was turned down on financial grounds and the cost of constructing bombproof underground storage facilities was also considered prohibitively expensive.

Almost too late, Britain woke up. In the event of war with Germany it was recognised Italy was likely to come in on the German side, yet the focus remained on a likely confrontation near the Franco-German border. Little attention was devoted to Malta. In 1939, Churchill's voice as the newly appointed First Lord of the Admiralty was a lonely one when he insisted Malta was vital to Britain's control of supply lines through the bottleneck of the central Mediterranean. Cunningham, now in his HQ at Fort St Angelo, shared his views, but what could he do?

With an ill-defended Malta, the Mediterranean Fleet's war location was at Alexandria in Egypt, with the Anglo-French strategy being to control the Mediterranean from the east and west with their superior fleets. The greatest threat came from the Regia Aeronautica, with tactics honed in Spain. In July 1939, the Committee of Imperial Defence ruled Malta should be defended by 112 heavy and 60 light anti-aircraft guns and by four squadrons of fighters. This was referred to as Scale B. Very little resulted from this ruling at a time when Britain's production of modern guns and fighters was woefully inadequate. This left Malta and its population of 220,000 terribly vulnerable.

If Italy became an enemy, her need to reinforce her Libyan colony would be paramount, which should have indicated Malta's importance as a base from which to attack. Malta was, however, not a priority. The RN and the Merchant fleet, as well as the Maltese, would pay heavily for Britain's neglect of Malta's defences. As would another band of the few. At the political level, the Prime Minister, Neville Chamberlain, and his French counterpart, would do all they could to keep Italy out of any war, to keep her neutral. It was a forlorn hope.

For Christina, Sheila and Vera, all enjoying the summer of 1937, their thoughts were focused on their futures. They did not opt for the free journey back to England to which they were entitled, but looked for further adventure. They obtained a contract to dance for fifteen days at the Tabarin Tunis. Once there they were assured they would be engaged for further work in Casablanca. Casablanca in 1937 certainly evokes an image. Gianni was very sorry to see Christina go, insisting she would return and work in the beautiful nightclub he intended to build, the finest in Malta he said. Christina was 24–years–old when she left Malta. At some stage, she travelled further to dance in Dakar, in what is now Senegal; in its heyday it was a major city within the French colonial empire. She also spent some time in Gibraltar. Her dancing shoes had taken her a long way from Dukinfield and they weren't through yet. She had seen fascists in Italy, experienced civil war in Spain and saw life in Vienna before the *Anschluss*. She had visited many capitals soon to experience the horror of total war. Christina's stepping stones to Malta were steps through a Europe and a system of colonial government soon to be torn apart. As she sailed away that September evening and watched Malta slowly disappear out of sight, little did she realise Gianni's words would ring true. Christina would return, but by then Britain would have been at war with Nazi Germany for six months.

Michael Longyear was at home on Sunday, 3 September 1939, listening to the Rediffusion, Malta's radio network, which transmitted in English and Maltese. As Britain was tied by treaty to Poland, many on the island had probably been doing the same ever since the unprovoked German attack on Poland two days earlier. The announcement by Neville Chamberlain came at 11.15 am British Summer Time: Britain was at war with Germany. 'I rushed out full of excitement to friends to tell everybody that we were at war. I had quite different ideas about the reality of war.

To my mind war was deeds of bravery and skills as shown in the books of "*Biggles and Co*" and represented by a painting in a book that I had seen depicting the God of War in a chariot. How all of that was to change.'[6]

Rediffusion, a radio system unique to Malta, transmitted from radio sets and amplifiers in Valletta to thousands of loudspeakers in village squares, barracks and houses. It had two channels: Channel A relayed a BBC programme and Channel B broadcast in Maltese, relaying concerts which took place on the island as well as talks and announcements in both languages. Transmissions from England were virtually impossible because of atmospherics and, in the absence of a first-class radio, most people preferred Rediffusion. From that Sunday everyone became news-minded and demands for loudspeakers were enormous. Priority was given to villages as Rediffusion was often the only means of giving an air raid signal or sending essential information rapidly. Soon the Longyear family were issued with gas masks and a mobile gas chamber came to the married quarters to test the masks.

Malta's Governor was Sir Charles Bonham-Carter. As far as administration and welfare were concerned, he reported to the Colonial Secretary in Whitehall, but as Commander-in-Chief (C-in-C) of Malta's army garrison he reported directly to the War Office. Bonham-Carter did not command the naval or air force units on Malta; they had their own single-service C-in-Cs in Egypt. He could not therefore give direct orders to Malta's senior sailor and airman, but nor could their C-in-Cs give orders directly to him. Although the three services cooperated, the command arrangements could hardly be described as unified. This impacted Malta's ability to present a united front concerning her role or her defence, or to speak with a single voice to the military planners in London.

The Mediterranean Fleet left Malta to concentrate at Alexandria, leaving only a few submarines and torpedo boats. In November, Admiral Cunningham returned with some cruisers and destroyers. Malta was defended by 4,540 British and 1,552 Maltese troops reporting to Bonham-Carter through a General Officer Commanding (GOC). They came from four British infantry battalions and one Maltese regiment: the King's Own Malta Regiment, although one of its companies was made up of Boy Scouts. Two more battalions of the regiment were soon raised and, with some reinforcement from Britain, the status of the garrison was raised to that of a division. This was still inadequate.

From January 1940, the senior airman was a New Zealander, Air Commodore 'Freddie' Maynard, appointed as Air Officer Commanding (AOC) (Mediterranean). His remit covered a wide geographical area but he had little to command on Malta. The first line of Malta's defence against air attack was fighter aircraft. There weren't any. If some were found, the island's airfields were in poor shape.

---

6. *Malta 1937–1942*, by Michael Longyear, page 9.

The seaplane base at RAF Kalafrana was useful for resupply and boasted large engineering workshops and stores facilities. Of greater importance was the able team of experienced Maltese aircraft fitters, retained after the base's London flying boats were moved to Gibraltar when war was declared. Kalafrana had anti-aircraft guns for localised defence; it needed them as the substantial workshops, barracks, messes and large hangars were tempting targets. There was also a specially widened road connecting Kalafrana to Hal Far; aircraft like the Hurricane could be towed along the road minus their wings. But there weren't any Hurricanes, only some Swordfish biplanes, mostly of the floatplane version. These were used for air-sea rescue, working alongside Kalafrana's eight RAF high-speed launches.

Ten years after becoming an RAF station, Hal Far, like Kalafrana, boasted a fine Officers' and Sergeants' Mess, but it had no fighter aircraft. Nor did it have paved runways, while its take-off and landing runs were limited in direction. Near the centre of the island, unintentionally built on the bed of an ancient lake, was Ta' Qali. Some said it reminded them of a giant soccer stadium with a huge grandstand – the high ramparts of Mdina – to one side. The view of the airfield from above was indeed excellent, especially if potential attackers knew it well. The pilots of *Ala Littoria*, the Italian national airline, knew it well, as they operated from there alongside other civilian airlines. Like Hal Far, Ta' Qali had no concrete runways and its surface soon showed its origins in bad weather, becoming virtually unusable. At the outbreak of war it had no fighter aircraft either, but the airfield's offices were good. The facilities for airmen were, however, extremely poor.

About a mile inland from the head of Grand Harbour was Luqa, Malta's third airfield. Also built as a grass landing field, paved runways were added in 1938, the only ones on the island. The longest measured 3500 feet, a good length in those days. Luqa had small but modern barracks about a mile distant. The airfield commanded a magnificent view of Valletta and its harbour to the north-east, but the combination of the slope in that direction, a deep valley at one end of the main runway and a quarry at the other, would have ruled it out as an airfield in Britain. Nevertheless, it was a masterpiece of civil engineering surrounded by hills and valleys, quarries and ravines, all of which nudged one another for space. Where there was a little room, a village had grown. The narrow, steep-sided, dry, stony valleys were often the scene of rushing torrents in the heavy winter rains.[7] Once the concrete runways were operational, Luqa became Malta's civilian airport and *Ala Littoria* duly moved in from Ta' Qali, broadening further its pilots' familiarity with Malta's airfields. In 1939, Luqa had no fighter aircraft either but it was set to become the island's principal RAF station.

---

7. *Briefed to Attack*, by AM Sir Hugh Lloyd, pages 24–6.

In April 1939, the first radar – radio direction finding – outside Britain became operational in Malta. It was located on Dingli Cliffs, one of the highest places on the island. It was not continuous and had to be shut down every few hours. A second set arrived in July and was erected nearby. The two radars now provided continuous coverage and could detect aircraft at 10,000 feet at a range of seventy miles, although aircraft at 2,000 feet could only be picked up at thirty miles distant.

This then was the situation on the outbreak of war: three airfields with limited facilities but no fighters, a single radar station and one seaplane base. And there were some packing cases on the slipway at Kalafrana. Despite the Committee of Imperial Defence's ruling concerning Scale B, there were only twenty-four heavy anti-aircraft guns to defend the entire island; the city of Coventry had forty-four.

Christina arrived back in Malta on 10 March 1940 on a three-month contract at the Morning Star. She moved into the same house as before, but the circumstances were now very different. She had no companions to live and work with, gone was the Mediterranean Fleet on which many of Valletta's nightspots relied, and Britain was at war with Germany. The Mediterranean seemed to be a backwater and Malta was quiet; it felt almost empty. Christina had come from her parent's home in Cheshire, although in the early part of 1939, she was in Morocco where she was engaged for a time to a French judge. For some reason she left, her father assisting her with a passage from Casablanca on a cargo ship, perhaps to, or via, Gibraltar. There is a suggestion she had plans to return to North Africa after her contract in Malta to finalise arrangements for her marriage, although she later said Morocco was definitely off. What had changed her mind? Did the outbreak of war precipitate a desire to return home, or was it a change of heart?

'The first few weeks went by at a funereal pace. I spent a lot of time wishing I had stayed at home and a good deal more longing for the expiry of the contract … in Gianni's gin palace. The situation was vastly different from that of 1937 when, with the other girls, I had stood at the beginning of a road to adventure – when there had been a purpose to our performance in what, after all, was nothing more than a low dive… . I was conscious, as I had not been before, of the sordid atmosphere of my surroundings.'[8]

Three years earlier, with five other English girls to work and socialise with, it was fun. Yes, the wild unruly crowds were now gone and it was no longer an ordeal to walk home unescorted at night, but something else had gone too and not just the 'Hi Blondie' calls and the wolf-whistles, now scarcely audible. The atmosphere and the sense of self-worth Christina had previously felt had also gone. Now, of all the ships of His Majesty's navy, only three remained in Grand Harbour: the monitor HMS

---

8. *Carve Malta on my heart and other wartime stories*, by Frederick Galea, page 25.

Terror and the gunboats *Aphis* and *Ladybird*. Christina longed for her contract to end so she could return to England.

Gianni Fetini's sentiments and those of other businessmen could not have been more different. They needed ports full of ships and dancehalls full of sailors. Empty harbours meant loss not profit. There were still soldiers and airmen on the island, but gone were the thousands of sailors manning the fleet. It was not quite the done thing, 'for any decent Maltese citizen to spend his evening down the Gut and there were not enough indecent ones about to keep Gianni's place running at a profit. It just had to be admitted that it was Jolly Jack who sent the big money rolling into the cash registers. But these days Jolly Jack, the playboy, was now very much the earnest warrior, with a mission important enough to keep him away from the bars and cabarets of Malta.'[9] Not surprisingly, Gianni was often very glum indeed.

The only other occupants of the old rambling three-storey house in Floriana were a young English couple, Cecil and 'Babs' Roche. Cecil was a comedian, Babs a dancer and they performed in another of Gianni's cabarets. With time on her hands by day, Christina found Rediffusion a godsend. The announcements in Maltese on Channel B were usually followed by an English translation, which was a great way for her to learn the language. The late evenings often found her and the Roches on their roof high above Grand Harbour, or sometimes on Christina's balcony at the front of the house looking inland. As April turned to May their discussions turned to worrying events all too close to their homes in England.

On 7 April 1940, Hitler unleashed his armies on Denmark and Norway; the Phoney War was over. In the Middle East, in the event of war with Italy, the RAF had less than 260 aircraft covering an area stretching from Malta to Kenya in the south and to Iraq in the east. Many, such as Gladiator fighters and Wellesley bombers, were obsolete. The number of heavy guns in Malta had only risen to thirty-four, with the War Office deciding any increase be provided to Alexandria to better protect the Mediterranean Fleet. This was a major setback for Malta's defenders. The general provisioning of Malta in the previous nine months was also inadequate, with Britain assuming unimpeded access from Gibraltar.

Air Commodore Maynard enjoyed a good working relationship with the senior service, having stayed with Admiral Cunningham for six weeks before the latter moved back to Alexandria. This relationship developed further with Vice Admiral Sir Wilbraham Ford, Cunningham's representative. Maynard felt when, not if, Italy entered the war, Malta could be held, even though on a clear day the Sicilian coast is visible as a faint line on the horizon. So began for Maynard and his successor a series of difficult strategic decisions made on the most tenuous resources. Determined to

---

9. *Ibid.*

offer some opposition in the event of an Italian strike, Maynard focused on the wooden packing crates at Kalafrana. They contained Sea Gladiator biplanes. At one stage there were twenty-four, transferred between freighter and Kalafrana, Kalafrana and aircraft carrier, then back again. Some were unpacked, assembled and flown to the carrier *Glorious* as it headed to the North Sea and the Norwegian Campaign.

Cunningham agreed to Maynard's request for four of the remaining eight aircraft, which were quickly assembled. The Hal Far Fighter Flight was born on 19 April, twelve days after Hitler invaded Denmark, and a call immediately went out for volunteer pilots. They were placed under the command of Squadron Leader 'Jock' Martin. Four other pilots volunteered: Peter Keeble, the Irishman William 'Timber' Woods, and John Waters and Peter Hartley, who were Swordfish floatplane pilots from Kalafrana. They were soon joined by George Burges, a former flying-boat pilot now serving as *aide-de-camp* to Air Commodore Maynard, and Peter Alexander, a Canadian previously operating radio-controlled target drones. This was Malta's first line of defence; four obsolescent biplanes and seven volunteers untrained in the art of air-to-air combat. The Gladiators may have looked archaic but their pilots were unanimous in their opinion of them, considering them first-class aircraft. John Walters said, 'they could turn on a sixpence and climb like a bat out of hell. Other aircraft all had their nasty little ways, but the Gladiator had no vices at all.'[10]

News soon reached the island of Hitler's *Blitzkrieg* on 10 May and the German rapid advance into the Low Countries. The British Expeditionary Force (BEF) advanced from its prepared positions on the Franco/Belgian border, but soon afterwards there was a sudden and decisive breakthrough at Sedan in France, and the French Army began to show signs of collapse. Belgium surrendered. Many French units, separated from the main French Army, continued to fight hard and supported the BEF under Viscount Gort as it retreated to Dunkirk. A very battered RAF, which had suffered catastrophic losses operating from France, withdrew to the British mainland having lost 900 aircraft and 430 aircrew. The 'miracle' of Dunkirk soon followed, but there was no disguising the bitterness of defeat.

Cunningham was told the Gladiators were required for service in Norway. Training was interrupted, the aircraft dismantled and repacked. Shortly afterwards the Norwegian Campaign ended disastrously for Britain with another evacuation and the loss of HMS *Glorious* and 1,519 seamen and airmen, as well as Hurricanes and Gladiators successfully re-embarked from Norway not long before. The four Gladiators of Fighter Flight were again reassembled and training restarted. With Sir Charles Bonham-Carter back in London with pneumonia, a temporary

---

10. *Red Duster, White Ensign*, by Ian Cameron, page 43.

successor, Sir William Dobbie, arrived on 28 April, but it became clear Bonham-Carter would not be returning so Dobbie became the effective Governor on arrival. Aged sixty, Dobbie was listed for retirement. Although Malta was still largely untouched by war, Dobbie quickly saw her vulnerability to airborne assault and urgently requested reinforcements. An additional battalion arrived within a few days. Admiral Cunningham stressed the need for long-range air reconnaissance aircraft based in Malta, while the Admiralty expressed concern about the lack of fighter protection for the island. The Air Ministry's response was Malta would have to make do; all modern fighter aircraft were needed for home defence.

Meanwhile, Christina and the Roches were 'frittering away their days on the golden sands of Ghajn Tuffieha, bathing in the cobalt blue Mediterranean, fattening ourselves with foodstuffs long listed on the ration cards in Britain – all that was nice work if you could get it but having it we were quite prepared to trade it for a ticket back to England.'[11] Christina was due to return to England on 17 June.

Although London considered Malta had six months' food reserve, if Italy concentrated her forces, the island was unlikely to withstand more than one serious seaborne assault. Nor could it be used as a naval base until better defended. As the possibility of France being knocked out of the war loomed large, the problem of building up Malta's defences became all too apparent. Once the direct air link to Malta was severed, no fighter had sufficient range to reach the island from Britain. At the time, RAF North Front, Gibraltar's airfield, was unsuitable as an air-staging post; it was simply a landing strip for aircraft disembarked from the navy's carriers. Convoys were needed if Malta was to be held, regular convoys to improve on and replenish the defences and to sustain the population.

In Britain, the RAF was soon preoccupied and fighting for survival. With the country braced for invasion, it is little wonder scant thought was given to reinforcing Malta, except perhaps by Churchill. If France was knocked out of the war, the window of opportunity – wide open for nine months – would close, leaving Malta largely isolated. The enormity of the calamity taking place in France would not have been widely known amongst the civilian population in Malta; even in Britain there was censorship, but as far as they could the Maltese followed events and continued to hope and pray. With Italy not having entered the war, for most civilians life remained quiet, but there was intense military activity as the authorities did what they could to prepare for the inevitable: war against Italy only sixty miles away.

Facing Malta on Sicily alone were over 250 aircraft. The Italians were well aware of Malta's unpreparedness and lack of fighter defence. On the evening of 9 June, the regular Italian airline service took off from Marsaxlokk Bay overflying Hal Far and Luqa, probably taking photographs on its way to Sicily. Hal Far's four aircraft

---

11. *Carve Malta on my heart and other wartime stories*, by Frederick Galea, page 26.

were dispersed amidst the prickly pears. Given the highly successful use of German airborne troops against the Dutch, wrecked vehicles and old junk was scattered at Hal Far, leaving only a narrow strip for the Gladiators which were flown as often as possible by their novice fighter pilots. Practice blackouts were held, anti-aircraft units reorganised, and air raid and interception exercises carried out in cooperation with the RAF HQ, then located in St John Cavalier in Valletta.

Malta lacked any centralised setup from which to conduct its defence. Having different HQs, each working in isolation, was not the way forward. A Royal Artillery officer was appointed as anti-aircraft defence commander working directly for Air Commodore Maynard, and he set up a small HQ and the rudiments of a gun and searchlight operations room within St John Cavalier. The radar at Dingli could detect most aircraft, friendly and hostile, unless they were flying extremely low, but there were inevitable gaps in coverage. With the arrival of three low-looking beam radars, most of the gaps were plugged. One problem for the technicians was the high rate of consumption of transmitter valves. Fortuitously, *Ala Littoria* came to the RAF's aid by bringing a dozen valves on the last civilian service they flew into Malta before the outbreak of war. It was just as well the Italian authorities did not look too closely at the cargo manifest.

Friendly aircraft were equipped with IFF – Identification Friend or Foe – which allowed them to be differentiated from other potentially hostile radar plots. Few people in Malta realised to what extent their lives depended on radar. Malta's experience would soon benefit other theatres of war with the pioneers of Dingli having lit the way. St John Cavalier also housed intelligence, wireless/telegraphy, code and ciphers, meteorology, and a RN liaison officer. Landlines connected the ops room to the airfields, and the artillery and searchlight officers had their own links to units. The small plotting table was very much a makeshift affair compared with those in use in Britain. In the event of an air attack against Valletta or Grand Harbour, a red flag (*bandiri hamra*) would be hoisted on the flagpole on the roof of the *Auberge de Castille* as a last minute warning for people to take cover.

The civilian authorities also geared up with the formation of a 2,000-strong volunteer Special Constabulary to ensure people reacted to warnings and to enforce blackout and curfew regulations. A Passive Defence Corps was established to deal with the feared threat of the use of gas, along with twelve centres with first-aid posts, decontamination chambers and medical staff. The Malta Volunteer Defence Force, a forerunner of the Home Guard, was also formed, as were three demolition and clearance squads, each of about forty men, who would hurry to the scene of destruction to recover anyone trapped beneath debris.[12]

---

12. *Gladiators over Malta*, by Brian Cull & Frederick Galea, pages 22–3

By the end of May, only weeks after having taken post, General Dobbie was again warning London of what he saw as serious and extensive deficiencies in Malta's defences. Anti-aircraft guns were far short of the requirement and the infantry was stretched. He highlighted the absence of fighters as the real danger. He was advised his requests for additional defences could not be met because of the situation in Britain and the risk of invasion.

Once war was declared, accompanied postings for married service personnel ended and arrangements were made for families to return home. Inevitably, this was a low priority. The island's governing council considered the matter early and plans were in place to move families away from military targets. Some limited evacuation took place in May, but many families chose to stay put. There was no compulsory evacuation for fear this would demoralise the local population. Service families would move into St George's Barracks and others to the Parisio Palace in Naxxar. Owned by the wealthy Scicluna family, the palace had enormous rock-hewn cellars, ideal air-raid shelters in the eyes of the planners. The plans were tested and wives and children from Kalafrana were moved to the palace. Yugoslavian-born Tamara Marks, married to a squadron leader, was required to pack personal belongings and taken to what might become her new home in Naxxar. The evacuees found it untypical of a palace. Tamara regarded the place with a sick feeling.

The sleeping accommodation was split between rooms for up to twenty and smaller ones for six. The beds were simply constructed three-tiered wooden bunks. Knowing this was an exercise, and hoping war would never come, few paid much attention to the 'rules'. Those new to barrack room life were introduced to 'biscuits' – the service name for the coarse canvas bags used as mattresses. Although Tamara only stayed one night, the reality of her surroundings slowly began to sink in. If they were required to live there, it would be very different from life at Birzebbugia, which was a happy community in a beautifully situated village with comfortable houses and well-stocked shops nearby. They could bathe from their own doorsteps and play tennis at the well-kept and popular courts at Kalafrana and Hal Far while, 'the tongue wagging was not any more venomous than it usually is in circumstances where everyone knows everyone's business.'[13]

---

13. *Women of Malta*, by Frederick Galea, page 32.

Chapter Five

Enter the Italians

aving determined the war was all but won, Benito Mussolini decided to join in, declaring war on Britain and France on Monday, 10 June 1940. For the Maltese, and everyone else now trapped on the island, so began the second siege, or, as the Maltese called it, the Greater Siege. On that Monday, Christina had seven days of her contract left to run. Despite the continuing bad business, Gianni had implored Christina to renew for another three months but she refused; she was definitely returning to England, or so she thought.

At 4.30 pm, the British Ambassador in Rome, Sir Percy Loraine, stood before Count Ciano, Mussolini's Foreign Minister, in the latter's elegant office. He was informed the King of Italy would consider himself in a state of war with Britain from midnight. Ciano described Sir Percy's reaction as 'laconic and inscrutable'. Sir Percy's supposed exit line was, 'I have the honour to remind Your Excellency that England is not in the habit of losing her wars.' Later, Mussolini appeared on the balcony of the sumptuous Palazzo Venezia to announce the news. Within the Italian population reaction was muted. Count Ciano said the news didn't surprise anyone, nor did it arouse very much enthusiasm. Yet he was very, very sad. 'The adventure begins. May God help Italy,'[1] he said.

Christina was at work when the blow fell. It was quiet, with the few customers outnumbered by waiters and hostesses. What business was being done could be counted by the number of glasses on three tables. A sailor sitting on his own appeared more interested in a crossword than his beer. Near the bandstand, four young soldiers celebrated a birthday with belts off and tunics unbuttoned, quietly enjoying themselves. Christina sat in an alcove near the entrance with Charlie Farrugia, a young, highly respectable Maltese man. His main purpose, or so he said, was to help Christina learn Maltese. Since Christina's arrival in March he had dropped in at the music hall almost every evening to teach Christina a few more words. At least she was able to make good use of what otherwise would have been some very boring hours. As they sat talking quietly, the volume on a radio in a bar across the street was turned up and a torrent of Italian came hurtling through the open doors of the Morning Star. It was the voice of Mussolini.

1. Quoted in *Churchill and Malta's War 1939–1943*, by Douglas Austin, page 50.

'Immediately there was a hubbub and the waiters and bandsmen led by Gianni came charging down the room to the doorway, where they stood listening with cocked ears… . The ranting was perfectly clear to Charlie, if not so much to me. My knowledge of the *dolce idioma* was such that I could not keep pace with the fast and furious speech, but I got the gist of it all right. Had I not, Charlie's white face, as he took in every word, would have warned me that something disastrous had happened. So too, would have the muttered oaths, the *Maria santissima's* of Gianni and his employees.'[2] As soon as the voice went off the air, Christina checked with Charlie whether she had understood correctly, that it meant war for Malta. Charlie confirmed the grim news; war was coming to the island.

Mussolini had chosen his moment well, or so he thought. He was determined to enter the war only if he could be certain he was on the winning side. With the imminent collapse of France, and the widely held belief that Britain would seek terms, the Italian dictator wanted a share of the spoils without risk. He wanted to continue expanding his 'New Roman Empire' and saw a great opportunity to take British dominions in Africa. The impact of his speech on the Maltese was dramatic and shocking: Italy was Malta's nearest neighbour and, until a few years earlier, Italian was the language of the 'educated' in Malta.

Charlie Farrugia was visibly upset and left quickly saying he would see Christina the following day, perhaps. Christina felt very, very lonely. The news spread like wildfire and Rediffusion programmes were interrupted by special announcements. Notices ordering all service personnel to report for duty were flashed on cinema screens and military police visited bars, restaurants and other public places clearing them of those servicemen still blissfully unaware of what had been said in Rome. Two military policemen – Red Caps – came into the Morning Star and a few words of command soon had the soldiers on their feet, fastening belts and tunics. They left at the run. Servicemen had been warned if Italy entered the war the first blow might fall on the island.

Tamara Marks and her husband Ronnie were at the 8.00 pm film at the Capitol Cinema in Kingsway, Valletta. Halfway through, the film was cut and a notice appeared on the screen directing all military personnel to report to their respective stations immediately. As they left, a cinema official validated their tickets so they could use them at another time. They never did. Outside, the streets were crowded but uncommonly quiet. The three red danger bulbs illuminated on the *Auberge de Castille* mast brought home the meaning of the words on the cinema screen. They sat in silence throughout the eight-mile bus journey home. There was nothing to say, the worst had happened. Although they had been expecting it for some time it was still a blow. 'How inadequately we were protected, no one knew better than we,

---

2. *Carve Malta on my heart and other wartime stories*, by Frederick Galea, page 27.

the wives of the men in the services. Although everyone laughed at the Eyeties and their bombastic threats when there still was a faint hope that they would see sense and we would only have the Germans to fight a good many miles away, it was no joking matter now that war was on our doorstep.'[3]

Gloom descended on those left at the Morning Star. Christina discussed the situation with a couple of dance hostesses. As an English woman, her opinion was eagerly sought, but she knew no more than anyone else. Outside in the narrow street, Gianni, his face ashen, was surrounded by the bandsmen and the other staff. They were all worried and anxious and pressed Gianni for more information about their jobs. Would the Morning Star have to close? Or would it be business as usual? Gianni, the businessman, was at a complete loss, but so was everyone else. He stood with his hands in pockets, eyes focused on the ground, as he moved his weight from one foot to the other. He may well have been thinking about the impact on his trade. He mumbled something about having to wait and see. Christina added her quota of questions, but before Gianni could reply a wild commotion broke out where an angry crowd had assembled outside an Italian barber's shop. They soon became an enraged mob, their voices reaching fever pitch, and Christina feared for the poor Italian's safety. Her thoughts went back to the Spanish Civil War where neighbours became enemies and respectable, law-abiding citizens were dragged into the street to be humiliated and reviled, then taken away to an unknown future. Thankfully, that evening in Valletta, the Maltese police were quickly on the scene and took the barber into custody, and inevitable internment.

It all seemed senseless and futile to Christina, all because people were of different nationalities. Once the incident was over, they all trooped back into the empty cabaret and Christina sat with Gianni as the bandsmen took their places on the rostrum. In an effort to be cheerful the band struck up a lively tune, but Gianni was in no mood for such levity and scowled at the bandsmen, angrily shouting at them to stop. 'The gloom in the place deepened. Faces grew longer. The conversation took on a melancholy tone. It was a long time since I felt so depressed. Why, for Heaven's sake, didn't somebody laugh or crack a few jokes? We were all behaving as if we'd lost the war and as yet it hadn't even started.'[4] When asked if they should come to work the next day, Gianni simply shrugged his shoulders; tomorrow was another day. Christina's comment that the war hadn't even started shows how little impact the ten-month long war had had on Malta. Most on the island felt remote and untouched by events in France. Now there was the sudden and shocking realisation the curtain on Malta was about to go up.

As Christina walked home that evening she was deep in thought. Between *Porta Reale* and Floriana, 'the war memorial pointed to a cloudless, indigo sky, a sky

3. *Women of Malta*, by Frederick Galea, page 27.
4. *Carve Malta on my heart and other wartime stories*, by Frederick Galea, pages 28–9.

interwoven with the beams of searchlights. It was a celestial scene that in recent weeks had become part and parcel of the Maltese night. By now we had all grown accustomed to searchlight practice, just as we had grown accustomed to having Rediffusion programmes interrupted by the seemingly far-fetched statement that the island was about to be attacked from the air. When the novelty had worn off, few of us paid much attention to the practice announcements broadcast in English and Maltese: Air Raid Warning – *Sinjal ta l-Attakki mill-Ajru*. I, for one and there were many others, never seriously believed that the day would come when the somewhat bored, matter-of-fact tone of the announcer's voice would take on a ring of more compelling urgency – the day when the mock air raids would be substituted by the real thing.

'Arriving at the residential area, I made my way along *Strada Capuccini* – a short, steeply-rising street, at the top of which a huge wooden cross mounted on a ten-foot plinth stood silhouetted against the sky. It was a beautiful evening but very warm and people in no immediate hurry to retire into the heat of their homes were sitting about the doorways – some on the steps, others in chairs placed out on the pavement. From the snatches of conversation I overheard, in which the name of Mussolini cropped up repeatedly, it was evident that the main topic was Italy's entry into the war. Every now and then came the low murmur of prayers as the members of some family circle, united for the evenings' devotions, recited litanies and counted their rosary beads. I saw no signs of panic anywhere along the route, yet an unmistakable atmosphere of foreboding hung heavily in the air of that warm June night.'[5]

Once home, Christina found Cecil and Babs had invited Billie, a pretty blonde dancer, to stay the night. They all spent some time discussing their situation. With war on their doorstep would they be able to leave the island? What would happen to them if they couldn't leave? Would there be any work for them to do? Question followed question, but none could be answered and, with their problems unresolved, they retired for the night; they would simply have to wait and see.

At their home in Birzebbugia, Tamara helped Ronnie pack a small bag and he left to report for duty. After he had gone, Tamara felt very small and lonely, unsure when they would see one another again. She went outside. 'It was a beautiful night, as June nights usually are in Malta.... Little clusters of people were on their doorsteps discussing animatedly. No one thought it would be serious. The island was too small, they said, for any bomb to fall on it. It was one chance in a million that could happen. Look at it on the map. A mere pinpoint, surely nothing could hit it, especially if it was dropped from any height. This view was held by a great number of people and curiously enough testified to by the pilots. No, there was nothing to worry about.'[6]

---

5. *Ibid.*
6. *Women of Malta*, by Frederick Galea, pages 27–8.

Yes, Malta is small, but, as the pilots knew all too well, it couldn't very well be missed. The RAF stations of Luqa, Ta' Qali, Hal Far and Kalafrana were all very close to one another, their proximity dictated by Malta's terrain. The Italian Air Force knew exactly where they were, having been given the intelligence gathered by their national airline. And how could they possibly miss Grand Harbour and the dockyards? Many of the Italian aircrew had learnt their trade well in the Spanish Civil War. With Malta's very obvious military targets closely surrounded by towns and villages, 'collateral damage' was inevitable and every civilian was now on the front line. Yes, the pilots knew what could befall Malta; their words were worthy but the reassurance offered was misplaced. It would have been better had they talked about precautions and being prepared. The only hope in the coming days was that Italian aircrew did not share their leader's enthusiasm for war against their small island neighbour. They had the skill and the courage for the task, but would they be willing to press home their very obvious advantage?

Tamara was woken up by the sound of guns the next morning. She dressed quickly, desperate to find out what the commotion was all about and hoping they were merely testing the guns. 'There was a disquieting roar of aircraft but it seemed unlikely that it could be the Italians. They were too well-known for their *dolce far niente*; they could not possibly start a war so early in the morning when they had the whole day to do it in. I looked out of the window. Flashes of fire and great sheets of smoke were coming from the direction of Kalafrana. The noise was terrific; the doors and windows were rattling as if they would jump off their hinges. I ran into the street. There was no one to be seen, not a soul. I wondered where everyone had got to. If only the guns would stop a minute, I could collect my wits and do something. Another sickening thud … that was near. I had heard that under the table was the safest place. Yes, I must hide under a table. I shut the door and climbed the stairs four at a time. No, the door was rattling too much. I had better leave it open.

'Down I rushed, opened it, dashed upstairs again and slipped under the dining-room table, which was of thick mahogany. After a minute in a very cramped position, the ridiculous sight I must have been struck me forcibly. I could not possibly cower like a rabbit, it was too silly. Besides, it would have been better for me to do some packing. Another salvo. The aircraft were coming nearer and nearer. If only I had someone with me. Anyone. I had to get away. Then, just as I ventured out of the door, the guns would go off; the door nearly slammed in my face and I did not have the key. Then, for five minutes nothing could be heard. The police station – that was it. Why had I not thought of it before? There was bound to be someone there. I ran for sheer life, little metallic sounds clicking off all round me.'[7] The metallic sounds were shrapnel; war had come to Malta.

---

7. Quoted in *Call-Out*, by Frederick Galea, pages 25–6.

The air raid siren didn't awaken Christina, it was the Roches shouting desperately that the air raid warning had sounded and they were heading for the basement. She acknowledged their anxious calls but, 'lay back in the pillows and listened to the clip-clop of Babs' heels on the stone steps as she and her husband hurried below. For a while I stared vacantly at the ceiling, not quite certain what all the fuss was about. Then slowly, I got up... . Ten to one this was just another practice raid. And anyway, I had not heard the siren – maybe Babs and Cecil had been imagining things. Perhaps I ought to go down, though. I sat at my dressing table and began to undo my curlers. I didn't like being seen in curling pins.

'Then it happened. Without further warning there was a deafening crash, and the building rocked and shook as if it were about to collapse. Another crash, the roar of aircraft, the drawn out whine of a bomb followed by an ear-splitting explosion, a loud salvo of gunfire. For a few seconds I sat where I was, terrified. Then, I got up and made a mad rush for the door... . More crashes and roars. I never realised it was such a long way down to the cellar and I began to feel that I would never get there alive. But I made it... .

'"Billie, where's Billie?" demanded the Roches when they saw I was alone. Their concern for her safety was unnecessary. Before I could reply she came bounding down the last flight of stairs at breakneck speed; a vision of loveliness clad in a flimsy pair of chiffon cami-knickers, which left nothing at all to the imagination. Like me she had been caught napping. But at that particular moment none of us had a mind for the niceties of dress. The main thing was to save our skins; with or without the covering.

'The cellar was full of junk; including some pieces of old furniture. In one corner there was a solid-looking marble-topped table festooned with cobwebs. I suddenly got the bright idea that we would be a good deal safer crouching beneath it than standing where we were. Another loud crash and I was certain beyond doubt. Under I dived, quickly followed by Babs and Billie. Cecil was left to brave it alone.

'The din of battle grew louder and more terrifying as we sat huddled together beneath the old table. I was firmly convinced that our last moments had come... . At long last ... the racket subsided and only the faint drone of aircraft could be heard. At the OK from Cecil we crawled cautiously out of our hideaway, trailing yards of dirty cobwebs behind us... . I was thankful for Cecil's presence and his steadying influence. And I'm sure Billie was doubly grateful. Few men in similar circumstances would have done what Cecil did. He gathered up several sheets of dusty brown packing paper that were lying around the floor and before Billie knew what was happening she had been wrapped up into a neat parcel of respectability – and warmth. For it was decidedly cool in the sun-starved cellar, despite the red-hot atmosphere of the world above.

'A few minutes later the anti-aircraft guns opened up again, but this time we girls remained where we were; Cecil reassuring us that there was really nothing to worry about because you never heard the bomb that hit you. And as the smoke of gunfire grew to a crescendo he attempted to dispel our fears still further by providing a running commentary. There was a series of thunderous roars: "That's the *Terror.*" Another series not quite so deep in tone: "That's the ack-ack." Then suddenly: "Quick – under the table. This is a bomb." But before we could get back under our marble roof, the bomb exploded, proving to Cecil's great satisfaction that his theory was correct.

'"What did I tell you?" he grinned, a trifle sheepishly, I thought.

'Although the first alert of the war lasted only twenty minutes, it seemed as if we had been down the cellar for many hours when finally there came the long, steady drone of the All Clear. A few minutes of silence followed: the sort of profound, almost eerie silence that follows the sounding of the *Last Post.* Then came the *Reveille.* The silence was broken by a chorus of high-pitched voices and a terrific clatter on the iron grating in the pavement above as our next-door neighbours rushed out of their house… .

'On reaching my room, I ran to the balcony… . I expected to be confronted by a scene of devastation and havoc, with at least half the buildings of the district reduced to ruins. But life is full of surprises. Dust there was in plenty, the roadway was strewn with the glass of shattered windows and a strong smell of cordite hung about, yet from where I stood I could see nothing to detract from the familiar pattern of the surrounds.

'I studied the people milling about in the street, curious to see how they had taken this sudden attack on their homeland by their former friends. From their actions, as well as their words, it was manifest that their anger and indignation bordered on the flash point. The usual decorum of my neighbours was thrown to the winds as they shook their fists at the now deserted sky and rained down curses on the whole Italian race. The air grew blue with blasphemy as a hunchbacked old grandmother expressed in no uncertain terms her personal opinion of the love-child Mussolini.

'From the people below, my roving eye wandered to the top of the front wall of St Francis Barracks just across the way, where a young soldier stood surveying the roofs with a pair of binoculars. In due course his sights were set on my balcony. A few seconds later I heard a loud chuckle. When I thought about it afterwards, I realised the soldier had every reason to chuckle. Not only was I dusty, dishevelled and covered in cobwebs, but half my head was still in curlers. No pin-up by any means. But I hadn't got round to caring.'[8]

Christina asked about casualties, but the soldier didn't know. He pointed to the site of one explosion, a near thing, right on Christina's doorstep. That was the bomb Christina heard as she sat at her dressing table. It landed near *Porte des Bombes* of all places, claiming the first victim of the war from a group of Maltese workmen.

---

8. *Carve Malta on my heart and other wartime stories*, by Frederick Galea, pages 29–31.

For Michael Longyear life changed suddenly that morning: 'My mother had been designated as an air raid warden and was given a large hand bell to ring around the married quarters as an air raid warning. She continued ringing long after the first bombs were dropping until she was unceremoniously bundled into the makeshift shelter. These were dug in the grassed area between the road of the quarters and the bastion. The shelter was really a slit trench covered with corrugated iron and further covered with earth. Seating was on an army bench on either side of the trench so that we all faced each other. On that first day a soldier was detailed to sit outside the open entrance with no protection, other than his tin hat, because it was thought that we civilians might panic. When the sound of shrapnel dropping from our AA guns was heard hitting the ground near us, it was suggested that he should come inside with us. He agreed to the suggestion only when assured that we would not panic, but he still sat at the bottom of the steps in case we did.'[9] The old monitor, HMS *Terror*, anchored in Marsamxett Harbour, seemed to Michael to fire every gun it had, the black smoke quickly drifting across the creek bringing with it the acrid smell of cordite and powder.

Tamara made it to the police station. Soon afterwards the all-clear sounded and she returned home where she was met by Ronnie. She packed ready for evacuation to Naxxar before taking a last look at her small but compact and convenient flat with such a lovely view of Kalafrana Bay: 'The sun streaming through the French windows and glistening on a sea of burnished cobalt made this sample of Italian "morning hate" seem so very imbecile.'[10]

The early morning 'hate' was the first of the day's eight air raids. Ten Savoia-Marchetti 79 (SM.79) aircraft bombed Hal Far. Another fifteen attacked the dockyards thirty minutes later, as ten more targeted Kalafrana. The bombers had fighter escorts – Macchi C200 (MC.200) single-engine, modern monoplanes. As soon as the raiders were spotted by radar, three Gladiators were scrambled. As they lifted off, the first bombs fell behind them. Long before they reached the level of the attackers, bombs fell on Valletta. The Gladiators all attacked, but without apparent result, then their pilots sat and watched helplessly as the Italian bombers simply accelerated away. The Gladiators were simply too slow. How could they gain more speed?

No bombs fell on Floriana in the second or third raids and the Roche's friend Billie returned home. By then, feeling considerably bolder, Cecil suggested a stroll into Valletta for a meal and to find out the form from Gianni. They had no sooner reached the city gates than the sirens sounded and their leisurely pace broke into a trot as they joined a fast-moving stream of people heading toward the Royal Opera House. Eventually they found themselves in a long tunnel, a relic of the one-time

9. *Malta 1937–1942*, by Michael Longyear, pages 10–11.
10. *Women of Malta*, by Frederick Galea, pages 32–3.

railway between Valletta and Rabat. This raid was particularly heavy; so much so that hundreds of people herded together in the tunnel bowed their heads in prayer, calling fervently upon the Holy Virgin to deliver them from harm. Later, when walking down Kingsway, Christina saw the shops were still closed, leaving them to predict the Morning Star would not be open either. It was bolted and barred. The street called Strait was as silent as a pathway to the grave. They returned to Floriana.

At Birzebbugia there were three buses to take the RAF wives and children, Tamara amongst them, to Naxxar. Halfway there, the buses stopped dead; the drivers shouted it was an air raid: 'Panic seized us... . We did not know what to do. We got out of the buses carrying the children and their luggage. We scanned the sky. The sun was at its highest and it was a strain to look into the intense sunlight. Some sat down on stones; some lay flat... . I had found a flat stone and made myself comfortable in the ditch. We could see the aircraft like small dots very high up.'[11]

Tamara thought they were British as there was no anti-aircraft fire. Another lady said they must be Italian as there were too many to be British. Tamara was astonished, more so when the lady said the RAF only had three fighters. She thought that ridiculous and said so. But the other lady insisted the RAF only had three ancient but gallant Gladiators. Tamara hoped it was not common knowledge there were only three defenders. To her it seemed madness to carry on with Sicily only sixty miles away. But such was the reality of Malta's fighter defence.

Tamara was soon joined in the ditch by others: 'It was quite pleasant sitting there in the sun chit-chatting to the muffled sound of the anti-aircraft guns in the harbour. The aircraft had disappeared over the sea and the white puffs caused by the shell bursts were slowly flattening out and looking like innocent cloudlets.'[12] Once the all-clear sounded they drove hell for leather to Naxxar.

On that first day more than 120 bombers struck the dockyards, Hal Far and Kalafrana. There were various claims and counter claims, but no aircraft were shot down. Six bombers suffered damage from the guns in the afternoon raid on Hal Far. They all returned safely to base, their crews reporting being intercepted by biplanes which apparently numbered twenty at one stage. The bombers claimed varying degrees of success, including a direct hit on an anti-aircraft battery which killed six members of the Royal Malta Artillery. Six Maltese naval personnel were also killed when two launches were sunk. Damage to military property was relatively slight, although many civilian buildings around the dockyard were hit. Eleven civilians were killed and 130 injured.

The obsolete Gladiators may not have shot down any enemy aircraft, but they were seen opposing the Italians and this had a profound impact on the morale of

---

11. *Ibid.*
12. *Ibid.*

a fearful civilian population. The biplanes, together with the guns of the Royal Malta Artillery and the Royal Artillery, helped break up the Italian formations and disrupt their aim. As a result, many bombs fell harmlessly into the sea. Bombing from between 10,000 and 15,000 feet also contributed to inaccuracy. Nevertheless, the Italians had been challenged and they knew it. While the first air raids awakened the islanders to the reality of modern war, it was the very last air raid that day which demonstrated its totality. The primarily residential areas of Gzira, Zabbar and Cospicua were heavily bombed, and this raid had a dramatic impact on the civilian population, with thousands seeking safety elsewhere.

Tamara was not surprised to find life in the Parisio Palace was to be 'ordered', with the husband's rank determining status and who was in charge. The wives of those in the RAF HQ had preceded the main group and, beneath fine murals and between sculptured pillars, they organised bewildered looking women and wailing children, all under the control of a group captain's wife who commanded attention with the aid of a wooden mallet. Each group of ten was put under the charge of an officer's wife and many wore their husband's rank from that point onwards. Officers and other ranks' wives had separate dining rooms. Only women with children were allocated rooms; those without, like Tamara, slept on landings. Buckets served as lavatories placed at the corners of balconies. There was one just outside the window on Tamara's landing. There were three air raids the first night, which saw everyone without exception scurrying to the shelters in the old cellars. Most people felt like wrecks the next morning.

The previous evening, after the all-clear had sounded and when it was still daylight, Christina and the Roches collected bedding and went back to the tunnel. The road was crammed; everyone had the same idea – get beneath good, solid rock. They joined a slow-moving procession of hundreds of people of all ages and from all walks of life. Old and young alike staggered along carrying blankets and pillows, cushions and folding seats. Some balanced rolled-up mattresses on their heads as others pushed heavily-laden wheelbarrows and prams. A man pushing an iron bedstead on its castors had Christina's admiration.

The railway tunnel was now a vast dormitory with rows of mattresses and deckchairs. Pictures of the Holy Virgin and the Sacred Heart of Jesus adorned the walls, interspersed with cards bearing the words *Ikun Imbierek Alla* (Blessed Be God). As darkness fell, the tunnel, illuminated by oil lamps and candles, became more crowded. When Christina decided to lie down she found she had lost her floor space. 'Collecting my rolled-up blanket and pillow I went … in search of new lodgings … tripping occasionally in the darker patches over the legs of some prone body and now and again barging into the end of a camp-bed…. . I came across a few feet of bare ground right up near the entrance. While not the safest of places, there was a certain amount of solace in the fact that the crowd up here was not quite so thick, the air not nearly so foul as further down…. . I sat down very tired yet in no mood for sleep.

'I looked around at my bedside companions. On my right a family of four, husband and wife and two little girls, lay huddled together on a mattress, all of them sound asleep. Beyond them, a young mother sat propped up against the wall, feeding a tiny infant at her breast. Down by my feet two boys, about ten and twelve years old, were curled up on a blanket and a woman who looked as if she might be their mother sat dozing above them in a deckchair. On my other side a wizened old man was making a fuss of getting himself ready for bed. I watched, fascinated, as he struggled slowly out of his shirt and trousers, folding them neatly and placing them at the side of my pillow. Standing in underpants and singlet he scratched his head thoughtfully for a few moments then he picked up the sheet covering his folded blanket and wrapped it round his shrunken body. After making the sign of the cross he sank to his knees, shook up his pillow and firmly settled down at my side.

'Sandwiched in among total strangers, I lay awake for a long time trying hard to imagine what the future held in store for all of us in Malta. My thoughts became morbid, as not unnaturally I wondered if I would live to see my mother and father and brothers again. Whether I would be killed outright or horribly maimed. I tried to cheer myself up by thinking how the girls at the Theatre Girls' Club would have laughed if they could have seen me tucked up for the night next to this wizened old man. At length, to a lullaby of subdued conversations and loud snores, I fell asleep.

'It must have been about two hours later when I was awakened, not by the sound of the air raid warning, exploding bombs, gunfire, or the all-clear, but to the mischievous giggling of the two lads at the bottom of my makeshift bed, one of whom was in the act of tickling my bare toes!'[13]

The following morning, Christina and her friends returned home before setting out once more to Valletta to see if they could find their employer. War or no war, they needed to earn a living. When they reached the main Valletta-Floriana thoroughfare they were confronted by a scene similar to the previous evening, except this time the crowds were moving in the opposite direction. So far there had been no raids and people were doing their very best to get as far away from Grand Harbour as possible. Some were on foot; some were on wheels, as hundreds of citizens streamed away to what they considered safer towns like Hamrun, Birkirkara, Naxxar, Rabat and St Paul's Bay. They took all their worldly goods; lorries and horse-drawn carts all stacked high with furniture, bedding, carpets and cooking utensils, all heading out of the city in a continuous stream.

In scenes similar to those seen in Belgium and France, Malta now faced the shocking sight of refugees streaming away from where they felt threatened.

---

13. *Carve Malta on my heart and other wartime stories*, by Frederick Galea, pages 33–4.

Thankfully they were not strafed from the air to cause panic; in fact there were no air raids that day. 'The road leading from Cospicua to Zabbar Gate presented a pitiful sight. Women with bundles on their heads, or with bundles hanging from their arms, carrying babies, with one or two children holding to their skirts, with a boy or a girl pushing a pram loaded with the most essential belongings, crowded the road, walking without destination in view, but leaving their beloved homes, abandoning the city, going anywhere, as far as possible from the target area. Buses, touring cars, cabs, and horse-drawn vehicles carrying the more fortunate families who either owned a vehicle or could afford to hire one, moved in the crowd of walking and less fortunate humanity also proceeding in the direction of Zabbar.'[14]

People fled to anywhere away from the bombing, but few places on such a small island were completely safe. In those first few days, it was estimated about 100,000 people left their homes. To begin with, the situation was chaotic until some sort of order was imposed. Churches were opened to house refugees, as were schools and other buildings. How was the civilian population likely to react if the bombing intensified? How could morale be kept high?

In Valletta, Christina and the Roches found all the shops and offices, the market, the bars and restaurants still closed. At Gianni's home, the only information was from a woman on the balcony of the house next door. With upturned eyes and hands she simply said, 'mhux hawn': Gianni had hopped it. They returned home worried, jobless and stranded; they were also hungry and their cupboards were bare. How long the shops would remain closed was anyone's guess. Then there was a knock at the door. They opened it to the Mallias of the Queen's Store, who had not forgotten the Inglizi in their hour of need. Their kindness in bringing welcome foodstuffs left Christina and her friends deeply moved.

They spent the next few nights in the railway tunnel, although there was no bombing at night. At the end of the week, a number of people returned to their homes. Rock shelters were increasingly made available and the efficient air raid warning system usually allowed time to take cover. Despite the personal danger, Christina very much preferred the comfort of her top floor room to that offered by the former Malta Railway Company.

The RAF tried to improve the Gladiators' performance with the largely Maltese-manned aircraft repair section at Kalafrana working wonders. Modifications increased the engines' boost and although this would do them no good in the long term, it gave the pilots what they needed: more speed and a fighting chance of catching the bombers. One Gladiator had its two-bladed wooden propeller replaced with a three-bladed metal one in a further attempt to improve performance.

---

14. *Gladiators over Malta*, by Brian Cull & Frederick Galea, page 32.

The respite from bombing on 12 June was a godsend, but the Italians returned the next day with a series of nuisance raids which had little effect. The Italians again suffered no losses. The following day they were back and lost a bomber and its crew of six, not to the island's defences, but to airframe icing causing loss of control. Hurricanes were seen for the first time, with three landing at Luqa. Unbelievably, they were not reinforcements, but the first of a group of five on their way to Egypt, which was seen as having greater priority. The Hurricanes were expected and two days earlier Sir William Dobbie sought agreement from the War Office to retain them. The War Office agreed, but unbelievably the first three were allowed to continue to Egypt. This serious breakdown in communication was perhaps indicative of the command arrangements on the island. By then Fighter Flight had two more Gladiators unpacked and ready to fly.

Dobbie visited six villages on Sunday, 16 June, a day when attacks intensified. He arrived in Zetjun in the middle of an air raid and finished in Mosta soon after bombs landed nearby. His visits were a much needed morale boost, but he harboured doubts about how long morale would hold up under intense, indiscriminate bombing. Often affectionately referred to as 'Old Dob Dob', Sir William was described as the simplest and humblest of men. He was a devout member of the Plymouth Brethren, a teetotaller and did not smoke. He was judged by his men as always fair and had no 'sides', always exuding an inner calm others found hard to explain. His calmness was needed now.

There was more bombing the day after, with four out of the five bombers involved being damaged by Gladiators. There were almost 150 civilian casualties in the first week, two thirds of them women and children. Things were then quiet for a couple of days. A dozen RN Swordfish biplanes arrived at Hal Far on 20 June, their pilots perturbed when they saw their destination covered with an assortment of vehicles, barrels and drums. Nevertheless they landed safely. Bombing resumed that night, focused on Grand Harbour. The Italian crews reported very heavy defensive fire and blinding searchlights. The following morning saw one precious Gladiator crash on take-off and a second overturn when landing, having lost its tailwheel due to ground debris. One pilot was slightly injured, but the loss of two aircraft was a bitter blow. Thankfully, they had an experienced and highly efficient team of Maltese ex-dockyard apprentices and Auxiliary Air Force mechanics to call upon, formed around a nucleus of RAF fitters and riggers. This team had been welded together by Flying Officer Collins, a former warrant officer. They may have lacked experience on Gladiators and had no spares, but they were great improvisers.

The defensive strength was soon up to three, with the engineers actually creating one working aircraft out of the two wrecks. Thankfully, on the same day, two more Hurricanes destined for Egypt arrived and this time Air Commodore Maynard ensured they were retained. The following day six more arrived from Bizerte, although one was damaged after a night landing at Luqa when it hit a bus. Two Blenheim bombers also arrived. The six Hurricanes and two Blenheims were all that made it out of twelve of each type which left England four days earlier. The Hurricane pilots were not from a formed fighter unit but from a pool of ferry pilots. Some were bomber pilots who now needed to learn a new trade and learn it fast. But becoming a fighter pilot was not a skill to pick up overnight, and Malta was no longer a benign training environment.

Fighter Flight had its first success on the evening of 22 June when George Burges and Timber Woods shot down an Italian reconnaissance aircraft. This was witnessed by many as the action took place over Sliema and Valletta. It caused quite a stir. Two of the Italian crew were rescued from the sea off St Thomas Bay; the other four were lost. Burges had further success the following day when he shot down an MC.200 fighter far superior in performance to his Gladiator. The Italian pilot was taken prisoner. This success took place as Luqa was being heavily bombed. Although the bombing was inaccurate, Malta's gunners were not and four bombers were damaged. 'The Maltese were jubilant over the shooting down of the Italian aircraft, and Fighter Flight in their turn felt they had justified the confidence everyone at Hal Far had shown in them and the hard work which the mechanics from Kalafrana, with their army helpers, had put in to keep them flying.'[15]

There were now eight Hurricanes, although only five were serviceable. As Malta now had more Hurricanes than Egypt, three had to be sent to Alexandria, leaving Malta with only two. The three ferry pilots remaining were attached to Fighter Flight. Two had no previous fighter training; the third had not distinguished himself in Britain, having damaged two aircraft when serving on a Spitfire squadron. That may well have been why he found himself as a ferry pilot. It was often all too easy for squadrons in Britain to 'unload' pilots they did not want into such pools and some inevitably found their way to Malta. The island needed formed units, operational fighter pilots trained in their art, along with experienced engineers trained on the types in use. Thankfully, the existing team of engineers and support staff were able to work with great flexibility, initiative and resolve.

London anticipated French capitulation and the Admiralty considered abandoning the Eastern Mediterranean and concentrating the fleet at Gibraltar. Churchill strongly opposed this as it would spell doom for Malta. Cunningham also warned Egypt could not be held for long without the fleet. On 24 June, France capitulated and the balance of power in the Mediterranean changed significantly. The route for Hurricanes to reach Malta through France was now firmly closed.

Two days later Italian bombers hit Luqa, Hal Far and the dockyards. The returning crews reported accurate bombing, intense anti-aircraft fire, but no sign of

---

15. *Gladiators over Malta*, by Brian Cull & Frederick Galea, page 32.

the RAF, although Fighter Flight did make an interception. The so-called accurate bombing resulted in a bus being hit by an incendiary bomb at the Marsa crossroads; thirty civilians died. Francis Cordina's 26-year-old brother Joe was on his way home on board that very bus. With the bus on fire, he escaped from the carnage, taking cover in a nearby store. The store then received a direct hit. Having heard of the tragedy and with Joe having failed to come home, Francis, along with his father and an elder brother, went to a local hospital to see if they could find him. They were met with harrowing scenes of rows of mutilated and burned bodies laid out in rows. They found Joe.[16]

The dockyards and Luqa were again hit on 30 June. The Italians noted five RAF monoplanes – Hurricanes – were airborne, but failed to make an interception. That same night Malta's newly-arrived Swordfish hit back, striking an oil refinery in Sicily. It was almost three weeks since Mussolini's declaration of war.

At Naxxar, everyone settled in and Tamara was amazed and pleasantly surprised at the friendliness and adaptability of her companions. She had not enjoyed her three years' experience in England, whereas her contacts at Birzebbugia had been superficial. 'Seeing them at close-quarters, I liked them. They were clever at makeshifts, polite and kind to each other. It was like being back at boarding school again.... We were sorely tried by the lack of bathrooms.... Only three bathrooms were available for about seventy women and an equal number of children. Old pruderies had to go by the board. Two or three women had to use the same bath at the same time and they did. Children washed *en masse*.'[17] When six bathrooms were built out of sacking and corrugated iron, three were labelled 'Other Ranks' and three 'Officers wives only'. Duties were assigned and came round by rotation. One lady was taken to hospital to have a baby, her fourth, and then returned to Naxxar with her newborn son. Life went on. They got used to the order of the raids.

There were no restrictions on husbands visiting by day, but they were only allowed in the garden. No one infringed this rule. To begin with the curfew began at 6.00 pm, but this was extended after a month to 8.00 pm. None of the residents stirred from the Parisio Palace for the first week; their imaginations far too active even though no bombs had fallen within a mile. They all expected to be killed and they worried constantly. It was this worry that produced their only casualty, a warrant officer's wife who drove herself out of her mind with worry and died at Mtarfa Hospital a month after Italy declared war.

Everyone soon realised they needed to venture out. Their reappearance into the world after a week's seclusion was something of a revelation and, from that day onward, they grew bolder. Every day a group would go downtown to eat, or shop, or go to the cinema. If they did not return by 8.00 pm they were locked out with little

16. *The People's War Malta: 1940/43*, by Laurence Mizzi, pages 59–61.
17. *Women of Malta*, by Frederick Galea, page 35.

chance of getting in unless they bribed the gardener. Some of the 'inmates' dubbed the palace 'the concentration camp'; although Tamara thought it rather unjust as the Entertainments Committee was very active. Concerts were organised and there were whist drives and tombola, although they were often interrupted by air raids. 'One night we had a carnival party. Everyone was to dress up but was to use only material to hand; nothing was to be brought from outside…. . I decided to go as Eve and for two days, had three carefully picked fig leaves in a vase by my bedside. They were to be sewn one on a pair of pink panties and two on a pink brassiere. I thought the idea simple and effective, but was dissuaded from putting it into execution as Sgt Baker had been invited too…. . A "caught in an air raid", which consisted of two towels wrapped around hips and breasts, was a big success.'[18]

By the end of June some confidence had been restored and life began to return to normal with shops reopening and people beginning to go about their business. When the sirens sounded, the shutters came down, but were lifted just as quickly with the all-clear. A great fillip to morale was the success of Fighter Flight and the arrival of the Hurricanes. At the beginning of hostilities the islanders went to their shelters as quickly as possible on hearing the siren; now they stood on their flat roofs and other vantage points to witness thrilling aerial battles.

The early raids hadn't bothered Michael Longyear: he and his friends still enjoyed the same activities as before. They attended school and went into Valletta with few worries despite the blackout. 'I remember well, going into Valletta with my sister in the evening, she carrying a torch which was suddenly painted with a deep blue lacquer by somebody who came out of the dark as we entered the *Porta Reale*. It was some chap who was either employed or took it upon himself to carry this out. The torch shed so little light that it was virtually useless. He put his life at risk by leaping in front of cars and bicycles to paint their headlights with a similar result.'[19] Michael had seen at first hand the work of a locally recruited special constable.

Britain's situation in the Mediterranean was now extremely serious. The RN held both ends with strong forces at Gibraltar and Alexandria. Italy held the centre with strong naval, land and air forces on either side of the narrow gap separating Sicily from North Africa. While the British had two aircraft carriers, the air defence of the Italian fleet depended entirely on land-based aircraft. The Italians significantly outnumbered the RN's cruisers and destroyers and had over 100 submarines to the RN's eight. In the crucial area of aircraft, the Regia Aeronautica could call upon 2,000 whereas the RAF and RN combined had about 200, precious few of which were based in the all-important centre ground – Malta.

The ninety-mile wide Sicilian Straits effectively splits the Mediterranean in two, as well as dividing Europe from Africa. The sea between Sicily and the Italian island

18. *Women of Malta*, by Frederick Galea, page 54.
19. *Malta 1937–1942*, by Michael Longyear, page 12.

of Pantelleria is shallow and could easily be mined. With only thirty miles separating Pantelleria from Cape Bon in Tunisia, this narrow strait is easily patrolled by land-based aircraft, submarines and destroyers, but is the only channel that could be used to connect the British fleets. It would also have to be negotiated by any merchant ship attempting to reach Malta from the west. Would the RN risk its capital ships in such a channel?

The RN could only concentrate its total fleet in the Mediterranean by abandoning Alexandria or Gibraltar, whereas the Italian fleet could be concentrated at will. The Italians also had an army on the Egyptian border within striking distance of the Suez Canal, an army that relied on communication and reinforcement through the sea lanes between Italy and North Africa. Only in Malta could air or naval forces be based to disrupt that reinforcement. But there was a harsh lesson for Britain from the Norwegian Campaign: no surface fleet could hope to establish control in waters dominated by enemy air power. Also, if Malta fell or was neutralised, Egypt would surely follow. Britain faced a significant challenge.

At the end of June another Italian air force group moved to Sicily for operations against Malta. It included many of the Regia Aeronautica's top units, all commanded by Spanish Civil War veterans. Half the pilots were also veterans. Their Fiat CR.42 biplanes were slower than the MC.200 fighters already in use, but their manoeuvrability was considered more suited against the Gladiator, none of which had been 'claimed' by any MC.200 pilot. On the same day as their first missions – 2 July – four Vichy French aircraft conducted recce flights over Malta from French North Africa. What was the purpose of these missions from a supposed neutral country? Were the Vichy French sharing intelligence with their former foes?

Churchill was deeply concerned about the widely dispersed yet powerful Vichy fleet, fearing it might fall into German hands despite assurances to the contrary from Darlan, the French Navy Minister. The French President, Marshal Pétain, had obtained a concession from Hitler that French warships would be allowed to disarm in French ports in Africa, and Darlan had instructed all of his captains never to surrender any warship intact to Germany. Churchill was unaware of these things and felt compelled to act.

In the early hours of 3 July, the RN boarded French vessels in British ports. In Plymouth, the crew of the French submarine *Surcouf* resisted and two British officers and one seaman were killed; one French seaman was also killed. The RN delivered an ultimatum to the French fleet at anchor in Mers el-Kébir in Vichy French Algeria. One of a number of options offered was for the fleet to be put beyond use by entrusting it to the United States until the end of the war. Unless the French accepted one of the options contained within the ultimatum within six hours, the fleet would be sunk. Negotiations were protracted, not helped by the admirals on both sides failing to negotiate with one another personally. Importantly, the French admiral did not pass on to his government the full text of the various options offered by the British, including the crucial American one.

In an attempt to block the French fleet's escape from its anchorage, Fleet Air Arm aircraft dropped mines in the channel leading to the open sea. French fighters shot down one aircraft killing the crew. Soon afterwards, the British fleet, under Admiral Somerville, opened fire. The attack was devastating: 1,297 French sailors lost their lives and 350 were wounded. James Somerville later described the action as shameful and a political blunder, although his decision not to negotiate personally with his French opposite number may have influenced the French response. At Alexandria, French warships formed an integral part of the Mediterranean Fleet and Admiral Cunningham strongly opposed the Admiralty's suggestion to seize the ships, successfully negotiating the disarming and de-fuelling of the French vessels.

If the British Cabinet had known of Hitler's concession, or Darlan's directive, would its attitude have been any different? At the time, could Britain afford to take Hitler at his word? Admiral Cunningham did show what could be achieved by diplomacy. The decision to use force rekindled Anglophobic feelings in France and aroused deep animosity throughout the French Navy, although it also clearly demonstrated Britain's resolve to continue the war alone. That was noted particularly across the Atlantic.

Over Malta on the same day, an Italian recce mission with CR.42 escorts was intercepted by John Waters in a Hurricane. One SM.79 was shot down. The crew of six perished despite parachuting from their aircraft. Waters was then attacked by the escorts and his aircraft was badly damaged, crashing on landing. Although he was unhurt, his precious Hurricane was a write-off. The Regia Aeronautica now had confirmation of the presence of Hurricanes and responded by sending twenty-four CR.42s to strafe aircraft at Hal Far. They claimed eight aircraft destroyed. In fact only two Swordfish were damaged, but these were repairable; there were no casualties. The Fleet Air Arm retaliated that night, bombing Catania and Comiso airfields; thirty men were killed including five Italian pilots.

An unexpected reinforcement arrived on 5 July in the shape of a French *Latécoère* torpedo bomber, a floatplane. It was crewed by *Premiere-Maître* (Warrant Officer) René Duvauchelle and *Quartier-Maître* (Sergeant) Jacques Méhauas of the French Navy. They had escaped from the Vichy French base at Bizerta in Tunisia to join an increasing number of Free French who, despite the earlier action at Mers el Kébir, rallied to the Allied cause. René and Jacques soon exchanged their uniforms for the 'light blue' of the RAF and were attached to 230 Squadron to operate alongside the latter's Sunderland flying boats now at Kalafrana.

Bombing raids continued with Italian aircrew describing defensive fire over Grand Harbour as 'infernal'. Malta's gunners had been waiting their chance to show their worth and they took it in both hands. In fact, they fired at such an intensity there were concerns ammunition would only last thirty days. The Italians, thankfully, lost their enthusiasm and the situation improved. On 7 July, one bomber was damaged and, falling behind the rest of the formation, was shot down by Timber Woods. It crashed twenty miles south of Kalafrana with the loss of its crew of six. Eleven people, nine of them civilians, were killed on the ground in the bombing and six others wounded.

Over the next couple of days, the Italians carried out more recce missions. George Burges claimed a bomber shot down, but it actually made it back to Sicily very badly damaged. Its pilot, the unit's commanding officer and one other crew member lost their lives. Following this attack, Rome Radio claimed Italian aircraft shot down one of two intercepting 'Spitfires'. Two days later, the Italians tried again with SM.79s, who were meant to be escorted by CR.42 fighters. With the bombers almost an hour late reaching their rendezvous, few of the escorts had sufficient fuel to accompany them to their targets. Zabbar, Tarxien, the dockyard and the submarine base at Manoel Island were bombed, although casualties were light, with only one civilian killed. The Italians paid heavily for their very poor coordination. Three RAF Hurricanes were waiting for the bombers and they promptly shot down two whose crews were killed. One was the first Italian aircraft to come down on Maltese soil. Unfortunately, it crashed onto an army post and two soldiers later died from burns. The Regia Aeronautica claimed three 'Spitfires' shot down by their bombers, but the RAF suffered no losses that day.

The Italians then changed tactics, turning to night bombing and day recce flights, although their main problem was lack of coordination between bombers and fighters rather than wrong tactics. The Maltese population who saw the shooting down of the Italian bombers were jubilant and anti-Italian feelings ran very high. More scrambles occurred over the following days with Italian crews claiming more 'Spitfires' shot down and also Hurricanes; again Fighter Flight suffered no losses, but nor did the Italians. On 12 July, George Burges, the former seaplane pilot turned fighter pilot without the benefit of formal training, was awarded a Distinguished Flying Cross (DFC) for gallantry and devotion to duty. He became a 'pin-up' overnight. He had six confirmed victories and his photograph, published in a Maltese newspaper, found its way into many Maltese homes. Malta needed a hero and now they had one from Yorkshire – George was born in Sheffield and educated at Sheffield Secondary School.

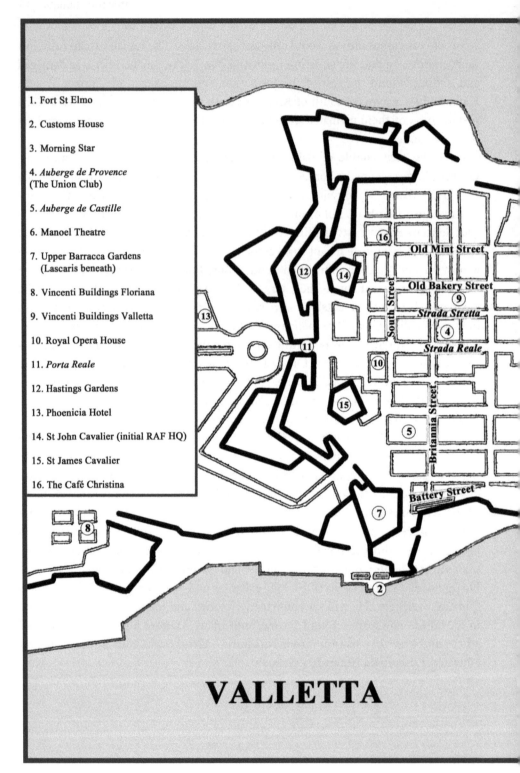

1. Fort St Elmo

2. Customs House

3. Morning Star

4. *Auberge de Provence*
(The Union Club)

5. *Auberge de Castille*

6. Manoel Theatre

7. Upper Barracca Gardens
   (Lascaris beneath)

8. Vincenti Buildings Floriana

9. Vincenti Buildings Valletta

10. Royal Opera House

11. *Porta Reale*

12. Hastings Gardens

13. Phoenicia Hotel

14. St John Cavalier (initial RAF HQ)

15. St James Cavalier

16. The Café Christina

Old Mint Street

South Street

Old Bakery Street

Strada Stretta

Strada Reale

Britannia Street

Battery Street

VALLETTA

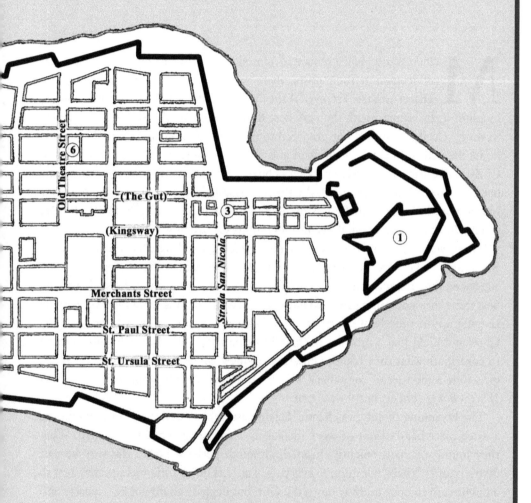

MARSAMXETT HARBOUR

Old Theatre Street

⑥

(The Gut)

③

(Kingsway)

Strada San Nicola

①

Merchants Street

St. Paul Street

St. Ursula Street

GRAND HARBOUR

MJMcD

Chapter Six

The *Whizz-Bangs*

Malta's music halls remained closed and, with a curfew in place and servicemen at their posts, there was no hope of employment for the cabaret artistes. Yet, even if they were out of work, Christina was not one to admit it. In keeping with the very best traditions of the theatre, she was merely 'resting'. Cecil Roche was not prepared to rest for long. One afternoon he arrived home dressed in khaki drill uniform and wearing a blue forage cap. In answer to Christina's question, his eyes sparkled as he described how a few days previously he had gone to see Major Shephard, the Provost Marshal, who made arrangements for him to join the RAF. Now he was dressed to kill as Aircraftman 2nd Class Roche, Cecil. He was posted to No 8 Sector Operations Centre in Valletta.

There were many who had the same idea as Cecil. Two English comedians, Chris Shaw and 'Vicki' Ford, went to see the Provost Marshal to offer their services. He suggested they form a concert party. They were in for a long war, he said, and the best thing they and other stranded entertainers could do was serve their country by keeping up the morale of the troops and the many thousands likely to arrive soon. Chris and Vicki had a meeting in their Floriana flat with others who also wanted to contribute what they could, Christina amongst them. The four men and seven girls were a mixture of comedians, singers and dancers. The appropriately named *Whizz-Bangs* concert party was born.

The beginning of July was hectic. Having assembled a talented team, including a three-piece band of out-of-work musicians, a rehearsal venue was needed. What they found was 'conveniently' located, although perhaps not in the very best of districts and perhaps not quite to everyone's taste. The Victoria was situated next to a public convenience midway down the Gut, but beggars could not be choosers and it was ideal for their purpose. It had a good stage, a fine set of plush curtains and a piano – what more could they ask for, for nothing?

Rehearsals were held at a frantic pace made all the more challenging by temperatures topping the eighties. The Provost Marshal was a regular visitor, roping in his wife to help. Each artiste provided their own costumes for individual acts but many others had to be made, for which Chris Shaw and Vicki Ford advanced funds from their savings. With a dressmaker engaged, and cheap silks and satins available from the Indian shops, some very good costumes were produced. Scores of props were also made on a self-help basis. There was a lot riding on the first show and they were all very keen to ensure it was successful.

Major Shephard persuaded the owner of the newly-built Regent Cinema to open for one afternoon performance of the first show. The cinema was small but had a large stage and perfect acoustics. He invited senior officers who wanted to ensure the show was fit to serve the troops. The *Whizz-Bangs* were delighted to have the opportunity to display their efforts to best advantage and, as they suspected theatres and cinemas might not open for some time, they did everything possible to promote the show. Handbills were produced and distributed in the streets and shelters.

This very first show was a huge success and the Regent Cinema was packed to overflowing despite the threat of air raids. For the audience the war seemed a long way away, 'as songs and dances, sketches and ensembles brought forth cheers and applause such as had not been heard in Malta since the last carnival. Long before the interval we guessed what the verdict of the service chiefs would be. And at the end of the two hours' run we were left in no doubt at all. The entire audience stood up and registered its approval in no uncertain manner. Overjoyed, we were convinced that we were well on the road to success, that our concert party was no longer the gamble it had seemed a couple of weeks ago.'[1] On 13 July 1940, the official Diary of the War on the Malta Front included an entry stating the first entertainment in wartime Malta was presented by the *Whizz-Bangs* concert party. They were off!

With the *Whizz-Bangs'* triumphal debut, Major Shephard became their booking agent. Long before he decided on potential venues, the troupe were asked to put on a show the following afternoon for Maltese troops at Fort St Elmo. A miniature version of the previous day's show was performed. Even though many did not understand English, they roared with laughter at the comedy scenes and applauded enthusiastically after all the songs and dances. It was another great success and, after a prolonged bout of cheering at the end, one Maltese soldier went round with a steel helmet collecting a substantial sum of money which he proudly presented to the *Whizz-Bangs* as a token of appreciation. Until then very little thought was given to remuneration, but it was obvious a charge had to be levied if the show was to continue. None of the performers had earned anything for over a month and they had to eat and pay rent, war or no war. Major Shephard agreed. The hat may have been traditional, but it was far too precarious a way to earn a living. A charge of sixpence was levied on anyone attending future performances.

This was the beginning of the *Whizz-Bangs* concert party which was destined to go on strongly throughout the most difficult period in Malta's wartime history. The troupe toured all the barracks, gun-sites, searchlight batteries and aerodromes, not once, but many times. Their repertoire consisted of burlesque singing, Arab dances, ballet, impersonations and speciality acts, and the cast included some very talented singers. Later, the *Whizz-Bangs* was taken over by the NAAFI – the Navy,

---

1. *Carve Malta on my heart and other wartime stories*, by Frederick Galea, page 38.

Army and Air Force Institute – resulting in performances staged free-of-charge. With the entertainers then on a fixed salary, they toured the island putting on shows wherever they could mount their makeshift stage. When the tour was over, they simply started all over again.

With the authorities having coped with the first weeks of the crisis, voluntary evacuation was begun with assisted passages for women and children to South Africa via Egypt. Tamara put her name down as she felt she was of no use and yet, only an hour before she was due to leave, she changed her mind. Her late refusal created a major fuss which only strengthened her resolve to stay, but her decision proved fortuitous; a few weeks later, the billet where her husband Ronnie would have been sleeping had she left, received a direct hit; four of its occupants died.

In Britain, the RAF was fighting a battle that determined the outcome of the war. It became known as the Battle of Britain, but only after it was won. If it had been lost, with a field army still shattered after Dunkirk, Britain would have been occupied. Until that summer of 1940, public opinion in the United States was against involvement in another European war; the Battle of Britain changed that. Without the Americans, there would have been no D-Day, no liberation of Western Europe. If the Luftwaffe had won in the skies above south-east England in the summer of 1940, Europe would be a very different place. That was the period in which the fate of the western world was decided. The whole pattern which followed was shaped by a few young men. Few indeed: 'Their shoulders held the sky suspended.'[2]

Those same summer days saw another handful of young men in Malta, though far less numerous, fighting desperately. Fewer still were trained fighter pilots and they lacked equipment and engineers. Yet they faced a fully trained, well-equipped and well-maintained, numerically superior Regia Aeronautica. While events in Britain would prove critical to the outcome of the war, events in Malta would prove critical to the war in North Africa.

One evening in July there was a discussion between the Gladiator pilots about naming their aircraft. 'Someone apparently suggested Pip, Squeak and Wilfred; but this wasn't received with much enthusiasm. It was John Waters ... who made the inspired suggestion. "How about Faith, Hope and Charity?" he said. The names caught on.'[3] To the Maltese, these old aircraft captured their spirit of defiance.

The first of Fighter Flight to fall was Peter Keeble. On 16 July he and George Burges scrambled to intercept twelve CR.42 fighters; two against twelve, Burges in a Gladiator, Keeble in a Hurricane. The ensuing dogfight was witnessed by many, including Wing Commander Robert Carter Jonas, Luqa's Station Commander, and an anti-aircraft gunnery officer.

---

2. From *Epitaph on an Army of Mercenaries*, by A.E. Houseman.
3. *Red Duster, White Ensign*, by Ian Cameron, page 47.

Having fired at the Italian aircraft, Keeble was attacked by two others. His aircraft's engine was hit and it began to smoke badly. Now unable to outrun the Italians, he tried to out-turn his more manoeuvrable assailants, but to no avail. Descending lower and lower, twisting and turning for all he was worth, Keeble fought desperately to keep out of range of his pursuers' guns, but a jink from one brought him close to the other in a desperate fight for life. Only the terrain which he rapidly approached might shield him. He shook off one pursuer, but the other stuck to him like glue, even though he was down almost to ground level. In a last desperate attempt to evade, Keeble dipped beneath the wireless aerials at Rinella, perhaps in the hope his pursuer would hit a cable. He didn't. The Hurricane flattened out for a few seconds as if Keeble was attempting a crash landing, but then it dived into a field killing Keeble instantly. His tactic of trying to use terrain was a wise one, he simply ran out of luck. So did his assailant, who was unable to pull out of his final attack and crashed in the same field. The equally unlucky Italian died soon afterwards in hospital in Hamrun. This marked the end of Fighter Flight's charmed life after six weeks of bitter fighting.

'Peter was our first casualty and a day or two later we buried him in the quiet little cemetery up at Bighi, with the wind sighing in the fir trees overhead.... It was difficult to adapt oneself to the fact that only the evening before Peter's death, I had been sitting talking to him in the Mess; and now all that was left of Peter was in that flag-draped box before us.'[4] The conversation the evening before was about costly war memorials versus more hospitals, with the names of the fallen engraved on plaques over the beds. At the time of Peter's death, his father, Squadron Leader Noel Keeble, was serving at RAF Felixstowe, whose personnel made a donation to endow a bed in Peter's name at the Blue Sisters' War Memorial Hospital in Malta.

For the remainder of July, sporadic raids continued. Hardly any Hurricanes were now available and the main defence was left to the guns and the Gladiators, which rose to meet every challenge. No kills were claimed, but one damaged bomber ditched twenty miles from Sicily on its way home.

There was a single Italian recce mission on 31 July with an escort of twelve CR.42 fighters. All three available Gladiators were scrambled. In the ensuing dogfight, the leader of the Italian formation was shot down and killed, and one Gladiator was hit. Wing Commander Carter Jonas was watching the Gladiator when, after 'a burst of fire in its petrol tank, the whole aeroplane appeared to blow up and dive vertically like a flaming torch, leaving a long trail of black smoke in the sky to mark its path The pilot, fortunately, as the tank exploded in front of him, stood up in his seat and went headlong over the side. We watched him dangling on the end of his shroud lines until he disappeared below the cliffs at Hal Far where he was rescued from the

---

4. Memoirs of Air Cdre Robert Carter Jonas, page 19.

water, more dead than alive, forty-five minutes later.'[5] Peter Hartley was terribly burned, only wearing a shirt, shorts, knee-length socks and shoes. Carter Jonas visited him at least once a week in the months he spent in Mtarfa Hospital, where to begin with he was not expected to survive. 'I remember well my first few visits to the hospital, with Peter lying rigid and motionless, speechless with pain; only his half-closed eyes moved, restless and frightened, beseeching for relief. Youth and a strong constitution, however, combined with devoted nursing, eventually won through, and many months later a somewhat scarred Peter was flown back to England.'[6]

That was the only Gladiator lost in combat and Carter Jonas determined it was *Charity*. There were certainly more than three Gladiators involved in those early months, perhaps as many as six, but it is unclear when, or even if, the pilots used such names for a particular aircraft. But there was no doubt about the positive effect the names had on the population.

By the end of July, the defenders were considered to have accounted for at least twelve Italian aircraft but, by then, the RAF was in a desperate situation. With no spares or ground crew trained and experienced on the specific aircraft types in use, it took much hard work and improvisation to keep them flying. They were kept in the air by 'robbing', removing spare parts from broken or wrecked aircraft, or by trying to manufacture parts locally. There was a limit to this and it had been reached. Despite every effort, only one Hurricane and one Gladiator were fit to fly. With so few pilots trained in air combat, they all desperately tried to acquire new skills 'on the job', tools of a very demanding and deadly trade in the face of an experienced enemy. There were no prizes for coming second, not in this game.

Malta's reliance on regular convoys was almost total; single ships making fast runs could only supply some essentials. More fighter aircraft were needed, and soon. The island could not simply rely on faith, or hope or even charity. With the RAF engaged in a desperate fight for survival at home, could any precious fighters or their pilots be spared for an island many considered indefensible? For the moment, the fate of Malta largely rested on a band of courageous defenders and the seamen who provided their lifeblood.

The three military commanders on Malta all made recommendations to London. With nearly half the garrison Maltese, Dobbie's main concern was civilian morale. He judged it could only be maintained with improved air defences and suggested a minimum of fifty good fighter aircraft as well as additional anti-aircraft guns. Maynard and Ford's views were similar, although Maynard viewed Malta as largely defenceless. Ford strongly opposed any suggestion of abandoning the island, but warned no action could result in disaster. Aware of the views of the three senior officers, Churchill demanded action.

---

5. *Ibid.*
6. *Ibid.*

When Italy entered the war, few in London thought much of Malta's chances, yet against all expectations the very poorly defended island was doing rather well. Even the obsolete Gladiators were giving a good account of themselves. This was unlikely to last. Malta desperately needed more aircraft and combat-trained pilots. Churchill pressed the matter. Despite the difficult situation for Britain that summer, the RAF made twelve Hurricanes available for delivery from HMS *Argus*. The navy insisted it was too dangerous to ship anti-aircraft guns through the Mediterranean; instead they would have to go the long way round, via the Cape of Good Hope and Suez; it would take seven weeks. The Hurricane delivery, on 2 August, set a pattern for the future, with all twelve successfully launched 380 miles from Malta, all landing safely at Luqa. They and their pilots were soon amalgamated with Fighter Flight to form 261 Squadron. How long could a single fighter squadron hold off the Regia Aeronautica? More importantly, how long could their aircraft survive on the ground? Four days later, Winston Churchill addressed the House of Commons:

'Never in the field of human conflict was so much owed by so many to so few. All hearts go out to the fighter pilots, whose brilliant actions we see with our own eyes day after day.'

These words were as applicable to Malta as they were to Britain. It was, however, what he then said, often overlooked, which showed the means, the only means at Britain's disposal in 1940 of taking the war to the heart of Nazi Germany:

'But we must never forget that all the time, night after night, month after month, our bomber squadrons travel far into Germany, find their targets in the darkness by the highest navigational skill, aim their attacks, often under the heaviest fire, often with serious loss, with deliberate careful discrimination, and inflict shattering blows upon the whole of the technical and war-making structure of the Nazi power.'

Those words were prophetic and also summed up Malta's potential role: attack. Her position astride Axis shipping lines could dictate the outcome of the war in North Africa. To do so it would need bombers and submarines, and of course the island would have to be defended sufficiently well to be able to operate as an offensive base. The gallant pilots of 261 Squadron, Malta's very thin blue line, were hardly enough.

The problem for both Britain and Malta was one of supply. Britain had fighter aircraft, but was short of fighter pilots; Malta was short of both and also needed regular supplies. The first convoy to attempt the run after Italy declared war left Alexandria on 29 August. The size of the escort indicates the effort involved: three battleships, one aircraft carrier, four cruisers, and seventeen destroyers, all to protect four merchantmen. The merchant ships were bombed on their second day out in a skilful and carefully coordinated strike by Italian SM.79s. The 10,600-ton SS *Cornwall* was hit three times and left drifting without engine power, listing and with several fires. A number of crewmen were killed and others badly wounded. After the ship's ammunition locker exploded, more fires began and the ship was considered lost by onlookers. To begin with, her Master, Captain Francis Pretty, thought the same, but he was not a man to give in easily. Awarded the DSO as a RN Reserve officer in the First World War, Captain Pretty and his crew fought valiantly to get the ship underway and it limped onward, straggling well behind the rest. Despite being close to disaster, with an increasing list and fires not fully under control, she pressed on, gamely arriving in Malta on 1 September. The *Cornwall* set the standard to be followed by Allied merchantmen under increasing difficulties for the next two years.

The convoy was successful with only one merchantman damaged. The word 'damaged' disguises the reality of what many merchant ships suffered. In this case, *Cornwall* did not sail again for six months. Some escorts came from Alexandria, others sailed from Gibraltar to meet the merchant ships as they closed on Malta. The Gibraltar escorts also delivered eight heavy and ten light anti-aircraft guns before going on to reinforce the Mediterranean Fleet. This first supply run delivered 40,000 tons to the besieged island. To fulfil Malta's needs, Admiral Cunningham calculated two 40,000 ton convoys were needed *each month*. When would the next arrive?

The Gladiators' story did not end with the arrival of the Hurricanes from *Argus*, especially as it took some days for the new aircraft to be made combat-ready. Italian recce flights continued and soon the first Junkers 87 (Ju87) Stuka dive-bombers from an Italian squadron put in an appearance. Bombing of Valletta and the airfields continued with Gladiators and Hurricanes scrambled. On 18 September a Hurricane shot down a CR.42 fighter and a week later another Hurricane shot down an Italian MC.200 fighter. Dobbie continued to express his concerns to London emphasising the island's vulnerability to invasion from the sea or from the air. Churchill pressed the War Office to strengthen the island, although the situation was made more complicated when, in September, the Italians began a slow advance against considerably smaller British forces in Egypt.

By the beginning of October, the Maltese, always an adaptable people, were learning to take things in their stride; they did not consider the efforts of the Regia Aeronautica of any great magnitude. If Italy's intent was to overwhelm the island's defences, or frighten the islanders into submission, then their plans were foiled by a handful of fighters, manned to begin with by volunteers, and the sterling work of the gunners, British and Maltese alike. Quiet spells for the pilots were interspersed with frequent scrambles and the Hurricanes began to suffer significant wear and tear with a lack of spares a pressing problem. On 17 October, the island's Ministry of Information said the total number of Italian aircraft destroyed was twenty-five, with twenty so severely damaged they would probably have been unable to reach their bases. RAF losses were three fighters and two pilots. The tally of Italian losses was increased by one on 27 October when six Hurricanes and two Gladiators met nine MC.200 fighters, one of which was claimed as probably shot down.

The Air Ministry was trying to solve the problem of the number of aircraft available in the Mediterranean theatre. At the time, the use of North Front airfield at Gibraltar was extremely limited by its size. Fighters could only be delivered to Malta by aircraft carrier, or to Egypt dismantled and crated as deck-cargo following the lengthy sea route around South Africa. Only medium bombers and reconnaissance aircraft could reach the island by overflying France. For eight months Alex Woods was embarked with the Fleet Air Arm's 816 Squadron on HMS *Furious*, ferrying fighter aircraft from the UK to Gibraltar, and then to West Africa for the lengthy and challenging Takoradi air route to Khartoum in Sudan and then on to Egypt.

The mainstay of the RAF's medium bomber force in 1940 was the twin-engine Wellington, ideal for night bombing, and the smaller and more manoeuvrable Blenheim for day bombing. These began to make an increasing appearance in the Mediterranean theatre, with some in London at last recognising Malta's potential. The navy also wanted to use Malta for offensive operations, but could not do so until the island's defences were strengthened. Churchill always had his eyes on the offensive and insisted the air defence of Malta must be regarded as the very first priority. As a result, it was agreed to establish the island with the full Scale B of air defences laid down in 1939. The estimate for this to be achieved was April 1941. Until then offensive operations would be limited. One aircraft type which found its way to the island in September was the American-built Glenn Martin Maryland and its use in the reconnaissance role soon brought significant success. This aircraft would be linked with a man they called Warby.

With increasing numbers of army units, there was plenty of work for the *Whizz-Bangs*. They had already given over fifty performances and their second revue was in production. Wherever they went, they were entertained well with regular parties in their honour. They attended a formal dinner at Fort Ricasoli. At Mellieha, the after show entertainment from the King's Own Malta Regiment was boisterous with cabaret turns from members of the regiment and community singing. The most elegant venue was at Hal Far. In the Mess, after a buffet supper, the carpets were rolled back for dancing. Their host, a Fleet Air Arm squadron commander, almost stole the evening by dancing a Russian *gopak*, 'with an ease and grace that drew tumultuous applause from an admiring audience.'[7] Mtarfa, Tigne and St

---

7. *Carve Malta on my heart and other wartime stories*, by Frederick Galea, page 39.

Andrews Barracks were among the larger locations visited and service families often outnumbered uniformed members of the audience. Wherever the *Whizz-Bangs* went, they were well received, with the possible exception of Italian prisoners-of-war, who, unsurprisingly, were unable to grasp the English sense of humour.

Robert Carter Jonas recalled one evening in September when the *Whizz-Bangs* came to Luqa to entertain officers and airmen with a concert in the canteen. Robert sat at the back of the room, among the officers and their wives and friends, and found the experience particularly reflective: 'For stretching out below me I could just discern the dark silhouettes of hundreds of heads, with grey clouds of smoke rising above them from their pipes and cigarettes, and the sounds of creaking and scraping as the men shifted their bodies on the hard wooden benches. At the far end of the long narrow hall was the improvised stage, with its makeshift curtain, the homemade scenery, and the crude lighting. It wasn't a West End production and the players would not have got a job in Shaftesbury Avenue. Yet the atmosphere was there; men down below in the gloom were obviously enjoying the show, but I felt their thoughts were thousands of miles away. The hardworking actors and actresses this evening … were bringing to their audience vivid thoughts and perhaps painful memories of happy and forgotten days, of a world at peace… .

'Now the troops joined in the chorus of *It's a Lovely Day Tomorrow*, led by a dark-eyed brunette, in a long satin dress, whose rich and lovely voice carried her audience far beyond the boundaries of our little world. Sitting there in the gloom at the back of the room, I quietly wondered to myself whether it really was going to be a lovely day tomorrow, or whether we were going to be bombed to hell?'[8]

With the show over, Carter Jonas walked across the airfield toward the far end of the runway where two Hurricanes were on alert in case of night raids. Although the night was chilly, it was hot and stuffy in the canteen and he was glad of the fresh air. Despite the quarter moon, 'the night was dark, and it was not until I had almost reached the far end of the black tarmac runway that I was able to distinguish the dark forms of the two Hurricanes, and the fire tender and the ambulance; while the red glow of cigarette ends indicated where the waiting airmen were passing the night. The pilots, John Waters and Timber Woods, I found on two stretchers, inside the ambulance, reading and smoking, waiting for something to happen.'[9] Usually something did. Would tomorrow be a lovely day?

For the Parisio Palace ladies 'the great events of the season were the concert parties given by the *Whizz-Bangs* who … had an unlimited supply of *joie de vivre* and the knack of "putting it over".'[10] Tamara, and about a dozen others attended a show at Kalafrana which they all enjoyed, even though there were, 'scenes and jokes

---

8. Memoirs of Air Cdre Robert Carter Jonas, pages 36–7.
9. *Ibid.*
10. *Women of Malta*, by Frederick Galea, pages 54–5.

at which no lady should have laughed and yet, although there is not a more prim and proper person than the serviceman's wife, we all laughed uproariously and slyly remembered some of them for future airing.'[11]

With the Sergeants' Mess well known for its hospitality, they all looked forward to a lavish tea afterwards. Tamara was anxious to meet the newly-arrived Free French crew. 'Jacques was busy with Gallic gesticulations explaining something to Christina Ratcliffe, the star of the *Whizz-Bangs* show, a striking blonde.'[12] As the two Frenchmen could only speak French, Tamara was in her element. Christina was also a fluent French speaker and the young Frenchmen made quite an impression on her too: 'René was about twenty-eight years old, dark and handsome, with great green eyes and a brilliant smile. Jacques was much younger, a lightly built youth with light brown hair and grey eyes. His pale face was drawn and wore a most solemn expression. After we had exchanged a few words in French, Jacques sat down beside me, apparently pleased with the opportunity to converse in his own language.... . Some five minutes later René joined us with an RAF officer and a very attractive girl whom I had noticed in the audience during the show. The couple were *le ménage de Marks* – Ronnie Marks, a squadron leader, and his Yugoslavian-born wife, Tamara. Tamara spoke perfect English and French, and I learned later that she knew four other languages almost as well.'[13]

Tamara and Christina listened avidly to the Frenchmen's story and saw a great deal of them over the days that followed. Not all Frenchmen accepted defeat or the formation of the puppet Vichy Government. Many escaped to join the growing ranks of the Free French. Others elected to join the RAF like René and Jacques. Their story was not untypical.

René was a 28-year-old pilot and Jacques the 19-year-old Wireless Operator/Air Gunner (WOp/AG). When France collapsed, René was in Tunisia, where his small single-engine floatplane, a *Latécoère* torpedo-bomber, was lying in Bizerta Bay without fuel. The Armistice came as a blow to him and many of his non-commissioned officer (NCO) colleagues who were in favour of continuing the fight. Few officers supported the idea, preferring to lay down their arms and wait, no one knew for what. This lack of action, with hangars full of aircraft, but with little fuel, was more than many could bear, but the majority, married and accompanied by wives and children, feared reprisals on their families. Isolated escapes had a chance of success, but mass escapes without a leader and good plan risked bloodshed. Very few were prepared to take the risk.

The *Latécoère* operated with a crew of two, pilot and WOp/AG who also acted as the observer. René succeeded in gaining the support of a few trustworthy and

---

11. *Ibid.*
12. *Ibid.*
13. *Carve Malta on my heart and other wartime stories*, by Frederick Galea, page 42.

enthusiastic NCOs, but getting sufficient fuel was far from easy. Eventually they were able to half-fill the tanks. The nearest British territory was Malta, but René was none too sure of their likely reception. He elected to take Jacques with him as he was the only member of their group who was unmarried. Under the cover of darkness, they took off at 8.00 pm one evening. At that point the guns opened fire, but René believed they were purposely aimed wide. Would their luck hold? With no one in Malta aware they were on their way, and no way of contacting Malta's defences, would the British open fire?

At 10.00 pm they sighted Malta. They were tired and anxious, having heard the island's gun batteries were second to none. René asked Jacques to signal the word F-R-A-N-C-E. They were quickly caught in the searchlights, but the guns remained silent. After landing they clambered out of their aircraft covered with oil, as a pipe had burst. They were wearing shorts and shirts and no flying gear, as they had had to walk nonchalantly to their aircraft so as not to arouse suspicion.

In Malta they were welcomed with open arms. Following a trade test, René was given the rank of sergeant in the RAF, although he was a warrant officer in France. They were stationed at Kalafrana flying the *Latécoère* on reconnaissance missions, but they hoped the RAF would soon give them a better aircraft as the *Latécoère's* performance was inferior to all the Italian fighters. He later told Tamara, 'It is a good little ship, but I do not like being the rabbit every time.'[14]

Tamara was admitted to Mtarfa hospital for a minor operation and spent ten days there. René visited three times, once immediately before a secret night mission. He gave Tamara his diary, and £20 for expenses, and asked if he did not return, she return his diary to his mother telling her his last thoughts were of her. The following morning, he returned and presented Tamara with an enormous bunch of flowers, as a thanksgiving he said. His mission had involved a return flight with Jacques to Bizerta to disembark a French agent under extremely hazardous conditions. René and Tamara soon became firm friends. She convalesced for a week with her husband at the Riviera Hotel, Ghajn Tuffieha. They never felt threatened, even though enemy aircraft frequently passed nearby. With an army rest camp half a mile away, the hotel bar was lively and most evenings, raid or no raid, Tamara and Ronnie danced in the moonlight on the open air terrace. So far, damage to property through bombing was slight and there were relatively few casualties. When Ronnie was posted to Luqa, Tamara decided not to return to the Parisio Palace. She moved into the Metropole Hotel in Sliema while looking for somewhere to share with Ronnie.

In the autumn, Christina moved into a top-floor apartment in Vincenti Buildings, Floriana. She thought the view the finest in Malta, taking in from left to right, 'the still uncompleted Phoenicia Hotel, and across the way, the statue of Christ the King

---

14. *Women of Malta*, by Frederick Galea, page 57.

towering majestically at the top of a palm-lined avenue. The imposing pile of St John's Cavalier rising above Hastings Gardens, the old, narrow gateway to Valletta, with niches on either side, holding statues of L'Isle Adam, the first Grand Master of the Knights of St John to land in Malta and Jean de la Valette, founder of the city; St James' Cavalier, its ancient walls embracing a modern NAAFI shop and at its side the Vernon Club, a services' hostel for other ranks. The War Memorial to the dead of the First World War and to its right, St James' Counterguard with its picturesque turret and battlements. In the immediate foreground was King George V Merchant Seaman's Memorial Hospital, better known as the KGV and beyond were the Barracca Gardens and the Lift, its dizzy heights an irresistible lure to many a would-be suicide. The bastions of Lascaris and the Customs House were also in the picture. On view to the right were Fort Ricasoli, the Rinella Wireless Station, the naval Bighi Hospital, Fort St Angelo and, seemingly only a stone's throw away from my balcony, the Three Cities – Vittoriosa, Cospicua and Senglea. At the top centre and dominating the whole scene was the *Castille*, former *Auberge* of the Knights of *Castille* and Portugal.'[15]

Christina's balcony overlooked in part George V Gardens, facing the Three Cities. The only disadvantage of her idyllic location was the climb of eighty-eight stairs, also a very long way down, especially when in a hurry. It was also very close to Grand Harbour. Nearby was the Engine Room Artificers Club, known as the ERA Club, also on Vilhena Terrace. Before the war club membership was strictly limited, but now it was open to all service personnel, irrespective of rank, as well as their guests. It served meals and was very popular, the Wednesday and Sunday dances being particularly well attended. If an air raid warning sounded, the bar shut and many went to the Vincenti shelter; others simply ordered extra drinks and hoped for the best as the drummer and pianist played on.

Tamara eventually rented a third floor furnished apartment in Floriana at the corner of *Pietro Floriani* Street and *Piazza Miratore,* just round the corner from Christina's new home. Like many Maltese apartments, it had a covered veranda running all round the house. While it enjoyed beautiful views of Grand Harbour, Senglea and Fort St Angelo, it was desperately close to the harbour. Ronnie and Tamara became regulars at the ERA Club, and soon saw René and Jacques there with Christina at a Wednesday dance.

Life for the *Whizz-Bangs* must have verged on the surreal in 1940. The artistes were all stranded on an island at war. Bombing was regular but could hardly be described as intense. Targeting, as far as it went, was focused on the airfields and the docks, although inevitably the built-up areas suffered, given their proximity. Life went on. At the same time, Malta was full of young men in the prime of their lives,

---

15. *Carve Malta on my heart and other wartime stories,* by Frederick Galea, pages 43–4.

all eager for whatever relaxation and entertainment they could find when off duty. The *Whizz-Bangs* provided a perfect boost for morale and the former out-of-work entertainers worked hard doing essentially what they loved, staging two or three shows each week with rehearsals in between. They had guaranteed and appreciative audiences, and were well-hosted. War was put on hold for a few hours now and again and the *Whizz-Bangs* led very full professional and social lives. Who could blame them for living life as best they could, while they could?

Jacques took a keen interest in the *Whizz-Bangs*, often accompanying them to help out backstage. He and Christina became great friends. Even though Christina was six years older and initially described Jacques as a youth, friends were firmly of the view they fell in love. Perhaps falling in love in a siege was all too easy. Sadly for many, it was also short-lived. All things considered; 'it was not such a bad war after all. We still had plenty to eat. There were entrances to air raid shelters in almost every street. Our defences dealt effectively with the enemy bombers and no great havoc resulted. There seemed very little to worry about. Morale and spirits were very high in that autumn of 1940.'[16]

Jack Vowles was born in Halifax, Yorkshire, on 28 June 1921, the only son of Clifford and Bertha Vowles. Clifford owned an electrical engineering and retail business in George Square, and much of his work involved installing and servicing refrigerators in cold rooms in shops and hotels throughout Yorkshire. From his early teens, Jack worked with his father while attending Halifax Technical College. He joined the family firm at sixteen when he left school. With business prospering, Clifford, who held a private pilot's licence, regularly flew a Tiger Moth out of Yeadon airfield, now Leeds Bradford International. He would sometimes take Jack, who sat in the open cockpit being shown how to move the control column; for a time Jack's feet couldn't reach the rudder pedals.

Jack grew up as a skilled engineer with an interest in aviation. He also became increasingly adept at photography, often using his dad's cameras, including a cine camera. His interest stayed with him for the rest of his life. Wherever Jack went, so did his camera. From the age of sixteen, Jack began dating Barbara, also from Halifax. One Saturday, after working at a hotel in Malham, Jack arrived back at the shop and began unloading the car. His father was waiting outside and said: 'Everything alright? Why are you getting your stuff out of the car?'

'I'm meeting Barbara,' said Jack.

'You can't,' said Jack's father. 'There are things I need to discuss as I'm away for a few days next week.'

---

16. *Ibid.*

Jack explained he had a date, but Clifford would have none of it, saying he needed to talk to Jack about a list of jobs he wanted him to complete in his absence.

'Whose name is above that door?' asked his dad, pointing to the full-width neon side saying 'CLIFFORD VOWLES'.

'Yours,' replied Jack.

'Well, for as long as that is the case, then you do what I say,' said Clifford.

'Right,' said Jack, 'in that case I'm finished.'

Jack then announced his intention of joining the RAF. His father thought it would make a man of him; his mother was less pleased.

With visions of becoming a pilot, Jack reported to his local RAF recruiting office. Once he gave details of his education and engineering experience, he was told he would only be accepted for airman training as a fitter. Having burnt his boats with his father, Jack enlisted on 1 June 1939, four weeks short of his eighteenth birthday. Britain was at war three months later.

The following summer of 1940, 18-year-old Aircraftman 1st Class Jack Vowles was servicing Blenheim fighters of 235 Squadron at RAF Bircham Newton in Norfolk. His squadron flew convoy protection over the North Sea. High above, other fighter squadrons were desperately trying to save Britain from invasion. Jack was now a fitter qualified in the maintenance and repair of engines and airframes.

One morning, probably 19 October 1940, when Jack and his colleagues reported for duty, they noticed four new aircraft parked under the trees on the far side of the grass airfield. They had French markings. They were American-built Glenn Martin Marylands originally destined for France. Over 200 Marylands were delivered to France and used to good effect prior to the French collapse. The remaining aircraft of the original order were shipped to Britain.

Jack and his fellow airmen were called together by their Canadian squadron commander, who said all the Maryland technical manuals were in French, as were the metric instruments. A volunteer was needed who had an understanding of French to relabel the instruments. Jack volunteered and got to work, gradually moving from one aircraft to another. They were technically advanced and, as an engineer with some flying experience, Jack found them very interesting.

The Maryland was a twin-engine monoplane with a very narrow fuselage and a long, Perspex nose. The crew positions were in two isolated compartments: the navigator or bombardier's station was in front, with the pilot immediately behind; the WOp/AG was in a rear compartment separated by a bulkhead and a large fuel tank which gave the aircraft notably long range. Armament included four forward-firing light machine guns in the wings and one in a dorsal turret for rear defence. There was also a hatch in the deeply-cut rear fuselage behind the bomb bay for a hand-held gun. Two gunners could be carried. At this stage the aircraft were not fitted with cameras. Particularly interesting from Jack's perspective were the

Wright Cyclone engines fitted with hydromatic propellers. Later aircraft were fitted with the original Pratt and Whitney Twin Wasp engine. The throttles operated the French way, the opposite way to those of British aircraft. To increase power, the throttle was moved backwards not forwards, so full power was with the throttle fully back and idle was with the throttle fully forward.

One day, when Jack was in the cockpit a voice said, 'Hello, what are you doing?' The newcomer was Pilot Officer Williams, of 431 (General Reconnaissance) Flight, a unit Jack had never heard of. Jack explained about the labels. Over the next few days Jack often accompanied the young pilot, whom he referred to as 'Willie', on air tests and familiarisation flights, putting each aircraft through its paces and experimenting with the engines. In all, Jack flew four sorties totalling twelve and a half hours; three were with Willie, including a cross-country endurance flight lasting seven and a half hours.

The Maryland had an unusual control arrangement. The forward position, for the navigator, had a complete set of flying controls, with rudder pedals and throttles; there was also a selection of flight instruments which could be folded out from one side. A number of American-built bombers had similar features which allowed a bomb-aimer, with a good view ahead and below, to steer the aircraft for the last few minutes of a bombing run. On their flights together, Willie practiced asymmetric flying, flying on one engine in turn, which necessitated shutting down the engine and feathering its propeller. Feathering is a means of reducing the angle of the blade as it meets the airflow – to reduce drag. By experimenting, Jack discovered that by moving the lever initiating feathering only fractionally, the load was taken off the propeller. Although the engine began to vibrate, this stopped once the throttle was opened. Increased power was then available, resulting in an increase in speed. This was not covered in the aircraft's manuals.

One morning in mid-November the Marylands were gone; so was Willie. The word was they were on their way to Malta. These aircraft were most likely those intended to make up the second batch destined for Malta, the first having flown there in September. As far as Jack was concerned, he was done with Marylands. He wasn't, but he would have to wait nine months and meet a man they called Warby.

The Battle of Britain officially ended in October 1940 and the prospect of invasion of Britain receded. Later, Hitler's plans to invade were cancelled as he turned his eyes east. Londoners and others had suffered under the Blitz. The Battle of the Atlantic also began in earnest and this had consequences for Malta as well as Britain, both reliant on convoys. One consequence of Hitler's change of focus was soon apparent in the Mediterranean. There was now no need for the Luftwaffe to maintain a very well-equipped *Fliegerkorps* X in Norway and Denmark. Where else could this highly experienced air group be used to best effect?

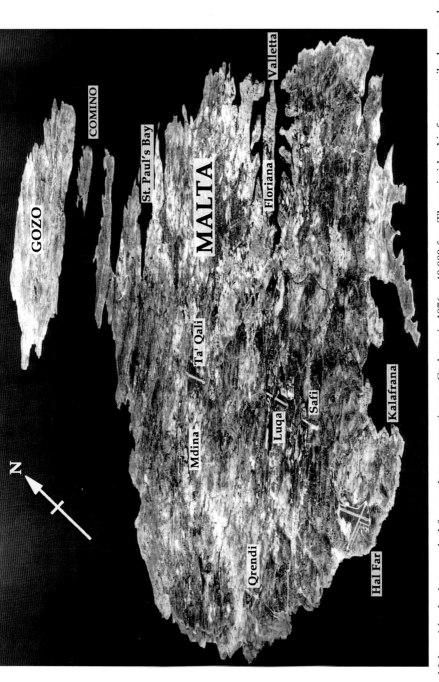

Plate 1. The Maltese islands photographed from a photo-reconnaissance Canberra in 1976 at 40,000 feet. The main island is fourteen miles long, and seven miles wide at its widest point. The six former RAF stations are highlighted: Hal Far, Kalafrana, Luqa, Safi, Ta' Qali and Qrendi. Kalafrana was the original seaplane base. In 1940, Luqa was the only airfield to have paved runways. Not shown is another airfield, Xewkija in Gozo, which was built in 1943 by the Americans.

Plate 2. *Strada Reale*, Valletta. The Royal Opera House is on the right with the Wembley Store opposite on the corner with the sign above its door.

Plate 3. *Porta Reale*, Valletta, mid-1930s. This is the main entrance into the capital and where, in 1942, Jack Vowles used up one of his many lives.

Plate 4. '*rowing boats with a hint of gondola about them....*' (Christina Ratcliffe). Grand Harbour; Floriana is on the skyline.

Plate 5. '*You can't see the fleet for the funnels.*' (Woody Woodhall). Grand Harbour; the Mediterranean Fleet can be glimpsed in the background toward Marsa Creek.

Plate 6. A Maltese lady wearing the Faldetta, in Upper Barracca Gardens, mid-1930s.

Plate 7. *Porte des Bombes.* The main entrance into Floriana, looking south-west from Floriana; this was the scene of Malta's first civilian casualty on the opening day of Malta's war.

Plate 10. The *Whizz–Bangs* concert party; Christina is third from the right in the front row.

Plate 11. '*churches, horse-drawn cabs with curtains….*' (Christina Ratcliffe). Floriana from Valletta; St Publius' Church is left of centre with Vilhena Terrace on the extreme left.

Plate 8. *Auberge de Castille*. This was the British HQ at the war's outbreak.

Plate 9. Lascaris Bastion and Upper Barracca Gardens; the SS *Knight of Malta* is in the foreground on the left and Customs House is on the right.

Plate 12. Al fresco entertainment from the *Whizz Bangs* 1941; Christina, with her striking blonde hair, is on the far left. Note the officer on the front row using binoculars, whereas two men on the back row are more interested in getting their picture taken.

Plate 13. '*He looked like a Greek God.*' (Christina Ratcliffe); Adrian standing behind a Maryland cockpit, 1940/41.

Plate 14. Glenn Martin Maryland of 431 Flight/69 Squadron at RAF Luqa, 1940/41.

Plate 15. Adrian Warburton on the wing of a Maryland, late 1940/early 1941.

Plate 16. Left to right; John Boys-Stones, Adrian & Frank Bastard outside 69 Squadron HQ. On 7 March 1941, after holding his stricken aircraft level so his navigator could bale out, there was insufficient height for John's parachute to deploy. He fell 200 feet onto solid rock. When found, the mortally injured pilot's last words were: '*I think I must have left things a bit late.*' (Robert Carter Jonas)

The Hurricanes and Gladiators of 261 Squadron began to operate from Ta' Qali, the first RAF aircraft to do so. Although Ta' Qali was disguised to avoid being identified as an operational airfield, it became the squadron's permanent base, although it remained Spartan. The officers lived in Torri Cumbo in Mosta; the airmen were closer to the airfield in Chateau Bertrand, known to many as the Mad House because of its strange, upside-down design. The move of 261 Squadron made room at Luqa for more twin-engine aircraft.

The arrival in September of three Marylands of 431 Flight, now fitted with F24 vertical cameras, was timely. Cunningham was particularly interested in the readiness of the large, modern Italian Fleet which could impact on his ability to support both the army in Egypt and shipping trying to reach Malta. Cunningham needed the services of recce aircraft. In Egypt, Wavell's outnumbered troops slowly withdrew ahead of the immense Italian Army. Wavell had plans to take the offensive, although he needed more information first about Italian dispositions, especially around Benghazi and Tripoli. Wavell needed recce aircraft too. He also wished Italian supply routes across the Mediterranean be disrupted but, as yet, there were very limited means to do so. The few RAF attack aircraft were not well suited to the task; the Fleet Air Arm had a sound doctrine but insufficient aircraft to be truly effective. Without air cover, the RN could do little. As a result, in the last six months of 1940, only a handful of Italian merchant vessels failed to reach North Africa.

The newly-arrived 431 Flight had a challenging task. Its aircraft were scarce in numbers and entirely new to the RAF. There was no one on the island trained in their maintenance, a problem far from unique. On arrival, 431 Flight absorbed the personnel of No 3 Anti-aircraft Cooperation Unit at Hal Far, which was disbanded. Spares were in very short supply, not helped by many being wrongly delivered to North Coates, where additional Marylands were being brought together and new crews trained. Very soon 431 Flight was reduced to 'cannibalisation', robbing parts from one aircraft to keep others in the air. Two Blenheims en route to Egypt were also 'acquired'. This established a trend for the RAF in Malta, and it was one which caused great irritation in Cairo and London. In addition to the three Marylands was a Blackburn Skua which had escorted six Hurricanes to Malta a month earlier from HMS *Argus*. As a result, command of 431 Flight was vested initially in the senior ranking officer, Captain Ford RN. An additional Maryland arrived in October.

At the end of October, a Wellington Flight was formed. On only the second night mission, they were already two aircraft and six men down. By then, Cunningham was increasingly focused on the well-defended port of Taranto in Southern Italy and 431 Flight was tasked to obtain photographic evidence of the strengthening of the already powerful Italian battle fleet. Cunningham intended to hit the Italians hard, using his elderly Swordfish biplanes launched at night from *Illustrious*. Surprise was essential given the Swordfish's desperately slow cruising speed of eighty-five knots. It was equally important their crews knew exactly where each major warship was berthed so the assault could be planned properly and coordinated effectively. On the night of 11 November the Swordfish struck with devastating results. Three battleships were hit. The Italian capital ships were soon withdrawn to Naples. After the Battle of Taranto, any Italian admiral encountering a force which included an aircraft-carrier felt himself to be fighting at a disadvantage, even if he was superior in other types of ships.

The RN victory was highly significant and provided a great boost to morale. The move of the Italian heavy units also had a major impact on its ability to intercept ships heading for Malta. The victory may also have served to obscure one very important aspect: the dominance of the air over the sea. The Japanese military attaché in Rome carefully noted the lessons of Taranto. Did anyone else?

In November, with their faithful *Latécoère* now unserviceable, René and Jacques joined 431 Flight, which was now also operating a Hudson. More French personnel also made their escape from Bizerta. One aircraft, with a crew of three, reached Malta safely, but two others went missing in the attempt. The arrival of the French submarine *Narval*, with its crew of forty, expanded the French contingent on the island significantly. René and Tamara got to know many of the crew and spent many hours on the rocks facing the submarine, 'we would see her gliding softly in, looking shiny and black like a sea-lion.'[17]

Air raids continued spasmodically. There were two or three raids every few days, with slight casualties and damage, and then no raids for a week. Tamara attended a two-month first aid course, becoming qualified as a Voluntary Aid Detachment (VAD) nurse working a morning shift in the Floriana Medical Inspection Room. She stopped going to the shelter in daylight and only rarely went at night. She and her friends held the Italian prowess as fighters and bombing experts in utter contempt as the fighters seldom gave fight and many bombs fell in the sea. 'Greatly appreciated was the joke of the Italian bomber pilot, who returned to his base in Italy with his bombs still in their racks because, as he said himself, "I could not very well drop them, the raid was over; the all-clear had gone." It was a good war.'[18] The 'good war' did not last much longer.

René and Jacques, with an English observer, George Taylor, enjoyed their work on the Maryland, but reconnaissance by single aircraft was highly dangerous. Tamara and Christina feared for their safety knowing it was often René's skill that got them out of many a tough spot. 'Jacques only laughed at our concern, apparently enjoying the excitement and risk involved in the operations. He never spoke to me of his own gallant deeds over enemy territory, but he was full of the dare-devil exploits of his companions in the flight, one of whom he held in particularly high

---

17. Quoted in *Call-Out*, by Frederick Galea, page 45.
18. *Women of Malta*, by Frederick Galea, page 68.

esteem. *"Il est absolument magnifique. Formidable"*, he would say, his eyes shining. One day he told me how this pilot, in order to get really clear pictures of an Italian battleship in Taranto harbour, had dived down to within fifty feet of the decks, taken his photographs amid the flak of anti-aircraft gunfire and then made off for home chased by a heavy formation of fighters. Later he was again flying over Taranto harbour when an engine cut out. Nevertheless, he completed his mission and managed to get back to Malta, his photographs proving to be of the utmost value.... . Jacques's friend appeared to be ... intrepid and death defying, fearless in the face of the enemy, mad as a hatter.'[19]

Tamara thought René was in his element flying the Maryland: 'He was as pleased as a dog with two tails because, as he explained to me, "A plane is like a horse, it must answer to your smallest whim and this one is a thoroughbred and a thoroughbred will never let you down."' Tamara asked others about the Maryland as she thought René's enthusiasm would make him biased. Most thought it a good aircraft although there was room for improvement. René made light of other's views.

After René came back with an engine on fire, Tamara was never again happy when he was flying. She had become very fond of the Frenchman; perhaps she even allowed herself to fall a little in love with him. 'He was known as a reckless pilot; he deemed it a disgrace ever to turn back without bringing the information he had gone out for. "It is like a glorious game of hide and seek," he would say. "I have to fly very steady and low over the target to take good photographs. I can see the gunners below waiting for me, cocking their guns, firing. The flaming onions, revolving on themselves, come up slowly, slowly. One almost feels like putting one's hand out and pushing them out of the way. They take their time. They know where they are going to hit. Nothing can stop or deflect their course now. They explode at the spot where I was only a few seconds ago. More come up. But they are always too high or too low, too much forward or too far behind me. It is a battle of wits. I put myself in the gunner's place and fool him every time. Besides, these Eyeties are too temperamental. They would much rather fire first and calculate afterwards."'[20] René had a different tale to tell when the Germans took over. They had developed the box barrage, with a certain number of guns firing within a calculated area at the same time, each one at its respective aiming point, making a solid box of fire.

In mid-November, a British fleet traversed the Mediterranean from west to east, dropping off three merchant ships carrying troops and 20,000 tons of cargo. Following the highly successful action at Taranto this resulted in growing confidence on the island, although anti-aircraft defences still only amounted to seventy heavy and thirty-four light guns, still well short of the Scale B requirement. There was

---

19. *Carve Malta on my heart and other wartime stories*, by Frederick Galea, pages 44–5.
20. *Ibid.*

also reassuring news from the Western Desert where the British Army, under Wavell, expelled the Italians from Egypt, taking some 30,000 prisoners.

Mussolini, having annexed Albania in 1939, was desperate for more territory. Disappointed at having gained little with the fall of France, he began looking toward Greece, but Hitler was secretly planning his move against the Soviet Union and did not want another conflict on his southern flank in the Balkans. His success in restraining Mussolini was temporary; in a surprise and foolish move, Italian forces moved into Greece from Albania at the end of October. It soon went badly wrong and the Italians were expelled within a month. Britain was committed to supporting Greece and inevitably that support came from Wavell's forces in Egypt. Reinforcements earmarked for Malta were therefore diverted, although with Mussolini's new focus, the threat to Malta diminished for a while.

There were some privations, but food and drink was available, even alcohol if one knew where to get it. Transport was scarce, but there were dances, concert parties and even a flourishing amateur dramatic society. Some women wore evening dresses and were escorted by officers dressed in Mess kit. As for the many children on the island, like Michael Longyear, they didn't worry about the war at all, doing much as they had done previously and still attending school. The blackout was something of a limitation, but it was almost as if the 211 air raids between June and the end of December were something of an irritation that could be lived with.

A second operation to deliver Hurricanes took place in November. This again involved HMS *Argus*, with escorts from Gibraltar commanded by Admiral Somerville. By then there were only four serviceable Hurricanes and one Gladiator left. In the early hours of 17 November, intelligence was received of a move by the Italian fleet, so the embarked Hurricanes were launched forty miles further west than originally intended. This was at the very limit of their range. It took fifteen minutes for the aircraft to assemble before they set off in two groups, each headed by a Fleet Air Arm Skua. Once out of sight, Somerville reversed course to return to Gibraltar, thinking this second delivery of Hurricanes an unqualified success. Soon, a series of signals came in with disturbing news. The operation had turned into a disaster. Only five Hurricanes arrived, nine others being lost having run out of fuel. The first formation was lucky – only two aircraft ditched with one pilot rescued. The crew of the Skua leading the second group had to watch helplessly as one after another, the Hurricanes ran out of fuel and attempted to ditch. None of the seven pilots were ever found. Major lessons needed to be learned from this tragedy. Despite this, the last few months of 1940 were considered a period of great success for the RN and the Italian Navy now gave Cunningham's vessels a wide berth.

With the curfew lifted by December, the cinemas reopened. The Parisio Palace shut its doors with the inhabitants having been evacuated, or, like Tamara, moved elsewhere. Meanwhile, the *Whizz-Bangs* remained the only live entertainment on the island. The manager of the Manoel Theatre in Valletta agreed to host a typical English pantomime. This was the concert party's third production and they planned to take the pantomime on the road afterwards. *Cinderella* was chosen and Christina's long blonde hair made her the natural for the lead role. The Manoel was perfect: adapted for use as a cinema, it was originally an opera house and reputed to be one of the oldest in Europe, having been built in 1731 by Antonio Manoel de Vilhena. The stage was large, the acoustics excellent and it seated over 700 in the stalls, then with tier upon tier of ornate boxes topped by a sky-high balcony. The number of dressing rooms allowed everyone to spread themselves out in comfort, quite a luxury compared to many other venues. The pantomime was another huge success and the audience was alternately spellbound by ballet or roaring with laughter. A dancing school acted as the ballroom crowd, one of whom was the daughter of Major Shephard, making her stage debut.

Elsewhere dressing rooms were non-existent and often a single room divided by a curtain hung up on a string was used by everyone: 'Often it was so cold, that the make-up would not run out of the tubes. Once, when there had been no dressing room provided at all, the artists undressed and made-up in the bus and waded through ankle-deep mud before getting on the stage.... And yet they never broke an engagement. The show went on raid or no raid. Sometimes, if playing for an anti-aircraft battery detachment, they went to the slit trenches, the crews being recalled to their guns.'[21] At a camp in Boschetto Gardens they gave al fresco entertainment in true concert party style, changing into their costumes among tangerine and lemon trees, hidden from their audience by army blankets suspended from the branches.

Christmas 1940 was a happy time for Christina and many others. She was invited by Tamara and her husband 'Marko' to join them for Christmas Day. 'They were splendid hosts and spared no effort to make things go with a swing. There was an abundance of food and drink, and their flat lacked nothing in the way of decorations, an illuminated tree, balloons and streamers, holly and mistletoe combining with the great red poinsettias of the season to make a truly festive scene. René and Jacques were among the guests and they were deeply grateful for the hospitality showered upon them by *le ménage de Marks*. Away from their loved ones, alone in a strange land, they shrugged off their homesickness with a philosophical *c'est la guerre* and enthusiastically joined the rest of us in the fun and games.'[22] Life was almost normal – apart from the rationing and the raids. Tamara gave Christina a potpourri jar for Christmas and its undying fragrance would provide her with, 'a poignant reminder of the Christmas spent in the company of those two brave French boys.'[23] René was something of an artist, sensitive too, and he rented a small flat in Valletta to which he

---

21. *Women of Malta*, by Frederick Galea, page 83.
22. *Carve Malta on my heart and other wartime stories*, by Frederick Galea, pages 46–7.
23. *Ibid*.

could escape from the boisterous surrounds of the Sergeants' Mess. He also began a sketch of Tamara.

For the islanders, and especially for the people living in Valletta, there was something of a Christmas bonus when Admiral Cunningham arrived in Grand Harbour on the afternoon of 20 December on board his flagship HMS *Warspite* with a destroyer escort. News spread quickly and as the *Warspite* slowly made her way to her berth, with bands playing and the crew assembled, the Upper and Lower Barracca Gardens were full of cheering Maltese. Cunningham stayed for almost forty-eight hours, untroubled by air attack. To the watching people of Malta, what better indication could there be that Britain was in control of the situation?

Between Christmas and New Year the Free French submarine *Narval* failed to return. René and Tamara hoped in vain; she had gone down with all hands off Tunisia. Soon there was more troubling news. Not long after the New Year festivities, a pale and agitated Jacques arrived unexpectedly at Christina's flat. He had only a few minutes before returning to Luqa to prepare for another mission. 'He warned me that from now onwards I must take cover immediately the air raid warning sounded. He could not tell me why. The information he had was Top Secret, not even to be shared with me. He looked into my eyes. "Promise, Cherie", he pleaded. His own eyes were tired and strained. To please him I promised.'[24] *Fliegerkorps* X had arrived in Sicily.

---

24. *Ibid.*

Chapter Seven

Enter the Luftwaffe

By the end of 1940, the RAF strength in Malta was still pitifully inadequate, with fifteen Hurricanes for defence and sixteen Wellington bombers for attack. The Fleet Air Arm could field a dozen Swordfish. The small recce unit, 431 Flight, now had six Marylands, but this was well short of what was necessary to keep tabs on the Italians. This was evidenced by the Italian merchant fleet losing only a fraction of the ships sent to Libya since Italy's declaration of war. In fact Italy had successfully delivered some 47,000 troops to North Africa without loss.

With Malta's garrison and ground defences also inadequate, a more resolute opponent could have invaded the island with the gravest of consequences for North Africa and the entire course of the war. Instead, Mussolini sought to satisfy his territorial ambitions that had been thwarted following the fall of France, by prodding his unprepared army to move against Egypt and Greece. His focus should have been closer to home. Meanwhile, his sponsor, Adolf Hitler, was dreaming about doing what Napoleon had failed to do: conquer Russia.

Malta, nevertheless, had defended herself against superior forces with great determination while using its slender offensive assets whenever it could. Churchill refused to consider neglecting Malta and others gradually realised the island could play a vital role in weakening the Axis in North Africa, but only if it was properly defended and sustained. Following constant prodding by an ever-aggressive Winston, the AOC-in-C Middle East was directed to provide Malta with sufficient air power to maintain its defence and also take every opportunity to use the island as a base for attack. Malta's governing council never lost sight of this policy. Churchill rightly suspected it would not be long before Hitler focused on the Middle East. In fact, Hitler already had, prompted by Mussolini's failures and constant requests for support. The help Hitler offered to his ally came in the form of *Fliegerkorps X* which included specialist anti-shipping Ju87 Stuka dive-bombers. In total, some 350 Heinkels, Junkers and Messerschmitts moved to Sicily and Southern Italy in the final weeks of 1940. Their focus was Malta and the supplies trying to reach her, but the Luftwaffe's first priority was to sink *Illustrious*.

The first convoy of 1941 for Malta left Gibraltar on 6 January. It was to be reinforced with warships from Alexandria before two merchant ships docked in Malta. Eight others sheltering in Grand Harbour were then to join the fleet heading east to Greece and Egypt. The escorts included Cunningham's flagship *Warspite* and the aircraft carrier *Illustrious*. The rendezvous was at dawn on 9 January and, until then, the ships had gone unchallenged. Within an hour it was subjected to a coordinated and well-rehearsed assault by Italian bombers, which were beaten off. Soon the heavy escorts from Gibraltar left to return to base. At dawn the following morning, two Italian torpedo boats were encountered, one of which was sunk. Later, a series of feints by Italian aircraft successfully drew off the Fulmar fighters launched from *Illustrious*. This left a seven-minute window when no Fulmars were airborne, and it was then that *Fliegerkorps X* struck.

In a master stroke of careful planning and coordination described, 'as one of the great flying achievements of the war,'[1] forty Stukas fell on *Illustrious* in a devastating assault within that seven-minute window. The conditions on board the carrier afterwards were cataclysmic. Cunningham's pride and joy was disabled, crippled and on fire, having taken six direct hits from armour-piercing 1000lb bombs and three very near misses. Few on her escorts thought the carrier could survive as she careered out of line covered in smoke. Many of her guns were out of action leaving her a sitting duck. Remarkably, some of her heavy, ancient Fulmar fighters got airborne in the first few minutes and gamely tried to gain height to come to terms with their assailants. Some had no ammunition, yet they still tried to disrupt the Stukas' dives. Of the last formation of ten, five were shot down and four bombed inaccurately, but the very last one achieved a direct hit, right in the centre of the flight deck. This was virtually a deathblow to *Illustrious*. The Fulmars had no choice but to make their way to Malta, landing at Hal Far, leaving their carrier eighty-five miles from Malta with seven hours of daylight remaining. 'From her halyards fluttered a single pennant: "Not under control".'[2]

A further attack came early that afternoon, delivered by Italian bombers which thankfully stayed high. Their bombs fell wide. For the next few hours, damage control parties worked desperately as their ship slowly made her way toward Malta and relative safety. At 4.00 pm *Fliegerkorps X* returned, this time met by Fulmars from Hal Far, refuelled and rearmed. Outnumbered four to one, the Fulmars still shot down five German aircraft. Only a single Stuka, the very last one, was successful. Its 1000lb bomb hit the carrier, penetrating the armour-plating and bursting in a temporary sick bay. Between twenty and thirty seamen were killed instantly and fires previously extinguished flared up once more. For more than two hours the fires raged out of control and the stricken carrier took on a severe list. As darkness fell, Malta came into view. At 8.15 pm, on the evening of 10 January, *Illustrious* tied up at Parlatorio Wharf to cheering from the dockyard workers and the strains of *Roll out the Barrel*.

---

1. *Red Duster, White Ensign*, by Ian Cameron, pages 70–75.
2. *Ibid.*

The RN operation was actually a success in that the two merchantmen got through, delivering 10,000 tons of cargo. Importantly, the cargo included twelve crated Hurricanes, twenty-four heavy and eighteen light anti-aircraft guns. But it came at a cost of one cruiser sunk and another cruiser and destroyer damaged. *Illustrious* was very severely damaged and there was considerable doubt as to whether she could be made sufficiently seaworthy to make the long journey to Alexandria. Would *Fliegerkorps X* give the RN and the shipyard workers sufficient time to try? The crew of *Illustrious* suffered terribly, with 126 killed and 91 wounded. All night long the seriously injured were carried to hospital. Christina watched as the carrier, down by the stern and listing badly, was berthed only yards from her flat. In the wake of *Illustrious* being towed by another ship, 'came the very destroyer that had carried me away from the horrors of the Spanish Civil War, HMS *Gallant*. Her bow blown away by a mine at sea, she was now little more than a pitiful wreck, but living up to her name she struggled gallantly on and succeeded like the carrier in reaching port.'[3] HMS *Gallant* lost sixty of her crew killed and a further twenty-five wounded. She had sailed her last voyage.

The following day, Tamara went as planned for a sitting at René's flat, but he did not arrive at the appointed time. Tamara left after two hours with no misgivings as circumstances at Luqa sometimes meant he was late; she had often waited in vain. He could easily have been tasked with a short-notice mission with 431 Flight, designated 69 Squadron the previous day. On Sunday she waited another three hours; even René's landlady asked if she knew where he was. When she got home her husband broke the news that he, Jacques and George Taylor were missing on a mission to recce Taranto, Catania and Comiso. A message was received from them about shipping at Brindisi, but nothing was heard afterwards and their aircraft failed to return. On Monday, the Rediffusion announcer repeated an item from Italian radio saying an enemy aircraft of the bomber type was shot down over Catania on 11 January and the three occupants were dead. 'The announcer went on to talk about the weather and the crops. No fuss, no military honours, no big cortege, nothing. Three young men had died in the flower of their manhood. Their hopes and aspirations and their joy of living had been to no avail. Their contribution to a better, saner world ended. I felt stunned.... . René's death affected me more than I dared tell or show. We had believed so firmly in his lucky star. "Experience and a little luck, that is all one needs," he would say.'[4]

When Christina heard the news she was heartbroken. For the first time in her life she knew what it was like to grieve. Tamara knew Christina was very fond of Jacques; there was talk of them becoming engaged. When she visited, two other girls were with her. Christina burst into tears. 'It was heart-breaking to see the

---

3. *Carve Malta on my heart and other wartime stories*, by Frederick Galea, page 48.
4. *Women of Malta*, by Frederick Galea, pages 71–2.

racking sobs shaking her whole body. She was so slim and fair; it seemed impossible that such unutterable pain could be contained in so small a being without shattering it. With tears running down our cheeks we did our best to comfort her. Stories of men missing for months and then turning up were retold.... Hope eternal hope. There it was shining again through her swollen, tear-dimmed eyes. They were alive; she knew it. Jacques had promised her he would come back always. He was too much in love with her to go away like that, without saying goodbye. He was alive, she was sure. No matter what some silly Italian announcer had said. They were forever boasting of shooting our aircraft down.... She had better go and wash her face and powder her nose. What if they turned up this very moment and found her in that shocking state? Her high spirits were infectious. We started planning the rousing party we would have to celebrate their return.... We found a little solace in telling each other for the n'th time all the little traits that had so endeared the two boys to us. She talked herself into believing that they would come back some day. The other alternative was too horrible to contemplate. She firmly refused to entertain it.'[5]

Christina continued as a member of the *Whizz-Bangs*. Jacques had urged her to stop but she was now glad she hadn't. Her work made her mix with others and forced her to look happy and engage in cheerful conversation. This helped assuage her pain. Tamara had nothing for hers and sought work, which proved very hard to find. In the meantime, Christina agreed to Tamara accompanying the concert party on its travels. Because of restrictions on transport, many servicemen had no prospect of ever visiting Valletta. For some, the concert party was their only entertainment and they always made the entertainers welcome. No detachment was too small. Even audiences of seventy or eighty welcomed the troupe wholeheartedly. They never failed to put on a show, nor did they ever break an engagement regardless of rain or raids. Tamara saw for herself how hard the *Whizz-Bangs* worked and later reflected it was a good life; she couldn't harbour sad thoughts and pessimistic moods in their company. With Ronnie on duty every other night, Tamara often invited Marigold 'Pickles' Fletcher, a member of the *Whizz-Bangs*, to stay with her. An American by birth, Pickles was totally unruffled in air raids.

The war began in earnest for the islanders on the morning of 16 January 1941. The only surprise was that the Luftwaffe had waited so long after the *Illustrious* docked. Tamara went to see Christina immediately the sirens sounded. Like many others, they had got out of the habit of running to the shelter each time the sirens wailed, and had come to accept *Sinjal ta-l-Attakki mill-Ajru* as part of daily life. Much of their confidence was based on their assailants being Italian. Often attacks never materialised and when they did, the bombers were high and the bombing scattered, a large proportion falling into the sea. Also by then the gun defences

---

5. *Ibid.*

were increasingly effective. For some reason Tamara was scared, although she did not want to admit it. She found Christina on her landing, her sixth sense having alerted her. Christina had heard the Germans would try and finish *Illustrious* no matter what the cost. 'On this occasion there was something sinister in the wail of the siren, a deep note of foreboding that reminded me instantly of my promise to Jacques. With HMS *Illustrious* now berthed in Grand Harbour, the names of many of us might well be written on the bombs that were almost certainly to be showered on and around that sitting target. Tamara and I went below.'[6]

When they arrived in the cellar they found Gina Carter Jonas, the wife of Luqa's Station Commander, already there. She said the target was most likely *Illustrious*. 'More officers' wives arrived. "This was not a day to stay in one's flat," they hinted darkly ... and then it started.'[7]

'The din above Grand Harbour as the battle of *Illustrious* broke out will never fade from my memory. It was the noise of an aerial Armageddon that beggar's description. As I stood there with Tamara, saying nothing, only clutching her arm just a little tighter each time a bomb exploded, I realised the significance of Jacques' warning. These were none of your Italians flying at 15,000 feet, dropping their lethal loads into the sea and making off for home before our fighters could get at them. The German Luftwaffe was here on business and had brought along a very fine range of samples. But Malta was a little too quick with the orders and the Germans got far more than they expected when the harbour box barrage opened up with a terrific roar. The intensity of the assault was such that, when Tamara and I emerged from the shelter, we expected to find Floriana and Valletta wiped out of existence. It seemed incredible that anything could be left standing after the attack. Yet around us nothing had changed. The *Castille* was still in place, the Barracca Lift seemingly intact, the war memorial solid and straight as ever. And, by all that was wonderful, *Illustrious* stood unmoved at her berth.

'Then suddenly the streets were alive with people. Everyone started running wildly towards the ramparts of the harbour. Tamara and I joined them. It was only when we reached the bastion walls that we realised how devastating the attack had been; from where we stood we could see the terrible havoc that had been wrought upon the Three Cities. Dust was still rising in clouds from buildings that were no more and we knew that there must be hundreds of people lying beneath those piles of rubble, dead or critically injured. For a while we stood on the towering height, looking helplessly at the stricken scene beyond the water, each of us slowly realising that this was but a forerunner to the many perils that were to beset the island in the months ahead.'[8]

---

6. *Carve Malta on my heart and other wartime stories*, by Frederick Galea, page 47.
7. *Women of Malta*, by Frederick Galea, page 85.
8. *Carve Malta on my heart and other wartime stories*, by Frederick Galea, page 48.

This first raid on *Illustrious* lasted only an hour, but to many it seemed longer. The Germans unleashed a combined force of forty-four Ju87 Stukas and seventeen Ju88s escorted by fighters. That evening, in the shelter, an Army officer who acted as a raid watcher described how the gunners, both on land and on *Illustrious* herself, stayed grimly at their posts and put up a magnificent barrage through which the Luftwaffe had to dive to reach their target. He watched as one aircraft after another peeled off, diving straight into the flak; they never came up again. Six enemy aircraft headed for Luqa, perhaps hoping the defences were focused on protecting Grand Harbour. Not one made it back to Sicily, he said.

The following day was crisp and cold, but free from air raids with the Germans scouring the Sicilian Channel in search of missing airmen. Christina and Tamara ventured out, taking the ferry from Customs House steps across to Senglea. What they saw was beyond belief. 'The destruction that greeted our eyes was appalling, boulders everywhere blocking our path, half-hanging balconies at dangerous angles. It was a problem how to get from one street to another. Mountains of rock slabs had to be climbed with danger to life and limb. One street of about fifty houses had been razed to the ground. Pitiful remnants of frocks, shoes, hats and other oddments were mixed with the rubble. A string of washing flapped dismally against the only remaining wall of a three-storied house ... . We came away from Senglea feeling that war had started in earnest.'[9] The clock on the magnificent, now damaged, 400-year-old church of Our Lady of Victories, built by Jean de La Valette, had stopped at 2.20 pm in a silent reminder of the previous afternoon. Tamara and Christina came away from Senglea feeling sick. The three ancient and picturesque cities of Vittoriosa, Senglea and Cospicua were now cities of the dead, inhabited by ghosts and memories.

The Luftwaffe came back two days later, directing their assaults against Luqa and Hal Far. On the next day they came for *Illustrious* with about 140 aircraft. Again the Three Cities suffered and the already damaged church of Our Lady of Victories was reduced to a mass of crumbled masonry. There were more attacks the following day, and the carrier was again badly damaged. Two near misses lifted her out of the water and flung her against the wharf. Repair work intensified. The Axis aircraft did not have everything their own way; the fighters and anti-aircraft artillery claimed a total of seventeen aircraft shot down, one of which was brought down by a Gladiator. By then the Navy had taken over the Gladiators at Hal Far and were flying them as well as their own Fulmars and some Hurricanes.

Despite the bombing, the dockyard workers and sailors laboured desperately to get *Illustrious* sufficiently seaworthy to make her escape. Their efforts paid off. She slipped her moorings at dusk on 23 January and, by the following morning, was well

---

9. *Women of Malta*, by Frederick Galea, page 86.

on her way under her own steam to Egypt. A very battered and operationally useless ship arrived in Alexandria at midday on 25 January.

In their attempts to destroy *Illustrious*, the Luftwaffe mounted eight large scale raids in eight days. They used over 500 aircraft, of which they lost 61, about half each falling to the fighters and the gun defences. *Illustrious* was hit twice and suffered many near misses, but the area around the dockyard was reduced to a wasteland of stone and rubble with not a single building left standing. There were many casualties. Over 3000 houses were destroyed by 220 tons of bombs dropped in an area of only a few hundred square yards. Neither Coventry nor Stalingrad saw such a weight of bombs visited upon them in so short a time. The Three Cities was left utterly deserted.

Many observers now grew wiser and no longer watched the raids from rooftops, but headed for cover in the shelters. Many Maltese lost their homes, and some historic buildings were shattered beyond repair, but the people's spirit was intact. In fact, the survival of *Illustrious* and its escape was inextricably linked by many to Malta's spirit. On the morning of 24 January, everyone on the island heaved a collective sigh of relief when they realised *Illustrious* had gone. The Luftwaffe then turned its attention back to the airfields, but there was no doubt the Germans had come to stay and maybe what had fallen on the Three Cities was a sign of their intentions. First though, they needed to obliterate Malta's fighters. Two days before *Illustrious* made her escape, Commonwealth troops advanced westward through Libya and captured Tobruk. Perhaps this was another good sign.

On the evening of 24 January the ERA Club was unusually crowded. Many had stayed away the previous week because of the intense raids. There was no dancing and people were content to laze in the easy chairs and chat. Christina went there with Ronnie and Tamara.

'Suddenly the peaceful atmosphere was shattered by an outburst of raucous singing and yells. A group of unruly young officers stampeded down the entrance steps and crashed into the room. They appeared to have been celebrating on a somewhat grandiose scale. As they stood laughing and joking at the door I noticed that all the officers, apart from one, wore naval uniform. The exception was a blond RAF flying officer, good-looking and of medium build. The next thing I knew the RAF officer was coming towards us – towards me. After a quick word with the Marks, he introduced himself and then said in a quiet voice, "I'm so terribly sorry, Christina, about poor old Jacques and René. They were such wonderful fellows." I was puzzled. He had called me "Christina".

'"But how do you know me? And that I knew them?"

'"Because Jacques was always talking about Christina, of the *Whizz-Bangs*, and I've seen you in a show or two myself you know."

'Then the penny dropped. Here in front of me was Jacques' hero: "*Magnifique. Formidable.*" As we talked I noticed that he was wearing the ribbon of the DFC, beneath his pilot's wings. It seemed brand new. I noticed too how incredibly blue were his eyes. His mouth was full and sensitive. When he smiled a deep crease came into his left cheek and tiny lines crinkled about the corners of his eyes. His hair was golden and rather long, waving slightly above the ears. "He's like a Greek god", I thought.'[10]

His name was Adrian Warburton.

---

10. *Carve Malta on my heart and other wartime stories*, by Frederick Galea, page 50.

Chapter Eight

A Man They Called Warby

'A young Apollo, golden-haired,
  Stands dreaming on the verge of strife,
Magnificently unprepared
For the long littleness of life.'

By Frances Cornford

Jacques' hero was indeed Adrian, the pilot he described as great and wonderful. But what had Adrian done to earn such accolades? How had he become a recce pilot in Malta when, six months earlier in Lincolnshire, his personal life was in a complete mess and he was flying infrequently, and then only in ancient biplanes? To understand why, we need to go back to North Coates where Jos Braithwaite was wondering what to do with a pilot who had no place on 22 Squadron's modern Beaufort torpedo bombers.

In July 1940, the Air Ministry was under a great deal of pressure. Some came from Admiral Cunningham, C-in-C Mediterranean Fleet, who recognised Malta's potential, but could do little without first neutralising the very clear and present danger posed by the Italian battle fleet. He needed intelligence and asked the RAF to provide it. A cry went out for fast, modern, recce aircraft, but there were precious few. Following the French armistice, the Air Ministry had taken over a French contract for Glenn Martin light bombers. Perhaps they might have potential as general reconnaissance aircraft and could even be adapted to carry cameras.

The task of evaluating the aircraft was given to Braithwaite and on 14 August he flew to the aircraft assembly unit at RAF Burtonwood in Cheshire. Two days later, he returned in a Glenn Martin 167F. Two days after that he was directed to form a general reconnaissance flight using personnel from within 22 Squadron. He selected an Australian, Flight Lieutenant Earnest Whiteley, known as Tich, to lead the flight. Tich only arrived on 22 Squadron in June, but Braithwaite judged his man well. By 23 August, Braithwaite had four aircraft. As the Glenn Martins were new to British skies, Braithwaite personally toured various Hurricane units for fighter affiliation to ensure his aircraft would not be misidentified and attacked. On his return, 'Jos received an astonishing call from one Hurricane squadron – he had outpaced them! In all fairness Jos had picked the altitude and may have over-boosted his engines.'[1] The Glenn Martins were soon dubbed 'Bob Martins', after the famous dog condition powders, but were later officially known as Marylands.

Test flying and fuel endurance flights began immediately, occasionally interrupted by air raids. At dusk on 28 August, Tich was airborne practicing circuits when German air raids began. All the airfield lights on the East Coast were switched off, immediately replaced by searchlights and gunfire. Judging the safest place to be was over the sea, Tich flew east until met by searchlights and flak in Holland. Retracing his steps, the lone Maryland was again greeted by gun fire despite firing the colours of the day. In all, Tich made three return trips across the North Sea before landing at dawn to find he and his crew were listed as 'Missing on Active Service'. But Tich was well impressed by the aircraft's endurance. That quality, along with speed, manoeuvrability and armament was priceless in a recce aircraft.

Two Marylands flew to RAF Aldergrove in Northern Ireland for night flying in what should have been easier circumstances. The Maryland was not easy to master with its metric instrumentation and throttles that operated, 'the wrong way round.' It could swing viciously in a crosswind on take-off or landing and one aircraft crashed into a hangar killing the crew. These were the first casualties of 431 (General Reconnaissance) Flight, as the unit was now officially known.

Tich's next task was a challenging one: deliver three Marylands to Malta, each with a crew of three: a pilot, an observer or navigator and a WOp/AG. With his experience of the Maryland's excellent range, Tich was convinced they could reach Malta in one hop. With few specialist navigators available, pilots with navigation training were considered, including Adrian Warburton and one other, Paddy Devine; both had recently returned having completed the same Squire's Gate course. Jos Braithwaite asked Tich to take Adrian, suggesting this could be the new start young Warburton needed. He could then pay off his debts and perhaps rehabilitate himself. Braithwaite had clearly not completely written Adrian off.

Taking two pilots in place of two navigators would give Tich more flexibility, so he selected Devine and Warburton, tasking them with planning a route. Their work was meticulous; Tich later said their presentation of options would have done credit to Bomber Command. The route, timing and overall plan was accepted without alteration. 'Warburton had already demonstrated to me that he was a capable and reliable officer just looking for a challenge.'[2] Adrian was only too aware his position as a pilot, even as an officer, was tenuous to say the least and would have worked hard to satisfy Tich. Braithwaite had also judged Adrian well, Tich later describing Braithwaite as a brilliant commanding officer. On 3 September Adrian was re-

---

1. *Warburton and PR from Malta*, by E.A. Whiteley, published in *The Royal Air Forces Quarterly*, Spring 1978, pages 20–21.
2. *Ibid.*

graded as a pilot officer, but he was still on probation. The following day he was formally posted to 431 Flight.

The mission to Malta was unprecedented, attempting a non-stop flight over occupied France, mostly at night, in an aircraft largely unproven in RAF service and at the very limits of its range. The three aircraft flew to Thorney Island on 4 September, just over two weeks after Braithwaite was first directed to form a recce unit with brand-new aircraft. They intended to depart at night, crossing France to reach Sardinia at first light. They would then skirt Sicily, with its many fighters, to reach Malta. The distance was 1,300 miles following a route never attempted before in wartime conditions. Coincidentally, Thorney Island was only a few miles from Betty, Adrian's wife. In a two-day stay, Adrian made no attempt to contact her. He had closed the book on that short episode of his life.

They set off separately in the early hours of 6 September. The three crews were Flight Lieutenant Whiteley, Pilot Officer Devine and Corporal Shephard; Pilot Officer Foxton, Pilot Officer Warburton and Sergeant Gridley; and Sergeant Bibby, Sergeant Bastard and Sergeant Moren. A fourth aircraft was held in reserve. John Shephard, an experienced wireless and electrical mechanic, was another excellent choice. At first light, they flew diagonally across Sardinia exposing their newly-fitted F24 camera magazines. The navigation throughout was spot on and all three aircraft landed safely at Luqa, establishing a route for others to follow. Three more aircraft were meant to follow within a week or so, but in the event the next Maryland did not reach Malta until October. A fifth was shot down on the way in November.

Tich hardly knew Adrian yet had developed an instinct about him. And Adrian of course wanted to prove himself. Nevertheless, he was only being used for his navigational skills and had a long way to go to show he was truly worthy of his pilot's brevet. There was no doubt Adrian had drive and determination, and he desperately wanted to fly as a pilot, but could he ever develop the skill to master a high performance, twin-engine aircraft? Adrian's landings had always been described as weak and his instructors had given up on him after very few flights, even in the sedate Anson. What chance did he have of coping with the much faster and more demanding Maryland? Would Tich even give Adrian a chance?

On arrival, Tich presented Air HQ with the photographs taken en route. As if their ground-breaking 'transit' flight wasn't enough, their shots of Sardinia's ports and airfields were the first since war began. These were powerful credentials. Maybe doing something additional to the planned mission struck a chord with Adrian.

Intense training, running side-by-side with operations, began immediately. Maritime reconnaissance was 431 Flight's main role, but Tich placed equal emphasis on photography. The very first operational mission to Tripoli was within forty-eight hours, with Adrian as navigator. Tich appointed him as the photographic officer and the flight's ship recognition expert, and Adrian took these new tasks very seriously.

He made a very positive impression on the photographic technicians and on Tich, who later said Adrian ensured no Maryland ever took off without cameras. If the weather precluded use of the vertical camera, either the navigator or the WOp/AG took oblique shots using Tich's Contax camera, or one of two Leicas borrowed from the Marquis Scicluna, owner of the Parisio Palace in Naxxar, Tamara's former home. Adrian also introduced a ship recognition training programme for all recce crews. Yet he yearned for more. He desperately wanted to get back into the pilot's seat.

Tich began training Adrian and Devine as Maryland pilots. The aircraft's dual controls were ideal for this purpose and should have made the task straightforward, but training under wartime conditions on an airfield under regular attack was demanding and hazardous. Nevertheless, Devine was an operational Maryland pilot by mid-September. Adrian, on the other hand, had not flown as a pilot for four months and struggled to master the Maryland's idiosyncrasies on take-off and landing. Once in the air his flying was fine, but his attempts to get the aircraft airborne and put it back on the ground were very poor and he had to beg for his training to continue. His take-offs were appalling: he was rarely able to control the Maryland's swing caused by the considerable torque from the engines combined with slipstream. His landings were little better, any crosswind usually making matters worse. It seemed coordination of throttles, control column and rudder was a skill Adrian was unable to master. On his first solo Adrian landed crosswind, trailing wire behind him from the airfield's perimeter fence. He then added insult to injury by completing a savage ground-loop – an uncontrollable and rapid swing, often through 360 degrees. This was witnessed by an irate wing commander and Tich was firmly reprimanded for risking a precious aircraft in the hands of such a 'ham-fisted idiot'. Tich now had grave doubts about Adrian and with little time to devote to such a training risk, Adrian found himself back in the navigator's seat.

Adrian had established a good rapport with everyone on 431 Flight and with the airmen, taking a keen interest in what they did. But to many of the officers at Luqa he was a loner who did not mix well. He avoided the Officers' Mess. This unwillingness to mix was always a quirk of Adrian's, but it seemed exacerbated within these early weeks. He was an 'odd-ball', a pilot who wore 'wings' yet flew as a navigator. Many would have seen or heard of his struggles and this would have been talked about; that's what happens in crewrooms and Messes the world over, and such talk can be cruel. Even Adrian's suspicion of such talk could have driven him further away from Mess life. He also had very little money. But he enjoyed his own company and soon realised the airmen accepted him for what he was; a dedicated individual anxious to learn more about photography and the airmen's tasks. This was the period when Adrian was a 'gash hand' with not enough to do.

For the moment, 431 Flight had sufficient pilots for operations without Adrian, who spent more and more time with the airmen. He gained their respect and this was something he never lost. He was often found with them, sometimes sitting on a workshop floor, playing cards. Yet he still had something to prove. He was lucky to have a leader of Tich Whiteley's calibre and he learned a great deal from him. But Tich went far beyond the norm; he took Adrian under his wing, sorted out his finances, and made arrangements to have part of Adrian's pay stopped in the UK to go toward his debts. Did Tich know Adrian was married? There is no evidence either way but it is most unlikely. If he had known, it is inconceivable he would not have ensured some money went to Betty, but he did not. After the war, Betty confirmed she never received a penny from Adrian. In fact, after their very brief meeting in Blackpool, Betty never saw Adrian again. All in all, Tich was a remarkable man, willing to invest much time and effort in Adrian despite the pressure of running a unit at war, on an airfield under attack. Yet it was most unlikely even Tich's faith and obvious liking for Adrian would ever have been enough to consider using Adrian as an operational pilot on his three precious Marylands. Until that is, 'Malta Dog' intervened.

Malta Dog is a stomach complaint similar to dysentery and sufficiently painful to reduce even the most seasoned and hardened veteran to impotence in three or four days. It can last weeks. Two of 431 Flight's pilots, Foxton and Bibby, were laid low with the bug. Tich now had a major problem. By then Admiral Cunningham was demanding up-to-date and regular intelligence on the Italian fleet and that was down to Tich. He had no choice but to use Adrian.

Tich sent Adrian as pilot on a recce mission in a fully-fuelled aircraft. The result was near disaster. Adrian's take-off was so bad it tore a wheel off the aircraft, forcing an immediate emergency landing. The Operational Readiness Book (ORB) recorded somewhat generously the flight was abandoned owing to 'hydraulic failure'. The aircraft – AR712 – crashed on landing. The following day it was hit by an incendiary bomb; the aircraft was a write-off. Tich then took the unusual step of asking Adrian's two NCO crew, observer Frank Bastard and WOp/AG Paddy Moren, if they were willing to continue flying with Adrian. They had already lived through circular take-offs and zig-zag landings but were prepared to fly with Adrian just once more, providing he completed some high-speed taxiing practice first. They thought Adrian was full of guts. So were they. They must also have had a lot of blind faith as their backing saved Adrian. He was airborne again as a pilot with Frank and Paddy on an operational sortie within three days.

Would Adrian ever truly master the art of taking-off and landing? He continued to swing wildly on take-off and, over a year later, his landings were described as a series of uncoordinated bumps. Once at night, he swung so violently from one side of the runway to the other he knocked over paraffin-filled goose-neck flares used to light the strip, turning the runway into a flaming flood. For some minutes afterwards, the burning paraffin stuck to the fin of Adrian's aircraft.

Despite this, Tich continued to back his judgement, especially as the demands for more photography continued to increase. All available 431 crews flew often. In October, Frank Bastard flew over ninety-two hours on operations, a staggering total in a single month. Adrian flew twenty operational missions the same month, although only six as pilot; perhaps Tich was laying an each-way bet.

Adrian's ability to recognise warships soon came into its own and on his return from one sortie to Taranto he reported twenty-eight warships all confirmed by his photographs. Tich insisted 431's overriding priority was to bring back 'the goods'. Crews were not to risk their aircraft by engaging unnecessarily in combat or by trying to shoot down enemy aircraft. The early Marylands were particularly vulnerable to incendiary bullets, as they had no self-sealing fuel tanks or armour plate. On a flight on 30 October, Adrian attacked and shot down an Italian seaplane before photographing the burning aircraft after it landed on the water. With the crew in their dinghy, Adrian ensured a distress call was broadcast. Publicly, Tich was critical, but as Adrian was over the sea, well away from enemy fighters, privately he was rather pleased. In order to encourage the staff assembling Marylands at RAF Burtonwood, Tich sent them a message: 'Your friend Mr Martin doing very nicely out here. Did some boxing yesterday and won by a knockout.'[3]

Adrian finally vacated the navigator's seat on 1 November. Now he had the opportunity to prove his worth. On 2 November, when flying with Sergeant John Spires and Paddy Moren, they were attacked by three fighters and a seaplane. Paddy claimed one fighter shot down; the seaplane landed on the water with a damaged engine. Adrian continued to attack the seaplane until it was destroyed, but his aircraft was also hit by defensive fire. A bullet hit the instrument panel before penetrating Adrian's harness, striking him in the chest and puncturing the skin over his heart to a depth of a quarter-of-an-inch. One engine also caught fire. Adrian successfully got the aircraft back to Luqa to be met by a medical team and an anxious Tich. Before being treated, Adrian produced the bullet he extracted from his chest on the return journey. He mounted it on a wristband which he invariably wore. People began to talk about 'Warby's luck'.

On 3 November, 431 reported three battleships at Taranto; four days later they reported four. Returning from another Taranto mission on 7 November with excellent photography, Adrian's Maryland was chased by four MC.200 fighters. In the twenty-minute engagement, Paddy claimed one fighter as damaged. Not surprisingly, Adrian and his crew were beginning to get noticed.

Adrian's regular navigator, Frank Bastard, flew to Taranto the following day with Sergeant Bibby. While being engaged by flak the aircraft's hood blew open. In attempting to reach it, Bibby broke his hand. Frank flew the aircraft clear of

---

3. *Warburton and PR from Malta*, by E.A. Whiteley, published in *The Royal Air Forces Quarterly*, Spring 1978, page 22.

the target area until his pilot recovered. With Bibby's left arm now useless, Frank had to manipulate the throttles for a successful landing at Luqa. His actions were instrumental in saving the aircraft and crew.

Admiral Cunningham wanted more information on Taranto so his Swordfish crews could avoid Italian defences and have a decisive impact. Only 431's increasingly expert crews could obtain such detailed evidence and it was they who brought back vital news about the extent and location of two lines of barrage balloons. Two Maryland missions targeted Taranto each day. Subsequent events confirmed the most important were flown on 10 and 11 November, two on each day. Tich flew the first, Adrian the second, crewed with Frank and Paddy. Adrian's aircraft was subject to intense flak and intercepted by a CR.42 which took twenty minutes to shake off. Frank confirmed in his logbook photographs of the Italian fleet were taken on this sortie. 'An aircraft from the *Illustrious* working from Malta then picked up full details of the enemy's dispositions, together with photographs showing the anti-torpedo nets and barrage balloons, and it was in the light of these that the Swordfish crews planned their attack.'[4]

The pilot of the morning sortie on 11 November was Paddy Devine. That afternoon, Adrian flew with John Spires as navigator. Tich later confirmed this trip was abortive photographically, but it did not stop Adrian from entering Taranto Harbour, not once, but twice. Years later, Spires left an account of the mission. He said the WOp/AG was Paddy Moren, but the ORB names Sergeant McConnell. Spires described the day as grey and still with hardly a ripple on the sea. With no breaks in the cloud, vertical photography was unlikely. Adrian was unperturbed; they were going at zero feet, he said. He told John to get a sharp pencil and plenty of paper so he could plot the ships on the harbour map. John and the WOp/AG expressed their response in a single word.

'The weather was so bad the birds were walking and the fish were at anchor. But nothing, absolutely nothing, could get in the way of what Warby wanted to do.'[5] They referred to that particular Maryland as 'The Sardine Tin'; in the air, it became known as 'Whistler's Mother' because of the tunes played by the air going through the aircraft's many splinter holes. They achieved complete surprise, low cloud having deterred the Italians from raising their balloon barrage. The crew did their level best to count and note the names of the major warships and escaped unscathed, having flown twice round the outer harbour. When comparing notes, there was a discrepancy in the number of battleships: they counted six; there should only have been five. With no photographic evidence, Adrian decided to go back. Having lost the element of surprise, they were quickly spotted and the Italians opened up for all their worth. Despite the intense flak, they agreed on only five

---

4. *Royal Air Force 1939–1945, Volume 1, The Fight at Odds*, by Denis Richards, page 183.
5. *The Unknown Airman*, by Roy Nash, published in *The Star*, March 1958.

battleships, which, along with fourteen cruisers and twenty-seven destroyers, tried desperately to shoot their very vulnerable Maryland out of the sky.

Re-attacks in daylight, with alerted defences, are hazardous in the extreme. Adrian was not flying a single-seater and was responsible for the lives of two others. On top of that the Maryland was one of few specialist recce aircraft in Malta which the RAF could ill afford to lose. The second run was certainly courageous and Adrian showed resolute determination in the face of the enemy, but was it a little foolhardy? His actions can only be judged against the circumstances existing at the time. The Taranto task was the very highest of priorities and Adrian may also have suspected the Fleet Air Arm attack was imminent; in fact it went ahead that very night. Information there might be a sixth battleship present, and its precise location, could therefore have been vital. In the event he and his equally gallant crew were able to confirm visually there were five. But why did he do it? Was he trying to prove something to himself and live up to the family name? Or was he trying to show the doubters back at Luqa, and there would have been many though not on 431, that Adrian Warburton had what it takes? Maybe he also wanted to show Tich he was capable of coming back with the goods, that Tich's faith in Adrian was well-founded. Whatever the reason, Adrian laid down a marker that afternoon.

Early the next morning, a Maryland ran the Taranto gauntlet once more, unaware of the overnight attack. This aircraft was flown by Tich, now a newly promoted squadron leader. He reported one battleship partially submerged and another beached. Oil was pouring from many other ships and the harbour was in chaos. It was Tich's photographs, taken from 8,000 feet, which brought back proof three battleships had been hit. Admiral Cunningham wrote to Air Commodore Maynard on 14 November thanking him, 'for the most valuable reconnaissance work carried out by your squadrons, without which the successful attack on Taranto would have been impossible.'[6] In a single stroke, the attack on Taranto altered the balance of power in the Mediterranean. In announcing news of the attack to the House of Commons, Churchill spoke of, 'this glorious episode'. It was also a huge success for Tich and all of his crews. Cunningham's despatch on the operation, published in 1947, said, 'the success of the Fleet Air Arm attack was due in no small part to the excellent reconnaissances carried out by the Royal Air Force Glenn Martin Flight (No 431) from Malta, under very difficult conditions and often in the face of fighter opposition.'[7] Unfortunately, many of the aircrew involved did not live long enough to read Cunningham's fine words.

Over the years a number of errors have been made, in good faith, about Adrian's involvement at Taranto. He played an important part, but some accounts unnecessarily embellish his involvement perhaps at the expense of other crews. Many

---

6. *The Air Battle of Malta*, by the Ministry of Information, page 17.
7. *Ibid.*

writers understandably relied on 431's ORB as a primary source. ORBs, sometimes referred to as the Form 540, are normally compiled by a junior officer and verified and signed by the unit commander at the end of each month. By November, Tich was in sole charge of 431 and it was his job to sign the ORB before sending it to Air HQ. Unfortunately, the first ORB covering 1940 and much of 1941 was lost or destroyed. 'The rewrite had inaccuracies which we tried to correct in an air raid shelter during bombing attacks. When the rewrite was reported lost or destroyed, one of my new officers did his best to prepare a third submission which I reluctantly signed knowing it had many obvious inaccuracies. Winning the war tomorrow was my first priority – not writing history.'[8]

Adrian's performance up to and including Taranto formed the basis of a growing reputation. A man called 'Warby' began to emerge and was talked about more and more, and in very positive terms. This was the first time in his short RAF career Adrian was noticed for doing something right and it gave his confidence an enormous boost. His contribution was significant, although Taranto was primarily Tich Whiteley's and 431's success. Later, when word of Adrian's later successes began to spread, many of the pre and post attack recce missions of Taranto were incorrectly attributed to Adrian.

Adrian did not return to Taranto until 20 November. The ORB records his crew as Sub-Lieutenant Smith and Paddy Moren, and says they experienced poor visibility with haze up to one hundred feet as well as low cloud. By then the Italian battle fleet, previously berthed in rows, was now scattered haphazardly within the harbour. So haphazard, and so low did Adrian fly, a W/T cable from an Italian ship was found wrapped around his aircraft's tailwheel when he landed. He again delivered another first class visual report. Some accounts suggest this occurred on the 11 November. This is perfectly possible, although the 20 November ORB entry includes the comment, 'W-T aerial snapped.' The Maryland's W-T aerial stretched from a mount on the aircraft's upper fuselage behind the cockpit to the top of the fin. It could have snapped, but would such a relatively minor occurrence have been recorded in the ORB, especially on the document's third rewrite many months later? It is much more likely this referred to the aerial from the Italian ship, an incident which would have been well remembered and talked about long afterwards. Regardless of which flight, it shows just how low Adrian was prepared to fly. Later that month, Adrian was confirmed as a pilot officer – he was no longer on probation. Soon afterwards, a cartoon appeared in the *Times of Malta* which featured an Italian admiral hurling his sword in rage at Adrian's aircraft. A legend began to develop and, from then on, it appeared as though Adrian could do no wrong.

8. *Warburton and PR from Malta*, by E.A. Whiteley, published in *The Royal Air Forces Quarterly*, Spring 1978, page 30.

In mid-December, he attacked a surfaced U-boat and on Christmas Eve, flying with Sergeant Jimmy Alexander and Paddy Moren, he pounced on a solitary Italian aircraft: 'I was entering the Bay of Naples from the south-west at 1,500 feet when I saw an SM.79 with brown mottled camouflage heading across my track. The clouds were at 2,000 feet in a solid bank, so if the fighters appeared I could retire. I therefore made a stern attack; some pieces of the tail flew off and my rounds started going into the fuselage. I closed the range and concentrated on the starboard engine which started to smoke and eventually stopped. My rear gunner wanted to try the new turret, so I broke away and drew parallel to the SM.79, slightly above and about a hundred yards to his starboard. My rear gunner put in a burst of about twenty rounds which ignited the petrol, and the SM.79 burst into a mass of flames and dived into the sea from 1,000 feet, disappearing immediately. I then carried on with my recce of Naples and returned to Luqa.'[9] The aircraft was in fact a SM.75 transport aircraft. Its crew of four, including the squadron commander, and four passengers were killed.

Throughout these missions, Adrian was always well supported by his crew, his most frequent WOp/AG being the very talented Paddy Moren and they became close friends. December also saw two additional Marylands joining 431 Flight: 'Willie' Williams, whom Jack Vowles last saw at Bircham Newton, arrived on 19 December, and another Maryland arrived a few days later. By then the Frenchmen, René Duvauchelle and Jacques Méhauas, had been flying with 431 for almost a month and had become well aware of Adrian's exploits. They had little need of Jack's labels so carefully written and fixed in the cockpit.

On 27 December, Malta gained two more decorated heroes: Pilot Officer Adrian Warburton was awarded a DFC and Sergeant Frank Bastard was awarded a Distinguished Flying Medal (DFM) for his actions during the incident with Sergeant Bibby. The awards were gazetted in February. Adrian was in very good company, one among many heroes on 431 Flight. He was promoted to flying officer at the beginning of January 1941.

So this was the man they called Warby, aged twenty-two, an 'accidental' operational photo-reconnaissance pilot and the man Jacques described as *magnifique, formidable*. By January 1941, Warby was also very much part of Malta's wartime scene.

---

9. *The Air Battle of Malta*, published by the Ministry of Information, page 21.

Chapter Nine

1941 & New Arrivals

A New Year football match, to raise money for the RAF Benevolent Fund, was such a success other methods of raising funds were considered. Encouraged by the popularity of the *Whizz-Bangs* formed seven months earlier, the *Raffians* was formed with Christina's friend Cecil Roche, now a flying officer in Air HQ, as producer. It included officers and men from Air HQ and other Lascaris girls all working in their spare time. Like the *Whizz-Bangs*, they toured airfields and outstations often using the bomb disposal lorry when transport was short. Both concert parties brought amusement and relief, sometimes appearing together as the RAF *Fly Gang*.

January 1941 ended well for Malta's RAF defenders with six awarded DFCs. One went to Irishman William 'Timber' Woods, who had flown with Fighter Flight from the start; he was credited with five enemy aircraft shot down. Also honoured was Captain Francis Pretty, appointed as an Officer of the Most Excellent Order of the British Empire (OBE) for his gallantry in command of the *Cornwall* the previous August. He left his ship within a week of arriving in Malta as masters of his calibre were in short supply. He took command of the brand-new MV *Nottingham*. Six days out on her maiden voyage across the Atlantic, she was attacked by U-74. *Nottingham* was hit in the stern after attempting to ram the U-boat. Although they took to the lifeboats, Captain Pretty and his crew of sixty-one were never seen again. It was, 'a sad end to a man who initiated a tradition.'[1]

The post of AOC was upgraded to air vice-marshal and the newly-promoted Maynard was created Companion of the Order of the Bath (CB) prior to his relief. The choice of successor was important if Malta was to fulfil the new directive from London of taking the war to the enemy, but the arrival of the Luftwaffe in Sicily quashed any early hopes of taking the offensive. At the end of a month in which General Dobbie reported the spirit of the Maltese people was as strong as ever, 261 Squadron had twenty-three out of twenty-eight Hurricanes, and three out of four Gladiators, serviceable. Flying from Hal Far since the departure of *Illustrious*, 806 Squadron of the Fleet Air Arm also had two out of three Fulmars available.

February saw heavy bombing of the airfields with many aircraft damaged or destroyed on the ground. The Luftwaffe knew its business. From then on, day after

---

1. *Red Duster, White Ensign*, by Ian Cameron, page 38.

day, it attacked with careful deliberation, pressing home its bombing runs against fierce anti-aircraft fire. With over 150 modern fighters and 180 bombers to choose from, the skies above Malta were rarely empty of the enemy. With relatively few defending fighters, German fighters often flew low, machine-gunning anything they wished on the ground and paying particular attention to parked aircraft. And all the time, the relentless bombing of the airfields, hangars, and dockyards continued with great precision. Craters in the landing strips were promptly filled in, and British and Maltese ingenuity saw damaged Hurricanes quickly repaired to struggle into the air against odds of up to twenty-to-one.

A new cinema, the Coliseum, opened in February. Construction started before Italy declared war, but the owners decided to press on with it, war or no war. The largest cinema in Valletta, from the moment it opened the public flocked to the three performances each day, often playing to a full-house. Tamara watched a newsreel of the Battle of Britain with a raid raging outside. The sound of guns and explosions on screen, matched by the sound of guns and explosions outside, were perhaps a trifle too realistic. Yet very few Maltese spectators left their seats for shelter and fewer still service personnel. This was rather foolhardy, but without doubt it demonstrated the spirit prevailing in Malta at the time.

General Dobbie continued to press London for more fighters. In requesting another infantry battalion, he expressed concern about how the Maltese might react if faced with invasion. He hinted the army might have to be used to control the civilian population. His pessimism had the desired effect and two battalions of infantry were despatched from Egypt. A relatively little-known German general, along with some advance units of the formation he now commanded, arrived in Tripoli. His name was Erwin Rommel. His unit was the Afrika Korps.

The *Knight of Malta,* involved in convoy duties since hostilities began, ran aground east of Tobruk. She was abandoned under bombing; so ended another valiant vessel, this one having brought many newcomers to Malta over the years, including Christina. HMS *Terror*, one of the three RN ships to defend Malta against the first Italian raids the previous year, was also sunk off Tobruk the same month.

Axis sorties continued to increase and the RAF's Mark I Hurricanes struggled against the latest cannon-armed Me109Es which they met in mid-February. In the next three months, one small but battle-hardened unit of nine Me109Es claimed forty-two British aircraft destroyed. Maynard pleaded for Mark IIs, or better still, Spitfires. Attempts were made in February and March to operate Wellington bombers from RAF Luqa. They desperately tried to redress the balance after heavy bombing raids by day and night. They achieved some success with their night attacks, but many were destroyed on the ground by day. It was impossible to base bombers on the island on a permanent basis and they were withdrawn to Egypt. One heavy bombing raid against Hal Far left two Swordfish and one Gladiator totally destroyed and other aircraft damaged. The only Gladiator left was *Faith* and she was relegated to meteorological flights. But the biplane fighters had served the island well. Sometimes faith is enough.

To cope with the increased air activity, a filter room was built in a small cellar at 3, Scots Street, Valletta, a corner house overlooking South Street. It was manned entirely by RAF personnel and fitted with extra telephones. Information on radar contacts, giving their location, height and an estimated number of aircraft, was passed to the filter room, an essential hub. Here, the tracks were analysed and given appropriate labels: 'H' for Hostile, 'X' for Unidentified and 'F' for Friendly, before being passed to fighter control. Information was also relayed by visual observation from places such as the rooftop of the *Auberge de Castille*. A new plotting table was added with a UK-type grid system painted on the table. The work in this residential location in the middle of the capital was top secret and RAF policemen carefully vetted all personnel who worked there, although it was clear the facilities were insufficiently secure. More tunnels at Lascaris were therefore excavated and equipped. These opened as summer approached, and the filter room and the Scots Street staff were transferred to the new facility.

With increased calls for photography, 69 Squadron's tasks expanded. It became the one squadron resident at Luqa which never left until after Malta's war was won and, under Tich Whiteley's leadership, it gained a reputation it would never lose. On paper, the squadron had twelve Marylands, but was terribly short of spares and on some days only one aircraft was ready to fly. In contrast to earlier months, Frank Bastard flew only twice in February and once in March. Adrian achieved his fiftieth operational mission in February. The squadron's ranks were swelled further with the transfer of George Burges, a founder member of Fighter Flight, who became the next senior pilot after Tich.

At the beginning of the year, on his return from a short visit to the Air Ministry in London, Tich smuggled in some lipsticks, as well as other precious commodities no longer available on the island. He intended to give the lipsticks to a young lady, but when she failed to appear at a party, they ended up going to his second love – his aircraft. By then, the supply of Lockheed hydraulic fluid, on which his Marylands relied, had given out. The only alternative was medicinal castor oil, 'but the army doctors refused to surrender what they had. So George Burges visited some nursing sisters with the last of my lipsticks – and came back with the island's entire supply of castor oil.' Tich's second love was satisfied.

Adrian's reputation of always returning with the goods was now well established and, throughout the early part of 1941, he was selected for special tasks. He constantly varied his tactics to achieve the best results, sometimes flying at height

---

2. *The Whiteley Papers*, by Gp Capt E.A. Whiteley, quoted in *Wings of War*, by Laddie Lucas, page 123.

and often extremely low. He took photographs of the Tragino viaduct near Calitri in Southern Italy, the target for an experimental raid by paratroopers. According to Paddy Moren, some of Adrian's photographs before and after the raid were taken at the near-suicidal height of twenty-five feet.

On 7 March, a Maryland returning from a mission was intercepted by six Me109s just as it crossed the Maltese coast. The rear gunner was killed and the aircraft was soon on fire. John Boys-Stones, who delivered the last Maryland in December, held the aircraft level long enough for his navigator to get out, but when he himself jumped there was insufficient height for his parachute to deploy. He fell 200 feet onto solid rock. Ten minutes later, Luqa's doctor was kneeling beside the young, still conscious pilot. Although he was dying of multiple injuries John said, 'I think I must have left things a bit late.'[3]

Christina discovered many facets to Adrian's character. What struck her most was his love of adventure, his devil-may-care attitude and what she described as his cool cheek.

On the same day Boys-Stones so tragically lost his life, Adrian went missing. Tamara Marks heard the news in a telephone call from her husband. Her heart sank. Were they to lose all of their friends? Knowing how fond Christina had become of Adrian, Tamara went to her flat to offer support. Christina looked quite perturbed, but Tamara felt she was not as heartbroken as she expected her to be. By then Christina was sharing her flat with Pickles and all three of them enjoyed an evening at home. There were, however, some very glum faces at the ERA Club. Christina had every reason not to be glum. The night before, Adrian said he was flying the next morning, but if she heard later he was missing she was not to worry. His favourite drink was 'Horses Neck', made up of brandy and ginger ale, and he was embarrassed at having drunk all of Christina's very limited stock. As his planned trip would take him close to Athens, he intended to develop engine trouble and land there to pick up a few bottles of Greek brandy before returning the next day. He asked Christina not to tell a soul.

The following morning, knowing Adrian's secret, she played things straight, but inwardly she was having a good laugh. Then someone said news had been received Adrian's aircraft had actually been shot down in flames. Christina was horrified, heartbroken. Had he been shot down after all? Later, Luqa's intelligence officer received a message from Adrian saying he had been chased by enemy fighters and ended up short of fuel. He therefore landed at Menidi in Greece to refuel. He would be back in a couple of days after some small repairs were completed on his aircraft. By then, a small RAF contingent was operating in support of the Greeks. Significant numbers of British troops were also being transferred there from Egypt

---

3. Memoirs of Air Cdre Robert Carter Jonas, page 129.

anticipating a German strike. The news Adrian was safe spread like wildfire and his friends celebrated at the Monico bar in Valetta. Malta lacked many things at the time but liquor could still be found. Tamara and Ronnie, whom Adrian and Christina called 'Mara' and 'Marko', were there, but Tamara left early with the party still in full swing. An hour later the air raid siren sounded and a 500lb bomb hit the Sergeants' Mess next door. The party-goers heard the blast but carried on regardless. There was nothing left of the Sergeants' Mess.

A grinning Adrian duly presented Christina with seven bottles of brandy and half a dozen bottles of Greek champagne, perfectly timed for his twenty-third birthday on 10 March. He restocked 69 Squadron's depleted cellar and, for Christina and her friends, there were cosmetics, reels of cotton, press studs, gramophone records and an ashtray he had 'lifted' from a hotel. He also brought a brooch for Christina in the shape of an Evzone's shoe; Evzones being the Greek ceremonial guards who wear traditional dress. The prized gifts for the ladies, by some margin, were the press studs, which could not be had in Malta for love or money. It wasn't often Adrian could provide the essentials of dressmaking. Christina improvised where she had to, even repairing Adrian's threadbare service hat with threads extracted from the seam of his uniform. Afterwards, Adrian was rarely without his beloved service dress cap, wearing it even in the air on top of his flying helmet. Sometimes he wore a pair of baggy, casual, grey flannel trousers, or long, sheepskin trousers, his choice often dictated by the temperature he was likely to experience on his low or high-level missions. By contrast, for the rare formal functions he was required to attend, he was immaculately dressed in his No 1 service dress uniform.

Personal appearance and dress on 69 Squadron were important to Tich who thought his officers should set the right example. After Tich left Malta things changed, but it also became nearly impossible to obtain replacement items of uniform. Adrian's attire became an expression of his individuality and he often wore an army battledress blouse with his RAF rank on slides on the shoulder tabs. He wore a cravat rather than a tie, and rarely wore uniform shoes, preferring something more comfortable. Cravats and scarves would soon became a normal part of RAF flying kit, so important was it to constantly swivel one's head in the air looking for 'the hun in the sun'. A tie and shirt was totally inappropriate for a pilot in combat. With flights often lasting many hours, who can blame Adrian for his relaxed dress? Yet this was very much against the RAF 'norm' even in those testing days in Malta.

By now Adrian and Christina were recognised as a couple, and a very glamorous one at that. This was a relatively quiet time for both of them. They both worked hard, Christina with three or four *Whizz-Bangs* performances a week and Adrian flying on most days, but they still had time to spend together. Adrian did not drink a great deal and smoked little. In fact some of his colleagues never saw him drink alcohol at all. Although they both openly enjoyed parties they were probably conscious they should live up to the glamorous life with which they were quickly labelled. There was a shy side to Adrian's character, often masked by his 'front', and he was easily embarrassed. Adrian and Christina were not constant party-goers, often preferring their own company and a quiet life in Christina's apartment overlooking Grand Harbour. Indeed, an early photograph of Adrian shows him in the apartment winding wool for her.

Adrian was also a fine horseman, often borrowing a horse from the army stables in Valletta to ride down to the Marsa racecourse. Christina sometimes accompanied him having taken riding lessons in Gibraltar. She was glad to be able to wear her jodhpurs again. As they rode to the Marsa racecourse Christina grew very nervous. The horse Adrian had chosen for her was anything but a slow-mover – it appeared to have all the makings of a Grand National winner. She wondered what it would be like when they reached the track, but Adrian assured her he would stay alongside after having one good gallop round the course. 'With that he shot off like an arrow, leaving me alone with my steed. The horse broke into a slow trot and we followed, all very calmly and peacefully. Then it happened. I let go of the reins to fasten my hair-slide which had come undone and, before I knew where I was, the horse was carrying me at breakneck speed after Warby. How I remained on that animal I don't know, I dug in my knees, gripped the front edge of the saddle and hung on like grim death. It could have been only a few minutes but it seemed like hours before Warby came to the rescue. Once alongside he swooped down, grabbed the dangling reins and somehow managed to bring the horse to a halt.'[4] From then on, whenever they were out, he was discreet enough to refer to his favourite drink as a 'brandy dry' and no longer 'a horse's neck.'

In March, four merchantmen delivered another 45,000 tons of cargo. The cost was two cargo ships sunk and one cruiser damaged. The Italian fleet then set sail to strike a blow at Allied convoys from North Africa to Greece. There were misgivings in London about supporting Greece with troops drawn from Egypt, but the risks were accepted. Admiral Cunningham received intelligence advising when the Italians left port, and Adrian was tasked to fly to the area and confirm the enemy fleet was at sea. He was then required to radio its location. The ensuing Battle of Matapan was Italy's greatest defeat at sea with the loss of two heavy cruisers and three destroyers. The RN picked up 1,105 survivors and, on leaving the scene, broadcast the location of other Italian survivors while granting safe passage to an Italian hospital ship. The Italians lost 2,303 sailors; the RN, by contrast, lost the three-man crew of a torpedo-bomber.

Although Adrian deserved his reputation for always coming back with the goods, this action confirms the location of some of his targets was already known. With

---

4. *Carve Malta on my heart and other wartime stories*, by Frederick Galea, page 51.

69 Squadron's crews living and working together, it would not have taken long for these intelligent individuals to 'compare notes' and realise there was more to some of their tasks than met the eye. Perhaps 'Warby's luck' could be used to protect the existence of another intelligence source a little longer. He was not always taken at his word, so heavy was this layer of secrecy, as illustrated when he reported an Italian ship by name and the harbour in which it was berthed. The RN did not accept his report. A few days later, he presented the senior service with a photograph of the ship in question, taken so low and at such close range its name could clearly be read.

Four more Marylands arrived in March, as well as twelve Hurricane Mark IIAs. A month later, twenty-four more were launched from HMS *Ark Royal;* only one failed to arrive. The Hurricanes arrived after pressure from Churchill to use *Ark Royal* against resistance from the Admiralty, which was concerned about resources being removed from the Atlantic to support the reinforcement operation. Around the same time, a detachment of six Blenheim bombers arrived and were immediately employed on day anti-shipping and coastal operations. A third attempt was made to send more Hurricanes by running a single merchant ship, flying initially Spanish then French flags, with twenty-one crated Hurricanes on board. Sadly, the ship hit a mine and was lost, with eighteen survivors interned by the French.

The successful outcome of the action at Matapan offers an indication as to why Adrian was occasionally briefed by senior officers for specific missions. That reason was Ultra, a top-secret source of British intelligence, although the story of British attempts to break German and Italian ciphers went back a long way. The British first cracked Italian naval ciphers in 1937, resulting in an accurate picture of Italian naval and shipping movements. This lasted until mid-July 1940 when the Italian Navy introduced new codes. From then on signals intelligence regarding Italian naval matters was thin, although the British retained an intermittent ability to read Italian low-grade codes and ciphers. By then a new and very important source of similar intelligence was coming from a former stately home in Buckinghamshire, known as Station X. It was Bletchley Park.

The foundation for Bletchley Park's success lay with Poland. Only Churchill and a few others knew Polish cryptographers provided the initial breakthrough when, in July 1939 and two months before the beginning of the Second World War, Poland presented Britain and France with a replica of Germany's Enigma machine. The Poles had been reading German military and political communications for six years. By then, the Germans had added a new complexity to its ciphers but, even so, what the Poles provided allowed Bletchley Park to build the code-breaking system known as Ultra, which began to come on line from May 1940, although the source, even the codename, had to be protected at all costs. Air HQ in Malta began to receive a lot of intelligence from Bletchley Park, although this was retained at the highest level. It was decrypts of the Luftwaffe's Enigma signals which had first given warning of the arrival of *Fliegerkorps X* in Sicily. Were further decrypts sometimes the reason why recce aircraft were sent to very specific locations where enemy vessels were known to be? If this information could be contained, perhaps by using a carefully briefed, slightly secretive pilot, what better way was there to protect the existence of the intelligence source? The pilot himself would be unaware of the true source and most would put it down to 'Warby's luck'.

The intelligence situation was improved further in the summer when an important Italian cipher was broken by Ultra decryption. The British in Malta now had advance notice of the departure dates of almost every Italian convoy and individual sailing. This information often included the composition and planned routes as well. No longer did the RAF and the Fleet Air Arm have to conduct widespread shipping sweeps for potential targets, which was wasteful of precious aircraft and fuel. Now assigned vessels known to be at sea could be directly targeted, having been 'found' by a recce aircraft first. Once found, did Malta have sufficient strike assets to attack?

For Tamara, evenings were often spent at the cinema, followed by dinner and a few drinks at either the Monico or Cilia's on South Street. 'Walking back from Valletta to Floriana in an air raid was an arduous and lengthy job. In normal times, the walking distance does not take more than twenty minutes. In an air raid it took usually twice as much, sprinting from one slit trench to another, waiting until the guns in each area boomed a little less loudly and looking skywards to see if any more shrapnel was likely to fall.'[5] At least the alerts were only for air raids. At the time rumours of invasion were rife and everyone expected to hear one long unending siren – the invasion signal when everyone would rush to their posts.

One April night, Vincenti's shelter was packed and Tamara and Ronnie struggled to find space and to sleep in the stifling, noisy atmosphere on concrete floors. 'Suddenly, after what seemed to be the heaviest bomb ever dropped right in the backyard, the siren went off: one long, piercing, unending wail. The whole cellar woke up with a start. One thought was uppermost in everyone's mind – INVASION. It could not be anything else. It was the signal which was to be given in such an emergency. So it had come at last. We were all prepared to give a good account of ourselves. Mothers clutched children tightly to their bosoms; men grabbed tin hats, gas-masks and made for the exit although the barrage was terrific. The bombing went on. Bombs whistled continuously. Some of the men were undecided as to whether their duty did not rather lie in staying where they were to protect the women and children. At this moment a most unmartial looking Royal Artillery sergeant burst into the cellar. Although his face was begrimed, a big smile was spread over it. We all looked up at him, resenting his cheerfulness in such serious circumstances. "Relax, relax," he

---

5. *Women of Malta*, by Frederick Galea, pages 96–7.

said. "False alarm; a bomb has short-circuited the Dockyard siren and it won't stop. They'll repair it as soon as the air raid is over".[6]

The siren blew for two hours and few within its hearing slept. This was a serious scare, and living under such conditions was gradually taking its toll on people physically and mentally. On 8 April, Tamara witnessed the terrible demise of a small Admiralty buoy-tender, *Moor*. 'I was at home idly watching the traffic of tugs, ferries and smaller craft in Grand Harbour. The sight never ceased to fascinate me. It was a lovely evening just after sunset. A moment of respite before the night raids, a leisurely high tea on the balcony and a little light reading. Suddenly the whole house was shaken as by a terrible earthquake. A swirl of water, the aft end of the ship showing for a minute and then it was gone. One survivor was picked up.'[7] *Moor* had hit a mine; twenty-eight people lost their lives.

As each week went by, from Tamara's perspective, the raids seemed to grow in violence with both Grand Harbour and Marsamxett Harbour targeted regularly. With Floriana situated between the two, bombs intended for one or the other inevitably landed in this densely populated, residential area. The tale of one Floriana girl Tamara knew, and her boyfriend, is especially haunting. Just as they left their house, the bombs began to fall and they debated whether to go to the shelter or not. She was in favour of the shelter; he was in favour of staying where they were. As the noise of the approaching bombers grew louder, she instinctively rushed down the road. When the raid was over, she came back to find her house in ruins and her boyfriend dead. All she was left with was what she was wearing. From then on, the tragedy continually played on the girl's mind. For two months she was seen constantly rushing to and from the shelters. She finally lost her reason and a year later was still being treated in hospital.

Tamara joined a more advanced first aid and nursing class in order to gain her bronze medallion as a VAD. Lady Dobbie and her daughter Sybil attended the same course. Tamara also joined an amateur dramatic society started at the ERA Club, with rehearsals often continuing by candlelight.

In mid-April, Adrian experienced his first 'friendly fire' incident. He took off in Maryland AR735 for what should have been a routine air test prior to a recce mission. Shortly afterwards, two Hurricanes were scrambled to intercept a low flying intruder heading for Luqa and one pilot spotted a large twin-engine aircraft over Kalafrana apparently under fire. He attacked. Almost immediately he recognised the aircraft as a Maryland, which banked away and dived steeply for the sea. But damage had been done to the Maryland's starboard engine and to the hydraulics. Adrian was forced to land wheels-up.

---

6. *Ibid.*
7. *Ibid.*

Toward the end of April, everyone noticed a reduction in air raids and a slackening in their intensity. Rumour had it the Germans needed their aircraft on other fronts. This was true; Axis offensives opened in the Balkans and in Libya. The Luftwaffe had also sustained heavy losses and needed some respite to recover. Whatever the reason, there was a sense of relief. This was the very moment when concentrated raids by the Luftwaffe might have had a telling impact. Instead, the hard-pressed defenders were given a breathing space and the RAF made good use of it. Wellingtons took off from Luqa on most nights to bomb targets in Sicily and North Africa, notably the ports and port installations. Night fighters also arrived and worked well with the powerful searchlights. By day, Blenheim bombers added their weight despite mounting losses. A detachment of fifteen anti-shipping Beaufighters operated for a period of three weeks from Malta in May, to give long-range protection to convoys. At the beginning of May, 69 Squadron was further reinforced with four additional aircraft and carried out the all-important pre-strike recces of the Beaufighters' targets. But the transfer of troops and aircraft from Egypt to Greece in an effort to halt the German advance from Romania would soon have a telling impact. More troops were also sent from Britain and Jack Vowles soon found himself caught up in the mad scramble to help Greece.

Jack was still working on Blenheim fighters at Bircham Newton. He joined 272 Squadron, formed from two flights of the existing Blenheim squadrons. The squadron moved to RAF Aldergrove in Northern Ireland, but was soon recalled to the mainland to reform with Beaufighters at RAF Chivenor in Devon. The airmen were given boat tickets to Liverpool and rail tickets. A troop carrier landed at Aldergrove flown by a Dutch pilot and Jack found out it was due to fly to Doncaster, only thirty miles from Jack's home. The pilot agreed to give Jack a lift; he would make his way to Chivenor after seeing Barbara and his parents.

For the flight, Jack sat up front and after they passed Liverpool under very low cloud, Jack warned the pilot of a barrage balloon directly ahead. The Dutch pilot had to bank hard and climb to avoid it. They then followed the Mersey inland until they cleared cloud and Jack used a ruler and a compass to plot a new course to Doncaster where they landed safely. Jack spent one night at home and saw Barbara, the girl he had been courting since he left school. He then met up with his colleagues. On arrival at Chivenor they found their squadron still with Blenheims, although they were replaced by Beaufighters three days later. The engineering staff had to learn about the new aircraft quickly as their pilots began conversion training. The squadron included three Polish pilots. The aircraft flew with full fuel and ammunition as a matter of routine, but instead of practicing 'circuits and bumps' as directed, the Poles made off down the Channel to fire at anything they could identify as German. They returned only when they ran out of ammunition. From then on the Poles were only allowed to take off with a small amount of fuel and ammunition until their conversion was complete.

Within days, the squadron was warned of a move and the first aircraft flew out within twenty-four hours, heading for Egypt where they were rushed into action to support Greece. Jack and his colleagues were given a few days leave, and this was just enough for Jack to get back to Halifax where he and Barbara were married by special licence two weeks before his twentieth birthday. Their time together was short. Jack was soon on his way to Greenock in Scotland to join a convoy.

By then there had been a costly retreat and evacuation from Greece, which was followed by more bad news in the shape of the German airborne assault on Crete. Another Allied defeat followed. In the Greek campaign, Britain suffered 12,000 casualties. The RAF lost over 200 aircraft and the army again lost almost all of its equipment. The navy suffered heavily, particularly in the Crete evacuation, losing over 1,800 sailors killed, three cruisers and six destroyers sunk by aircraft, with many others damaged. There was a lesson to be drawn from here: if shore-based aircraft could not cover the fleet, it must carry its own fighters. Before the year's end, the Japanese would demonstrate they had learnt this lesson.

For London, balancing priorities was a constant challenge. In May, General Dobbie again reported on the inadequacy of Malta's air defences, which were causing him considerable concern. He asked for senior officers of quality to replace those who were tired and jaded and in need of relief. The best type of fighter aircraft was needed, in greater numbers, and they needed to be manned by pilots more experienced than some of those sent. Hundreds more engineers were needed to operate and maintain the myriad aircraft types now using the island. Dobbie's appeal was fully supported by Maynard, and Vice Admiral Ford added his weight saying that the Axis was becoming bolder having gained air superiority over the island. Later that month, Dobbie went further, saying the air situation had gravely deteriorated, with morale on one fighter squadron having been affected to such an extent it had almost been destroyed. In London, Churchill concluded Air Vice-Marshal Maynard should be rested. He had served Malta well. Like other commanders in the early years of the war, he had no choice but to send young men into battle poorly prepared and with the inadequate resources provided in peacetime by governments who failed to heed the lessons of history.

On 12 May, 261 Squadron was amalgamated with 1430 Flight – flown in a few weeks earlier – to form 185 Squadron, which was unique in the RAF, as its motto is in Maltese: *Ara Fejn Hu*, 'There it is'. In its nine months in Malta, 261 Squadron was credited with over 100 aircraft shot down, but success came at a price with twenty-two of its pilots killed – a squadron's worth of pilots. At the end of May, 249 Squadron and its Hurricanes arrived from Egypt to operate from Ta' Qali. Also in May, HMS *Ladybird* was the second of the original three defenders of Malta to be sunk off Tobruk.

A number of 69 Squadron's NCOs were commissioned in May, including two of the founder members of 431 Flight: Frank Bastard and Bob Gridley. Bob also married a Maltese girl. The number of aircraft available on 69 Squadron was a continuing problem. Despite ten Beauforts being established on paper, very few actually appeared. Even though some additional Marylands had arrived, with losses and unserviceability there were rarely more than four available each day. Two crews, including Adrian, flew to Gibraltar to collect two more that had reached there from Vichy territory. Adrian spent two weeks in Gibraltar conducting photo-recce missions of the French bases at Casablanca, Oran and Mers el-Kébir. At 3,000 feet over Casablanca Adrian was intercepted and pursued by aggressive French fighters. After the shelling of their fleet a year earlier, they most definitely viewed Britain as an enemy. Adrian again returned with the goods. From Gibraltar, Adrian and Paddy Moren travelled the short distance across the Straits to neutral Tangiers. In a nightclub, the waiter presented them with a free round of drinks with the good wishes of Luftwaffe crews, who, like them, were wearing borrowed civilian clothing and enjoying a relaxing evening away from war.

Tich Whiteley, the man who saved Adrian from himself and who displayed such faith and confidence in him, flew with 69 Squadron for the last time on 1 June and travelled back to the UK via Gibraltar where he met Adrian; theirs must have been a fond farewell. Tich was awarded a DFC soon after leaving Malta. Adrian had lost a very good friend, but by then he had developed into a very capable reconnaissance pilot with an enviable reputation.

Adrian arrived back in Malta on 8 June, immediately making use of a lone Hurricane that 69 Squadron had acquired. It was painted blue and converted locally to the recce role with its guns removed to give it more speed and a higher ceiling. Adrian doesn't appear to have had any problem with it despite precious little time for training. By then the Mark I Hurricane was obsolete as a fighter and even the Mark II could no longer hold its own against the later marks of Me109. Yet the increasingly worn-out Hurricanes were all the valiant RAF fighter pilots had.

In early June, German attacks stopped. For over a week there were no raids. Then the spotters reported something not seen for months: bandits approaching the island at 20,000 feet; they were identified as SM.79s. The Italians were back, along with their slightly lackadaisical, medium-level bombing experienced the previous summer. Hitler was now gazing east to the Russian steppes and the allure of Caucasian oil. Everyone in Malta rejoiced. From then on, for a while at least, the civilian population made the most of it. The bars filled up once again, especially popular venues like Monico's and Cilia's on South Street. Meanwhile, RAF bombers relentlessly took the war to the enemy despite heavy losses.

In daytime, the Maltese emerged from their shelters to watch the air battle from their rooftops once again. Some even returned to what was left of their damaged homes. The pre-war air power theorist, Giulio Douhet, had long argued the infliction of high costs from aerial bombing could shatter civilian morale and unravel the social basis of resistance. The Maltese proved him wrong. There was a message there if anyone was listening, particularly the strategic bombing theorists in Britain and the United States.

Adrian's growing knowledge of enemy warships extended to merchant vessels and the ports they used. He and his colleagues became familiar with the berthing and loading arrangements, resulting in very accurate estimates of when enemy cargo ships were likely to leave port. Assessments that specific ships were, or were not, at their usual berths were invaluable. Adrian was also involved in trialling a secondary role: dropping bombs from the Maryland. On the very first training sortie at Filfla, off the southern coast of Malta, while practicing dive bombing from 12,000 feet to 6,000 feet, the pilot's hatch blew off, damaging Paddy's turret and also the tail of the aircraft. On a later mission, Adrian achieved a direct hit on an Italian cargo ship which was confirmed by a shadowing aircraft. In total, Adrian carried out twenty-one bombing missions against targets from North Africa to Northern Italy, although these were very much on top of the squadron's primary photographic missions. Adrian – and his crew – never failed to return with excellent photography of every port and airfield within Malta's area of interest.

A mission came up where Adrian was meant to fly as part of a coordinated package of aircraft. Adrian's allocated aircraft was out of action and his departure, in a notoriously underpowered Maryland, was much delayed. He flew on his own to the target area and joined a formation of German Ju88s acting as convoy escorts. This was another example of the Maryland being misidentified by enemy aircraft. One other 69 Squadron aircraft involved was shot down and the crew of three killed. Once again, 'Warby's luck' held, and he and his crew returned unscathed.

Adrian was sent to find the remnants of some merchant ships previously hit in shallow water to confirm the vessels were sunk. When he got there, he thought one was missing and went off in search of it. Knowing enemy ships often sought refuge in so-called neutral ports, he undertook a reconnaissance of the Vichy French port of Sfax in Tunisia. There, they found the missing ship. Adrian discussed with his crew the implications of striking a ship in a neutral port before attacking, using an improvised wooden bombsight. Adrian's two 500lb bombs destroyed the ship in a devastating explosion which caused damage to their own aircraft because of the low altitude at which they were flying. Their target had been an ammunition ship.

Attacks on friendly aircraft were not uncommon, as Adrian had previously experienced, although they usually occurred in the heat of battle. With Adrian flying the Maryland, and later the Beaufighter, both similar to enemy aircraft like the Ju88, misidentification was a constant problem. Returning at dusk, Adrian was fired at from the ground and his aircraft damaged. Adrian's response was to telephone the battery commander to congratulate him on his shooting, before pointing out the error of his ways. He then invited the officer concerned for a drink. Adrian was also shot at by a Hurricane soon after take-off. Despite firing the colours of the day, and orbiting the prescribed 'safe' rocky islet of Filfla, the Hurricane pilot persisted in pressing home his attack. After his Maryland was hit repeatedly, Adrian ordered Paddy Moren to return fire. Only when the Hurricane had also been hit, did its now wounded pilot break off. The Hurricane pilot only just managed to get his damaged aircraft back to Hal Far. Adrian had to abort his recce mission because of damage, and after landing, he and Paddy counted thirty-six bullet holes in their aircraft. They were lucky; too often, friendly fire ended in tragedy.

Despite Adrian's growing reputation, he continued to foster a special, almost unique, relationship with the airmen. His earlier time as a 'gash hand' paid dividends. Tich had encouraged his aircrew to help in servicing their aircraft, but Adrian went much further, befriending many. Not only were there still those frequent times when he was found sitting on the floor playing cards, but he also shared his cigarette ration and was first to help any airman in trouble. To Adrian, the airmen were equals and, in their turn, many became devoted to him.

Adrian was now living on his nerves. Already an acclaimed recce pilot, he had proven his worth as an aggressive fighter pilot with a number of 'kills' to his credit and had shown aptitude as a bomber pilot. He was at the forefront of action for the best part of nine months, but the strain was showing. Poor food meant he was already thin and, like everyone else, he was living under regular bombing in demoralising conditions. The Officers' Mess and the airmen's barracks at Luqa were long gone, and tents were often the best that could be found, although Adrian spent ever more time with Christina in Floriana. All of 69 Squadron's crews were in constant danger whenever they flew, which was often in the summer of 1941. There was no avoiding the casualties his squadron and others were suffering, and the deaths of his colleagues affected him more and more. He knew he was not immune, despite the blasé front he put on. Against such a background, the escape and comfort he found with Christina was hugely important, even if it only lasted for a few short hours. He had found great solace and love, and there can be little doubt she provided a firm foundation from which he could express his individuality in the air. She also offered Adrian a safe retreat, where he could unwind whenever he was off-duty. Nevertheless, Adrian had flown three times as many sorties as anyone else on 69 Squadron and was long overdue an operational rest period.

Adrian and Christina knew the risks for both of them; tragedy was always close at hand. For the moment, and neither of them knew for how long, they spent whatever time they could together. With their vibrant personalities, love of life and determination, they soon became symbols of Malta's spirit. Christina, who Adrian called Chris, filled a vital part of Adrian's life. She called him Warby and provided an escape for him from the Mess life he had never felt part of and did not enjoy. She offered him stability. He was not a show-off, but Christina certainly provided him with a sense of self-worth from an early stage and, as a result of which, his flying achievements developed further. Those achievements were a great boost to morale amongst servicemen and Maltese alike. Adrian was also desperately short of money as so much was going toward his debts. Many were jealous of the way Adrian monopolised one of the most attractive girls on the island, although it was clear to anyone who looked that Adrian and Christina were genuinely fond of one another.

Many talked of Warby's so-called luck; others simply considered him slightly irresponsible, a reckless pilot who took too many risks. He continued to take risks, but as his reputation grew it is clear those risks were calculated. He planned his missions carefully and although he might alter a plan in the air quite literally on the wing, this showed flexibility, not necessarily any lack of responsibility. Adrian was also a very able navigator, having cut his teeth in the navigator's seat in the Maryland the previous September and October. His devil-may-care attitude did not, however, lie far beneath the surface. Although he always maintained an air of bravado, he also had a sensitive side to his nature, especially with regard to the losses happening all around him. Those that occurred on his own squadron affected him a great deal and, unusually, he recorded in his logbook the names of friends and colleagues killed or listed as missing. It was a long list.

Adrian may have lost Tich, but someone else with great power and influence was now on the scene – Air Vice-Marshal Hugh Lloyd – and his hand was crucial for Malta's future. He also gave Adrian free reign. It was Tich who gave Adrian the chance to show his talent and courage, but it was Hugh Lloyd who in due course ensured Adrian's light was given every opportunity to shine. Lloyd would, however, demand his pound of flesh and work Adrian very hard indeed.

On the same day Lloyd assumed command in Malta – 1 June 1941 – another important change took place in Cairo with Air Marshal Tedder taking over as AOC-in-C RAF Middle East. Interestingly, Tedder was not Churchill's first choice. That was Air Marshal Owen Boyd, but on his way to take command, his aircraft was forced down over Sicily by Italian fighters and he was taken prisoner.

Forty-six year old Hugh Pughe Lloyd was ideally qualified for his task, although he was another second choice, the first having become unfit before his appointment was confirmed. Nevertheless, Lloyd's selection was a clear indication the Air Ministry recognised the need to harness Malta's attack potential. Lloyd would need to make the island secure with the slender means at his disposal while at the same time taking the offensive. But he had little idea just how slender his means were, or the fragility of his new base.

Lloyd was a despatch rider in the First World War and was wounded three times before being commissioned as a pilot in 1917. He served with great distinction and was awarded the Military Cross (MC), the DFC and the Croix de Guerre with Palm and Star (France). The outbreak of the Second World War saw him leading a Wellington squadron on daylight raids against German shipping. He later commanded RAF Marham in Norfolk before becoming 2 Group's Senior Air Staff Officer (SASO), planning and organising low-level, daylight operations. This was the man selected to command the RAF in Malta – not a fighter pilot or an air defender, but a man with bulldog courage trained and experienced in taking the war to the enemy. That needed to be Malta's role – if Britain could hold onto it. When interviewed about his appointment by Air Chief Marshal Sir Charles Portal, Chief of the Air Staff, Portal said that Lloyd's main task was to sink Axis ships sailing from Europe to Africa. Lloyd was to anticipate being in Malta for between six and nine months, by which time he would be worn out.

Three days after being asked if he was interested in the job, Lloyd was on his way. His journey highlighted one challenge in reinforcing the beleaguered island. It took the pilot of the Sunderland flying boat three attempts to get airborne from Plymouth. Once aloft, they missed a wall by less than ten feet and it took over a mile of countryside before the lumbering aircraft gained any height. They flew west into the Atlantic before turning south to avoid Brittany-based German fighters and Ju88s over the Bay of Biscay. Throughout their journey, they flew at 100 feet or less. Landing at Gibraltar was uneventful, but, even there, Lloyd was reminded of the difficulties of resupplying Malta by air. Gibraltar was more than 1,100 miles from Britain and the North Front airstrip was exactly that; a strip, not a runway built for reinforcement aircraft. It would take some time for that to be developed.

Lloyd had many hours to consider his task and reflect on the recent past. Until less than a year earlier he, like many others, never considered the possibility of fighting in the Mediterranean without France as an ally. Together they could have squeezed the Italians and Mussolini's North African adventure would not have lasted long. But with the fall of France, everything changed and 1,000 miles of North African coastline passed into Axis control. Britain also lost its vitally important air route to Malta over France. Britain enjoyed initial success against the Italians in Africa, but then attention was diverted into supporting Greece, a forlorn hope as many military men foresaw. Italian weakness there invited German involvement. The Greek campaign was a disaster that cost the navy and the air force dear. It also fatally weakened British forces in North Africa, leaving Rommel, with a single division initially, to push forward with relative ease, even leaving Tobruk isolated. To Hugh Lloyd's experienced eye, Malta seemed isolated and vulnerable. It was.

It took Lloyd's aircraft five attempts to lift off from Gibraltar and throughout the flight to Malta he could see enemy territory constantly, either to the south or to the north. They landed in Kalafrana Bay on the fourth attempt, losing a wing float in the process. For Lloyd, the journey was one of sober reflection; he was not reassured by what he found on arrival.

As he drove to Valletta, the damage to residential areas was obvious. He also noted some of the RAF's HQ facilities were above ground in different locations within the city, although by then the RAF's operational HQ was open for business at Lascaris. It was apparently a considerable improvement on what had gone before, but Lloyd described it as an underground stable. 'There was a long, winding, underground passage with a cavern at the end of it which accommodated one big table. This cavern … was without ventilation and smelt abominably.'[8] Lloyd discovered this was the ops room with two tiny offices at the far end separated from the rest by hessian cloth. One 'office' was for him; the other was shared by his SASO and three clerks. On this first visit, Lloyd watched the fighter controller handle an air raid. The aircraft plots were shown on a single table with all the other staff using the same table to coordinate their various tasks. He described the scene as bedlam and felt those staff who worked in the equivalent fighter ops rooms in Britain would have fainted on the spot.

The nerve centre of Lloyd's new organisation was at least underground and certainly well protected, but it needed significant expansion. He then embarked on a tour of his command. Kalafrana was well-found, with barracks, hangars and repair workshops. It also contained most of the RAF's spares and equipment, and was the location of the only engine repair shop on the island, as well as the only engine test beds. It was a near perfect target. A few well-placed bombs dropped there would end any prospect of Malta operating an air force. Hal Far was very restrictive with only one direction suitable for take-offs and landings regardless of the wind. It did have some substantial buildings and a few solid stone pens to protect the few fighters and a squadron of Fleet Air Arm Swordfish based there. Ta' Qali was a tightly contained airfield, with little protection, whereas Luqa was open and obvious. In Lloyd's view, it would not take many concentrated attacks to make all his airfields untenable. What could be done and done quickly?

The cry heard on RAF airfields in Britain was for aircraft dispersal. Most airfields had long since overflowed into surrounding countryside with dispersals hidden in woods using the thousands of workers available. In Malta, given the nature of the terrain and the lack of woods, what chance was there of dispersal? Maybe the aircraft could be better protected, but even if sufficient manpower were to be found, how would they complete their tasks when the places they were working on were bombed and strafed every day? Nevertheless, an answer was needed. Lloyd also visited Safi and Qrendi. Safi had two roughly made landing strips in the shape of a 'V' but they were so short, and the approaches so bad, even experienced pilots avoided using them if at all possible. Qrendi had two landing strips roughly marked out, but it would be a major task to make them usable even by fighters.

---

8. *Briefed to Attack*, by AM Sir Hugh Lloyd, pages 23–9.

Overall, Lloyd's inspection was depressing. The airfields were small, with little hope of expansion, and he thought the airmen's shelters were woefully inadequate. Underground facilities existed in name only, with the equipment needed by a modern air force stored above ground. Transport was inadequate and there were no underground fuel lines. In fact there wasn't a single petrol pump on the whole island. Petrol was largely distributed in five-gallon tins from small dumps open to the elements and the enemy. As Lloyd completed his tour he drove past a *gharry* – one of the one-horse carriages much in evidence. How long would they last, he wondered? He knew the well-looked after animals were the reserve meat ration.[9]

Lloyd's 'air force' numbered fifty-nine aircraft, a mixture of Hurricanes, Blenheims, Marylands and Swordfish. He had a grand total of 1,910 airmen. When in command of Marham's thirty-six Blenheims, he had 1,410 personnel. Now he had to spread his personnel to cover three active airfields, a seaplane base, an air-sea rescue unit, a radar installation, and HQ and operations facilities. The essential administrative tail reduced further the number of airmen he could call upon to maintain and service his aircraft. Even with the highly skilled Maltese workforce, Lloyd simply did not have enough to run the island's disparate air force, even had it not been subject to daily attack. It was a situation Lloyd felt was entirely due to Britain's long established custom of always being unprepared for war. He left no stone unturned in finding more personnel, recruiting civilians, including wives and daughters of service personnel, as well as stranded civilians. He hijacked personnel and aircraft on route to Egypt and sought support from the other services. Through Sir William Dobbie, Lloyd also tapped deeply into Malta's greatest asset: its people.

Malta's situation in the summer of 1941 was grim. In Sicily the Luftwaffe had 240 aircraft and the Regia Aeronautica had 220. The immediate problem was not a lack of RAF fighters, but how to protect the existing ones on the ground. This was highlighted one morning when Lloyd visited Luqa. He heard the sound of aircraft engines and since he was aware no British aircraft were airborne, it had to be the enemy. Within seconds, five Italian aircraft pulled up over the cliffs and flew fast and low toward Ta' Qali. They made a slight turn then dived before continuing north to clear the island. Not a shot was fired at them, their low approach having gone undetected. In their wake they left two Hurricanes on fire. There were too many gaps in radar coverage which were all too easily exploited. These gaps had to be filled to give better warning to the anti-aircraft defences and allow his fighters to scramble. Even that was unlikely to be enough. A defensive shield was insufficient for an island as small as Malta; it simply could not be defended in any depth.

Lloyd set about improving the Spartan and unsuitable facilities, including moving vulnerable stores underground. Dispersal and protection of aircraft was

---

9. *Ibid.*

given a very high priority, but with little earth moving equipment, and precious few tools, not even a single hydraulic drill, the task relied totally on manual labour. But Lloyd was completely frustrated in obtaining soldiers for the vital work as calls on manpower were already very great. Only the governor could dictate priorities. All Maltese men between the ages of eighteen and forty had already been conscripted and, of the remainder, thousands were employed building air raid shelters for the civil population and preparing defences for possible invasion. The fall of Crete only two days before Lloyd took over brought this latter task into sharp focus. The need for more manpower was Lloyd's most pressing problem.

For a few days he stayed with Sir William and Lady Dobbie at San Anton Palace declining a residence, or even an apartment. Instead he opted for a sleeping cubicle deep within the walls of Lascaris Bastion; only minutes and 160 steps from his ops room, so that he was on call, night and day. Being near the cliff face, there was a roughly made, if insecure, veranda from which to look down on a Grand Harbour often devoid of ships. Lloyd's home from now on was this cave hewn out of solid limestone. He made good use of it. Being constantly on call became routine and soon he thought nothing of it.

There was a major reinforcement in June with forty-eight Hurricanes launched from *Ark Royal* and *Victorious*; forty-three landed safely. As a result, Axis aircraft became nervous when approaching Malta and, despite fighter escorts, their reconnaissance aircraft suffered heavy losses. In a raid on Luqa, five enemy fighters were shot down for the loss of two Hurricanes destroyed and one pilot killed. Two of the enemy fighters crashed about fifteen miles from the Sicilian coast. Knowing a floatplane, probably with fighter escort, would soon be on its way to the downed pilots, Lloyd ensured Hurricanes were ready and waiting. Two floatplanes and a further four enemy fighters were duly despatched to the deep.

These were heady days for the Hurricane pilots who enjoyed success in the air and adulation on the ground. Men would raise their hats as they passed, and elderly ladies would curtsy or even step off the pavement to make room for an approaching airman. To many, the aircrew were modern Knights of St John. Of course, the Hurricane's success was principally against the Italians who were reluctant to press home their daylight attacks. As was found in London and other British cities, defending against night bombing raids was altogether more difficult. A Malta Night Flying Unit, comprising three or four Hurricanes, was established and worked closely with the searchlight units. Some of their early successes were attributed intentionally to the Hurricanes, even though the RAF knew their success was actually caused by a fault in a new type of Italian bomb which exploded as soon as it was released, destroying the bomber. To guard this information, all the bombers lost at night were credited to Hurricanes.

After months seeking meaningful employment, Tamara began work at the strange-sounding Standing Committee of Adjustment, housed on the ground floor of 3, Scots Street, Valletta. By then rationing was introduced to limit hoarding and black market activities, although food rationing was not yet stringently applied. It was still possible to find inexpensive places to eat in Valletta, provided one sought Maltese cooking. The British Hotel in St Ursula Street was one such outlet, popular with labourers and clerks as well as with Tamara and a new friend, Aida Kelly, who also worked for the RAF at Scots Street. They often met up there with Christina.

Tamara did valuable work, but it tore at her heart strings. Her job was to collate the effects of those RAF personnel killed or listed as missing. Most equipment went back to stores, but a letter was always sent to next-of-kin with any items of sentimental value. Sometimes, with the permission of the casualty's family, items were sold, with the proceeds going to the RAF Benevolent Fund. Any letters were read before forwarding to ensure next-of-kin didn't receive a tainted picture of their loved one. This work was hugely important for families trying to come to terms with the loss of a loved one far from home and Tamara was desperately keen to make whatever contribution she could. But was she strong enough emotionally to deal with such a task day after day?

Chapter Ten

Christina, Fighter Control RAF

With petrol rationing having an increasing impact, the *Whizz-Bangs* were restricted to three shows a week and the entertainers found they had time on their hands. Christina learnt from Cecil Roche that twenty British girls were needed for training in No 8 Sector Operations Centre, undertaking duties similar to those carried out by the Women's Auxiliary Air Force (WAAF) in Britain. Christina and Pickles Fletcher were two of fifty-nine applicants. Was Pickles the first American civilian to apply to work in an RAF control room? They were both successful and began in June along with Pauline Longyear, Michael Longyear's elder sister; she was 14–years–old. This was all part of Hugh Lloyd's push to alleviate his manpower crisis.

Christina's first days were spent as a telephonist, but soon she trained as an aircraft plotter. As the work expanded, Phyllis Frederick took over responsibility for training new staff. Phyllis lived in Sliema and crossed Marsamxett Harbour by ferry to get to and from work. When the ferry was cancelled because of raids, she used a rowing boat, despite shell fragments falling around the open boat. All the Lascaris ladies faced similar risks. From then on, Christina and Pickles combined plotting with concert party performances, often changing duties with their opposite numbers on another watch to make an engagement. It was tough going.

Their location was in the old communication tunnel built by the Knights of St John which had so unimpressed Hugh Lloyd; it had indeed been used as a stable. A signals unit, Y Service, was also housed there, which intercepted enemy radio communications and received similar intercepted communications forwarded from Alexandria. Ultra decodes from Bletchley Park were now playing an increasingly important part in Malta's operations. As the operational elements of the HQ were brought together, it became known to its occupants as the Hole. It was located 400 feet beneath St Peter and St Paul Bastion and Upper Barracca Gardens, at the south-eastern end of the ditch crossing the Sciberras peninsula which separated Valletta's inner and outer walls. The Hole remained under almost continual development with further chambers excavated deep into the rock.

In early autumn the main ops room was moved into a much larger facility within the same complex. It took its name from the nearby Lascaris Bastion, constructed in 1856 on the site of a garden built by Grand Master Jean Lascaris, he with the sour facial expression. What took place here was one of the best kept secrets of the

Second World War in Malta. The secure but dark and sunless rooms became the nerve centre of Malta's defence, the whole complex ventilated with metal piping and ducting retrieved from ships sunk in Grand Harbour.

The plotting table measured eighteen feet by twelve, and showed a map of Malta and the surrounding area, including part of Sicily and its main airfields, as well as the islands of Linosa and Pantelleria. The map was divided into lettered squares, each subdivided into numbered grids. Malta was within 'N' for Nuts and 'H' for Harry covered the area toward Sicily. 'M' for Monkey was west of Malta and became the scene of hectic activity whenever a convoy approached from Gibraltar.

Aircraft tracks, labelled in the filter room, were passed by telephone to a plotter. A typical message was, 'Hostile 15, H for Harry 4628, twenty-five plus at 15,000 feet, south-west.' The plotter placed a coloured pointed counter on the table at the appropriate reference. A wooden block giving details of the raid was pushed using a wooden rod to the marked position and updated as the blocks were moved along. The senior controller, sitting above 'the plot' in the centre of the dais, directed the fighters. Alongside him were his deputy, known as Ops B, the assistant controller and the guns and searchlight liaison officers.

The ops room was divided into A, B, C and D watches, each comprising up to fourteen girls. Everyone was sworn to secrecy, which extended even to admitting in which room they worked. Three listening stations picked up bearings from aircraft and passed them to the radio direction room, located under the dais. The resultant plots were marked on a blackboard to the right of the main table. Any 'mayday' call picked up by the direction finders resulted in the aircraft's position being quickly plotted. An air-sea rescue launch could then be despatched from Kalafrana.

Lascaris expanded into a network of tunnels and chambers accessed from the side of Lascaris Bastion. Another entrance was from the eastern end of the Valletta main ditch. In time, this excellent facility provided accommodation for fighter control, the filter room, combined operations, gunnery liaison, signals, the AOC and his staff and, of course, the inevitable NAAFI. But in the summer of 1941, Hugh Lloyd had to make do with an office within a stone building with a corrugated iron roof, located near the entrance from the ditch. Although it took many months before all the RAF's operational and administrative staffs came together, the new facility was a huge improvement, bringing together key staffs, including the anti-aircraft artillery control room only feet from the senior controller and the plotting table. The latter was soon operated almost exclusively by a very efficient team of ladies, British and Maltese, whom Lloyd considered the equal of any similar team in Britain. Malta now had a very capable nerve centre.

In mid-June, 69 Squadron received a second Hurricane, a Mark II, also locally modified for reconnaissance work. In the same month, Adrian spent some time visiting a Beaufighter pilot laid up in Mtarfa hospital following a crash landing at

Luqa. Adrian's motive was not entirely altruistic. In fact he plagued the poor chap with requests to have the Beaufighter repaired so he could fly it. The pilot eventually gave in and Adrian used volunteer airmen from 69 Squadron. Adrian flew a short test flight which was successful even though he had not flown the type before. He then sought and received approval for a special recce flight to locate a reported large convoy. For this to have been sanctioned indicates the extraordinary circumstances existing on the island at the time. Armed with six machine guns and four 20-mm cannon, Adrian failed to get the Beaufighter airborne and it ended up in a crumpled heap at the end of the runway. Thankfully, Adrian and his navigator were unhurt; mishandling was the probable cause. Perhaps Adrian's successes led to a degree of overconfidence from time to time.

In North Africa, with the British Army hard pressed by Rommel, 69 Squadron was tasked to photograph the entire 250-mile length of the coast road – the *Via Balbia* – from Benghazi to Tripoli. This was the only supply road for Rommel's panzers. It was thought the task would take six sorties to complete. Adrian did it in one, with every yard photographed and no breaks in coverage. This type of photography is immensely difficult to accomplish, even in peacetime, as any angle of bank applied to the aircraft results in an immediate loss of photographic coverage. Adrian's single flight saw him chased out to sea four times by enemy fighters from airfields along the road's length. Yet each time, having shaken off his pursuers, he picked up where he left off and completed the task, resulting in a complete mosaic of the coast road and its surrounds.

On the same mission, supported again by Frank and Paddy, as if Adrian didn't have enough to occupy himself, he also attacked a new airstrip they discovered at Misurata three days earlier. He calmly joined the traffic pattern and was promptly given a green light – clearance to land – by air traffic control, their Maryland having been mistaken for a Ju88. As Adrian overflew the airstrip, at a height of fifteen feet according to Frank, they fired at a line of Italian bombers, leaving three of them in flames and others damaged before exiting stage left as fast as possible. Maybe Adrian was relying on a degree of luck against the airfield, but he knew his enemy well. Perhaps though, it would have been wiser to have delivered his hard-earned and exceptional photography to Malta first.

Hitler unleashed his armies on the Soviet Union on 22 June. Death and devastation followed on an unimaginable scale. But it gave Malta's defenders the chance to reorganise and Hugh Lloyd enjoyed a lucky break – time to better prepare his airfields for the assaults that would surely come. A third fighter squadron, 126 Squadron, was formed at the end of June using recently arrived Hurricanes. It moved from Hal Far to Ta' Qali with a mixture of early Hurricanes and new Mark IICs. It enjoyed success, but like its sister squadrons – 185 and 249 – its operations were soon hampered by a lack of spares and shortage of aircraft.

There was more emphasis on disrupting Axis supplies heading for North Africa – there needed to be. Within the first six months of 1941, post-war Italian records revealed about ninety per cent of the supplies despatched arrived safely. Missions were mounted against Axis ships wherever they could be found – including in port. Sadly, the Blenheims were all too easy a target for any vessel with effective flak weapons. Surprise on those beautifully clear days of a Mediterranean summer was rarely possible. Nevertheless, the crews persisted with great courage and determination, despite mounting losses. The Blenheim squadrons rarely stayed long before being replaced and given time to recover.

One detachment of Blenheims arrived in early July. In its four-week stay, it lost thirteen of its aircrew, including the squadron commander. A replacement detachment of eleven arrived at the end of the month. In nine weeks the new team lost twenty-eight of its aircrew, also including its squadron commander. Squadron commanders did not simply send their junior officers and NCOs into battle; they led from the front. The Blenheim bombing missions were complemented by night torpedo attacks by the Fleet Air Arm's ancient Albacore and Swordfish biplanes. The courage displayed by their crews in their slow biplanes was extraordinary. The Swordfish crews often joked that as their aircraft's speed was similar to that of the ships they sought, they used a torch to identify the best target for their torpedoes. To extend the Swordfish's 200-mile range, an extra fuel tank was fitted in the only available place: the observer sat on it.

Southbound shipping was the very life blood of the Afrika Korps. Missions against Axis shipping certainly cost the Allies dear in terms of aircrew lives and submarine crews, but the loss of an oil tanker bound for North Africa could result in thousands of enemy vehicles stranded in the desert, halting an advance or turning a retreat into a rout. Enigma decrypts revealed that despite Rommel's startling success, his supply position was insecure and he was ordered to go on the defensive.

Despite the British aircraft losses, attacks against enemy shipping at sea or in port were essential. The work of 69 Squadron was vital and Adrian was often at the forefront, taking risks in order to bring back confirmation of targets. He suffered an engine failure over Taranto but continued photographing until the job was done, returning home on one engine. It was a 'shaky do,' he said. But these hair-raising episodes kept occurring and he simply carried on. On a mission to an Axis airfield near Tripoli, both of his engines cut out. He was 100 miles from land. He was down to 1,500 feet above the sea before the engines mysteriously picked up. Adrian simply pressed on with his mission. Others would have taken the prudent option and returned to base, cautiously. Again over Taranto, one of his cameras failed, so he overflew the harbour three times to ensure full coverage with the one remaining camera. On yet another recce of Taranto, in late July, he and his crew successfully shot down a Cant Z.506 seaplane. A few days later he took vertical photographs of three separate enemy airfields, photographed Palermo harbour, then dropped anti-personnel bombs. This mission ended in a fifteen-minute running engagement with an Italian fighter before finally shaking it off.

For the Maltese, the summer of 1941 was quiet and life went on much as it had in the past. Some tended their small fields, others laboured in the dockyards or at the airfields. There were anti-Italian slogans here and there, though these were more of an expression of annoyance at their near neighbour for making war on their small island than anything else. Many simply did not take the Italians seriously.

Operation Substance was mounted in July following concerns expressed by General Dobbie that Malta could easily suffer the same fate as Crete. He asked for two additional infantry battalions, more guns and substantially more personnel. With the Germans focused on Russia, now was a good opportunity for a fast convoy to include over 700 much-needed RAF personnel. In most convoys, cargo of different types was split between all the ships to avoid anything critical being lost if any one ship was sunk. The RAF personnel were critical, but the majority were embarked in a single ship, the troopship *Leinster*. On route to Malta one destroyer was sunk and a merchantman, cruiser and destroyer were damaged. A simple statement citing the loss of a single destroyer and damage to other ships masks yet another story of extraordinary heroism and seamanship.

The first air attack came on the morning of 24 July when a mixture of SM.79 bombers and torpedo aircraft struck. These raids were well planned and coordinated and the Italians pressed their attacks with courage and determination, in sharp contrast to their bombing attacks on Malta. *Ark Royal's* Fulmars disrupted the incoming aircraft, causing some bombers to jettison their bombs, but the torpedo bombers got through and scored hits. The destroyer *Fearless* capsized, while the cruiser *Manchester* limped back to Gibraltar with three of four engines disabled. Two further bombing attacks were fought off by the Fulmars. The convoy then took a calculated risk and steered through an Italian minefield, but in the early hours of the following morning, it was met by eight Italian E-boats from Pantelleria, all of which made determined attacks. Four E-boats were sunk.

The *Sydney Star* was carrying ammunition and nearly 500 troops. Her master was Captain Thomas Horn from Alnwick, Northumberland. After being hit by a torpedo, his ship was left without engines and abandon ship was called. While E-boats tried to locate the stricken vessel in the darkness, the troops and non-essential members of the crew were transferred to a destroyer. The chief engineer managed to restart the engines and, despite taking on water, the *Sydney Star* began to make headway. After being targeted by torpedo bombers, the ship started to list heavily. More attacks followed. By then she had taken on 10,000 tons of water, almost the same as her displacement of 12,000 tons. When within ten miles of Malta, with some RAF air cover, the ship was still threatened with near-misses coming within twenty yards. The already listing ship heeled over drunkenly. The engines stopped once again and the ship began to settle. The chief engineer got the engines going once more. Captain Horn realised they had little time before the ship foundered so called for 'full ahead'. At 2.00 pm, under a cloudless sky, with hardly a breath of wind, the *Sydney Star* entered Grand Harbour to a storm of cheering. Captain Horn had spent eleven days on the bridge, going without sleep for a seventy-two hour period. He and his chief engineer were appointed OBE.

Operation Substance was successful, and over 65,000 tons of cargo replenished food stocks and artillery ammunition, which was being used at a colossal rate. Aviation fuel was also nearly exhausted. Fighters consumed large amounts of fuel, but much more was being used by the bombers and to refuel the many aircraft staging through at night on their way to Egypt. With the safe arrival of the merchant ships, the Italian Navy planned a daring and surprising welcome. One ship, however, did not make it to Malta – the *Leinster*. As well as including an infantry battalion and an anti-aircraft artillery regiment, 665 RAF personnel were on board. One was a young airman from Halifax. He had an interesting and a painful journey.

Having arrived at Greenock earlier in July, Jack Vowles was directed to the *Leinster*, a steam packet of 4300 tons that had earned her living on the Liverpool to Dublin run. Fitted out as a troop and hospital ship, she was used in the Norwegian campaign. Few of those on board were aware of their destination other than vague references to the Middle East. They left the Clyde in the early hours, heading into the Atlantic. Despite the time of year, the weather was extremely cold and Jack soon found himself in agony as all the fillings in his double teeth shattered. The ship's dentist gave Jack the bad news: all of his double teeth had to be extracted. There was worse to come: there was no anaesthetic. For the ordeal, a medical orderly sat on each of Jack's knees with another holding his shoulders down. Afterwards, Jack was put into a bunk for bed rest. Three days later they headed south, the convoy having split into two. Jack's colleagues assumed they were heading for South Africa and the Cape before sailing for the Suez Canal as they were all aware the Mediterranean was 'a bit hot'. Jack took no interest as his gums were still bleeding. It was some time before he could eat anything solid. Soon he was using his cine camera filming the crew using flags to communicate with other ships.

Their destination became clear when *Leinster* was detached to Gibraltar to embark additional troops. By then Jack, only able to eat with his front teeth, was feeling a little better. On leaving Gibraltar at night, there were submarine scares with destroyers dropping depth charges in the confined waters made much worse by thick fog. At 2.00 am there was an enormous crunch; they were firmly wedged on rocks on the coast of Spain. Rumours about what happened were rife. Some said with visibility down to thirty yards, *Leinster* got so far out of formation she ran aground; others said torpedoes fired at a nearby battleship caused *Leinster's* captain to put his helm hard over, putting his ship on the rocks. Jack heard the captain had not been prepared to sail through 'bomb-alley' to Malta as the ship's plates, buckled in the Norwegian campaign, would not have survived a near miss. He was placed under close arrest and confined to the bridge with two armed guards for the voyage. In the fog, somehow the ship entered Spanish territorial waters and ran aground.

Soon afterwards, it was surrounded by Spanish soldiers using ropes to try and get on board. They posed no threat and were only interested in the leather shoes of the passengers and crew. At first light the captain told everyone to prepare for internment, but when the boats were lowered their crews rowed back toward Gibraltar. They were hailed from an approaching RN destroyer and, with Jack in the leading boat, they were taken in tow. As the small warship tried to make headway, it became apparent the combined drag of the boats was too much; there was a risk its stern would be pulled underwater. Jack and a number of others were ordered to clamber on board. Over the next couple of days, the airmen stayed on a French liner in Gibraltar before being taken back to the *Leinster* to collect their kit.

In Malta, Hugh Lloyd soon learnt of his missing airmen. He signalled the Air Ministry pointing out his total staff, including those sick, totalled less than that of any bomber station in England. Yet Lloyd had 174 aircraft and many more passed through on their way to Egypt. Some of these needed rectification before being sent on their way. The poor aircraft serviceability, exacerbated by a lack of trained mechanics, resulted in only one third of his Hurricanes and one fifth of his Blenheims being fit to fly. He desperately needed those missing airmen. Lloyd's signal was seen by Churchill. The Admiralty agreed to act.

The reduction in bombing was welcomed, but the island still experienced a couple of raids every day and more at night. Aida Kelly often spent the night at Tamara's flat, usually talking well into the night, unable to sleep because of their pet Bofors anti-aircraft gun fifty yards away. The raids had taken their toll on Tamara who had lost more than two stone in weight in eight months. Her mental health was also affected. The only relaxation possible was swimming, which carried with it risks if an alert sounded. The pre-war favourite of tennis was impossible as all open spaces not used for cultivation or airfields were cluttered with disused cars, empty oil drums, coils of barbed wire and the like, as a measure against paratroopers.

On 25 July, Tamara was in Kingsway and witnessed the only enemy aircraft ever to crash directly into Valletta. Many saw the Italian aircraft out of control above the city before it entered a steep dive. To many observers, it seemed as if the stricken aircraft was heading directly for them. 'The panic was terrific. It was 11 am and the street was filled with people who had been watching the raid. Everyone rushed madly for the nearest shelter. Some flung themselves on to the pavement. I followed suit. After what seemed an age, the machine dived into a crater made in an earlier raid, so that no one was injured. The crater was at the back of La Valette Band Club where, in peacetime, enjoyable dances had been held. At the outbreak of the war, Rosetti, the Maltese bandleader with Italian sympathies, had left for Italy. We got up and dusted ourselves, the light-hearted Maltese laughing at the fright they had had. As one wit said: "Rosetti had come back to conduct his orchestra for the last time."

'That same night, four air raids were sounded. My husband and I got up for every one of them.... Toward 5.00 am on the twenty-sixth, the all clear having sounded, we heaved a huge sigh of relief, gathered our shelter paraphernalia together, and made for home and bed. Just as I was trying to snatch an hour's sleep before getting up for work, heavy gunfire was heard again. I put my head under the blanket and swore that if this were to be the end, I would die in bed. I was too tired to worry. I could not help noticing, however, that the guns had somehow a different note, more rumbly than usual. My husband came into my room and asked me whether I had seen the thrilling sight out to sea. "What is going on?" I asked.

"'I think it is an attack by E-boats."

'I jumped out of bed and rushed to the veranda. The spectacle was worth while getting out of bed. The enemy craft could be seen plainly in the searchlights, which were all focused out to sea. The E-boats could not be farther than a mile from the mouth of the harbour. Tracer bullets made a fine firework display. Most of the missiles struck their targets effectively.'[1]

This was an attempt by the Italians to destroy the recently arrived ships as well as the submarine base at Manoel Island. Bletchley Park had given warning of an Italian naval attack and the Maltese-manned harbour defences were alert and ready. As soon as the enemy boats came within range, the guns of St Elmo and Ricasoli went into action. The Italians planned to use a human torpedo to blow a hole in the torpedo net protecting the harbour entrance, but it arrived late, so its crew exploded it as soon as it reached the net, sacrificing themselves for their mission. The explosion destroyed the net, but also the outer span of the breakwater viaduct, which collapsed, closing the gap almost as completely as the net had done. Six single-man explosive motor-boats then found their way blocked and were soon engaged by the coastal batteries. At daybreak, Hurricanes were scrambled against the retreating boats. All the Italian ships involved were wiped out and only eighteen Italians survived as prisoners. The Italian crews displayed great courage in what was a forlorn hope.[2] Vice Admiral Ford later said: 'The harbour defences of Malta, largely manned by Maltese, scored an outstanding success in this, their first action, and to them must go the entire credit for maintaining the security of the harbour.'[3]

Back in Gibraltar, Jack and his colleagues were split between four cruisers for the run to Malta, Jack being allocated to the oldest and slowest of all. The 'banter' – no

---

1. *Women of Malta*, by Frederick Galea, pages 101–2.
2. *Mines over Malta*, by Frederick Galea, pages 49–56.
3. *Victory in the Air*, by Richard Caruana, page 63.

doubt encouraged by the crew – was the back-marker, the slowest vessel, would be the first to 'cop it'. This tended to be true although, as it turned out, they were so slow a gap opened up and it was those up front which 'copped it'. Jack's passage was trouble free. On Saturday, 2 August, the RN disembarked 1,700 troops together with all of the stranded airmen. Jack felt lost and a little fed up when he was dumped with his kit bag outside the main guardroom at Luqa. His mates from 272 Squadron were, by then, well scattered. Then he heard a surprising and familiar voice: 'Hello Jack. What are you doing here?'

It was none other than 'Willie' Williams, the young pilot Jack last saw at Bircham Newton a year earlier.

'I had a difficult trip getting here,' replied Jack.

'Who are you with?' said Willie.

'I don't know who I'm with or what I'm doing,' said Jack.

'Well, you're with us now,' said Willie, '69 Squadron.'

Willie then went on to talk about what they had found out about the Marylands in those few short weeks at Bircham Newton. He also said there was much he had forgotten. Then he said: 'There's someone I want you to meet. His name is Adrian Warburton.'

That night Jack slept in a shack. The following morning he was taken to meet this man Jack had never heard of, a man Jack would refer to as 'Warby' and who would leave a mark on Jack that lasted the rest of his long life. They met in 69 Squadron's office. When Adrian came in, Jack thought what a handsome looking bloke. He was as tall as Jack, nearly six foot, and had blue eyes and a shock of light brown, almost blonde hair, which was not cut to regulation length, another thing Jack found Adrian got away with. The conversation was all about Adrian's favourite Maryland – AR733. He wanted Jack to make it go faster, to show him what he had found out with Willie. Jack's reputation had clearly preceded him to Malta. Adrian said if he overflew an enemy airfield which had Me109s on the ground, he had a good chance of making it home. If the Me109s were airborne at a similar height, he had an evens chance at best. But if they were higher than he was, he had a problem. He needed more speed. Adrian took Jack to AR 733: 'Show me what you told Willie about the propeller.'

'It's something we found out that's not in the books,' said Jack.

'I don't care what the books say,' said Adrian, 'I want you to make it bloody well go faster.'

Jack explained how the electrically-driven propeller pitch control worked, and showed by moving the pitch control lever from coarse to fine, halfway across there was a bracket to move the lever through to feather the propeller. At Bircham Newton, Jack discovered by moving the lever just a little, initiating the feathering phase, but only just, the weight was taken off the propeller. At that point, opening the throttle got rid of the resultant vibration and the engine produced more power. Jack was confident the aircraft would achieve an extra fifteen to twenty knots. Adrian said, 'let's go and see'.

Within a few minutes, they were airborne with Jack in the navigator's position sitting in front of Adrian. This was one of three or four air tests Jack flew with Adrian, and he was simply entered into the flight authorisation as 'AN Other'. The dual controls of the Maryland allowed Jack to describe what he had found out with Willie. Everything worked as advertised. On landing, Adrian said, 'I want you to look after this aircraft from now on'.

'He never ordered me to do anything though,' said Jack. 'He'd always say do you think it could do this or that and we'd discuss it.'

That first meeting with Adrian had a profound impact on 20-year-old Leading Aircraftman Jack Vowles from Halifax. At the time, Adrian was twenty-three. After his first night at Luqa, Jack was accommodated in a block very close to the aircraft pens at Siggiewi which also housed a radio station. One pen in particular was made of stone and this normally housed AR733. After a while, Jack had to move into a tent outside the main building.

Adrian's flair for mathematics impressed Jack and no doubt played an important part in Adrian's navigational skill. He also used his knowledge to counter anti-aircraft gun predictors and avoid their often lethal effect. On another air test, Adrian flew out to sea before turning back for Luqa. He then said to Jack: 'Watch this'. He switched off his aircraft's IFF as if he was on some peacetime training flight. Their aircraft was identified as hostile. As they approached Malta, Adrian watched carefully until he spotted a battery firing at them. He calmly lowered the aircraft's nose and accelerated. The shells, working on a prediction of the Maryland's height and speed, exploded above and behind. Jack, who went everywhere with his cine camera, filmed the explosions. After landing, Adrian went round to the gun battery concerned and told them they were 'rotten shots'.

Over the next few weeks, Jack developed a very comfortable, easy-going relationship with Adrian. When he arrived at the aircraft prior to a flight, usually with his regular crew of Frank and Paddy, in referring to the serviceability of the aircraft, Adrian would simply say, 'How is it?'

Jack would often ask, 'How long?'

Adrian simply shrugged his shoulders. Some flights lasted ten hours. According to Jack, Adrian generally had a mild manner and was a man of few words, without a temper, but he had a look that could rivet people to the spot. He never heard Adrian swear, apart from the occasional use of the word 'bloody'.

Paddy arrived at the aircraft one day with a box and Jack was horrified to see it contained bombs. Paddy reassured Jack it was ok, they were just smoke bombs. He explained that when they were over the sea near enemy territory they often came across fishing boats. Paddy would arm a few of the bombs and then throw them out. As the bombs fell, the fishermen would hear the unmistakeable whistle of falling bombs and leap into the sea to swim away as quickly as they could. This would always cause amusement to Adrian and his crew while causing terror for the poor fishermen. By comparison with what the Maltese were enduring, the fishermen suffered little. These were tiny, almost irrelevant economic blows to the enemy, but they offered a momentary boost to the Maryland crew's morale. It also did wonders for the squadron ground personnel who soon heard of the crew's antics.

One day, when Jack was waiting for Adrian and his crew, an air raid took place and, with bombers heading in his direction, Jack ran around the side of the pen to find better shelter away from the fully-fuelled aircraft. He saw the entrance to a small cave and threw himself inside. After bombs exploded nearby, he got up and, to his surprise, saw a soldier sitting in the corner of the cave with a kettle boiling on a small stove. The soldier simply asked Jack if he would like a cup of tea. Jack enjoyed the tea then crawled out of the cave to meet Adrian and his crew. Jack often returned to the cave, but never again came across the soldier.

Adrian's reputation as a superb recce pilot was well-established long before Jack turned up in Malta. 'I think he would have been a flying officer then – but it didn't matter, he sometimes wore no rank as well as some unusual clothes and clobber. He would turn up in any odd thing – old battle dress, Oxford bags and there was nothing exceptional about seeing him in carpet slippers. He wore flying boots, but he also had some sheepskin chaps, like cowboys used to wear. He wasn't boastful or overpowering – but overall, he was a most exceptional man.

'The work he did was so exceptional that everyone from the AOC downwards, just shrugged their shoulders and turned the other way because he did the work. He was told off very severely once, but then he was told to carry on and continue with the work he was doing. The fact is he could get away with anything!'[4]

On one visit to Valletta, Jack ventured down the Gut where a certain 'Yorkie' gave Jack a tattoo on his right arm. It reads 'The Fighting 69' mounted over an RAF eagle crest. Seventy years later the tattoo was still there, if a little faded. It is an unusual unofficial motto for a recce squadron, but one that recognised Adrian's uncanny skill in shooting down enemy aircraft. Only three people had the same tattoo: Jack, Adrian and one other.

Whenever Adrian flew to Egypt he always asked Jack and the other airmen if there was anything they wanted him to bring back. They invariably replied it didn't matter, as long as it was something to eat. Adrian would collect whatever money he could in order to buy food. Jack particularly welcomed fruit. Sometimes Adrian also

4. *Adrian Warburton*, by Tim Callaway, *Aviation Classics*, Issue 14, page 88.

brought back cigarettes; he was a smoker, but Jack did not think he smoked much and food was always far more important.

Jack's life revolved around work, food and sleep, and he had very little social contact with Adrian. He never saw him suffering from the after effects of alcohol and there was no gossip amongst the other airmen to that effect. The airmen's regard for Adrian amounted to hero worship. It was also well known amongst the lads that, with regard to his reconnaissance missions, Adrian had clearance from the top to, 'do it your way.' He took full advantage of it.

Many were lulled into a false sense of security in the summer of 1941. They had experienced German expertise, but thankfully the Luftwaffe was now busy elsewhere. Cargo was getting through, although the tenuous nature of the supply chain was well recognised at senior level. It would not take much of an effort on the part of the Axis to break that chain and the consequences would be quickly felt. In this time of relative plenty, now was the time to conserve, even to enforce stricter rationing, and certainly the Maltese civil population, as much on the front-line as the troops, should have been made more aware of the situation.

Lloyd pressed ahead expanding the airfields with whatever manpower he could find. There was no choice but to build on cultivated land even though this put further pressure on already limited food resources. Additional aircraft were flown in. They were no longer such easy targets on the ground, but it was impossible to hide more than a few and regular Axis recce flights soon revealed when new dispersals contained aircraft. Physical protection was all that could be done but, given the size of aircraft like the Wellington, this was a major challenge. Their hiding places had to be connected by taxiways and this was an even greater challenge, especially at Luqa, given the surrounding undulating terrain. There was no concrete available, and the steam rollers were lightweight and archaic. Even if dispersals were rolled, when a heavy aircraft remained in the same position for many days it would sink in and be impossible to move under its own power. With no tractors, this task was far from easy. Manpower, more manpower was Lloyd's constant cry. Progress was made, but his target of 240 dispersals, complete with blast walls and slit trenches, seemed a long way off.

At Luqa, aircraft were dispersed to the west, east and south, with taxiways linking the airfield through a section called the Loop-way to Stirling Valley, then to Safi Strip and eventually to Hal Far. But it took months before the route was available for anything other than relatively light, fighter aircraft. From the air, Luqa increasingly began to look like a huge octopus, the central part of the airfield being the body, with the tentacle-like taxi tracks winding round through fields and between quarries and farm buildings. Many pilots found they needed full throttle going uphill and full brake downhill to avoid running off the track into one of the many quarries.

The terrain was not quite so rugged at Ta' Qali and soon dispersal points covered a wide area with aircraft pens cut into the rock on the steep slopes up to Mdina.

Caves were carved out to house equipment and repair facilities, even when the airfield was being bombed. If possible, other exposed facilities, such as the repair shops, were moved underground or into caverns. Shortage of miners slowed the work, especially on expanding Lascaris where buckets and ropes were used to haul the excavated stone which was dispersed in bombed out buildings to disguise the ongoing work from the all-seeing cameras of recce aircraft.

The arrival of the additional airmen transformed the position for Lloyd and allowed him to accept more aircraft and turn his attention to the task he was sent to accomplish – attack Axis ships. Like his RN opposite number, Vice Admiral Ford, Lloyd was now in regular receipt of intelligence from Bletchley Park and both men worked closely together coordinating recce flights, submarine attacks, and torpedo attacks using Swordfish, some of which were now fitted with a short-range radar to detect surface vessels. Lloyd's principal weapon of attack was the Blenheim and he was expected to use these aircraft with the greatest determination.

Despite the gulf in ranks, Adrian's relationship with Hugh Lloyd was crucial. Air Vice-Marshal Maynard had earlier realised that to get the best out of Adrian he needed to be given a free hand and briefed Lloyd accordingly. Adrian was allowed to continue doing things his own way with Lloyd turning a blind eye to Adrian's involvement with Christina, of which he must have been well aware. As far as Lloyd was concerned, Adrian was a single man involved with a single lady who happened to be a member of his staff. There did not appear to be anything improper in the relationship. Service attitudes toward what was termed 'social misconduct' by officers were extremely strict; it was simply not tolerated, war or no war.

An example had already been made for all to see. One of the original and decorated members of Fighter Flight, credited with a number of aircraft destroyed, became involved with the wife of a naval officer serving away from the island. When word of this reached Sir William Dobbie, the individual concerned was history. Regardless of Malta's shortage of experienced fighter pilots, he was posted within twenty-four hours. He went to Greece, adding to his total of aircraft destroyed before being shot down and killed. Little wonder that, for the moment, Adrian guarded his secret well. Hugh Lloyd had the same attitude as Dobbie. A few days before he took over as AOC, a highly decorated senior officer and veteran of the Battle of France and the Battle of Britain, arrived as a controller at Lascaris, which was desperate for such men. He also arrived with a 'reputation'. When it appeared he may have been becoming inappropriately involved with his subordinate female staff, many of whom were the wives and daughters of servicemen, he too was history, posted away from Malta within twenty-four hours. Malta was desperately in need of such men, but the hierarchy would not tolerate any behaviour amongst officers that might impact adversely on morale.

Adrian was therefore very careful about his past; even Christina may not yet have known of his marriage. As he had the AOC's ear, as well as his patronage, other senior officers had little choice but to leave Adrian well alone, even if they had misgivings. There were some who did not take to Adrian, whom they saw as eccentric. Seldom in the Mess, he rarely socialised. Of course he had very little money. He continued to spend time with the airmen who worked on his aircraft and he was worshipped by many, not just for his exploits, but also for the interest he displayed in them and their work. And he kept Christina under wraps away from many. She was of course incredibly busy as a plotter and with the *Whizz-Bangs*, but the haven she provided was vital and there can be no doubt what she brought to their relationship ensured his survival from mounting physical and mental strain. Every pilot who arrived at the same time as Adrian had been rested having flown their operational quota. So too had many others who arrived months after him and had flown far less. By the summer, Adrian had flown three times as many operational sorties as any other 69 Squadron pilot, yet he soldiered on.

With Lloyd's support, Adrian's position was secure, although his frequent visits to Hugh Lloyd's office in the ditch did nothing to suppress the feelings of jealousy felt by some. In fairness to Adrian, Lloyd often did business directly with his pilots. He later described how Adrian would often 'breeze' into his office and give him the benefit of his views on how to deal with Italian merchant ships and their use of ports like Palermo and Tripoli. Adrian, of course, was a consummate planner, but so was Lloyd and one can well imagine the benign smile on Lloyd's face as he allowed his young subordinate to hold forth. He later recalled: 'There was something about his fair-haired good looks that reminded you of Lawrence of Arabia, and like Lawrence he was absolutely unorthodox and a complete individualist. You had to let him do things his own way. On and on he went: tireless, controversial, cynical, aloof. But in value absolutely beyond price.'[5]

Lloyd liked Adrian and was impressed by his character. Perhaps Lloyd recognised Adrian's unorthodoxy, seeing in Adrian some of his own qualities when he was a young operational pilot. Whatever his task, Adrian was never deflected from achieving it and invariably returned with first class photography and very detailed descriptions of his targets. If Adrian was late in returning from a mission, even by ten minutes, Hugh Lloyd, a man with far reaching responsibilities over many hundreds of personnel, often drove to Luqa to await Adrian's return. This was not simply because Lloyd was eager for the information Adrian brought, nor was he a soft touch overly concerned for one man. Lloyd couldn't afford to lose a man like Adrian, who was far from having an easy time under his AOC's patronage. Adrian was flying constantly and working desperately hard. In August he flew his 100th Maryland operational sortie. Lloyd described Adrian as, 'the absolute king of photographic reconnaissance, the pearl of the Mediterranean.'[6] Little wonder

---

5. *Photo Reconnaissance*, by Andrew J. Brookes, page 125.
6. *The Unknown Airman*, by Roy Nash, published in *The Star*, March 1958.

this remarkable young man was becoming Hugh Lloyd's recce pilot of choice in the battle of supply, the key to the contest in the Mediterranean. On its outcome, victory in North Africa for either Allies or Axis depended.

As long as Adrian delivered the goods, Lloyd closed his eyes to how Adrian dressed, although he never seemed to be without his beloved service dress cap so carefully repaired by Christina. When Adrian went to see Lloyd he invariably wore a scarf. Sometimes it was clean, sometimes it wasn't. Adrian was also very thin and Lloyd never thought he had enough to eat. But what Adrian did have was a magic all of his own, as well as courage and flair.

When Lloyd arrived there was not a single, trained photographic interpreter on the island. He soon rectified that by having two posted out from RAF Medmenham – Howard Colvin and Raymond Herschel. Such was his confidence in the value of reconnaissance when the two interpreters arrived he had his office in the ditch divided into two so the interpreters had ready access to him. Not only did Lloyd want to know the location of Axis cargo ships, but he also wanted to know when and what they were loading, and when they were likely to sail. So began a constant watch by Marylands of Axis ports.

One night when Howard and Ray were hard at work using their desk lamps to illuminate their photographs, someone silently entered their room and asked if they were looking at the latest cover of Naples. Ray replied, adding, 'sir'. The response from the fair-haired, extremely good-looking RAF officer was, 'Don't "sir" me, old boy.'[7] That was their first introduction to the Warby they had heard of. All three got to know one another well. Ray later described Adrian as a natural photographer who often returned from a target with only about fifty frames exposed out of a roll of 500.

Adrian was awarded a Bar to his DFC at the beginning of August 1941. Christina was very proud, 'to accompany him to Griscti's military uniform outfitters in Valletta, for a small silver rosette to sew on the blue and white striped ribbon he was now wearing.'[8] Christina was kept busy with her needle. So much had changed for Adrian in the eighteen months since he gained his pilot's brevet with a below average assessment. Upon awarding this second DFC, Hugh Lloyd was quoted in the *Times of Malta* as saying Adrian and his crew of Sergeants Moren and Bastard had a price on their heads, having shot down a total of eight Italian aircraft. Adrian's two DFCs and each of his sergeant's DFMs made them unique. The AOC's comment was widely reported. Maybe now was the time to rest this very able crew.

The Malta Night Fighter Unit was now operating twelve Hurricane Mark IICs, eight of which were armed with four cannons, with the remainder having twelve machine guns each. Working closely with the searchlights, and with such

7. *Evidence in Camera*, by Constance Babington Smith, pages 129–130.
8. *Carve Malta on my heart and other wartime stories*, by Frederick Galea, page 50.

firepower, there was a noticeable decline in night bombing raids. More detachments of Blenheims arrived in September, which included some fighter variants to act as convoy escorts and conduct anti-submarine patrols. There was an inevitable Axis reaction to the success of the Blenheims. All Axis merchant ships were equipped with anti-aircraft guns manned by well-trained gunners. The loss rate of Blenheims increased alarmingly, reaching an unsustainable twelve per cent in August and September. At the time, the Blenheims came for a relatively short stint with very few engineers and none of the normal support a UK-based squadron would enjoy. The crews all lived in the same Mess and, with aircraft being lost at the rate of six each week, it did not take them very long to realise they had little chance of surviving a six-week detachment. Theirs was a very conscious courage.

Casualties among other crews were also heavy, but they never reached the scale of loss experienced by the Blenheims. Everyone was aware of how critical the war in the desert was and how vital it was to strike every single Axis merchant ship with great vigour and determination. The crews never shirked from their aim, even when Axis merchant ships were escorted by Italian fighters, or the longer range Ju88 bombers converted to fighters. Given the constant lack of fighters in Malta, the Blenheims were never afforded the benefit of an escort. At one stage, Lloyd refused to send his Blenheims against strongly escorted vessels saying it was, 'sheer murder'. Although Admiral Cunningham rebuked Lloyd for his comment, Lloyd had a point and from mid-October the Blenheims were only used against unescorted cargo vessels. The Blenheims did not just fall victim to enemy fire. There were many other hazards, not least operating hundreds of miles from base at very low altitudes. The only realistic tactic was to drop their four 250lb bombs from 100 feet or less before overflying the target. The eleven-second delayed-action fuses should give them just enough time to clear the debris hemisphere. To achieve success, a section of three aircraft often targeted one ship, all aiming to release their weapons simultaneously. A second section went after a different ship some seconds later. It was in one such attack that the risk was highlighted.

The first section hit their target, which was in the process of altering course. The stricken vessel swung wildly toward its neighbour then exploded; directly in front of the second section of Blenheims. Two of the aircraft took the full force of the explosion. The leader was Wing Commander Pepper, and he and his two crewmen were killed. His number two was very seriously damaged and only just made it back to base; the aircraft never flew again. The loss of Pepper was a serious blow. Already the holder of the DFC, he was a master tactician who spent hours discussing tactics with his crews; 'his losses were far less, and his sinking much greater, than those of any other squadron commander.'[9] Of the five ships which Pepper's squadron

---

9. *Briefed to Attack*, by AM Sir Hugh Lloyd, pages 74–5.

targeted, only two made it to Tripoli. Pepper's detachment of 139 Squadron was withdrawn soon afterwards. The Blenheims continued to do what they could with units absorbed into one another because of devastating losses.

Despite the additional measures taken by the Italians to protect their shipping, including sailing longer routes taking them further away from Malta, their losses mounted. In the battle of wits, Ultra and the recce Marylands searching far and wide gave the Allies the edge. At one stage, the Italian Navy were questioning whether their lack of shipping might force them to abandon North Africa entirely. Clearly the Blenheims and the few submarines operating from Malta were having a telling impact on Axis supplies. Their work was complemented by the Wellingtons hitting enemy ports and harbours, principally Tripoli, which was bombed for six to eight hours every night for several weeks in the late summer. With the Marylands also sometimes dropping bombs, this contributed to the insecurity felt by the Italians. These constant assaults resulted in turnaround times for merchant ships increasing three and four fold, with sunken ships in harbour forcing unloading in open water. All of these delays in the enemy getting supplies to their front line were important and could critically affect the outcome of the conflict in the desert. The German liaison officers with the Italian forces were describing the situation by September as catastrophic, and were urgently demanding the return of the Luftwaffe to Sicily in greater numbers.

The 69 Squadron Marylands contributed further to Axis insecurity in the air when they discovered an Axis air supply route to the west of Pantelleria and Lampedusa. Hurricanes were fitted with long-range fuel tanks and, along with RN Fulmars, enjoyed great success against enemy transport aircraft using the route. The route was diverted via Greece.

Hugh Lloyd visited Luqa every day to talk to personnel, especially those about to be launched on night missions. By then the ditch through which he drove was adapted for an additional purpose; the solid limestone walls on either side now contained rows of little holes, each containing a Maltese family or two. Lloyd's Maltese driver, Sergeant Aquilina, always made a point of sounding the car's distinctive horn, resulting in scores of small children lining the ditch as he drove past. Lloyd described the salutes from these young children as straight from the Guards Depot.

The RAF took additional measures too. A detachment of Beaufighters had arrived and these powerful aircraft, armed with eight cannons, offered close protection to ships within range of Malta. The Beaufighters, with their excellent range, were particularly useful against enemy aircraft, especially torpedo aircraft, when they thought they were safe on the ground in Sicily and even farther afield in Sardinia. Hurricanes also added their weight, with some converted to become 'Hurribombers', modified to carry eight 20lb bombs which were useful against aircraft parked in the open. Even trains in Sicily were vulnerable to strafing.

The Marylands continued to get in on the act by shooting down Italian aircraft, despite being discouraged by Hugh Lloyd. He was right to do so; the Marylands were precious assets and the RAF could not afford to lose any in air combat that could be avoided. Sometimes Lloyd would 'reprimand' Adrian for chasing and shooting down the 'poor Italians', as Lloyd referred to them. 'And he would answer a little shamefacedly: "Well, sir, it was too easy." Then later on he would come into my office and say rather sheepishly: "I've shot down another one." "You mustn't do that Adrian," I told him.'[10] This reveals something of the unique relationship between an air vice-marshal and an officer seven ranks his junior.

For a time, Hugh Lloyd offered a bottle of champagne for each aircraft shot down. The Lascaris staff also demanded a bottle for every ten aircraft shot down. Inevitably, in the heady days of summer and autumn, the supply of champagne ran out; it was good while it lasted. But everyone understood that with the Italians once again struggling, there would be an inevitable German response.

Lloyd's most pressing problem was how long operations could be supported. They were consuming more than was being delivered, which was unsustainable for more than a few weeks. They needed convoys, more convoys; but the Italians and the Germans knew that too. Thankfully, September saw one arrive from Gibraltar with eight merchant ships delivering an impressive 85,000 tons of supplies. It was greeted by spontaneous and moving applause from a crowd who cheered the gallant ships and their escorts as they entered Grand Harbour. Seamen paraded on deck and Royal Marine bands played as if they were returning from a peacetime cruise. One merchantman, the *Imperial Star,* was lost en route. Malta now had sufficient fuel, ammunition and food for four to five months and was in a very different position to a year earlier with her garrison now numbering almost 25,000. Her three squadrons of Hurricanes were more than a match for the Regia Aeronautica, but how would they fare against the later marks of Me109? How long could the latest welcome supplies be made to last? Six months? Seven? Or eight? Or nine?

Adrian often reassured Christina about being safer in the air than on the ground. This was partially true as Allied aircraft often had a better chance of survival if airborne when daylight raids took place. More aircraft were destroyed or put out of action on the ground than were ever shot down. In fact, it was losses on the ground that brought the RAF and the whole defence of Malta to crisis point. The Wellingtons in particular, which usually flew at night, suffered badly in the daylight raids on Luqa. For Adrian and his 69 Squadron colleagues, often the most dangerous part of their missions was close to home, when they were 'bounced' by marauding enemy fighters. Nor, as we have seen, were they immune from 'friendly' fire.

---

10. *The Unknown Airman*, by Roy Nash, published in *The Star*, March 1958.

Much was made at the time of Warby's luck. He was fortunate many times, especially when his aircraft was damaged, although many of the risks were calculated, based on thorough planning and preparation. He spent hours with intelligence staff learning about 'his enemy' and would use whatever tactic was appropriate to give him best advantage. Sometimes he flew at high-level, other times at extremely low-level. He also had the advantage that a number of his later missions were based on information from Ultra, although this was known to very few. Having found a particular ship, in order to protect the intelligence source, he often had to radio a message back to Malta confirming the ship's location, immediately giving his position away. A number of 69 Squadron pilots questioned the rationale behind this. The response that an anti-shipping strike awaited the recce report only went so far. That Adrian always came back with excellent photography, regardless of weather, or enemy action, was certainly not simply down to luck.

Inevitably, Adrian's self-confidence increased with his continuing success. He may have become overconfident on some of his missions and often accomplished something extra, something more than obtaining images of his target. Had a pattern been set long ago on the transit flight led by Tich from Britain to Malta? Their task was one of aircraft delivery, yet, on top of that, Tich elected to photograph military installations in Sardinia. Time and time again, Adrian added something more to his tasked mission by maybe attacking an airfield, or actively engaging, rather than avoiding, enemy aircraft. If he judged the circumstances favourable, he would 'mix-it' with the enemy and his score of downed enemy aircraft was very unusual for a recce pilot. For a while he was the top scoring pilot in Malta, although his 'kills' sometimes involved his gunner, usually the extremely able Paddy Moren. In another calculated risk, Adrian repeated the ploy of his earlier attack on the Italian airfield, doing the same to the Luftwaffe airfield at Catania in Sicily. He was successful, destroying one large transport aircraft and damaging two others. With Axis airfields notoriously well-defended, the similarity of the Maryland to the Ju88 could only work in his favour so often, so perhaps it was time to stop.

Christina continued with regular rehearsals and performances with the *Whizz-Bangs*. Inevitably, with arduous shifts at Lascaris, something had to give and she had to consider giving up one or the other. Living within walking distance of Lascaris had its advantages. It could also be dangerous, as she found out. At the end of a night shift, when she was tired to the point of exhaustion, she walked home despite the fact an air raid warning was still in force when she left the operations room. As she carefully made her way back to her Floriana flat, fighter-bombers swooped low overhead, dropping anti-personnel bombs indiscriminately over the whole area. Living and working in this area might be convenient, but it was becoming especially hazardous.

Adrian had ten days local leave in September, which was one of the quietest months of his first tour of duty on the island. Expecting a posting back to Britain, Adrian's last trip that month saw him once again teamed up with Paddy Moren for a reconnaissance over Sardinia. They were intercepted by a Macchi fighter which they shot down. A week earlier they had shot down another Cant Z.506 seaplane. This increased Adrian's total 'kills' to ten. At the end of September, Wing Commander Dowland, 69 Squadron's Commanding Officer, assessed Adrian as an exceptional photo-reconnaissance pilot. Adrian had come a long way in a year.

Autumn in Malta is often a pleasant season once the harsh, dry winds from the south abate. Rationing resulted in belt tightening, but it was Malta Dog which laid low those unacclimatised to conditions. Local leave was possible and an RAF rest camp was established at St Paul's Bay. This was popular, especially with ground crew who did not benefit from the same rotation as aircrew. In fact, many airmen saw out their war on the island. Hugh Lloyd soon made periods in the rest camp compulsory for all ranks. Swimming and sunbathing were favourite pastimes, but sailing had obvious limitations. Dancing in the evenings was also well liked, as was the cinema, and the concert parties remained extremely well attended. The volunteer 'artistes' from Air HQ did a magnificent job.

For Jack, days and dates meant nothing; it was work, work, and more work. There were frequent changes of accommodation as he was either bombed out, or moved for unknown reasons. After the tent at Siggiewi, Jack lived in the former Poor House next to the old lunatic asylum on the right of the main road from Luqa down the hill to Marsa. He thought his new home appropriately named. Their beds were made out of wooden poles and chicken wire. Not long afterwards Jack was struck down with appendicitis and spent a week in the RN Hospital Mtarfa. Following some days in the rest camp, he was placed on 'light duties' and organised whatever sport or entertainment he could. A true Yorkshireman, Jack set about getting a rugby team together and marking out a pitch. The pitch proved a waste of time; instead they played at the former Marsa racecourse. The Poor House did have a stage in what was a cinema and Jack organised some film evenings. He also obtained some curtains and it was here he watched a performance given by the *Whizz-Bangs*. That was the first time he saw Christina.

The airmen recognised Adrian and Christina as an 'item' but it caused no comment; they said much more about Adrian's outrageous dress. Jack described Christina as a lovely person, good looking and pleasant, and Jack and his friends often saw Adrian with Christina in Valletta. They would be walking arm in arm, the tall handsome pilot and the very attractive, and always smartly dressed, blonde. They smiled at everyone, and despite the hardships, everyone smiled back. Jack said people sometimes applauded as Adrian and Christina passed and he described their attraction for one another as magnetic. 'She looked after him. By the time he arrived at the airfield each morning, he was ready for anything.'

As wartime postings went, there were some plusses to being in Malta at that time, discounting the risk to life and limb, but there were also minuses. There was no welfare along the lines well-established in Britain. Accommodation was always a problem, with servicemen crammed in blocks with every piece of floor space in use. There were not enough beds, rarely any electricity and certainly no heating in winter. Often, troops bombed out of their blocks lived in whatever they could find. Cooking arrangements were inadequate and they got worse. Gone were the days when coal could be obtained, even on the black market. As Tamara said, 'The only way to keep warm was to go dancing and that is what we did.'[11]

Christina then got her wish: her Warby was sent for a rest. He was posted, not back to Britain as expected, but to Egypt to become an instructor. Maybe Lloyd had a hand in this, knowing a return to Malta was unlikely if Adrian went back to the UK. In Egypt, Adrian was still close and well within Lloyd's sphere of influence. Adrian left on 1 October 1941, along with Frank Bastard and Paddy Moren. By then, Adrian had flown 116 operational missions in the Maryland, plus others in the Blenheim and Hurricane. The only other Maryland pilot who came close to this number was Jack's friend, Willie Williams, who achieved 115 some months later.

11. *Women of Malta*, by Frederick Galea, page 102.

Chapter Eleven

Determination

October saw another detachment of Blenheims arrive for anti-shipping duties. They attacked with great courage, but lost twenty-nine personnel in a few weeks. They were withdrawn to Egypt where the squadron was disbanded. More Wellingtons arrived in mid-October to continue night bombing. Thankfully they carried with them some much-needed ground crew. Autumn and early winter saw continued successes against Axis shipping. This was a particularly important period prior to the long anticipated Allied offensive in the desert. In answer to further prodding from Churchill, Force K, comprising two cruisers and two destroyers, arrived in October, as well as eleven Albacores flown in from *Ark Royal*. This was all part of a plan to disrupt further Axis supply routes. It wasn't long before Rome learnt of the reinforcements. With the Luftwaffe committed to supporting Rommel's planned offensive, it was left to the German Navy to provide more support to the Italians. Over the next three months, twenty-seven U-boats were sent to the Mediterranean.

At the end of October, 69 Squadron moved to Ta' Qali to make room for more aircraft at Luqa. An important addition to Hugh Lloyd's offensive capability came from Cornwall; a detachment of three new ASV Wellington Mark VIIIs equipped with radar. Originally belonging to 221 Squadron, they were officially the Special Duties Flight, but were unofficially referred to as Goofingtons. Their task was to find enemy surface shipping at night. One Wellington pilot was Tony Spooner, who later said of Lloyd: 'Some held that he was too brutal and unrelenting; others swore by him, declaring that he was the finest leader we could possibly have.'[1] Lloyd quickly won Spooner's support by regularly being on the airfield in the middle of the night to meet him and his crew following long and hazardous missions. The AOC was also very anxious to learn about the elementary radar fitted to the Wellingtons and with good reason: he wanted Spooner to work with Force K. They proved highly successful. Bletchley Park provided information about an Italian fleet of seven merchant ships with escorts heading for Tripoli. To protect the intelligence source, a recce aircraft from Luqa was sent to the general area and it duly made a 'chance' sighting. Force K left Malta that night and after working closely with Spooner's Wellington, all seven of the merchant ships, along with two escorting

---

1. *In Full Flight*, by Tony Spooner, page 170.

destroyers, were sunk without loss. There was a similar successful operation in November. These attacks placed Rommel's operations in jeopardy.

Tony Spooner often found himself in the same position as Adrian, working directly for Hugh Lloyd. It was Lloyd who bypassed the normal chain of command, not the other way round. Spooner considered Lloyd, often seen with a long black cigarette holder, to be part showman. And of course Sergeant Aquilina drove him everywhere in a distinctive pale blue car with white-wall tyres. Tony thought Lloyd had certain, almost theatrical gestures: 'the proud throw of his head, his clipped yet dynamic powers of speech, and the same Churchillian sense of history and drama.'[2] Interestingly, Spooner completed a course at RAF Squires Gate, Blackpool, at the same time as Adrian, although they never met. Tony's first Wellington squadron was also based at RAF Bircham Newton at the same time as Jack Vowles worked on Blenheims. In Malta, like Jack, he was regularly bombed out of his accommodation and he too spent a few nights in the former Poor House. Tony also spent a prolonged period of ill health on the island, recovering at the rest centre at St Paul's Bay before his detachment ended.

Late October and early November became known as the 'Great Deluge' and torrential rain returned in December, which lasted into the New Year. Within hours taxiways were washed away and it was often unsafe to move aircraft. The lack of tar and bitumen had very serious effects with some aircraft dropping a wheel straight through the taxiway surfaces. Shipping strikes were delayed or cancelled as aircraft became bogged down. With no tractors or ground equipment to help, it was very labour intensive to move aircraft and to repair the damaged surfaces. It was particularly miserable for the hard-pressed airmen. Desperately needed aircraft repairs were postponed due to the needs of manual labour, with the ill-equipped airmen working in very difficult, wet and muddy conditions. The only shelter was under the wings of aircraft with rain pouring down for hours on end. Afterwards, there was nowhere to dry clothing. There were a few days of sun before the rain returned. Jaundice and sickness rates soared; maintenance rates fell.

It was no longer safe to taxi Wellingtons at night when they returned from a mission, which meant holding them like sitting ducks on the runways until it was light enough for the pilots, who stayed with them, to follow a safe route to dispersals off the airfield. The strain on the pilots following their often long bombing flights was enormous. As the Wellingtons eventually moved toward their dispersals, they often met Blenheim day bombers trying to reach the runway. Adding to the confusion were the aircraft transiting through Luqa on their way to Egypt. On average sixty Wellingtons each month staged through, and always at night to avoid the threat from enemy fighters. With all refuelling carried out using five-gallon tins,

---

2. *In Full Flight*, by Tony Spooner, page 208.

the situation bordered on the chaotic. By the end of November, Ta' Qali's grass surface was deep in mud and resembled its origin: a lake. There was no choice but to move 69 Squadron back to Luqa and many of the fighters soon followed, to be parked in rows where they were terribly vulnerable. Hal Far was also unusable for days at a time, which compounded a very difficult situation.

The Allied offensive in the desert began in mid-November and throughout the four-week preparation period, and afterwards, the Wellingtons from Luqa bombed targets in support of the army. Their crews performed well, but this was only possible because of the work of their dedicated engineers. As troop-carriers did not exist, when the detachments arrived on the island they brought a few airmen with them. The Blenheim and Wellington squadrons of sixteen to twenty aircraft could carry fifteen and twenty-six ground crew respectively. They then borrowed whatever airmen they could from other units and operated, in appalling conditions, four times the number of aircraft they would have served in Britain. Their efforts emphasised how much more than an unsinkable aircraft carrier Malta had become, supporting a powerful bomber force night after night, month after month.

It followed, as night follows day, that Malta's growing attack strength and its success in staunching the flow of supplies from Italy to North Africa would draw down retribution. Mussolini's position in North Africa was untenable without significant German support. In fact, Mussolini's future relied upon him holding on to his empire. Neither the Italians nor the Germans could stay there without supplies and the combined offensive action of Force K, RN submarines, RAF bombers and the Fleet Air Arm's Swordfish and Albacores denied the Axis a huge amount. Shipping losses were enormous and many damaged ships never sailed again. The ports of Tripoli, Palermo and Trapani had, to a large extent, been turned into graveyards. It was abundantly clear to the Axis high command that, as long as Malta retained her power of offence, there was little chance of Rommel leading and sustaining an offensive capable of defeating the Allies.

With the onset of winter on the Russian Steppes came stalemate for the German armies, which had, until then, blitzkrieged their way across most of Europe. Denied the quick victory he anticipated, Hitler turned his attention back to the Mediterranean and the tiny rock that stood in his way. Malta needed to be crushed as a base for offensive operations. He gave the task to *Generalfeldmarscall* 'Smiling Albert' Kesselring. It was Kesselring who directed the Luftwaffe throughout the Battle of Britain and he was now in command of all German air forces in the Mediterranean. His task was simple: obliterate Malta. He even decreed in his orders that Malta was to be 'Coventrated', the term devised by Goebbels to describe the scale of destruction the Luftwaffe achieved in one night in Coventry.

Previously, Kesselring's command was limited to a single *fliegerkorps* of 400 aircraft. A second *fliegerkorps* of battle-hardened veterans withdrawn from airfields facing Moscow and Stalingrad soon moved to Sicily and Southern Italy. They were joined by others withdrawn from Belgium and France. This increased Kesselring's command to about 900 aircraft. Preparations were soon in hand for an aerial assault – Operation Herkules – the invasion of Malta, with General Kurt Student in command of airborne forces. As a number of personnel based on the island had forecast, Malta was about to 'cop it'. At the time dozens of Spitfire squadrons were based in Britain, many flying offensive fighter sweeps over Occupied France and the Low Countries, yet not a single Spitfire fighter squadron was based anywhere within the Mediterranean theatre. As Kesselring was preparing to unleash the latest marks of Me109s over Malta, the RAF was relying on outdated Hurricanes kept in the air by a band of intrepid pilots and hard-pressed engineers.

On 13 November, perhaps as an indication of Malta's change of fortune and shortly after launching another Hurricane delivery, *Ark Royal* was torpedoed. At the time, Alex Woods was embarked with 816 Squadron's Swordfish. The single torpedo created a hole 130 feet long and the ship began to list severely. Earlier in the war, the carriers *Courageous* and *Glorious* sunk rapidly after being hit by torpedoes with heavy loss of life. Remarkably, of the *Ark Royal's* complement of 1,437, only one sailor died having been killed in the initial explosion. The *Ark Royal* sank in the early hours of 14 November and post-war investigation confirmed nothing could have been done to save the ship. Alex Woods ended up at Gibraltar. Could he and his colleagues strike a blow against the U-boats trying to enter the Mediterranean?

The successful delivery of 242 and 605 Squadrons could not make up for the loss of *Ark Royal*. Chaos still surrounded Malta's reinforcements, demonstrated by the fact the support staff of both squadrons were sent to the Far East. Malta's new aircraft therefore needed to be serviced by the already hard-pressed airmen from the existing Hurricane units. Throughout the autumn, 69 Squadron continued to enjoy success, but always at a cost, with a number of crews lost. Wing Commander Dowland was shot down in a Hurricane by Italian fighters and baled out over the sea. Luckily he was picked up by a Swordfish floatplane after an hour. By the end of November, 69 Squadron had seven serviceable Marylands and two Hurricanes.

The loss of *Ark Royal* heralded a dire time for the RN. It altered the situation not only in the Mediterranean, but also impacted on the Far East where the situation was becoming critical. *Ark Royal* was due to head there to provide air cover for the RN's two battleships operating from Singapore, being replaced in the Mediterranean by *Indomitable*; unfortunately the latter ran aground in Jamaica. Later, in November, the battleship HMS *Barham* was sunk by a U-boat off Egypt with the loss of 841. It took two months before the Admiralty admitted her sinking and the horrifying film of her last seconds was not released until after the war. Despite the losses, Force K had shown what could be achieved by warships operating from Grand Harbour and, at the end of November; Admiral Cunningham provided reinforcements in the shape of Force B – two more cruisers and two destroyers.

The lull in bombing was over by the beginning of December. The authorities knew of the German moves, but the news was kept secret with no official announcement made. Yet everyone was aware the Germans were back. For over a month Tamara said, 'shelter suits (we called them "siren" suits) were being made right and left. Warm, strong material was run up into two-piece trouser and battle dress top affairs. Some used lightweight blankets, others their husband's discarded civilian suits. Ingenuity had full scope.'[3] The full-scale evacuation of British civilians was now underway and a number of Lascaris plotters were now Maltese girls. Pickles became Captain of B Watch and Christina, Captain of D Watch. As it was rarely possible to change their new duties to fit in with concert party performances, they decided to give up the *Whizz-Bangs* at the end of the year and remain with the RAF. The concert party was an important part of their lives for eighteen months, but now they were involved in something far more crucial. There were other artistes waiting in the wings, but fully trained plotters were rare.

Dive bombing by Stukas announced the Luftwaffe's return and, despite heavy losses, they continued with typical persistence. To the civilians, the bombing appeared indiscriminate with incendiary, as well as high explosive bombs, being used, many of which fell in residential areas. The harbours were often mined too. As the year drew to a close, the raids went on increasing. Not surprisingly, more and more people used the shelters, not just at night, but also by day. Unless one actually lived in a shelter it was often difficult to find space.

In December there was a particularly sad end to the Hudson which led the first Hurricanes to Malta in June 1940. Since then it had been doing valuable long-range reconnaissance work operating as part of 69 Squadron. It was accidentally shot down by a RN Fulmar and its crew of four were killed. By the year's end the former 431 Flight, now 69 Squadron, had lost ten aircraft in the air and many more destroyed on the ground. Twenty-one of its aircrew were killed. The Hurricanes were struggling desperately now, always outnumbered and increasingly outperformed by the later marks of Me109 employed against them. The only answer was Spitfires, but still none had been allowed out of Britain.

There was good news from North Africa where the long-awaited and overdue Allied offensive was underway. The siege of Tobruk was lifted. By the end of December, Benghazi was in Allied hands for a second time. Everyone thought Rommel and his Afrika Korps were doomed. Then bad news arrived from the Far East: Japan struck Pearl Harbor, Hong Kong and Malaya, and HMS *Repulse*, along with her consort HMS *Prince of Wales*, became unwitting testaments to the

---

3. *Women of Malta*, by Frederick Galea, page 102.

vulnerability of these mighty ships to air assault. Without an air umbrella, both were sunk by Japanese aircraft north of Singapore; 835 members of their crews were lost. This caused great sadness in Malta where both ships were well known. The impact of the Japanese onslaught was soon felt in North Africa where, once again, and just like Greece when Allied forces were on the verge of victory, they were denuded in order to reinforce failure, and an abject failure at that. Nevertheless, the surprise attacks in the Far East resulted in the United States entering the war.

The activities of the RN's surface ships from Malta – sometimes as Force K and sometimes the larger Force B – were controlled by Vice Admiral Ford, and he coordinated their missions closely with Hugh Lloyd and his Blenheims and Spooner's radar-equipped Wellingtons. In November, Spooner, who was now commanding the Wellington detachment, was awarded a DFC. In the first two weeks of December, the RAF/RN combination was highly successful, sinking Italian cargo ships and a tanker heading for Benghazi. Italian warships were not immune either and two cruisers were also sunk. Then disaster struck. On 17 December, Force B ran into a newly laid minefield near Tripoli and the cruiser *Neptune* went down with the loss of 765; only one survivor was picked up five days later. A destroyer was also lost and the two original cruisers of Force K, *Aurora* and *Penelope*, were both damaged. Force K was crippled. In the same month, six Italian frogmen entered Alexandria harbour and successfully attacked the battleships *Queen Elizabeth* and *Valiant*; they were out of action for months.

Alex Woods was now a lieutenant commander in command of the Swordfish of 812 Squadron. The squadron was allocated to *Argus*, but for a seven-week period from 27 November, it was disembarked to RAF North Front, Gibraltar. German U-boat crews soon felt the impact of 812. On the night of 30 November, Swordfish damaged *U-96*, which took a week to struggle back to St Nazaire for repairs. The German war correspondent Lothar-Günther Buchheim was on board *U-96* at the time and his experience of the attack formed part of his bestselling novel and the acclaimed film *Das Boot*.

Two nights later similar treatment was dished out to another U-boat. In the run up to Christmas, three more were attacked by 812 Squadron and damaged sufficiently that they had to return to port for repairs, significantly reducing the U-boat threat to those ships running the gauntlet to Malta. On 21 December, 812 Squadron's perseverance paid off when *U-451* was sunk off Tangier, the first U-boat to be sunk at night. Alex Woods was awarded a well-deserved DSO in the New Year for his leadership and there were awards for a number of his crews. Later, the squadron re-embarked on *Argus* in support of fighter deliveries to Malta.

Hugh Lloyd had now been in Malta for nine months, the maximum envisaged when he was appointed. Tedder did not intend to lose Lloyd, whose post was renamed AOC Air HQ Malta. At the same time Air Vice-Marshal Keith Park, the former AOC 11 Group throughout the Battle of Britain, was appointed AOC Air HQ Cairo. If Tedder harboured any doubts about Lloyd's performance, this was the ideal time to make a change and he had a candidate more than capable of replacing Lloyd as Malta's air defence commander. Tedder made no such change; he was more than satisfied with Lloyd's performance.

Command arrangements on the island remained unchanged. Army units remained under General Dobbie through his GOC. Dobbie had been in post for over a year and a half and had concerns about his inability to direct the senior sailor and airman on the island, who continued to report directly to their respective C-in-Cs in Egypt. Ford and Lloyd's relations with Dobbie were largely of an administrative nature; he was not consulted on operational matters, being routinely advised as a courtesy. Lloyd later acknowledged this arrangement was curious and led to tension; 'it had its good and its bad points – good, in that there was no interference whatsoever, but bad when it came to deciding how many soldiers or airmen, and what equipment, should be sailed on the next convoy.'[4]

From Sicily Kesselring set about his task of destroying Malta carefully and deliberately. Many Axis reconnaissance sorties were flown in the early part of December until he had a clear picture of Malta's defences. Probing raids gradually increased until the year's end. For most people on Malta, Christmas 1941 was a cheerless affair with little food or anything to protect them from a cold wind howling through broken and pane-less windows. When an air raid warning sounded on such a small island, everyone was affected, even those living in relatively remote villages. Only Gozo and the tiny island of Comino were raid-free, as neither island had any targets of military significance. November and December were torrid months for the RAF with thirty bombers shot down, a rate of attrition that simply could not be sustained. Malta's air defence fighters also suffered heavily. The defenders were not receiving sufficiently early warning of raids and, despite Hugh Lloyd's best efforts, the ground facilities were still inadequately equipped for resistance to bombing. By the end of 1941, there had been a total of 1,169 alerts. Many wondered what 1942 would bring.

Christina knew all about the mischievous side of Warby's nature. Sometimes it was pointed in her direction. She quite enjoyed that; he made her laugh easily. And she was never happier than when she saw him laugh or smile. Heaven knows he had been under such strain given what he did every day and with so many of his friends having 'bought it' or 'gone in'. Many were her friends too. They hid the horrid reality of what happened behind such terms. But through her work she knew how they died, and it was often a horrible and lonely death. In the few quiet moments

---

4. *Briefed to Attack*, by AM Sir Hugh Lloyd, pages 89–90.

they shared, Christina knew the losses affected him. She also knew there was no escape for any of them, not until this terrible war was over. If she was his sanctuary when he was in Malta, even a temporary one, then she was happy. She had missed him terribly when he was in Egypt, but inside she was pleased for his sake.

It was quiet on the bus that late December morning. They were going to Ghajn Tuffieha in the north. Some of the boys and girls were asleep, or maybe they just had their eyes closed. Perhaps they were partying until the early hours and were catching up on their beauty sleep before the show in front of the 8th Manchester Regiment. She was tired too, very tired, but she hadn't been partying, she had been on duty. There were only three raids, but they were quite enough to keep D Watch busy with little chance of any shut-eye on the ops room floor.

She had today and tonight free, before reporting back tomorrow morning, free except for today's show, her very last regular concert party performance. Christina had known for months she couldn't continue; she had to give up either the *Whizz-Bangs* or her work in Fighter Control. Even though she had loved her eighteen months with the troupe, and often thought her performances were the most important of her career, she never had a moment's doubt about what she would do. Her work had never been so important, so needed, as when she was on shift at Lascaris. More and more dependants had been evacuated and they had lost many from the ops room. Thank goodness for the Maltese girls who volunteered; they were very good. There was no way she could bring herself to leave, especially now she was about to take over as Captain of D Watch.

In many ways, she wished he would be posted away permanently. But now he was back, typically with no advance warning and to everyone's surprise, especially hers. There was just a small parcel waiting for her in the ops room, neatly wrapped and tied with string. It was a 'blitzed' parachute which she could easily make into a nightdress. Warby was such a thoughtful man and so caring. Few knew what he was really like.

As their ancient bus made its way slowly through the open countryside, with the tiny fields on either side, some of her friends simply stared out of the broken windows. Unbroken windows were a rarity in Malta these days. They were as rare as hens' teeth! Hens! What a joke! Suddenly there was a squeal of brakes as the Maltese driver brought the bus to a shuddering halt. 'Air raid! Air raid!' he yelled. That woke everyone up! They all made a hasty exit. The driver stood for a few seconds in front of the bus pointing excitedly at the aircraft he had spotted. He then made off like a madman down the road, leaving them to their own devices. By then they were all out of the bus, standing to one side, putting the bus between them and the approaching aircraft. Not that it would afford them any protection as the Germans shot up any vehicle they spotted. They were also more than a little exposed, in open country with no sign of any shelter whatsoever.

Christina peered around the side of the bus looking closely at the aircraft that seemed to be coming their way. What type was it? Was it German or Italian? She was now very good at aircraft recognition, better than some of those who manned the guns, Warby once said with a laugh. The aircraft was making directly for them. It was a fast, twin-engine monoplane. Was it a Junkers 88? No, and this aircraft was painted pale blue which was unusual. 'No need to panic everyone. It's one of ours.'

Christina recognised it as a Beaufighter, a photo-reconnaissance Beaufighter, a very rare bird in Malta. Then it dawned on her, it was Warby. He had said he might call and say hello if given the chance. He was bound to find a rather unique way of doing so. They all watched fascinated as the Beaufighter got closer and closer. Some of them waved the gaudy, frilly costumes they were carrying. Then suddenly, when the Beaufighter was directly overhead, it went into a vertical dive! 'Look out,' someone screamed, 'he's crashing!' Some of the group threw themselves onto the ground and covered their heads with their arms. With an ear-splitting roar, the Beaufighter skimmed over the bus, missing it by what seemed like inches. Christina closed her eyes, sick at heart, and waited for the sound of the crash. It never came. When she recovered her senses she saw the pale blue aircraft was climbing steeply upwards, the sun glinting off the Perspex canopy, the roar of the aircraft's engines coming back at them like a loud mocking laugh. Sometimes, she wished Warby wasn't quite so mischievous.[5]

Adrian arrived back the day before his impromptu, yet typical, call on Christina. Almost three months earlier, on 1 October, his flight from Malta to Egypt was his last with Frank and Paddy. In Cairo, they were summoned to meet Air Marshal Tedder who wanted to hear first-hand about conditions on the island. Adrian was then granted ten days leave, which he used to visit his father, Geoffrey, still serving in Port Said. Afterwards, Adrian joined 233 Squadron at Shandur as a gunnery instructor; Frank and Paddy were also instructors. Operating a mix of Marylands and Blenheims, 233 was an operational training unit with most instructors coming from the South African Air Force. They undertook the final training of South African and Rhodesian crews before they moved to squadrons in the western desert.

Adrian did not take to instructing, logging few flights; he rarely flew with students. Once he found out No 2 Photo Reconnaissance Unit (PRU) was based at Heliopolis he arranged a posting there. Frank and Paddy stayed with 233 Squadron. Like 69 Squadron, Adrian's new unit struggled for aircraft. Originally designated to fly Marylands, the ship carrying all of its aircraft was sunk the previous January. With no further Marylands available, the unit was assigned three Hurricanes modified locally by having two cameras fitted and the guns removed. Adrian soon felt at home

---

5. *Carve Malta on my heart and other wartime stories*, by Frederick Galea, pages 51–2.

and within four days was flying the Hurricane, working for someone else who gave him a degree of leeway. Squadron Leader Hugh McPhail's approach was one of simply getting the job done; he got on well with Adrian and appreciated his many fine qualities as a recce pilot.

The unit acquired two Beaufighters which were given to Flight Lieutenant 'Johnnie' Walker for conversion and use as recce aircraft. This involved removing guns, cannon and radio equipment to increase the aircraft's speed and ceiling. The intention was to use them over Crete now it was in German hands. They flew with a crew of two including a photographer skilled in maintaining the camera and replacing its large magazine. Adrian's claim to know all about Beaufighters was not examined too closely. By mid-November, he was back on ops, his rest period having lasted just seven weeks. On his very first trip over Crete, with the recce Beaufighter flying much higher than it was ever designed to operate, the starboard engine failed due to the engine oil freezing; the port engine also malfunctioned. They only just made it to a landing strip in North Africa. Warby's 'luck' had travelled well.

With the war in the desert going in favour of the Allies, thoughts turned to the possibility of an Allied landing in Sicily. Photographs of all potential beach landing sites were needed and Beaufighters were ideal, with Malta being the obvious location from which to mount such missions.

Despite his many hours on the Maryland, Adrian had not overcome his problems taking off or landing a twin-engine aircraft, and his new flight commander, Johnnie Walker, considered him ham-fisted, although he never flew with him personally. Leading Aircraftman Norman Shirley did; he was a photographer regularly crewed with Adrian and earlier shared 'Warby's luck' over Crete. He described Adrian's take-offs and landings as the clumsiest he ever experienced. Yet in the air, Adrian was in his element, totally and completely at one with his aircraft. Despite Walker's reservations, Adrian's knowledge and experience of operations over Sicily were second to none. He was an ideal candidate for the detachment, which was led by Walker, and included one other pilot and three volunteer ground photographers, one of whom was Norman Shirley.

The C-in-C personally briefed Walker about the importance of the Sicily task. Tedder knew Hugh Lloyd well and suspected he might try and divert the Beaufighters, and especially Adrian, from the primary task to keep track of Axis shipping. Tedder did not wish Walker's detachment to be sidetracked in any way. Designated T Flight of 2 PRU, the detachment left Heliopolis for Malta on 29 December. They landed at Timini, west of Tobruk, to refuel and there received news of poor weather ahead. As Adrian knew Malta well, he pressed on. Walker waited for better conditions. In fact, it was nine days before he got to Luqa. By then, Adrian and Hugh Lloyd had used the nine-day period rather well.

Lloyd had his own ideas about using the Beaufighters, but he is unlikely to have ignored or deliberately gone against any known directive from Tedder. The situation in North Africa was, however, changing as the desert pendulum swung back in favour of the Axis. How far the pendulum moved came as a major shock. As a result, preparations for a possible invasion of Sicily were no longer a priority. What Lloyd wanted, what he always wanted, was to attack Axis ships wherever they could be found, especially those heading for Tripoli. Now he had his premier recce pilot back under his command in an aircraft even the best of the Luftwaffe had little chance of catching. Within twenty-four hours of arriving, Adrian was off revisiting and photographing many of his old haunts, including Tripoli and all of Sicily, and Southern Italy's ports. He also photographed those airfields in Sicily from which an airborne invasion would most likely be mounted. By the time Johnnie Walker arrived, Adrian had flown over a dozen new missions.

When Johnnie touched down at Luqa he found his mission of photographing Sicilian beaches had already been overtaken by events. Even as he slowed to a stop, he was confronted by the unmistakeable figure of Adrian shouting up at him, telling him to get the aircraft to dispersal as quickly as possible. This was the reality of life on Malta's airfields; too much time spent on runway or taxiway invited a bombing or strafing attack from prowling enemy aircraft just waiting for a sitting duck. And there were insufficient Hurricanes to keep the skies clear to cover either the launch or the recovery of Allied aircraft.

Within Adrian's second stint on Malta, he flew all of his sorties bar one in the dark blue Beaufighter that so startled many of the *Whizz-Bangs*. The Beaufighters, now fitted with three 20-inch cameras, operated alongside 69 Squadron and to a large extent both units operated as one. Adrian found himself under the direct control of Hugh Lloyd, who dictated Adrian's role. For each of his missions, Adrian maintained his supremely professional approach using a combination of meticulous planning, instinct and carefully calculated risks. To the photographers who flew with him, Adrian showed no outward sign of fear.

The particularly bad times began in January and 69 Squadron suffered more than most. In the middle of the month, Wing Commander Dowland was returning from an early morning flight when two German Me109s pounced, badly damaging his Maryland. Dowland's navigator was Pilot Officer Potter and his WOp/AG was Pilot Officer Bob Gridley, who as a sergeant accompanied Adrian to Malta in 1940. Bob Gridley's return fire caused the fighters to break off. Dowland ordered his crew to bale out over the island but only Potter did so; Bob may have been wounded. Dowland ditched his crippled aircraft largely intact only forty feet from Tigne Point, east of Sliema. A Maltese gunner from a nearby gun battery, Gunner W. Izett, swam out into the rough, cold sea and although he was able to access the cockpit, he was unable to release the injured Dowland's straps. Izett had to watch helplessly as the aircraft slipped beneath the waves taking with it Bob Gridley and the courageous John Dowland GC; his George Cross was awarded for removing live enemy bombs from ships on two separate occasions. Izett searched in vain for twenty minutes and was hauled out of the water exhausted. Dowland's body was recovered later, but Bob Gridley was never found. Having flown in the Battle of Britain, Bob served continuously on 431 Flight and 69 Squadron for fifteen months. He was 20-years-old. The day after his death, his Maltese wife Doris gave birth to their son.

At the time Jack Vowles was working nights, sleeping by day in the Tower House Hotel in Sliema. He and some colleagues went across to the gun battery soon afterwards; there was nothing they could do. They then helped the crew change a gun barrel, taking cover in an air raid thinking they were the target. There were near misses, but most bombs fell behind them in Sliema itself. One hit the back of the Tower House Hotel and Jack returned to find a colleague badly cut by glass while having a bath, a cold bath. Lloyds Bank was also hit, its front wall collapsing into the street. Paper money was blowing about and being picked up by passers-by. Jack collected a wad of notes and walked into the bank which was deserted, almost. The manager's office was wide open and behind his desk the manager was sitting motionless, covered in dust. He had no obvious injuries but was quite dead, a victim of blast. Jack left the wad of notes on his desk with a stone on top to keep them in place. He tried not to dwell on such sights.

Two days later there was another tragedy for 69, one that hit Jack very hard. It occurred because Jack's friend, Flight Lieutenant E.J.A. 'Willie' Williams, DFC, did a favour. On that particular day, Willie was the duty pilot in air control at Luqa. A Maryland returned and the crew reported they had photography and information that needed to be acted upon immediately. The pilot was therefore instructed to taxi to air control and shut-down rather than taxiing to a distant dispersal. After the crew were whisked away to be debriefed, Willie volunteered to taxi the aircraft to dispersal. No one will ever be sure what happened, but, as Willie's aircraft passed close by a bomb trolley, loaded with four 500lb bombs, they exploded. Willie and two airmen were killed instantly.

The new squadron commander for 69 Squadron was Wing Commander Eric Tennant and he and Adrian got on well from the start. Tennant sometimes signed Adrian's logbook as the CO of 69 Squadron and sometimes as the CO of 2 PRU suggesting Air HQ considered Tennant in command of both. The reality for Adrian was he worked for Hugh Lloyd and, as was his habit, Lloyd communicated directly with Adrian, or through his SASO, by-passing 69 Squadron and its CO. And that's how Adrian often reported his results, directly to Air HQ.

His famed luck continued. Three days after the tragic loss of Willie Williams, Adrian was fired at by Allied ships approaching Malta from the south-east. Shortly afterwards the Hurricane patrol over the convoy, led by Sandy Rabagliati, Ta' Qali's wing leader, attacked the lone Beaufighter five times until the colours of the day were fired by the Beaufighter. Later, Adrian was reported as saying to Rabagliati he thought it rather a poor show as he only found one bullet hole in his aircraft's left aileron. Adrian often stayed with Christina, driving to and from Luqa in a battered old car, sometimes driving to work in pyjamas and slippers; that was perhaps taking his relaxed style of dress a little too far. His reputation was such that his idiosyncrasies were overlooked; what he 'delivered' was far more important. Few knew exactly where Adrian lived, although when he arrived at dispersal one morning after a night raid he told Corporal Cyril Wood, 'Some bastards blew us out of bed.'[6] He later told Luqa's adjutant the same thing.

Christina loved to dance, but as Adrian was a poor dancer he sometimes brought Johnnie Walker along to dance with her. This indicates something of the strength of their relationship. Johnnie said he never saw Adrian touch alcohol. Some said Adrian was boastful or a show-off, although these views rarely came from those who worked closely with him. Adrian was often disconcerted by the respect shown him and the fame that surrounded him. At the Union Club, Johnnie introduced Adrian to Lieutenant Commander Wanklyn, captain of HMS *Upholder*, the most successful RN submarine commander of the Second World War. Recently awarded the VC, he also held the DSO and the Distinguished Service Cross. When Wanklyn referred to Adrian as 'the great Warburton', Adrian was highly embarrassed.

There was another wind blowing that harsh winter, a wind of change. The previous autumn, a senior RAF officer from Britain was attached to Tedder's HQ in Egypt, advising on the latest bomber and fighter tactics. His name was Basil Embry. Tedder directed Embry to break his journey home in Malta to review fighter tactics and air defence. A Catalina flying boat delivered Embry in the early hours of 14 January. No sooner was he ashore than the sirens began their mournful wail. The guns were quickly in action and bombs began to fall. Lloyd asked Embry to observe the raid from Lascaris. Embry's first comment was the ops room was overcrowded, with spectators distracting the duty staff. They also contributed to the ventilation system being taxed beyond capacity so the air quickly became fouled, affecting everyone's efficiency. From that moment on, the Lascaris control room was placed out of bounds to all except those on duty.

Embry discussed tactics with the fighter squadrons and spent hours studying raid reporting and the methods used for fighter control. The problem centred on the performance of the Hurricanes, which came as no surprise to anyone. Even with their pilots at cockpit readiness, they could not gain sufficient height to engage the bombers before they were committed to fight the better performing Me109Fs, which often enjoyed an advantage of 5–10,000 feet. To gain enough height to engage the bombers, the Hurricanes had to climb away from the approaching enemy, posing a challenging problem of control. With no ground control interception radar, very

---

6. *Warburton's War*, by Tony Spooner, page 79.

good judgement was demanded of the controller, as well as a fair amount of luck. Many interceptions took place very close to Malta, often after bomb release. To then allow the fighters to attack meant forbidding the gunners to open fire.

The only solution was to intercept out to sea before the bombers reached their targets. This meant one thing and one thing only: Spitfires. Only they had the necessary performance to deal with the tactical situation, but there were no Spitfires to be had, not even in the Western Desert. Some in London thought Malta's airfields too small for Spitfires; Embry thought this nonsense. Nor did he agree Malta's topography was unsuitable for ground control interception radar and he suggested Lloyd signal the Air Ministry to ask for a siting team as a matter of urgency. Within a few days scientists arrived and selected an appropriate site.

Another of Embry's recommendations was for the Air Ministry to establish a group captain current in fighter operations to take charge of the Lascaris ops room. The new man would coordinate the fighter force along the same lines as sector commanders within Fighter Command in the Battle of Britain. At the time, there was no senior officer in Malta with up-to-date experience or knowledge of controlling fighters, and this was obvious both in the handling of the fighter force and in ops room procedures. 'The wing commander then in charge of fighter operations had recently been promoted from command of a squadron, and although he had a gallant fighting record, he had no experience of controlling from an operations room or of coordinating the activities of a number of squadrons.'[7] In Embry's view, the air defence of Malta was a sufficiently complex problem that if the RAF was to have any hope of air superiority, it needed a man of great experience. Lloyd was grateful for Embry's report and asked he discuss it in London. Embry delivered a copy of his report to the Director of Operations at the Air Ministry immediately on his return to London.[8] On the back of his staff visit, instigated by Tedder, the air battle of Malta began to turn, but it would take time. Now it was up to London.

What Embry witnessed was the opening round of Kesselring's plan. Having done his groundwork concerning the airfields and defences, Kesselring intended to gain air supremacy by making all three airfields inoperable. He also planned to knock out the Hurricanes either in the air or on the ground. His next step was to destroy all anti-aircraft gun emplacements to ensure a relatively trouble-free passage for gliders and paratroops to be positioned in Sicily. He was optimistic of early success, estimating six to eight weeks as sufficient to achieve his goal.

The increase in the Luftwaffe's missions was dramatic, with extremely well-planned and closely coordinated attacks. This marked the beginning of a long and bitter battle, ferocious in its intensity and of unparalleled duration. Although many Hurricanes were lost in air combat, it was the scale of losses on the ground which

---

7. *Mission Completed*, by ACM Sir Basil Embry, page 231.
8. *Review of Fighter Defences*, by Gp Capt Basil Embry.

demanded constant reinforcements. Over fifty were destroyed on the ground in January, which ended with only twenty-eight airworthy. With damage to hangars and repair facilities, it was more and more difficult to repair aircraft. The Hurricanes did their best, but their top speed was only slightly faster than the Ju88 bombers they were trying to intercept. These were heavily armoured and the .303 bullets of the Hurricanes had relatively little effect. In the same period that so many were lost, only twenty-three Axis aircraft were shot down. The RAF needed more cannon-armed fighters as well as something faster than Hurricanes: Spitfires.

The poor weather that winter also impacted to some extent on the Luftwaffe, but Lloyd was deeply worried by losses of aircraft on the ground despite the continuing efforts to build and rebuild shelters. He was always short of manpower to keep runways and taxiways operable, while at the same time trying to build more of the vitally important aircraft shelters. Unavoidably, manpower for these vital tasks had to be diverted from the equally important jobs of aircraft repair and maintenance. The total number of airmen stood at less than 4,000 and these were attempting to operate and maintain aircraft that in Britain would have demanded four times that number. Construction of the vital pens to protect aircraft had virtually come to a standstill as all available airmen were diverted onto trying to keep the runways and taxiways operational throughout the prolonged poor weather.

The airfields were now being subjected to an avalanche of bombs by day and night, with the night intruders flown in relays to try and catch aircraft on the ground. If the latter caught fire, and they frequently did, they formed a beacon for further raiders. Repairing the runways following these assaults was fraught, with delayed-action and anti-personnel 'butterfly' bombs making it extremely hazardous. Many personnel were killed and injured as more and more grounded aircraft were destroyed. This was the pattern for January, which brought 250 separate bombing raids involving 1,500 bombers. Under these constant attacks it was almost impossible to stop Axis ships getting through and this had an inevitable impact on the 8th Army's situation in North Africa. The bombing covered the sailing of two Axis convoys which reached Tripoli safely. The RAF was unable to do anything about them. A third enemy convoy was forced to turn back after coordinated strikes by Wellingtons, Swordfish and Albacores in very poor weather. The 24,000-ton *Victoria*, pearl of the Italian merchant fleet, was sunk.

The poor weather affected Sicily too, where the RAF Blenheims continued to press home their daytime raids against Axis airfields. On one mission, despite appalling weather, they destroyed thirty bombers. Wellingtons destroyed sixteen more at night. Hurricanes and Fulmars added their weight, intercepting Axis bombers at night as they returned to base after hitting Malta. These were important successes, but Kesselring still had some 800 aircraft available. Nor could the strikes against Axis airfields disguise the shortages being felt in Malta and Sir William

Dobbie was becoming increasingly concerned. Aviation fuel for the Hurricanes was short, as well as ammunition for the guns, which were often in constant action. There was also an increasing scarcity of food despite many attempts to resupply the island by ships making the hazardous journey on their own.

Rationing was increased, but this came a little late. Communal feeding kitchens were established in January. Further reductions in the ration were necessary and it may have been the case that the Maltese people were not sufficiently informed of the true situation early enough. Maybe this was another case of misplaced concern about how they would react or cope with the reality of what they faced.

Another convoy had to be attempted despite the weakened state of the RN in the Mediterranean after the losses of the Greek campaign and Crete evacuation. With the Luftwaffe firmly in control of all the approaches to Malta, any convoy was at serious risk. Three merchant ships were successful in making the passage from Alexandria in mid-January. But Malta's problems paled into insignificance when news began to emerge from North Africa where the situation swung very much in favour of Rommel, although he took a huge risk. The Axis ships that made it to Tripoli in January allowed Rommel to advance in force, initially on a reconnaissance. He met with surprising success and simply kept going. Benghazi fell to the Afrika Korps at the end of the month. Rommel kept going until he was stopped only thirty miles short of Tobruk, having advanced 250 miles in less than ten days.

When Rommel made his move he only had three days reserve of supplies but he captured vast quantities of fuel and equipment, thousands of guns and enough ammunition to sustain him for months. The impact of Rommel's success on everyone on Malta was devastating. It was particularly so for the bomber crews whose colleagues had given their lives trying to stop supplies reaching Tripoli. Almost overnight the Axis had another port available to them, Benghazi. At the same time, the Luftwaffe was far better placed to challenge convoys trying to reach Malta from the east and they successfully stopped a three-ship convoy from Alexandria. What occurred in North Africa was a catastrophe for Malta. In a broader context, however, there was some good news in that the Russians had stopped falling back and were now taking the offensive.

Back in London, there was much discussion about Embry's report and especially about how Spitfires could be delivered, and when; this aspect took weeks to resolve. In the meantime, focus turned toward a man who was already well-known, whose distinctive voice and controlling ability in the Battle of Britain was renowned throughout Fighter Command. He was none other than 'Woody' Woodhall, just ten years earlier a junior officer and Royal Marine pilot based in Malta. Now a group captain, his experience was unique. He served as a soldier in the trenches in the First World War – where he was seriously wounded – as a sailor operating from carriers, and was an experienced airman. All of this and he was no stranger to

Malta. In the Battle of Britain, Woody was Douglas Bader's Station Commander at Duxford; afterwards he was appointed OBE. In April 1941, he moved to Tangmere, where once again he was a first-class sector controller and station commander. By January 1942, he was in need of a rest, even his AOC agreed, saying he was the longest serving sector controller and station commander in the RAF. Woody was then contacted personally by the head of Fighter Command and asked if he was prepared to go to Malta at short notice. Embry's report had found fertile ground; there was no one better qualified to take on the newly created appointment of Group Captain Malta Fighters.

Woody realised his appointment would be no 'rest', but the briefings he received did not prepare him for the situation he found. Either he was misled, or the Air Ministry was in inexcusable ignorance of Malta's dire straits and the appalling situation Hugh Lloyd was trying to manage. Woody was told Malta's fighter defences were well organised, but needed someone with up-to-date experience to take charge and improve them. There were apparently five squadrons of Hurricanes on the island. In response to Woody's questions about serviceability, replacements and spares, the reply was vague. Serviceability was thought to be very high because the main workshops at Kalafrana had been augmented by various garages and workshops. Spares were being sent out by air and by submarine it was said, and a convoy could be expected in the near future. Spitfires would also be flown out from an aircraft carrier very shortly, he was told. Woody felt uneasy and wondered whether the Air Ministry was deliberately optimistic and vague, or whether they simply did not know the true situation. Given Embry's report, of which Woody was in ignorance, this vagueness about conditions must have been deliberate. If this was about rigorous application of the 'need to know' principle, then it was seriously misapplied. Woody would discover the true situation soon enough.

After a tortuous journey in a Sunderland flying boat at the beginning of February, Woody arrived at Kalafrana at first light. A raid was already in progress so the Sunderland held off until it was over. Met by Kalafrana's station commander, who invited him for breakfast, Woody was slightly perturbed by another raid taking place outside. His host assured him there was a chap on the roof who would tell them when to duck. This was Woody's introduction to air raid precautions in Malta, which seemed primitive, compared to those in Britain. His host told him, on such a small island, personnel only took cover when their immediate area was under attack otherwise essential work would come to a standstill. Woody later reflected this attitude was typical of the spirit on the island in troubled times.

Lloyd's first question of Woody was what he knew about fighters. 'I told him and his reply was, "they're all yours and God help you if you fail," … but I saw at once what a man he was.'[9] Nevertheless, it didn't prepare Woody for what he found at

---

9. *Soldier, Sailor & Airman Too*, by Woody Woodhall, page 168.

Ta' Qali. Not five squadrons enjoying good serviceability, but a grand total of seven aircraft with their pilots at readiness. This was the total available strength that day. Considerably shaken, Woody proceeded to Lascaris to take stock. There he found the plotters were civilians: wives and daughters of service personnel together with some Maltese girls. He described this unusual mix as extremely good. This was praise indeed from a man who knew how a fighter operations room should operate.

Woody discovered to his surprise that if those Hurricanes on standby on the ground were faced with a numerically superior force, the controller would often order them to disperse, i.e. to taxi to whatever 'shelter' they could find, stop their engines and wait until the attack was over. He considered this very bad for morale. That evening he called all the fighter pilots together and after a frank exchange of views, and having consumed the last of the Mess' beer, it was agreed that if four Hurricanes were available, they would always be scrambled. Anything less would leave one aircraft unprotected so they would be kept on the ground. The importance of always climbing into the sun before being vectored by the controller was also emphasised and this was a principle adopted whenever possible.

Jack Vowles' uniforms soon suffered under the harsh working conditions and, without an adequate supply system and no Station Clothing Stores to pop into to replace worn-out items, it was a case of having to 'make do and mend'. Little wonder Adrian was often seen in unusual, often bizarre attire, although perhaps he did take things to extreme. Once, when Jack reported for work, he was met at Luqa's main gate by an immaculately dressed RAF warrant officer. He was wearing a peaked service dress hat, khaki drill shorts and short-sleeved shirt, long stockings to the knees, and highly polished shoes. He was, of course, newly-arrived, but this did not stop him berating each passing airman for scruffy attire. That night someone stole the warrant officer's stockings. He was back at the gate the following morning but without stockings. He continued to berate passing airmen for their dress. That night someone stole his shoes. And so it continued. Within a week, the warrant officer looked like a veteran.

Jack's abiding memory of Malta was work, work, work – Malta's airmen got little time off, but nor did the soldiers and seamen. Many who flew in with temporary detachments found their stay permanent, given how desperate the RAF was to retain their skills. Some left when their detachment withdrew because of heavy losses. Most stayed. There were no rest tours for them, although some made use of the rest camp at St Paul's Bay. At other times, the best they could hope for was a few hours off to spend in Valletta. One free afternoon, Jack found himself going to Valletta 'by walk', as the Maltese described it. Approaching *Porta Reale*, he heard the click-clack of high-heeled shoes behind him. This was slightly unusual as most women wore sandals or walked barefoot. Having walked from Luqa, Jack was slightly out of breath and the lady overtook him walking briskly. She was very well dressed, wearing silk stockings with a black seam down the back. Jack thought she was Maltese. Soon afterwards, before getting to the bridge, something made Jack dive down onto the ground. He wasn't sure whether he heard aircraft or the whistle of bombs, or whether it was simply his well-tuned sixth sense, but he hugged the gutter for all he was worth. Bombs exploded nearby. When he got up, he looked ahead and said to himself, 'oh dear'. The smartly dressed lady was very obviously dead. He walked over to her and gently rearranged her clothing, pulling her dress down to cover her legs, and he placed her handbag beneath her head. There was nothing else he could do. Under the bridge, three horses also lay dead. Jack couldn't allow himself to think for too long about what happened, it was over, done with; there was no future in thinking about it. He continued into Valletta 'by walk', perhaps a little more slowly.

One day, when Jack was in his first-floor accommodation with one of his mates, there was the unmistakable sound of bombs falling nearby. They were getting closer. Jack's friend ran onto the balcony and promptly jumped to the ground below; he was followed shortly afterwards by Jack. Their barrack room was destroyed. Jack's lucky escapes were far from over.

On 13 February, Adrian's earlier favourite Maryland, AR733, flew its last trip in the hands of Terry Channon. Fortuitously, Terry had two gunners. Attacked only eight miles off Malta's southern coast, one gunner was killed by the first burst from one of two Me109s and the aircraft was seriously damaged. The other gunner, Sergeant R.J. Watson, who was also wounded in several places, managed to move his dead comrade and fired at the attacking fighters, causing one to catch fire. Watson then threw out items that were ablaze. He sustained severe burns extinguishing his dead colleague's burning clothing and a fire in the bomb bay. He was barely conscious when Channon brought the badly damaged AR733 back for a wheels-up landing.[10] Jack was on duty that afternoon and filmed the crash landing. Photographs were taken of the wreck and many expressed astonishment at the number of bullet holes, more than sixty. Sergeant Watson was awarded an immediate DFM. Jack later recalled a brief conversation he had with Adrian alongside AR733. 'How is it?' asked Adrian.

'It won't ever fly again,' said Jack.

Adrian took off soon afterwards in his Beaufighter on a mission to Taranto. He was accompanied by Corporal Ron Hadden. Most entries in squadron ORBs are brief, rarely covering two or three lines of abbreviated notes. The entry for Adrian's flight covers nine lines. It describes how he obtained photographs of two battleships, nine submarines, two destroyers, one torpedo boat, a hospital ship and a merchant ship. He also reported visually on four battleships, four cruisers, six to eight destroyers and nine merchant ships. The Beaufighter was subjected to intense ground fire

10. *Marylands over Malta*, by Brian Cull and Frederick Galea, pages 118–9.

from Taranto and the port engine had to be shut down owing to oil failure. They were then chased by four Macchi C.202 fighters, which they successfully evaded. Adrian then proceeded to Messina on one engine and reported the presence of three cruisers, four destroyers and five merchant vessels. At Messina they were fired at by heavy guns. On the way home he also spotted another hospital ship ten miles south of Reggio di Calabria.

Ron later said it took Adrian two attempts to penetrate Taranto harbour on a day of particularly low cloud. Once inside, he flew three runs at fifty feet despite intense flak which damaged the aircraft and caused it to bounce around. As a result, the armour-plated doors dividing the front cockpit from Ron's position were blown open. Adrian was sitting calmly with a cigarette stuck in the corner of his mouth. His elbows were propped up on the sides of the cockpit and he had his beloved RAF service dress hat pulled over his flying helmet. By this stage one engine had already been damaged and the other was running hot. Little wonder Adrian was Hugh Lloyd's recce pilot of choice.

On top of night bombing, Malta was also subject to regular night-time nuisance raids, all of which followed a similar pattern. Two Me109s would patrol a few miles off Malta before returning to base. They were immediately replaced by two more which would repeat the performance and this continued throughout the night. This resulted in wearying work for the Lascaris staff, especially the plotters, as any one of these nuisance raids could easily turn into an actual bombing raid. The pattern of attacks set throughout January continued into February, by which time some of the RAF's most experienced fighter pilots were lost. Tamara remembered the afternoon of 15 February well; her friend Aida wanted Tamara to go with her to the Regent Cinema in Valletta to see *North West Mounted Police*, but Tamara had seen the film so they didn't go. A direct hit on the cinema killed twenty-five servicemen and twenty-six civilians. A few had miraculous escapes. 'A sailor, who was at the bar of the picture-house at the time, was rescued after three days gloriously drunk. He was very surprised when they told him what had happened.... That particular raid did a lot of damage to Valletta and roused the Maltese to a frenzy of hatred against the Germans, for it was carried out in broad daylight and was another instance of wilful destruction of civilian property.'[11]

That morning the RAF had twenty-six Hurricanes; by the day's end there were eleven. The raids were so frequent it proved impossible to land, refuel and rearm before the next raid hit. The Hurricanes could manoeuvre extremely well, out-turning the Me109s with ease, but they were outclassed in terms of speed and firepower. They had had their day, yet their pilots continued to try and come to terms with their enemy. And Lloyd had no choice but to continue to scramble his

11. *Women of Malta*, by Frederick Galea, page 103.

obsolete fighters and their heroic pilots, knowing many were going to their deaths. He realised more than anyone when the Hurricanes were out of the battle, the RAF had nothing left; the Luftwaffe would dominate from the sky whatever was happening on the ground. Command can be a lonely place, but perhaps not as lonely as the cockpit of an outclassed fighter well past its best.

The number of service personnel on Malta had increased significantly, but they were out of balance. There were over 26,000 soldiers, of whom 6,000 served the artillery; the rest were infantrymen. With only 4,000 airmen employed on diverse tasks, little wonder maintenance, overhaul and repair fell well behind schedule, denuding even further the number of available aircraft. On top of everything else, every night, many of these same airmen were on duty dealing with the aircraft being ferried through Malta to Egypt to support the fighting in the desert. The solution to the manpower crisis came with the arrival of Major General Daniel Beak, VC, who took over command of the army as GOC. Another change occurred with Vice Admiral Ralph Leatham taking over from Vice Admiral Ford.

Poor weather continued into February, which thankfully resulted in a slackening off in raids. Even so, with, on average, two aircraft destroyed on the ground each day it would not take long before the island was defenceless. Hugh Lloyd appealed to General Beak for help, especially with regard to repairing the landing strips and building bombproof dispersal pens. Beak got on well with Lloyd from the moment he arrived and his response was immediate. He very quickly provided his infantrymen without which, at such a critical time, the RAF faced disaster. Each airfield was allocated two regiments. From that moment on, there were never less than 1,500 soldiers working on the airfields and sometimes as many as 3,000. Lloyd admitted, 'I'd have been out of business but for the soldiers.'[12] They were supported by civilians, officers, clerks, storemen and aircrew, by anyone who had a few hours to offer, regardless of the enemy or the weather. Gradually the work came together, the result of jointery at its very best, with soldiers, sailors and airmen supported by Maltese civilians and Maltese police.

Woody was impressed by Lloyd's leadership and considered him, 'a born leader and, more than any other man, I consider that he saved Malta in her darkest days. He worked all his subordinates hard, very hard, but he worked himself harder still. Wherever trouble was worst, there he would be found encouraging, helping and directing.'[13] Lloyd's piercing eyes seemed to take in everything, but there was always a twinkle lurking behind them. Always supportive of subordinates if they did their job, he was ruthless with those who did not, or who shirked their responsibilities. He led by personal example and was so quickly on the spot when one of his airfields was being bombed, many expected a raid as soon as he arrived. Woody saw Lloyd's

---

12. *The Air Battle of Malta*, by the Ministry of Information, page 46.
13. *Soldier, Sailor & Airman Too*, by Woody Woodhall, page 174.

distress when he noted how quickly some personnel took to their shelters. At the time, Section Officer Aileen Morris, MBE, a WAAF officer, was on attachment at Lascaris to organise the radio interception service known as Y Service. Lloyd asked her if she was afraid of bombing and she quite naturally said yes. Lloyd said so was he, but asked if she was willing to accompany him and try something out. During the next bombing raid on Luqa, the AOC and Aileen walked calmly up and down the tarmac. Their example was not lost on others.

Nevertheless, Hugh Lloyd recognised personnel serving in exposed positions on the airfields deserved better warning of raids. With the sirens warning of enemy aircraft within thirty-five miles of the island, he now established a system of flag warnings for the airfields similar to those used in the Dockyard. A red flag for example, hoisted prominently at Luqa or Ta' Qali, showed the enemy was making for that particular target. This was augmented by an officer with a portable radio posted on top of the Governor's Palace, which afforded a view over much of the island. He warned both the ops room and the fighters of the location of enemy aircraft, often remaining at his post until he actually saw bombs leaving the aircraft. He would then say he was getting down, quickly. Later, Woody established five posts along the lines of the Observer Corps. Manned in the main by Maltese university students locally enlisted in the RAF, they gave valuable service.

In late February, Tamara and her friend Aida Kelly made their 'escape' to the tranquil island of Gozo for three days leave. There was no bombing and plentiful simple food. It was an idyllic break away from the horrors of war and they returned rested and ready to take another six months of raids without flinching. It was obvious when they got back that Malta had had an awful time. Tamara described the number of raids at this time, and their violence, as unbelievable. Damage was widespread and casualties high. 'We went back to the usual routine. Raids, work, drinking parties to well past midnight. I don't know how we stood the pace, especially as rations were getting smaller and smaller.'[14]

The defending Hurricanes struggled valiantly on, but the few which were scrambled were no match for the Me109s and the fearful odds. Losses also continued on the ground. Often there were no available fighters at all and total reliance fell upon the guns. The long-awaited Spitfire supply was in hand, but the plans were subject to the most appalling bungling.

For the Lascaris plotters working the night shift, sleep became a rationed luxury because of the regular daylight raids. Nor were the girls immune either. Marigold Fletcher's home was destroyed when she was on duty. Patricia Cameron, an 18-year-old plotter, was killed in a bombing raid and her mother injured. Her elder sister Irene, also a plotter, was also hurt, but was back at work within days. In

---

14. *Women of Malta*, by Frederick Galea, page 105.

what spare time Irene had, she was also a member of the *Raffians*, sometimes on the same bill as the *Whizz-Bangs*, under the overall name of the *Fly Gang*. Despite her Lascaris duties, Christina also made the occasional guest appearance on stage with her friends. In 1942, one critic said their latest show was perhaps the best of all and a tribute to everyone's versatility. By then, after two years of constant performances, the *Whizz-Bangs* remained as popular and entertaining as ever.

In February, aircraft losses on the ground dropped from the previous month's high of twenty-eight to eleven, and in March that number dropped to nine, even though the raids were heavier than ever. At about the same time, another convoy attempted to get through from Alexandria, but it was forced to turn back by heavy attacks. The situation on the island was becoming very serious. Elsewhere for Britain, there was more bad news: Singapore fell.

General Dobbie submitted a gloomy telegram to London reporting some deterioration in morale and a critical point had been reached. London considered without further significant replenishment, operations from Malta would cease after the end of June. Churchill was extremely anxious. With the loss of Singapore and the surrender of its 75,000 strong garrison, he did not wish to contemplate the possible loss of Malta.

Chapter Twelve

Desperation

It had been fairly quiet since D Watch took over. They were all at their places, waiting. It was the waiting that often got to them, the tension. They all knew what to expect. Suddenly, the first messages would be heard in their earphones and the plots would appear. Everyone would then spring into action. But not yet, all was still quiet. The early morning 'hate' delivered by the Eyeties from on high was widely scattered. Any hits were called 'lucky' hits as the bombs went almost anywhere. It was hardly 'lucky' if it happened to be your location. There were often far more 'unlucky' hits on someone's home, or on a packed shelter. The pride of the Regia Aeronautica soon 'legged it' home for coffee and Chianti.

That took place long before Christina left her flat in Floriana, their flat. Adrian had left early, before she was awake. He always tried not to disturb her. Sometimes he didn't even fully dress before leaving; he was so considerate when she was tired, as she often was these days. He must be quite a sight sometimes when he got to Luqa. She smiled at the thought.

It was the siren that awakened her. It always did, but she didn't run down those eighty-eight stairs to the shelter like a mad thing, as she had in the past. That would probably happen again she realised, but not today. Had it really been a year and a half since she ran helter-skelter downstairs for the very first time? How quickly time had passed, and how much had happened since. She had no doubt about the identity of the early morning attackers; the Italians had a set routine. Her actions would have been different if they were Germans. Was she getting just a little blasé? She knew they were back en masse.

As she looked at the empty plot she knew he was airborne. Sometimes she actually moved his counter across the table as he headed north until Malta's radars could no longer see him. She had then removed him from the plot. She always hated doing that, it seemed terribly final. She desperately feared she would do that and that would be it. They had lost so many friends, and their recce aircraft had suffered terribly recently. They took such risks to get their photos, he took such risks. He laughed at her worries and said he was immune. 'Didn't you know about Warby's luck?' he said. But she still worried and hoped and prayed. Why had he been brought back? Couldn't he be posted away again even though it meant separation? Would he forget her and move on? She didn't care, she loved him too much, she wanted him to live and she doubted he would if he kept doing his sort of job. He said he was safer in the air, that there were greater risks on the ground where she was. She couldn't argue much with that, but she couldn't help but worry.

Everyone said he was too valuable; that's why he'd been brought back, that he was the one who always came back with the goods. And he did. Air Vice-Marshal Lloyd often happened to be around when he was due back, hovering, taking everything in while holding his long cigarette holder to one side. Did he actually smoke, she wondered? She hadn't actually seen him. She wondered if the cigarette holder was just something to make him stand out, the AOC, the man in charge, the man who held other's lives in the palm of his hand, the man who held her Warby's life in the palm of his hand.

Did Lloyd know about them, she thought, know they were living together? Once, when she was looking at him, it was as if he sensed her gaze and turned to look directly at her. He simply nodded. No smile, just a nod to one of his team. He must know, she thought, how could he not? There were so few secrets down here in the hole. He can't have minded, he could easily have put a stop to it and order him to live at Luqa with the rest. Maybe Hugh Pughe, as they called him, actually approved. He certainly gave Warby a lot of rope. Some of the clothes Warby now wore when he went flying were quite outrageous. He just laughed, but he could look so smart in his service dress uniform. But, please, please, sir, please send him away again, this time somewhere far away from Malta.

Things were happening. Something was beginning to build, messages were coming in and the girls were assembling the aircraft symbols. Christina was standing at one side of the plotting table wearing her headphones. Soon she too began to receive messages from the filter room. Aircraft – hostile aircraft – were forming up over Sicily. Things were different now the Germans were back.

She was always amazed by the calm voices that came through her headphones. Surely they must be as apprehensive as she was, but they sounded so relaxed. Maybe she sounded calm too, but often it was a mask; inside she sometimes felt like a jelly. Now the plots were moving south, approaching the island. She used her long stick, pushing out the small arrow-shaped blocks to grid positions, first in Harry and then in Nuts. She tracked the course of each of the raids, updating the information on the block as necessary. They did this for both friendly and hostile aircraft; those she was moving now were hostile and there were lots of them, bombers and fighters.

On the shelf, the 'chaps-in-the-gods', as they called the senior controller and his team, were getting ready for action, sitting high above the plotting table in the gallery, looking down as the picture below began to take shape. Then they would make their decisions. The senior controller on D Watch was talking rapidly to his right-hand man, Ops B. How on earth could Ops B listen in one ear and talk to Luqa or Ta' Qali or Hal Far at the same time? Had he already relayed that all-important word 'scramble' to the squadrons? She would know soon. When it was all over it was Ops B who had to do the boring bit, write up the operations log. She had seen the log often, all written in pencil in a hardback book, recording in fine detail, a minute–by–minute account of the air battle of Malta.

Other girls were now moving friendly plots as fighters scrambled. That was reassuring. Sometimes there had not been a single fighter to meet the hordes from the north. She noticed the AOC was up there now, his cigarette holder at the ready, standing quietly behind the senior controller. He wouldn't interfere, that wasn't his style. He was just there, supporting, reassuring. It almost looked as if he was holding a conductor's baton, looking at his orchestra, getting ready for the opening notes. In a way, he was. She found herself asking if all senior RAF officers had some sort of affectation like the cigarette holder. Come on girl; concentrate on the plotting table and the voice in your ear. Then she began to repeat the words she heard in her headset, through her microphone to the senior controller.

'Guns' – the gunnery liaison officer – was now also busy on the shelf. He was new, an army captain as usual. She hadn't seen him before, although he seemed to know his business. The air raid warning had sounded long ago and the signal flags she knew so well would be flying above the *Auberge de Castille*. The shelters would be full. And the guns would be busy high above their secret world. Bombs would be falling now, but not too close to cause any white dust to descend on them from the roof of the cave. They only rarely wore their tin hats. At least hers would protect her hair. It was underneath the plotting table, along with the bag containing her gas-mask, and her make-up. Make-up! That was another laugh these days, but she always tried to look her best. 'Guns' was becoming quite animated now, talking to the artillery. They needed to know where our fighters were; we couldn't afford to lose any of our precious boys to our own guns. But someone on the airfields was catching it. That's where the bombers were focused these days.

The plots began to converge, soon they would merge. Then it was up to the fighter boys. The senior controller was a Hurricane pilot, having a 'rest'. It was his job to interpret the plot, make the decision about when to scramble his handful of fighters and where to position them, and at what height, to give them the very best chance of a successful interception. Unlike some controllers who used first names, he stuck to the correct R/T procedure when he spoke to the fighter leader. Not that it mattered a great deal as they all seemed to recognise one another's voices. There was a familiarity that came across on the radio – respect.

There was never a dull moment in the control room when things were like this, but she and the other girls had to pay careful attention to what was going on and to listen carefully for the instructions in their headsets from the filter room. They all relaxed slightly when they heard the words 'Tally-Ho', then it was up to the boys. That's when the girls looked at one another and crossed their fingers and prayed a little. They were such brave boys and they were always against such awful odds. Yes, there were thrills when an interception worked like clockwork, but there were also some terrible shocks when you heard on the radio one of ours had 'bought it' or was 'going in.' So and so had been 'bumped' they would later say. All the fighter boys realised their chances of surviving a tour in Malta were very remote indeed; that was the awful truth.

The plots moved north again and our fighters headed for home, some of them damaged no doubt, and some of the pilots hurt. It was over. Perhaps Warby was right that the safest place for him when all hell was breaking loose over Malta and its precious airfields was far away in sunny Italy taking photographs. She knew what he did was no sinecure: 69 Squadron's losses demonstrated that.

She took the call on her headphones from the filter room and then pushed a new plot onto the table, a single aircraft. It was a friendly, heading south into H for Harry. She sensed it was him, she just knew it. Soon he called up on the radio: Stallion Two-Seven. That confirmed it. The senior controller answered in his normal calm manner. But there was another plot, only a few miles behind and it was a hostile. They were fighters. She hoped beyond hope they were Eyeties. He could outrun the best old Benito had, provided his faithful aircraft wasn't damaged. But his aircraft was often damaged. And they weren't Eyeties either were they? They were Germans, Me109s, and they were getting closer, ever closer. She felt the blood draining from her face but she had to stay calm, be professional regardless; others counted on her and looked up to her too. It was only a few miles from the Sicilian coast to safety, but it seemed to take forever. There was little they could do or say. He was descending, trying to gain more speed; he must have known he was being chased. Then the senior controller spoke once more:

'Look out, Stallion Two-Seven, two 109s on your tail.'

He didn't acknowledge; he would have his hands full, trying to get every possible knot out of his aircraft; twisting his head left and right to check if either of his assailants was within range for that killing shot. As he closed the island, Christina continued to plot his course trying not to think too much, just getting on with her job. He was now in N for Nuts. She also plotted the course of the two Messerschmitts. They were dangerously close. Then all went silent in the Ops Room; a deadly hush as all eyes were focused on the table. It was as if they were all up there with him. The hostile and friendly plots merged. Then Christina heard words she hoped never to hear in her headphones:

'Plot on Stallion Two-Seven faded.'

Her heart thumped. But she was determined not to show the tension she felt inside.

'Plot on Stallion Two-Seven faded,' she repeated to the controller.

The Senior Controller's face was grim, fearing the worst. Christina was having the utmost difficulty in carrying on. But she had to. Personal feelings didn't count in this game. There were no further plots on Stallion Two-Seven, only on the Me109s. She knew what that meant. Her Warby had been 'bumped'. It was the end.

Five minutes later a message came from Luqa airfield:

'Stallion Two-Seven landed safely.'

He had flown in so low the radar stations were unable to detect his aircraft; he had to stop the pursuing 109s getting into a killing position. I bet he'll laugh about the worry he had caused, Christina thought. And he did.

'Didn't they know about Warby's luck?' he said.[1]

The first attempt to deliver Spitfires was made in February. Lloyd's urgent requests, supported by Embry's recommendations, were at last acted upon. The operation was an abject failure. The launch from HMS *Eagle* was abandoned desperately late in the day after a fault was discovered in the Spitfires untested overload fuel tanks. This appalling error resulted in the fleet returning to Gibraltar with a precious carrier having been needlessly placed at risk in waters that now washed over *Ark Royal*. The failure showed the RAF in a very poor light.

In anticipation of the Spitfires' arrival, a few battle-hardened pilots were flown in. These included the able Canadian, Stan Turner, and Laddie Lucas, a Fleet Street journalist before the war. As they walked from the jetty at Kalafrana, the siren sounded. Within minutes they saw four antiquated Hurricanes desperately trying to climb through the early morning haze. That was the sum total of Malta's fighter defence that morning. Circling high above the lumbering machines were a dozen or more cannon-armed Me109Fs. Soon they swept down fast from their lofty perch, their characteristic 'blue note' an ominous precursor of what was to follow. It was a chilling spectacle for the new arrivals. Somehow they would have to mount a defence with those clapped-out Hurricanes for another month. Turner made his views plain within days of arriving: 'Either sir,' he said to Lloyd, 'we get the Spitfires here within days, not weeks, or we're done. That's it.'[2]

Lessons appeared to have been learnt from the first embarrassing attempt and the beginning of March saw fifteen Spitfires safely delivered. They were Mark Vbs armed with two cannons and four machine guns – exactly the mark of Spitfire needed and a match for the Me109Fs. It was impossible, however, to keep *Eagle's* movements hidden from prying 'neutral' Spanish eyes. Once at sea between Vichy French territory to the north and south, it was not difficult for the Axis to chart the carrier's progress. Kesselring had ample time to plan. His recce aircraft also spotted the new and improved dispersals, although they proved extremely difficult to destroy, only a direct hit had the desired effect. Smiling Albert therefore turned his attention to the landing strips themselves to make it impossible for any RAF aircraft to use them. Once again, the contribution of General Beak's soldiers was vital. As soon as a raid was over, up to a thousand men swarmed onto the airfields armed with

1. *Carve Malta on my heart and other wartime stories*, by Frederick Galea, page 55.
2. *Malta, The Thorn in Rommel's Side*, Laddie Lucas, page 47.

buckets and spades, filling in the craters and doing their best to level the surfaces. The Luftwaffe kept at its task, losing many aircraft. The pounding of the airfields went on and on, day and night, making aircraft maintenance a nightmare. One comment that did the rounds was, 'yesterday's all-clear lasted all of ten minutes'.

Two weeks later, nine more Spitfires arrived from *Eagle* and a few days later, another seven. But a single squadron of Spitfires did not make a Maltese summer, or even a spring. In theory, the RAF had thirty-one Spitfires by the end of March; the reality was very different. Despite the deliveries themselves being successful, the operation was poor and lacked coordination. The aircraft should have been launched to arrive as early in the day as possible; they were not. They should have arrived serviceable and combat capable; they were not. They should have been met by a new pilot who could scramble as soon as refuelling and rearmament were complete. They were, but those Spitfires that arrived serviceable were not combat ready until significant work on them took place. There were also not enough bombproof shelters available, each with a team of engineers and a replacement pilot ready, from the moment each aircraft landed. These tasks were far from easy to accomplish when the airfields were actually being bombed, but there were nevertheless too many failures concerning the whole operation. As a result only a handful of Spitfires were able to take to the air and they were not enough to make the slightest difference.

On top of that, within days, those Spitfires not destroyed by bombing were grounded through lack of spares. And where were the specialist Spitfire ground crew? It was a far more complex aircraft than the Hurricane. A Hurricane, for example, could have its wings removed and still be pushed or towed, as the main wheels were attached to the aircraft's fuselage. The Spitfire's main wheels were wing-mounted, so moving a damaged aircraft was a much more difficult affair.

Spitfires in far greater numbers were needed, but so were spares, skilled Spitfire airmen and a far slicker organisation on the ground. Aircraft delivered in dribs and drabs were not the answer. They needed to be delivered in strength so they could have an immediate impact and begin to create a favourable air situation. In the meantime, Lloyd was left with no alternative. He had to ask his courageous Hurricane pilots in their worn-out aircraft to hold the line.

In an attempt to run the remaining Hurricanes out of fuel, Kesselring sent over dozens of fighters in advance of the bombers to lure the Hurricanes into the air. After the main bombing raid, he then sent further fighters to try and catch the Hurricanes at their most vulnerable, coming into land, very short of fuel and with little ammunition. In one week, eight Hurricanes were destroyed in this way, with many others damaged. Others had to be written-off after crash landing out of fuel. The RAF could do little to stop the Luftwaffe and it was obvious to everyone the bombing was moving toward a climax. A raid in late March scored a direct hit on the *Point de Vue* Hotel, Rabat, which was in use as an RAF Officers' Mess. Five pilots and an intelligence officer were killed. By then only eleven Hurricanes were left. At the end of the month, a small reinforcement of twelve got through from Egypt. This number, especially of Hurricanes, could never save Malta, but every little helped.

Outnumbered by about twenty to one, the RAF's air defences were almost at breaking point, but they held. Kesselring was well behind schedule. It is interesting to speculate on what would have happened if the attacks on the airfields had continued. At best the RAF would have been able to hold out for another week, perhaps two, but at the moment of most serious weakness, Kesselring switched tactics and ordered the Luftwaffe to target Grand Harbour, where prizes just arrived from Egypt awaited.

More could and should have been done in London to get many more Spitfires out to Malta and much earlier. In the first three months of 1942, Britain experienced only 151 daylight enemy sorties, a substantial proportion of which were reconnaissance flights involving a single aircraft. Yet it was defended by dozens of Spitfire squadrons. Between February and April, 17,000 Axis sorties were flown against Malta, defended at best by three squadrons whose total serviceability never exceeded twenty-six aircraft on any one day. In those months, with all the heat turned on Malta, Churchill considered the island worn down and pressed to the last gasp. He intervened directly, seeking a solution for the 'dribs and drabs' by looking across the Atlantic.

The early months of 1942 were desperate for anyone trying to operate from Malta's airfields. For 69 Squadron, having lost their squadron commander in January, there were changes of command, other losses and more Marylands damaged or destroyed on the ground. With so few Marylands available, many fitters were attached to other squadrons. Jack Vowles spent a lot of time servicing the torpedo-carrying Wellingtons which operated mostly at night. For a time an attempt was made to operate them from Ta' Qali, but it was much too small and they returned to Luqa. Jack changed accommodation often and spent various periods in what was referred to as the millionaire's house at Ta' Qali and another near the submarine base on Manoel Island. Having been bombed out of there, he ended up back at the Poor House.

A new recce aircraft arrived on 7 March, one which from now on would make a major contribution to Malta's war. It was a PR Spitfire and it landed at Ta' Qali on its way to Egypt, or so its pilot, New Zealander Harry Coldbeck, thought. He was delighted to be met by his friend Laddie Lucas. It came as a shock to Harry, but didn't surprise anyone else, when Hugh Lloyd commandeered both the aircraft and its pilot for service at Luqa. Nominally, Harry became part of 69 Squadron, but was left very much to his own devices. He worked in a tiny office with the intelligence staff and went largely unacknowledged by 69 Squadron or Air HQ. In fact, Harry didn't know where 69 Squadron's offices actually were and he just got on with his job as best he could. In fairness, there wasn't a great deal left of 69 Squadron by then.

March saw a change in the command arrangements. Ever since Sir William Dobbie's appointment, he had reported to separate departments in London. At the beginning of March, he was placed directly under the control of the Middle East C-in-Cs. At the same time, Admiral Henry Harwood succeeded Cunningham as C-in-C Mediterranean. With General Auchinleck under pressure in Egypt to mount an offensive, it fell to Air Marshal Tedder to focus on Malta. London was quick to point out there was no lack of confidence in General Dobbie, referring to his inspirational leadership, but there was an undercurrent of tension at a senior level in Malta, principally between Dobbie and Lloyd. This would soon surface.

Christina was always desperate for sleep. One night, when she was particularly weary, she determined to enjoy a double ration. Wearing her favourite nightgown made from the 'blitzed' parachute given her by Warby, she intended to sleep through whatever the Luftwaffe threw at them. But she had tempted the devil and awoke with a terrific start to the roar of aircraft, gunfire and the sound of crashing masonry. After one tremendous explosion, her bedroom door burst open and the bedroom window splintered into fragments. The whole building rocked as if it were going to collapse. Christina's only thought was to run for it, to get out of the place before it caved in and crushed her to death. 'I rushed out of the flat and flew down those eighty-eight steps. When at last I reached the hall I paused for a few minutes. The firing had ceased; perhaps the raid was over. Then with a terrific roar, the harbour anti-aircraft guns opened up – the battle was on again.

'The shelter, I must make for the ERA shelter. I ran out into the street and stood there absolutely dazed, shrapnel dropping all round. Should I run on or go back?

'"Quick, miss, come in here," a voice called out.

'It belonged to a soldier who was sheltering in the hall of the next door flat. I dashed in and stood beside him, shivering with cold (I refused to call it fear), blissfully unaware that all I had on was my transparent nightie. But the soldier was very gallant. He took off his greatcoat and army boots and made me get into them. Then he offered me a cigarette and we saw the rest of the raid out together.

'When the all-clear sounded we viewed the damage around us. The corner flat, two doors away from mine, had been hit and the coping stone lay in pieces on the pavement. Later that afternoon Warby arrived breathlessly at my flat.

'"Was I worried," he said. "They told me when I landed it was your flat that had been hit."

'Still suffering from the effects of shock, I sobbed out my story. But Warby never had time for tears. Seeing that my emotions were getting the better of me, he said sharply, "You mean to tell me that you 'ran' all the way down those stairs in your nightie?"

'I nodded. "That was a very silly thing to do, wasn't it? You should have baled out of the window. You had your parachute on."

'Not long after that incident Warby was posted on temporary special duties to Egypt. I was sorry to see him go, but on the other hand I was relieved. Without

Plate 17. Air Vice-Marshal Hugh Lloyd, Air Officer Commanding (Mediterranean), 1941. '*I found him … the personification of aggression…. While raiders circled above … he made the aerodrome a lighted target to help us, and stood on the runway in the open while flares hung overhead and the bombs fell, making every effort to bring his aircraft safely down.*' (Patrick Gibbs)

Plate 18. '*a born leader and more than any other man, I consider he saved Malta in her darkest days.*' (Woody Woodhall). Signed photograph of Hugh Lloyd with his characteristic cigarette holder.

Plate 19. View from 'the shelf' of the main ops room of No 8 Sector Operations Room Lascaris.

Plate 20. The '*chaps-in-the-gods*'. (Christina Ratcliffe)

Plate 21. '*Bright sunlight lends an added dignity to the bombed streets and squares of Valletta through which Christina is walking. And on her way to the shops she meets an officer friend.*' (*Times of Malta*). Christina talking to Cecil Roche, October 1942.

Plate 22. '*Bombs bursting on Valletta, left-hand side. Others bursting by the harbour and Marsa Creek on the right. Distance 2¼ miles.*' (Jack Vowles)

Plate 23. *'Part of Malta's Harbour Barrage during an attack on the harbour Dec 18. Each one of those black puffs is worth about £10 to £15.'* (Jack Vowles)

Plate 24. *'Taken four minutes later. Dust from bomb explosions can be seen to the left and right of the hut. Harbour 3½ mls away.'* (Jack Vowles)

Plate 25. *'This one got a little closer than we expected; 45 yards away HE bombs being used.'* (Jack Vowles)

Plate 26. '*On reaching Kingsgate, tears sprang to our eyes. The Opera House, dear to every Maltese heart, had received a direct hit during the evening raid of 7 April. The woodwork was burning fiercely, charred or still-burning bits of material from the stage curtains were falling in the street. People were paralysed with grief and just stood there with bewildered faces.*' (Tamara Marks)

Plate 27. Life goes on, places to go.

Plate 28 . SS *Talabot* burns. Floriana is beneath the smoke.

Plate 29. Looking toward a devastated Senglea from Floriana. '*The destruction that greeted our eyes was appalling, boulders everywhere blocking our path, half-hanging balconies at dangerous angles.... One street of about fifty houses had been razed to the ground.*' (Tamara Marks). The damaged Vilhena Terrace is on the right.

Plate 30. Vincenti Buildings, Floriana, in the summer 1942. '*All around* Pietro Floriani Street, *only Christina's house was standing. "Standing" is a euphemism ... it looked more like the Leaning Tower of Pisa than the real thing itself. There were four small craters in front of the door and a couple more round the corner. I could not imagine why Christina still insisted on living in it.*' (Tamara Marks)

Plate 31. St Publius' Church Floriana after a bombing raid.

Plate 32. The paraffin queue.

Plate 33. Queuing for food outside the Victory Kitchens in Britannia Street, Valletta.

Plate 34. Christina using a coupon for her daily meal at the Britannia Street VK, October 1942.

Plate 35. Christina in front of the Britannia Street VK, October 1942.

Plate 36. Members of the RAF *Fly Gang* with Christina.

Plate 37. Christina collecting water, October 1942. The young girl is called Lisa and was the daughter of a Valletta neighbour.

Plate 38. Flight Lieutenant Adrian Warburton. Note the 'flying boot' emblem on his left breast pocket. This was unofficially awarded to crews who crashed in the desert and walked out.

Plate 39. Christina on the Valletta-Sliema ferry. This photograph, signed '*Christina, Fighter Control RAF*' is displayed in the Club Bar of the Phoenicia Hotel in Floriana.

Plate 40. Having breakfast in bed. This photograph is also displayed in the Club Bar of the Phoenicia.

Plate 41. Squadron Leader Adrian Warburton between August and November 1942.

Plate 42. *'The famous AR733; a story I can't write here. But take a close look and try and think how it flew so full of holes.'* (Jack Vowles). Sgt Bob Watson, a WOp/AG, was awarded an immediate DFM for gallantry for his actions prior to the crash landing.

Plate 43. Beaufighter *'A for Apple TK 227 Sqn 1943 1 ship 4 kites.'* (Jack Vowles). It was an action by three aircraft of 227 Sqn on 14 October 1942 with which this story opened. Adrian's response as events unfolded contributed to the award of his third DFC. He also flew the unarmed recce variant of the Beaufighter from November 1941 until March 1942.

Plate 44. *'The most valuable pilot in the RAF'* (Lord Tedder) and *'Christina of George Cross Island.'* (*Times of Malta*). Adrian and Christina on the roof of her Valletta apartment block, November 1942. This is the only photograph known to exist showing them together.

Plate 45. Adrian on the roof of Christina's Valletta apartment block, November 1942.

Plate 46. 'Young Jack'; Jack Vowles sitting on the wing of a captured Me109.

Plate 47. Corporal Jack Vowles.

Plate 48. Photo-reconnaissance Spitfire; similar to those flown by Adrian between August 1942 and October 1943.

Plate 49. P-38 Lightning. This is a fighter variant of the type in which Adrian was lost. Note the port engine has been shut down and the propeller feathered. The recce variant of the P-38 suffered regular engine failures. Could such a failure have had an impact on Adrian's last flight?

Plate 50. P-38F5b Lightning serial number 42-67325 at Mount Farm. This is the actual aircraft in which Adrian met his death.

Plate 51. The crash site near Egling-an-der Paar, Bavaria, 12 April 1944.

Plate 52. Wing Commander Adrian
Warburton DSO and Bar, DFC and two
Bars. The photograph was taken in 1943
before the award of his American DFC.

Warby to worry about, both on and off duty, I felt I could get on with the war in peace.'[3]

Before he left, Adrian was again subject to a friendly fire incident. Flying a Beaufighter, he was attacked by four Hurricanes, with one pilot actually claiming to have shot the 'enemy aircraft' down. Adrian took delight in personally escorting the pilot concerned to his Beaufighter, which was undamaged.

Adrian flew out to Egypt in the middle of March, ending his ten-week detachment. Even though this second tour of duty was short, he had flown forty-three operational missions and produced some of the best and most important photography of his career. Three weeks later he was listed in the *London Gazette* as being awarded the DSO. Adrian had been a flight lieutenant for two months. Such an award to a junior officer not in command was often regarded as an acknowledgement the officer had only just missed out on the VC.

Also returning to Egypt were the two stalwart Beaufighter camera operators, Corporal Ron Hadden and Leading Aircraftman Norman Shirley. Both proudly wore DFMs, which made them unique, as neither were aircrew. Norman later recalled a recce mission over Catania's main runway, with Adrian flying at below hangar height. The Beaufighter was hit by machine-gun fire and Norman's hair was parted by a bullet which sliced a groove out of his helmet.

One of Malta's regular supply vessels was the *Breconshire*. She made the run more than most and could carry 10,000 tons, including 5,000 tons of fuel oil. By March she had completed five trips, sometimes on her own, sometimes with others. Her captain was a regular RN officer, Captain Colin Hutchison. At the end of the month, she formed part of a convoy from Alexandria with three merchantmen: *Clan Campbell*, *Pampas* and *Talabot* with an escort under Rear Admiral Phillip Vian.

The ships were shadowed immediately they left port and were soon attacked, albeit ineffectively, by Italian bombers. Vian was then notified the Italian fleet was at sea, heading in his direction. When it began to close, he led most of his outgunned escorts directly at what he knew was a superior enemy force. After a brief engagement, the disconcerted Italians swung away. Meanwhile, his charges were heavily bombed, but Vian had taken the precaution of leaving six destroyers and an anti-aircraft cruiser for protection. No ships were hit despite carefully coordinated Luftwaffe assaults. Soon afterwards the Italian fleet, including the 35,000-ton battleship *Littorio*, closed. A single broadside from the *Littorio* outweighed the entire firepower of Vian's vessels. Once again Vian attacked. In what became known as the Battle of Sirte, the RN achieved an unqualified tactical success seeing off a much superior force with light cruisers and destroyers. The Italians went home.

---

3. *Carve Malta on my heart and other wartime stories*, by Frederick Galea, pages 58–9.

The merchant vessels were targeted later by enemy bombers, five of which were shot down. They resumed course hours behind schedule, a problem exacerbated by *Clan Campbell's* relatively slow speed. On the evening of 22 March, and as outlined in Vian's orders, Captain Hutchison ordered the merchant vessels to make their own way at maximum speed. The following morning, with dawn breaking, they were twenty miles from Malta in poor weather with low cloud. Hutchison was disappointed at the lack of fighter escort, but he knew nothing of the RAF's desperate situation. That grey and overcast morning the RAF had a total of twenty-five Spitfires and Hurricanes available.

The Luftwaffe found the divided ships about to enter the narrow channels between the shore and mine fields. Within twelve miles of Malta, *Breconshire* was hit and was soon without power. Hutchison did all he could to restore the engines or secure a tow from an escort, which continued to try and beat off further attacks. All that day he and his crew fought valiantly to save the ship. To Hutchison, there seemed to be no fighter cover at all despite being within nine miles of Grand Harbour. The poor visibility meant he was unaware of the efforts being made by the remaining fighters to hold off hordes of Axis aircraft.

Throughout that night and all the following day, efforts to take *Breconshire* under tow failed. One escort hit a mine and was left without power; she was soon sunk. On the morning of 24 March, the RAF fighter strength stood at eighteen; by the end of the day it was nine. Despite further attacks, *Breconshire* was slowly towed into Marsaxlokk Bay, a temporary refuge at best as it had no facilities for unloading. *Clan Campbell*, lagging well behind the others, was sunk long before the RAF got anywhere near her. There were constant attacks the following day and *Breconshire* was hit many times. As darkness fell, Hutchison realised he and his crew could do no more; he ordered them off the ship, which soon turned turtle. The loss of *Breconshire* was a tragedy. What befell *Pampas* and *Talabot* was far worse.

The arrival of supply ships usually heralded heavy bombing and this was an exemplary case. In a failure at the highest level, the authorities failed to ensure *Pampas* and *Talabot* – both of which arrived on 23 March at great human cost – were unloaded as promptly as they could have been. Rather than being berthed alongside a wharf, the ships were moored initially in the middle of Grand Harbour to be unloaded by lighters. The ships' exhausted crews could do little; unloading also ceased when warning was received of another raid. Damaged derricks on *Pampas* also limited progress. Luqa's Station Commander, Wing Commander Powell-Shedden, aware much needed aircraft spares were on the ships, was appalled to find unloading ceased once it was dark. He appealed to Lloyd and also telephoned Sir William Dobbie personally. Lloyd doubted the accuracy of Powell-Shedden's report and Dobbie said nothing could be done that night. Neither Lloyd nor Dobbie took any action, although responsibility for unloading rested primarily with the

Superintendent of the Dockyard, Vice Admiral Leatham. Powell-Shedden sent his own airmen and aircrew to unload vitally needed aircraft engines and spares.

The inevitable happened and both ships were fatally hit. They were close to Tamara's apartment, and she vividly recalled *Pampas*' ammunition exploding all night and a sheet of burning oil spreading into the harbour. She and Ronnie watched *Pampas* burn until morning. *Talabot* was anchored practically under the windows of their apartment when she was hit and began to burn fiercely. The thick, black smoke from burning oil enveloped their home. *Pampas* settled on the bottom, whereas *Talabot*, having caught fire, was scuttled because of the amount of ammunition on board, although its upper-deck remained above water belching fire and dense smoke, which became a nightmare for the people of Floriana. Many families were evacuated. *Talabot* burned for two days; Tamara was allowed back to her home after three. There were many individual acts of great courage by Maltese workers, some of whom lost their lives. One naval officer was awarded the George Cross and two Maltese policemen were awarded the British Empire Medal. The failure was not one of courage but of organisation; no orders having been given for unloading to continue in the hours of darkness.

Attempts at salvage continued until the end of April and Sybil Dobbie, the Governor's daughter, witnessed officers and men of the Cheshire Regiment retrieving barrels of fuel from the flooded holds. They swam in the cold, filthy mixture of oil, debris and water, pushing barrels to the side to be roped together and hauled out. They did this day and night, raid or no raid. When the cranes broke down or the power was cut off, everything was manhandled.[4] The Cheshire lads didn't stop until finally, just over half of *Pampas'* cargo was discharged. But only about a tenth was landed from *Talabot*. Despite what was saved, it was nevertheless a severe setback for everyone on the island. Something had gone terribly wrong in dealing with these precious cargoes and responsibility went to the very top.

At dusk on 26 March, made even darker by thick black smoke over Grand Harbour, the total RAF fighter strength on the island totalled eight. The only positive outcome was in the mind of Kesselring. He had thrown everything at the merchant ships and the airfields, and paid dearly. Yet two cargo ships successfully made port and it took his air force three days to sink them. He knew nothing of the debacle over unloading and assumed the arrival of the ships was a defeat.

It was recognised more widely than ever before that Malta's fighter aircraft were inadequate. The lack of even partial control of the air made it a miracle any merchantmen reached Malta at all. But the valiant ships were met with inefficiency beneath the weight of devastating enemy attacks; they deserved better and so did

---

4. *Grace Under Malta*, by Sybil Dobbie, pages 136–7.

Malta's heroic defenders. The many failings in the delivery of the first Spitfires also had to be addressed. A change at the top was needed.

Also in March, Tamara and Ronnie had a narrow escape when a bomb exploded within fifty yards of their home. 'I shall never forget the blinding flash of fire, the blast that picked me up and threw me against the far end wall of the drawing room. My husband and one of our friends were at home with me. The men rushed out before the raid was over to see if they could be of any assistance. After an hour or so they came back with their shirts blood-stained. They did not talk much all that day. The saddest tragedy in that raid was the death of a 19-year-old girl engaged to an army boy. They had been standing on her doorstep enjoying the sun and chatting when they heard the screams of the aircraft diving. She rushed down the incline towards the shelter. At that moment the bomb hit one of the buildings which collapsed, burying her. By some strange fluke the boy, however, escaped all injury and started his hopeless task of clearing the stones away in an endeavour to find her. After three days, during which he would neither eat nor sleep, he succeeded in discovering the body quite unharmed. The stones had fallen in such a way as to form a sort of niche. She had died of suffocation.'[5]

In the same month, Tamara had two further near misses: one when a bomb hit the shelter she was in and the second when another destroyed part of the palace in Valletta. 'Aida and I had only just left the heavy doorway which we had been sheltering behind, when the blast blew the iron doors down, killing ten people who had been taking cover there with us. I was starting to lose my nerve. Not so much in daytime but at night lying in bed, I would feel cold trickles of sweat running down my back as I listened to the bombs and the sickening thud that followed them, and yet I could not make up my mind to go and sleep in any of the public shelters.'[6]

The shelters were crowded, many people having lived in them since 1940. The old railway tunnel was ever popular; people gave birth there and others died of natural causes. Sanitary facilities were wholly inadequate and after a couple of hours at night, conditions were stifling and unpleasant. There were rarely any empty bunks, deckchairs often the only answer for those wanting sleep. The conditions affected Tamara badly, but her friend Aida was imperturbable, often watching raids from Hastings Gardens on top of the city walls; Tamara sought shelter. 'When I remonstrated with her, "don't worry," she would say, "only the very good die young and I am not very good, so it is all right." Her absolute fearlessness was contagious. Two or three times I went into the gardens with her, but I must confess I did not seem to take the same delight in watching raids as she did.'[7]

---

5. *Women of Malta,* by Frederick Galea, page 119.
6. *Ibid.*
7. *Ibid.*

One evening, Tamara accompanied a naval friend to the Customs House as he was leaving Malta on posting. When a raid began they crouched on the steps until the all-clear. After he left, Tamara tried to retrace her steps, but found the layout completely changed by the bombs. 'I stumbled along trying to find the steps we had used to come down to the quayside. They had vanished. Big puddles of water and enormous boulders were everywhere. I could hardly see. I felt hopelessly lost. Suddenly a light flashed somewhere in the distance. I made for it. It turned out to be a small ambulance slowly edging its way back to town. I signalled to the driver and he stopped. I asked him whether he would not mind taking me back to Valletta. He agreed and opened the door for me to climb in. The sight that met my eyes nearly made me faint. On the four bunks of the ambulance, four dead bodies were stretched out, partially covered with blood-stained sheets. I thanked the driver but said that I'd much rather walk. I was quietly sick over the side of the wharf into the water. I don't know how I ever reached home that night.'[8]

At the Union Club one evening, Tamara suddenly couldn't stand it any longer. She told Aida she had an awful headache and was going home. Aida wanted to come with her, but Tamara firmly refused. 'I walked home in a daze. Sleep, everlasting sleep, was the only thing I craved. On one of my trips to Egypt, I had been able, after a lot of wheedling, to buy a tube of Veronal. I don't know what made me buy the stuff, but I always carried it with me. Curiously enough, it gave me an enormous amount of courage in air raids. I knew that I could then kill myself painlessly if ever I was badly injured. I seemed to be acting in a trance. I quietly dissolved the contents of the small tube in a tumbler-full of water, undressed, opened the bed, swallowed the mixture, which tasted something like crushed aspirin and stretched myself comfortably on the downy bed. In about ten minutes my legs started to feel like cotton. I would move them about, but it was as if they did not belong to me at all. Slowly the numbness reached my arms and it could not have been more than a quarter of an hour before I was sound asleep.

'The next thing I remember is waking up in a strange bed. I was at the King George V hospital in Floriana. I had been unconscious for three days. Even then, I still had an overpowering desire to sleep. For another three days I slept most of the time. My husband came round to see me. He was looking wan and hurt. I apologised for all the trouble I had given him and tried to explain what had made me do such a silly thing, but words failed me. I could not explain it to myself. Nothing more terrible than usual happened and yet my resistance had snapped.'[9]

After Tamara left hospital Ronnie and Aida watched her closely, but her temporary madness was over. Ronnie now made desperate attempts to have Tamara evacuated. Everyone has their own personal limit of endurance; Tamara had gone beyond hers

8. *Women of Malta,* by Frederick Galea, pages 107–8.
9. *Ibid.*

and then she had simply snapped. Her descriptions of life under incessant bombing are fluent and moving, and she paints a shocking picture of someone struggling to cope. How many others suffered similarly and carried mental scars for the rest of their lives?

Very few buildings remained in Floriana which did not bear some trace of the indiscriminate destruction. Some were minus a balcony, others lacked a roof, not one had a pane of glass left yet people insisted on staying, refusing to abandon their homes unless they were razed to the ground. Pickles Fletcher was now renting a flat opposite the Floriana granaries and she had to move into her kitchen as it was the only place where she could keep comparatively dry when it rained.

Doris Camilleri was 9-years-old when death came to Mosta in March. When the alert sounded her family trooped to the shelter in Gafa` Street. Both entrances later took devastating hits. When Doris eventually clambered out, she passed the lifeless body of her 10-year-old brother Guzi. Her mother, pregnant with her seventh child, didn't see Guzi, staring instead at a leg wearing a heavy Army boot. Doris didn't at first believe it was her father's, but it was. They were brought out of the shelter by passing RAF personnel. As they picked their way through the rubble, they had to pass the mutilated but recognisable bodies of friends and neighbours. When Doris' mother found out about her husband and son she wept for three days. A few weeks later she gave birth to a healthy girl.[10]

One day Tamara received the call she dreaded; Ronnie had been injured in a raid. He suffered shock and a fractured shoulder blade resulting in a three-week stay in Mtarfa hospital. It could have been very much worse. During his stay, Saturday afternoon working was introduced in Tamara's office. On the very first afternoon, Tamara and Ronnie's apartment block was hit. But for her work, and Ronnie's injury, both would probably have been at home. Aida accompanied Tamara to her home. A bomb had fallen about five yards from the front of the apartment block, sucking one of the walls outwards. The block was cordoned off as it was unsafe, but Tamara got permission to enter with Aida to see what possessions could be rescued. It was very badly damaged and they were only able to retrieve a few items, clothes mostly, although some were burnt or scorched. During their search they ignored two further raids. The item Tamara especially wanted to retrieve was a gift from René, but as she tried to reach it, the floor collapsed leaving her dangling in empty space with a badly cut and bruised leg. Aida had to move very cautiously to pull Tamara up. René's precious gift had to be abandoned. Before they could leave, the floor collapsed, this time Aida making a lucky escape.

Tamara stayed with Aida while looking for somewhere else to live. This proved difficult as many landlords asked high prices for barely habitable flats without gas or

---

10. *The People's War Malta: 1940/43*, by Laurence Mizzi, pages 7–10.

water. Early one evening, as they made their way to Valletta after another futile attempt to find accommodation, they found Queensway strewn with rubble. There were three new big craters and people were running towards Porta Reale. They increased their pace to see what the commotion was all about. 'On reaching Kingsgate, tears sprang to our eyes. The Opera House, dear to every Maltese heart, had received a direct hit during the evening raid of 7 April. The woodwork was burning fiercely, charred or still-burning bits of material from the stage curtains were falling in the street. People were paralysed with grief and just stood there with bewildered faces.'[11]

The raid which destroyed the Opera House set an awful pattern for April, the cruellest month for many, as the blitz reached its climax; many historic buildings and monuments were destroyed, and many of Floriana's houses became ruins. Two days later, Sir William Dobbie was watching the progress of an air raid from the roof of his residence, San Anton Palace, when he actually saw a bomb strike the dome of nearby Mosta church. Knowing how attached the people were to the church, he was very distressed and went to see for himself. He expected a scene of great desolation, but to his great relief he saw the church apparently intact with a bomb lying on the marble floor. Looking up, he saw a neat hole bored through the nine-foot thick dome before the bomb fell onto the hard marble floor 200 feet beneath. A congregation of 300 was at worship at the time. That it failed to explode was celebrated as a miracle.

The Maltese regarded Sir William with a mixture of admiration and awe. A deeply religious man and member of the Plymouth Brethren, he did not smoke and was teetotal. He was often seen in towns and villages, threading his way through the debris of ruined houses and streets encouraging everyone. In all sincerity he told them all would come right if they worked hard and kept their faith in the Lord. His daughter Sybil also lived in San Anton Palace working as her father's secretary. She said this period was a horrible time that it was like, 'pain that recurs at regular intervals. In between whiles the sufferer forgets about it; then, with a cold sickening dread, feels the first warning pangs and knows that another paroxysm is coming on.'[12] The paroxysm was yet another raid. Tamara probably felt much the same; she eventually found a room in the top floor of a hostel. The bathroom was on the top floor, although the water tap was a hundred yards from the house.

Agnes Azzopardi was 7-years-old when the war began. She lived in Luqa village. On the same day the Mosta church congregation had their escape, she and her family had taken cover during a raid on Luqa airfield. A nearby shelter took a direct hit and twenty-three of the occupants were killed. One father was brought to Agnes' home mourning the loss of his nine children. 'I haven't got any left now,' he said, as he repeatedly counted on his fingers. But a daughter had survived.[13]

11. *Women of Malta*, by Frederick Galea, page 114.
12. *Grace under Malta*, by Sybil Dobbie, page 124.
13. *The People's War Malta: 1940/43*, by Laurence Mizzi, pages 2–5.

Ten days later, 18-year-old George Borg accompanied his father Antonio to buy flour wholesale to distribute to bakers in their neighbouring villages. They travelled by horse and cart, reaching Marsa just as bombs began falling in the dockyard area. George was terrified, but his father said they needed to press on to a proper shelter at the civil abattoir. No sooner had they got there when George heard the whine of a falling bomb. He threw himself flat and immediately felt his father's weight on top of him as Antonio instinctively tried to shield his son from danger. There was an ear-splitting explosion and splinters of rock flew all around, accompanied by clouds of dust and choking smoke. George was hit by flying stones. When the air began to clear there was no sign of Antonio or their horse. Even nearby buildings had disappeared, reduced to rubble. He finally caught sight of the dead horse some twenty yards away, with his father nearby. With blood flowing from his leg and his clothes in tatters, he staggered towards his father. Antonio was conscious but mortally wounded, his instinctive act having saved his son's life. George was at his father's bedside later when he died.[14]

The tonnage of bombs dropped in March and April amounted to twice that dropped on London in the worst year of the Blitz. *Fliegerkorps II* flew nearly 10,000 sorties in April alone, twice as many as in March, killing 339 civilians and 209 servicemen. Many judged the attacks as a murderous assault to break the spirit of the population. Little wonder life was coloured by whether the attackers were German or Italian. 'An old lady, crouching in a shelter during a bad German raid, was once heard to pray fervently, "O Holy Mother, send over the Italians".'[15]

Despite so much danger and devastation all around, work continued. There were now many women employed in the ops room at Lascaris. More and more young Maltese girls came forward. They did superb jobs as telephonists, typists, plotters, cipher clerks, secretaries and also supported a host of other clerical duties. Most lived in Sliema and the area around Grand Harbour. They got to and from work, usually on foot, regardless of air raids. A new Maltese plotter was Helen Cuell whose sister Betty was already there. They lived in Paola, often walking to Marsa and then by way of the harbour road. They had special passes because of the curfew. They also knew the location of every shelter by heart.[16] Carmela Galea was Maltese and personal assistant to Hugh Lloyd. Twice on her way to work, she was blown over by bomb blasts and injured, but both times, after receiving medical treatment, made her way to work. Lloyd was fulsome in his praise for the civilian staff he often saw making their way through a devastated Floriana to report for duty on time.

The Maltese dug themselves in wherever they could, into cliffs, or ridges, expanding cellars, or even burrowing into Malta's many fortifications. New homes

---

14. *The People's War Malta: 1940/43*, by Laurence Mizzi, pages 46–9.
15. *Grace under Malta*, by Sybil Dobbie, pages 32–3.
16. *The People's War Malta: 1940/43*, by Laurence Mizzi, page 65.

with stone floors and roofs and walls were carved out. Whole families lived like this, terribly cramped and on meagre rations, only venturing out to salvage what they could from their destroyed homes. 'When the all-clear sounded the narrow streets filled with white-shirted men and boys, black-cloaked women and barefoot children – a noisy, talkative, and excited people. As soon as the sirens screeched again, everything would stop, some did not hesitate and rushed for the shelters, but everybody else would stand waiting quietly, as if they were listening to the nerve-searing undulating wail covering the island. It was like a signal when the danger flag went up; the whole mass would stir, the excitement would spread like a bushfire, and within a few minutes the earth would swallow the people, leaving the narrow streets naked and empty.'[17] Many preferred not to come up in daylight in these months of heavy bombardment. Inevitably, this impacted on the manpower available in the dockyards or on the airfields. And all the time they prayed and hoped for long overdue relief from Britain. Meanwhile, their hatred for the Italians increased as their fear of the Germans deepened and spread.

The heavy fighter losses added urgency to the requirement for more Spitfires and Hugh Lloyd's requests became constant. Malta's situation was approaching desperation. The challenge for London lay not just in the numbers needed. By the end of March, not one British carrier was up to the task. *Eagle* was in for repair, the deck of *Argus* was too short for Spitfires and the lifts on *Victorious* were too small.

In order to press the case further, Lloyd despatched 'Jumbo' Gracie as his personal ambassador to ram the message home at the Air Ministry. Gracie pressed Malta's case hard. Some said there was no way Spitfires could ever be delivered to the island in sufficient numbers and suggested Malta should simply muddle through. Others said Spitfires alone would not be enough; engineering personnel and spare parts were needed, which only merchant ships could deliver. Gracie was not deflected and continued to stress Malta's case at the highest level. Churchill had also been giving the matter much thought, appealing directly to President Roosevelt for the loan of the American aircraft carrier USS *Wasp*. The President's response was immediate and positive. Gracie took his request for delivering spares and Spitfire ground crew to the Admiralty, which offered to use submarines. Inevitably, this was a slow and tedious process but, in the absence of a convoy, there was no alternative. Gracie then flew north to arrange the embarkation of Spitfires on board the *Wasp* in what was a unique demonstration of Anglo-American cooperation. Hopefully, Spitfires in numbers would arrive in Malta in mid-April.

Goering's promise to Hitler was Malta would be 'Coventrated'. The weight of bombs dropped on the island in April was the equivalent of thirty-six times the devastating bombing experienced by Coventry. Throughout that hellish month,

---

17. *George Cross Island*, by Charles Maclean, published in *History of the Second World War, Volume 3, No 5* (Purnell, 1967), page 1013.

nearly 6,000 bombers attacked the island, 1,638 in a single week. Even though the assaults were concentrated on the airfields and Grand Harbour, the surrounding residential areas suffered grievously.

At the beginning of April, King George VI wrote to General Dobbie saying he was following events very closely and, in recognition of the skill and resolution of the Royal Malta Artillery, the King assumed the Colonelcy-in-Chief of the Regiment. This move was without precedent and a clear signal, if one was necessary, Britain did not intend Malta to fall. On 15 April 1942, King George VI awarded the George Cross to Malta. This award, and its timing, was a master stroke. There was no better symbol of Malta's will and endurance. After that Malta was known as George Cross Island, and all who lived and served there were delighted with the distinction. Against regulations, many pilots on the island began to wear Maltese crosses sewn on their right-hand pockets.

Elsewhere in the Mediterranean the situation remained grim for the Allies. Having seized his chance at the beginning of the year, Rommel's success continued and the British Army fell back, leaving Tobruk isolated, eventually stopping the Afrika Korps just sixty miles short of Alexandria. Malta was on the verge of starvation with no convoys having successfully unloaded their cargo since the previous November. The loss of the March convoy brought matters to a head, with the reasons for its loss very much striking home. The RAF's ability to mount a credible defence from the island was now questionable and very few RAF bombers remained able to interfere with Axis convoys. The only factor limiting Kesselring's attacks on the island was the weather.

By mid-April, with only a handful of aircraft available, many aircrew teamed up with their army colleagues to fill sandbags and build blast pens to help protect the remaining aircraft. On some days the fighter strength was reduced to ten, then six, then sometimes four. Without the few precious engines and spares unloaded from *Pampas* and *Talabot* on the initiative of Luqa's Station Commander, there would have been no workable Spitfires at all. Once the fighter strength was down to less than four, they were kept on the ground with all efforts devoted to building numbers back to a dozen or more. To regain a fighter strength of twenty was beyond Hugh Lloyd's wildest dreams. The artillery defences were little better. The majority of the guns, except those very close to the airfields, were limited to fifteen rounds per gun per day. The unfinished airfield at Qrendi was turned into a decoy airfield, complete with a flare-path, and it was regularly hit by enemy bombers. Safi too played decoy, written-off aircraft being set up there as bait which often lured the Luftwaffe and the Regia Aeronautica.

Sir William Dobbie sent a series of urgent messages to London stressing the need for a strong force of fighters and more supplies. Initially he said Malta had sufficient wheat and flour until July, but anti-aircraft ammunition might be exhausted between mid-May and the end of June. He was advised a convoy in April was out of the question, although limited resupply by submarine would be increased. Dobbie replied saying it was impossible to carry on without further supplies of food and ammunition. He revised downwards his estimate of flour, which would only last until the latter half of May and said there was now only one month's supply of anti-aircraft ammunition. The very worst must happen if vital stocks were not replenished, he said, and if Malta was to be held, drastic action was needed. It was now a question of survival.

There was much disquiet at the top, seemingly between Dobbie and Lloyd; the sinking of *Pampas* and *Talabot* brought matters to a head. 'Lloyd, with his air of an attractive buccaneer, was a very different type from the equally valiant but strange, General Gordon-like figure of the Governor. He considered the Governor had not handled the question of Maltese labour with sufficient vigour; and being an outspoken man, he made his views plain.'[18] In referring to Malta's Governing Council as the 'Vichy Council', Lloyd said it, 'was possibly adequate in times of plenty, but in 1942 it was impossible to discuss administration without discussing operations, particularly when it came to starvation and surrender dates.'[19] Lloyd later said there was nothing 'Vichy' about the council and it was named in jest. If so it was a very curious jest given the desperate situation. Jest or no jest, there was no disguising the undercurrent of unrest. Lloyd never doubted Dobbie's physical courage, or that of Lady Dobbie. In fact he thought neither of them knew what fear was, but he thought Sir William had been in post too long.

Lloyd had earlier signalled Tedder, complaining bitterly about the failure to unload *Pampas* and *Talabot*, citing a lack of energetic leadership. Although unloading was primarily the responsibility of Vice Admiral Leatham, Lloyd was not entirely blameless, as he took no action following reports he received from Luqa's Station Commander. In fact his signal to Tedder may have verged on the disingenuous, although Lloyd had no authority to order unloading to recommence. Tedder learnt Lloyd's outspokenness was unwelcome when he received a private letter from Sir William Dobbie suggesting Lloyd be relieved, citing a lack of harmony within the governing council. Tedder rejected Dobbie's suggestion despite the evidence of a rift. He had the highest admiration for Lloyd's fighting determination and suspected Lloyd had been rightly outspoken. In signalling London, Tedder said Lloyd was the main driving force and inspiration in Malta's defence. 'What is needed is more leadership and less talk of harmony.'[20] Tedder would consider Lloyd's relief soon, as he had already served as AOC for longer than originally envisaged, but he had no intention of replacing him at this critical stage.

---

18. *Royal Air Force 1939–1945, Volume 2, The Fight Avails*, Denis Richards and Hilary St George Saunders, page 192.
19. *Briefed to Attack*, by AM Sir Hugh Lloyd, page 196.
20. *With Prejudice*, MRAF Lord Tedder, page 264.

On 12 April, Sir William Monkton, Acting Minister of State for the Middle East, and Air Marshal Tedder, paid a two-day visit to Malta. For Tedder this was an ideal opportunity to see conditions with the RAF on its knees. When on the veranda of the Xara Palace Officers' Mess in Mdina, he watched Me109s strafe RAF Ta' Qali in the valley below; some aircraft actually fired at the Xara Palace itself. Woody Woodhall was there: 'Sir Arthur asked if we had wired Kesselring to lay on a show for his benefit.'[21] Later Tedder visited Luqa only minutes after it was bombed. He saw at first hand the combined efforts of airmen and soldiers, as officers and other ranks, aircrew and ground crew, swarmed onto the airfield to fill craters left by the enemy bombers. 'That is the spirit of Malta,'[22] he said.

The main purpose of the visit was to assess whether to recommend Dobbie's relief. But Sir William urged that both Air Vice-Marshal Lloyd and Major General Beak be relieved at once. Tedder thought Lloyd's personal bravery and dynamic energy were having a widespread effect and, more than anyone else, Lloyd was the personification of Malta's resistance. The morale of the RAF personnel was one of the most stimulating experiences Tedder had ever come across. Major General Beak also impressed Tedder as a determined leader. Both Tedder and Monkton thought Leatham's staff and the staff at the dockyard deplorably weak. Within the governing council, all three military commanders, Leatham, Beak, and Lloyd, as well as Sir Edward Jackson, the Lieutenant-Governor, felt a change of governor was needed. Monkton and Tedder both thought Dobbie was exhausted.

Back in Cairo, General Auchinleck recommended the appointment of Hugh Lloyd as Governor and C-in-C, but Tedder advised against it. He needed Lloyd as a hands-on operational commander, one not concerned with civil administration. Yet it took Monkton seven days to submit his report to London. His telegram of 20 April said: '…General Dobbie should be relieved as soon as possible on grounds that he is a tired man, has lost grip of situation and is no longer capable of affording higher direction and control which is vital (R) vital to present situation.'[23] It was also proposed that after the current phase of the air battle was over, Hugh Lloyd should also be relieved, 'purely on the grounds that it was militarily unsound to ask any Commander to continue to exercise his command for too long a period under the conditions now obtaining in Malta.'[24]

Almost immediately there was troubling news from General Dobbie citing intrigue involving the influential Mabel Strickland, editor of the *Times of Malta*, and Lord Louis Mountbatten. This was based on Dobbie having sight of a telegram sent on 21 April by Ms Strickland to Mountbatten saying: 'Reference

21. *Soldier, Sailor & Airman Too*, by Woody Woodhall, page 182.
22. *Briefed to Attack*, by AM Sir Hugh Lloyd, page 170.
23. Personal telegram Serial No T596/2, held in NA PREM 3/266/1.
24. Defence Committee Aide Memoire, held in NA PREM 3/266/1.

our last conversation. That removal now vitally essential and urgent.'[25] Dobbie
asked for an explanation from Ms Strickland, who said she was urging a change of
governorship owing to alleged lack of coordination, which was responsible for the
disaster to the last convoy. General Dobbie took the strongest exception to what he
referred to as 'backstairs intrigue' involving a serving officer and asked his telegram
be shown to Churchill. This telegram was followed by a second quoting a reply
from Mountbatten: 'Arrangements made as requested.'[26] Dobbie strongly resented
Mountbatten's interference in a matter which did not concern him.

Churchill's initial reaction to the recommendations with regard to Dobbie, whom
he admired, was one of shock. He was also extremely unhappy it took seven days
for Monkton to make the Cabinet aware of his views. Nevertheless, over the next
few days Churchill accepted that after two years in post, Sir William had done more
than enough. Exercising such responsibilities in such an environment for so long
would have stretched the very best of men. It was decided he should be succeeded
by Viscount Gort. Dobbie had no thought of personal considerations, immediately
agreeing that only the public interest be served. He was a very honourable man.
Although it was largely the furore over *Pampas* and *Talabot* that precipitated the
change, all members of Malta's governing council bore responsibility for that
particular disaster. Those on the ground knew little of all of this; they got on with
their jobs, survived as best they could, eking out their meagre rations, and listening
for the siren; they didn't have to wait long.

It was now a desperate race to resupply Malta with Spitfires in quantity before
Kesselring's glider sites in Sicily were fully operational; it was assumed an Axis
assault would quickly follow their completion. On Malta's airfields, desperate
measures were undertaken to build more dispersal points. Soon there were over 600
connected by forty-three miles of taxi track. Very little of this was possible without
the support of the army. Every day, battalion commanders were on standby close
to the airfields with working parties complete with lorry-loads of stone, ready to be
called in to repair cratered runways and taxiways. Had enough been done? Were the
measures now in place sufficient to receive the desperately needed Spitfires?

At the end of the second week of April, fifty-two cannon-armed Mark Vb
Spitfires were loaded onto the USS *Wasp* at the King George V Dock on the Clyde.
They were joined by the pilots of 601 and 603 Squadrons. All the RAF personnel
were slightly overwhelmed by the operational efficiency on board the ship and the
hospitality shown by their American hosts. Sadly, the operational efficiency did not
extend to those authorities responsible for preparing the Spitfires for embarkation,
delivery and immediate use in an operational theatre. Essential aspects of preparing

25. Quoted in telegram No 158 from General Dobbie to Lord Cranborne (Secretary of State for the
    Colonies), held in NA PREM 3/266/1.
26. Quoted in telegram No 159 dated 23 April 1942 from General Dobbie to Lord Cranborne, held
    in NA PREM 3/266/1.

the aircraft had simply not been carried out. Over 90 per cent of the aircraft's long-range fuel tanks were defective and when the aircraft were fuelled in the carrier's hangar, serious flooding resulted. The US Navy, so thorough in its own preparations, was less than impressed. Nearly all of the Spitfires' guns were dirty and unsynchronised, and three quarters of the radios were inoperative. The aircraft did look nice in their tropical paint scheme, but this only served to undermine the secrecy of the whole operation. Some limited rectification was carried out at sea, but the RAF authorities in Malta would have to make good the deficiencies as soon as the aircraft landed. Would Smiling Albert afford them the time?

Gracie led the launch of forty-seven Spitfires on 20 April; forty-six arrived safely. Within twenty minutes, there was massive retaliation from the Luftwaffe which had followed the track of the incoming aircraft on radar. The timing of the attacks was perfect. Hugh Lloyd met all the new arrivals that first evening. He wound up by saying: 'You have come to a great little island and one of these days people will talk about Malta and you will be proud to say, I was there'.[27] At that point, a stick of bombs fell uncomfortably close, the last bomb whistling over the roof of the Xara Palace. The AOC didn't bat an eyelid and simply repeated: 'You will say. I was there.'[28] The following morning, twenty-seven Spitfires were available; by the evening, seventeen. Forty-eight hours after the reinforcements arrived, only seven Spitfires were left in working condition. This was Malta's nadir, and once again the island was left virtually defenceless, bereft of adequate air defences.

To make matters worse, photographic reconnaissance of Sicily by Harry Coldbeck revealed numerous glider strips prepared at Gerbini in preparation for an airborne assault. Matters seemed to be coming to a head. Heavy raids continued. The General Hospital at St Andrews was destroyed and other hospitals damaged. There was also much damage elsewhere. There was worse news. HMS *Upholder*, under the command of David Wanklyn, VC, was lost on its twenty-fifth mission. This was another bitter blow. *Upholder* had sunk almost 130,000 tons of enemy shipping, almost twice as much as any other submarine from the 10th Submarine Flotilla operating from Manoel Island. The flotilla was now forced, by weight of enemy air attack, to quit Malta.

The RAF still needed to learn lessons, and quickly, before any further reinforcement was attempted. The Spitfires should have been launched from the carrier much earlier in the day so they could be ready for combat immediately, before they were destroyed on the ground or grounded by cratered runways. Each Spitfire needed to be in full working order and combat ready as soon as it touched down. On top of that, a number of the newly-arrived Spitfire pilots lacked experience, provoking an immediate signal from Hugh Lloyd to the Air Ministry saying Malta was no place for beginners. A slicker reception process was also needed on the ground to

---

27. *Soldier, Sailor & Airman Too*, by Woody Woodhall, page 185.
28. *Ibid.*

quickly turn around arriving aircraft and scramble them within minutes. The RAF authorities, not just in Malta, had already had two chances to get this right. They were determined to succeed and detailed planning was initiated to mount a second operation using *Wasp*. Plans were also afoot to use the specially camouflaged HMS *Welshman*, a fast mine-layer, to deliver Spitfire engines and engineers to the island. Would the Luftwaffe give the RAF a third chance?

Tamara enjoyed an evening with Aida and her family in Hamrun, the day after Aida's twenty sixth birthday. Aida was in high spirits as everyone sat around the fireplace chatting and trying not to think about the war. The next day was the highlight of the week – pay day. Aida called for Tamara and together they went to collect their pay. Soon afterwards, the air raid warning sounded as a large enemy formation of 200 aircraft approached. Tamara wanted Aida to come with her to the shelter, but she wanted something from the office and promised to join Tamara at St Andrew's Scots Church. The raid was one of the heaviest Valletta had experienced. When it was over, Aida had still not arrived. 'I was getting quite uneasy, cursing inwardly her foolhardiness. I was sure she had gone to Hastings Gardens to watch the raid and stamp with joy at every machine shot down. She was blessed with the best eyesight of anyone I knew.'[29]

Tamara rushed back to HQ but Aida was not there; no one had seen her. The shelter next to Hastings Gardens had received a direct hit. Aida was not among the casualties in the sickbay, but no one was certain whether she had been in the shelter. All agreed she had rushed to take cover as soon as the aircraft started their dive. One airman said he heard Aida call out 'mother'. Desperately worried, Tamara went to the scene, where wounded were still being loaded into ambulances. She then ran to the Air Raid Precaution Centre on Merchants Street, praying nothing had happened to her dear friend. The building reeked of iodine and was full of casualties, some on stretchers, some lying on the floor. Aida's name was not on any list and no one recognised her from Tamara's description. A warden invited her to look at the many unidentified bodies. Tamara agreed, so desperate was she to find her friend.

'Our trek looking on sights, which I shall never forget as long as I live, began. I wished I had with me the pilot who had cold-bloodedly, in broad daylight, dropped his bombs on what he must have known was not a military target. Some bodies were so frightfully disfigured as to be unrecognisable. The only thing one had to go on was the clothes they wore. Aida had been wearing a grey skirt and a light green jumper. I searched on. I was feeling horribly sick and faint, but I forced myself to look at every casualty. Aida was not amongst them.... . Black despair gripped me, I, who was so cautious in my affection, seemed to be fated to lose all my friends.'[30] Tamara contacted all the hospitals, all to no avail. A few days later, Aida's handbag was found amongst the ruins of the shelter at Hastings Gardens.

---

29. *Women of Malta*, by Frederick Galea, pages 123–6.
30. *Ibid.*

The shock of losing such a truly supportive and loyal friend forced Tamara to make up her mind. She had endured enough and agreed to Ronnie's urging to leave the island. She no longer had the courage to stay. Over the next few days, she collected her few possessions, visiting Christina to collect the sewing machine she had lent her. It was only a week since Tamara was last in Christina's flat, yet she could hardly recognise the place. 'All around *Pietro Floriani* Street, only Christina's house was standing. "Standing" is a euphemism … it looked more like the Leaning Tower of Pisa than the real thing itself. There were four small craters in front of the door and a couple more round the corner. I could not imagine why Christina still insisted on living in it. Just as tea was brewed, an air raid warning sounded. We took the machine down to Vincenti's shelter, but Christina insisted on our going somewhere else. There was no reason for not staying there, we had used that shelter many times before, but Christina said she had a hunch and was adamant that we should leave. We took cover in another shelter a few yards down the road. In the middle of the raid, amongst other horrible sounds, we heard the hair-raising note of crashing masonry. When finally the raid ended, Vincenti's shelter was no more. My machine and Christina's few treasured possessions lay buried under a mountain of stones. Christina's sixth sense saved our lives.'[31] It was the second time Christina's intuition saved them, the first being immediately before the attack on *Illustrious*.

At the end of April, Bletchley Park reported some Luftwaffe units were to be transferred from Sicily to North Africa, Crete and elsewhere. This was not a moment too soon, as the RAF could only muster seven Spitfires; it was a struggle to maintain even that figure. Hugh Lloyd desperately awaited the next delivery, still some days away. Ultra soon confirmed two Luftwaffe groups withdrawn from Sicily. Nevertheless, Kesselring still possessed a very potent force which continually targeted the island, although London reassured Sir William Dobbie the danger of invasion could be discounted for the moment. There was still an ever-present danger: a danger of starvation. Rations could hardly be cut further. Mid-August was estimated as the starvation date, but without relief, surrender would come earlier. This was the effect of the loss of March's supplies. But if it came to surrender it would not be addressed by General Dobbie.

The Dobbies were required to make their preparations to leave secretly. There were to be no goodbyes, only a recorded broadcast to be transmitted after they had gone. This stipulation was a bitter blow to Sybil Dobbie after what she and her parents, the garrison and the islanders had been through together. 'We had shared fear and elation, anxiety and relief, victories and defeats, danger and escapes…. Together we had endured the increasing pressure of the war and the growing shortage of food. Together we had all won the George Cross. And now, while things

---

31. *Ibid.*

were apparently at their worst, while raiding and privations seemed still on the increase, we were leaving our friends without a word.'[32]

General John Standish Surtees Prendergast Vereker, 6th Viscount Gort, VC, GCB, CBE, DSO**, MVO, MC, flew to Malta early on 7 May. Gort was a former Chief of the Imperial General Staff and commanded the BEF in France until its evacuation from Dunkirk. His arrival was arranged so quickly he was unable to bring Malta's George Cross; it was sent later. Nevertheless, the impact of the award of the small silver cross was dramatic, and a perfect symbol of King George VI's regard for the island and its people. Nothing could better illustrate Malta's place in history. Having been Gibraltar's Governor, Gort was well aware of Malta's precarious position, the tenuous nature of its supply lines and its vulnerability to air assault. That vulnerability was brought home within minutes of his seaplane landing. As he stepped ashore, a bomb landed uncomfortably close and a number of people assembled to meet him fell flat on their faces.[33] In the middle of the ceremony to swear him in – held in the battered home of Kalafrana's Station Commander – more bombs fell. A number of officials hid beneath chairs and tables. Hugh Lloyd, who was present, said Gort blanched at such behaviour. Only a few minutes earlier, the Dobbies left. For Sir William it was always a case of job done, not rank or position that mattered, and he and Lady Dobbie had done their very best for Malta at a particularly important time.

Before they left, Gort had a brief meeting with Dobbie. As a result, he telegraphed Churchill emphasising Malta's plight and the need for the closest cooperation between local commanders over whom he needed to have supreme command. Within a few days, this was granted. It is interesting to speculate if such a decision had been made three or six months earlier. Gort's arrival was nevertheless perfectly timed. Three days after he stepped ashore Spitfires landed in Malta in numbers. To the islanders, this was close to a miracle.

Sir William and Lady Dobbie returned home to a very warm welcome. In a broadcast the same day, Churchill was fulsome in his praise of the man he described as, 'the heroic defender of Malta'. The following day, Dobbie called on the Prime Minister. At an audience with the King he was knighted Knight Commander of the Order of the Bath (KCB), awarded the previous year, and the King also invested him with Knight Grand Cross of the Order of St Michael and St George (GCMG). King George VI later said Sir William looked very old and tired. A few days later, Dobbie collapsed and was admitted to hospital. He made a very slow recovery. Churchill later ordered an inquiry into the circumstances which led to Dobbie's replacement. It concluded the intrigue was regrettable, but, by the end of April, Sir William was exhausted and had to be relieved.

---

32. *Grace under Malta*, by Sybil Dobbie, page 146–9.
33. *Ibid.*

THE MEDITERRANEAN & A

BELEAGUERED MALTA - SUMMER 1942

Chapter Thirteen

Salvation

Christina had no idea yesterday would turn out to be such a great day, although, like everyone else, she was very excited at the prospect of what might happen. It was an absolute joy to place on the plot no less than sixty-one Spitfires heading toward Malta, all launched from the *Wasp* hundreds of miles away to the west. This time, they arrived ready to fight, and the boys had them refuelled and rearmed in no time at all. Each aircraft was manned by a fresh, Malta-experienced fighter pilot ready to scramble within minutes.

It was now the morning after, and Christina wondered if their precious aircraft survived the night, so many were usually destroyed on the ground. At one stage, they weren't able to place a single fighter on the plot; they had nothing to stop the hordes from the north, nothing except the guns. Even the amount they could fire was rationed like everything else. Christina soon discovered she needn't have worried – the Spitfires were well-protected and well looked after. She focused on her duties, organising her girls so they were ready to play their parts. They were the back-room girls, well-hidden under Valletta's fortress walls, far removed from the harrowing scenes in the city and skies above. But they were often touched by what happened up there; that was where they lived and where they might die.

The last few months were totally one-sided; so many of the air boys they knew had bought it. Thank goodness Warby was well out of it. She often recognised their voices over the radio and it was heartbreaking to hear the emotion when they called up to say one of theirs had 'gone in' and there was no parachute. She felt numb when it happened. Her task was then to remove that particular plot from the table. She recognised the voice of a 603 Squadron Spitfire pilot, Bert Mitchell, a New Zealander. He called up on the radio just before he hit the water saying: 'So long Woody, I've had it.'

Recently, the days were fraught, busier than ever before, and it was relentless. Ever since January, raid after raid, even when the weather was poor, and every time the fighter boys were sent up against terrible odds. Each day their numbers were less than the day before. The girls grew weary of the same story day after day, week after week: 'Fifty plus bombers approaching the island', 'Visual on hostile fighters now crossing Gozo', 'One hundred plus milling up over Comiso'. There were always too many one-way tracks on the table, too many hostile plots pointing towards their tiny island.

Things began to happen quickly but they were ready, each and every one of them. It was as if a magic wand was waved over the ops room. Within minutes, the cavern was a hive of activity, with an amount of traffic on the plotting table never seen before. Two pairs of hands were not enough to cope with the mass of plots on the painted sea between Sicily and Malta, and a helper was positioned at each end of the table to rake off old tracks and set up fresh blocks. There was no time to change over or be relieved; those at the main plotting table had to stay where they were. Those involved in the vital task of gun liaison, or in the all-important direction finding room, had to stay at their places too. It was a case of all hands on deck and there was no time at all to powder one's nose or make a brew.

High above her on the shelf, the faces of the chaps-in-the-gods radiated delight as they went about their duties with renewed vigour and enthusiasm. There was an exultant note in the deep, powerful voice of the controller, Bill Farnes, idol of the plotters, as he shot out a volley of orders over the radio. Handsome, rugged, ruthless, Farnes could raise a girl up or cast her down, reduce her to tears or induce her to laughter – it all depended on his mood. He was one of their finest controllers; that's what mattered. Sitting next to him was Guy Westray, Ops B, with a telephone glued to each ear talking constantly to the airfields. All eyes were focused on the table, but how Bill Farnes could make head or tail of the chaos was beyond the comprehension of many. Hostile and friendly plots mingled with each other in what seemed one grand and glorious muddle. Yet the scene on the table was an accurate reflection of the picture in the sky above. It looked like the outside of some fantastic wasps' nest, with aircraft milling about in a clash of colonies.

Among all the happy faces on the shelf, perhaps none beamed quite as brightly as Woody's: Group Captain Woodhall, the officer-in-charge of the ops room, complete with monocle held firmly in place as if by magic. At long last, he had squadrons of Spitfires, manned by fully-trained and experienced pilots, to put up against the Hun. Only Christina and her fellow plotters knew of the dozens of dummy runs he staged over the radio with imaginary airborne squadrons. Once Woody put a Canadian with an unmistakable voice on the microphone at a stand-by radio set, then proceeded to give him dummy orders. The Canadian replied just as if he was flying his fighter. This resulted in two Me109s enthusiastically shooting each other down without any British aircraft airborne. Woody said to mark two 'kills' down to Pilot Officer Humgufery. Today there was no need for any such hoax.

As instructions from the filter room came one after the other through Christina's headphones, she feverishly pushed out plot after plot onto the table. She smiled inwardly; proud her efforts were of the utmost importance to the controller. She was thrilled at the wonderful stroke of luck that put D Watch on duty on this great morning. And her girls, by now all Maltese, were grateful for the chance to show their mettle, to explode the myth they would panic when put to the test. They carried out their tasks so well that when things quietened down, Woody came down from the shelf and thanked each plotter personally for the very fine show they put on. It was not until afterwards, when Bill Farnes added his own special blooms to the verbal bouquet that the girls went to pieces – and then there was swooning all round. Had her heart not belonged to someone else, Christina, like the rest of them, might well have measured her length at the feet of that fascinating *homme fatal*.[1]

This latest Spitfire delivery marked a turning point in the air battle, although the testing situation for the population continued. Once again, the delivery got off to a bad start with the embarkation authorities having failed to learn from earlier lessons. US naval officers asked for confirmation the external fuel tanks had been fully tested for leaks. When the captain of *Wasp*, Captain John W. Reeves, learnt they had not, he stopped loading; a spillage of highly flammable aviation fuel within the confines of his ship's hangar could have disastrous consequences. Work continued overnight to ensure as many tanks as possible were tested and, where necessary, repaired. Only then did Reeves agree to load the remaining aircraft and conduct further repairs using his own crew whilst en route. By the time *Wasp* reached Gibraltar, all the fuel tanks were serviceable, but this unnecessary episode created understandable doubts about British operational efficiency.

Like the previous effort, the operation benefitted from good weather and, early in the morning of 9 May, USS *Wasp* and HMS *Eagle*, operating together, launched sixty-four Spitfires. Sixty-one reached the island safely. Hugh Lloyd had successfully stretched his limited fighter resources until the reinforcements arrived. This time everyone was ready, with Jumbo Gracie in charge of the ground organisation. Lloyd made a final tour of Luqa on the evening of 8 May to ensure all was ready. As he left, he counted no less than thirty-three Ju87 Stukas and fourteen Ju88s diving on the airfield. Thankfully, there were no intruders overnight.

The first sixteen Spitfires arrived at Ta' Qali at 10.30 am. Within six minutes, Gracie was at cockpit readiness and all sixteen were ready to scramble within seven minutes, such was the speed with which the teams of airmen completed refuelling and rearming. Thirty-one Spitfires were scrambled before midday. Other alerts followed in the afternoon, but when the attackers were recognised as fighters only, Lloyd wisely kept his Spitfires on the ground.

One new arrival seeing Malta for the first time was Denis Barnham, a flight commander with 601 Squadron. 'Two islands, like autumn leaves floating on the water, grow larger and larger. The steep cliffs of the smaller and nearer, which must be Gozo with Malta lying beyond it, rush towards us. White walls crinkle a hilltop. The small fields are yellow. Blue water in front of my propeller and, as we cross the

---

1. *Carve Malta on my heart and other wartime stories*, by Frederick Galea, pages 59–63.

channel between the two islands, I can see the waves breaking on the sunlit rocks ahead.'[2] Within a minute or two Denis was, 'approaching some steep hills clustered thick with buildings that protrude into the sea: it's a harbour and there's a ship down there, low in the water, smoke coming from it. Peering down on top of its fore-shortened black masts I look deep into its splintered hold: tiny flames are dancing in it: it's blackened with fire.'[3] This was his first sight of Grand Harbour. The still smouldering ship was *Talabot*.

That night, only sixteen intruders bombed the island. For whatever reason, Kesselring had not unleashed his bombers when the Spitfires were at their most vulnerable. This gave the RAF time enough to prepare for whatever scene would unfold on 10 May. 'The life-and-death struggle for supremacy between two air forces provided a never-to-be-forgotten experience for those who were able to watch. Shelter seekers and others who did not see the "show" got a good idea of what they had missed from the next morning's *Times of Malta*. "Axis Heavy Losses", screamed the big black headlines. "Spitfires Slaughter Stukas – Brilliant Team Work of AA Gunners and RAF – 63 Enemy Aircraft Destroyed Over Malta Yesterday." All Malta went wild with joy at this great turn of events. Fresh hope sprang into the hearts of the people. Spitfires, for which we had been crying out for so long, were now here to defend us, shoals of them.'[4]

The Spitfires would not have been enough if not for HMS *Welshman*. Under the command of Captain William Friedberger, she embarked ninety-six Spitfire engines in Gibraltar, and other important cargo, as well as over 100 RAF technicians, all Spitfire specialists. Then, as soon as darkness fell on the evening of 7 May, the mine-layer was disguised as a French destroyer. On her fast voyage, she sailed within thirty miles of French North Africa. She was challenged by a suspicious German Ju88 which circled and even carried out what seemed to be a bombing run. Friedberger ordered his crew not to react other than to wave. Their disguise held. Later, an RAF Catalina arrived, but Friedberger ordered it – by Aldis lamp – to keep well away: a 'French' destroyer escorted by an RAF aircraft would have looked highly suspicious. Another Ju88 arrived, but again *Welshman's* disguise held, and when circled by a French aircraft and challenged by a French shore station, Friedberger ignored them both. That night, they ran at high speed through the difficult shoals which fringe the Tunisian coastline before steaming at full-speed to Malta, arriving two minutes after sunrise. Their greatest risk arose as they turned into Grand Harbour when their paravanes cut two mines which narrowly missed their stern. They docked on 10 May, the day after the Spitfires flew in.

---

2. *Malta Spitfire Pilot*, by Dennis Barnham, page 45.
3. *Ibid.*
4. *Carve Malta on my heart and other wartime stories*, by Frederick Galea, pages 59–60.

The scene the *Welshman* met was one of near total desolation. Wrecks were scattered left and right and masts of sunken ships pointed accusingly skyward. On the various wharfs rubble reached the water's edge. Friedberger was well aware Axis aircraft would soon spot his arrival and he wanted to unload as quickly as possible, hopefully within a single day, and be on his way. Thankfully, Gort was on hand, his presence felt everywhere, offering help and encouragement. All was ready. *Welshman* was soon surrounded by lighters, and working parties quickly began unloading. Two hours later, she was spotted by German recce aircraft and two hours after that, eighty enemy aircraft commenced a sustained and ferocious attack.

An important part of *Welshman's* cargo was six dozen crates of smoke-making compound, which was quickly used. The light winds helped and soon the ship was hidden by artificial smoke. The enemy aircraft were also met by the newly-arrived Spitfires, now in sufficient numbers to make a real difference to the air battle. Over French Creek, eighteen German aircraft were shot down. A few minutes after the raiders departed, Gort boarded *Welshman*. He found her listing, with holes above the water line and her decks covered with debris. But her cargo was on land and she was still seaworthy. That evening she cast off to steer between burnt-out and sunken hulks to a ring of cheers from the bastions of Valletta and Senglea, and the singing of *Roll out the Barrel*. She left behind her much-needed cargo. *Welshman* was back in Gibraltar two days later. This lonely ship served Malta well.

The battle was indeed furious, although the number of enemy aircraft destroyed, published in the *Times of Malta*, was exaggerated. There were also fewer complaints about the condition of the aircraft, although some pilots were returned to Britain because of their lack of operational experience. Fighter Command had a well-established habit of keeping the best and sending a number of what Tedder described as 'also-rans' to Malta.

On the evening of 10 May, Air HQ estimated twenty-three enemy aircraft destroyed, and a further twenty-four damaged, all for the loss of one Spitfire and one pilot missing. That evening, Rome Radio announced the loss of thirty-seven Axis aircraft against the destruction of forty-seven Spitfires. This was a huge success for the defenders of Malta, but that evening Hugh Lloyd found the atmosphere amongst the aircrew subdued. They knew their enemy, and they were all aware of the previous short-lived successes. Famine was not far away and many, even amongst the aircrew, harboured doubts about their ability to hold on to the day's advantage.

Surprisingly, Kesselring reported to Berlin his task of neutralising Malta as an offensive base was complete. His premature and ill-judged comment reveals how poor Germany's intelligence gathering strategy really was. He then reduced *Fliegerkorps II* in order to increase support for Rommel's planned offensive. Although it was not known at the time, Hitler postponed the invasion of Malta until after Rommel captured Tobruk. Kesselring, who always advocated the capture of Malta in order to guarantee supplies to the Afrika Korps, later wrote: 'The abandonment of this project was the first death blow to the whole undertaking in North Africa.'[5]

Viscount Gort's first task was to ensure the island did not starve its way to surrender. He took a firm grip. Yet more stringent rationing was introduced, nutrition experts were brought from Britain and dehydrated foods were flown in. Gas, electric and water supplies were badly affected across the island. In fact Valletta was without these services for five months. Hot drinks were a thing of the past for everyone, service personnel and civilians alike. There was rarely enough fuel oil for pumps to draw water from underground wells, which resulted in little water for drinking and even less for sanitation. Schools were closed, as were places of entertainment. Many of the streets in what had previously been main centres of population were blocked by thousands of tons of stone. Despite all of this, the determination and loyalty of the Maltese did not waiver.

Gort decided expanding communal eating was the answer to the food crisis and Victory Kitchens were established in every town and village. Dubbed 'VKs', they served one portion of food per person per day on a take-away basis in exchange for a coupon, a week's worth of which cost three shillings. At first the VKs did not enjoy much support and there were grumbles and complaints but, as the siege continued with little prospect of relief, they came into their own. As Christina noted, 'a shocking ignorance of culinary art was manifest in some of the dishes doled out.... *Balbuljata*, for example, which in normal times was a delectable Maltese speciality made with scrambled eggs, cheese, onions and tomatoes, had nothing at all in common with the unappetising powdered egg concoction masquerading under the name.'[6] The letters of complaint published in the *Times of Malta* did not go unheeded, but little could be done to improve matters. The Information Office emphasised the widespread use of powdered eggs in Britain, saying they were highly nutritious and strongly recommended by both the Ministry of Food and the Ministry of Health in London, 'the reaction to which was a V-for-Victory sign!'[7]

By May, there were forty VKs in twenty-three locations, with 4,000 people registered to use them. By the end of the year they catered for the majority of the population with 170,000 people registered. Pawlina Cutajar was a VK supervisor whose main task was to keep track of foodstuffs. 'From time to time the books were inspected by officials from the central office who went through the registers with a fine tooth comb. But in spite of every precaution, pilferage was rampant and abuses like presenting forged coupons were common. We pretended not to see through such tricks because we were afraid of reprisals should we lodge reports.'[8]

---

5. *With Prejudice*, by MRAF Lord Tedder, page 309.
6. *Carve Malta on my Heart and other wartime stories*, by Frederick Galea, pages 56–8.
7. *Ibid.*
8. *The People's War Malta: 1940/43*, by Laurence Mizzi, page 235.

The expansion of communal feeding was masterly. Despite the problems, there is little doubt the population owed its survival to the VKs through some very grim days. With a black market rife, control of supplies was essential. Even stocks available on the black market gradually reduced. Christina later recalled: 'When rabbit stew was offered, one did not ask what had become of the cat.'[9] With the lack of oil for cooking, people in their tens of thousands brought what little food they had to the VKs where it could be cooked in bulk, saving precious supplies of kerosene. Arguably, more stringent rationing introduced much earlier might have alleviated the desperate situation. Yet it would only have delayed matters, it would not have relieved them. Gort also pursued a vigorous campaign against waste, especially in the flour mills. There were many occasions when the supply of flour was only enough for ten days, but then the lonely *Welshman* arrived and the situation eased. Over the next two months, she successfully ran the blockade twice more. She was only a single ship, but the stores she delivered were crucial. After her third trip, twenty-one crew members received awards, Captain Friedberger the DSO. Nevertheless, even Gort realised that without a significant resupply effort, the outcome for Malta was inevitable – surrender.

Hugh Lloyd considered Gort a source of inspiration. Whether directing officials, meeting personnel, or cycling from one meeting to another, he was a tower of strength. In Lloyd's view, Gort did more than anyone else to ensure the safety and survival of Malta. Gort himself thought the Maltese showed a stoical determination to withstand everything that is humanly possible to endure, rather than surrender.

With few Marylands left, Harry Coldbeck in his lone PR Spitfire was often the mainstay of Malta's reconnaissance effort. The Air Historical Branch later recorded the first eight months of 1942 as, 'the heaviest and most sustained bombardment in the history of air warfare',[10] with photographic reconnaissance being the work of two or three trained PR pilots working from an airfield subjected to almost continuous attack. At the beginning of the year those pilots were Adrian and Johnnie Walker. Now the recce effort was in the hands of Harry, who was joined by Sergeant Les Colquhoun with another PR Spitfire, and from then on they shared the tasks. Later, two more aircraft and pilots arrived, but one was taken prisoner soon afterwards when his aircraft's engine failed over Sicily.

Day-to-day operations remained under Harry's control although he was not formally appointed as flight commander. The small unit performed extremely well, usually flying three or more sorties every day. The pilots lived together at Siggiewi Signals Station, about a thirty-minute walk from Luqa. Their main activity on the ground was bomb-dodging; there was no social life, although Laddie Lucas and

9. *Supreme Gallantry*, by Tony Spooner, page 212.
10. *RAF Narrative Photographic Reconnaissance, Volume II, May 1941 to August 1943*, by the Air Historical Branch, page 105.

other friends from 249 Squadron at Ta' Qali often visited. Two of the PR Spitfire NCO pilots were awarded DFMs and they were commissioned soon afterwards. Yet the Spitfire recce pilots continued to be ignored by 69 Squadron. Except for monthly signatures in their logbooks, there was no real link with 69 at all. It was only when Wing Commander Tennant's signature was replaced by that of a pilot officer as Acting CO that Harry, a flight lieutenant, became aware of the fact Tennant was posted missing on 15 June.

Harry was an effective and capable planner who could be relied upon to complete his allocated tasks on schedule. He presided over a carefully constructed flying programme to ensure tasking was shared between all available pilots. Very much a team player, he relied on good two-way communication with his pilots with whom he was popular. It was Harry and Les Colquhoun who first photographed glider sites being prepared in Sicily.

Discussion within Harry's small unit about their targets was inevitable. Harry thought it strange Air HQ often seemed to have advance information regarding the sailing, movement and location of merchant ships moving across the Mediterranean, and he also talked about this with Laddie Lucas and others.[11] Harry was puzzled by directives from Air HQ to seek out enemy naval units at specific locations. Invariably, the ships were found at the positions given. More puzzling was the requirement to report sightings at once over the radio in obviously coded language. Some suspected another intelligence source and speculated the Allies had an agent inside Italian naval HQ. Maybe some of their missions were a means by which the Axis could be fooled into believing their ships were simply stumbled upon by British aircraft, that there was no other intelligence source. For the moment, that was as far as it went, but idle talk, even amongst close friends, carried risks.

Despite having more Spitfires, Lloyd continued to martial his resources well, directing Woody to be selective. To begin with, whenever the Axis sent over fighters, or 'little jobs' as Woody preferred to call them, Lloyd kept the Spitfires on the ground, despite a clamour from his pilots to scramble. When the bombers were detected – 'big jobs' – then the Spitfires were released. Laddie Lucas described Woody as being in a class of his own.

Kesselring also varied his tactics, sometimes sending small patrols of up to thirty to circle the island. At other times, he despatched mass fighter sweeps involving every fighter he could muster, up to five times a day. Gradually the Spitfires asserted their authority and, with their airfields secure, they began to push the Axis aircraft further north. The Spitfires now intercepted enemy bombers out to sea by forward interception long before they could unload their lethal cargo. Malta's radar operators and efficient fighter controllers were in their element. The RAF could now pick

---

11. *Malta, The Thorn in Rommel's Side*, Laddie Lucas, page 187.

and choose when and where to give battle, using every tactical advantage available. Sometimes the Luftwaffe sent four or five Ju88 bombers escorted by dozens of fighters to fight their way to their targets. At others, enemy recce missions involved a single Ju88 escorted by eighty Me109s as well as a few dozen Italian fighters. The Axis was dogged and tenacious, but was met in equal measure.

One newly arrived Spitfire pilot said the tempo was indescribable. He said conditions were tough, but the morale of pilots, ground personnel and the army was magnificent. 'The bombing is continuous, on and off every day. One lives here to destroy the Hun and hold him at bay; everything else, living conditions, sleep, food and all the ordinary standards of life have gone by the board. It all makes the Battle of Britain and fighter-sweeps seem child's play by comparison.'[12] When it became clear to Kesselring he could not afford the casualties, he switched back to night bombing. By then, Beaufighter night fighters were well established and they also achieved significant success.

Shortages were affecting everyone and petty pilfering among civilian field workers prompted Jumbo Gracie, now in command of Ta' Qali, to take action by including the following in routine orders: 'A gibbet has been erected on the corner of the road leading to the caves. Any man, woman or child, civilian or service personnel, found guilty of sabotage, theft, or in any other way of impeding the war effort and subsequently shot, will be hung from this gibbet as a warning to others.' Pictures of the gibbet reached London's *Daily Mirror*. The Air Ministry intervened and the gibbet disappeared.

A further sixteen Spitfires arrived from *Eagle* in the middle of May, making seventy-six aircraft in the previous nine days. The resultant victories marked the turning point in the air battle of Malta. By the end of May, Hugh Lloyd estimated 154 Axis aircraft destroyed that month while the tonnage of bombs dropped reduced dramatically from over 500 tons in the first eight days to just over 100 in the remainder of the month. At long last, the airfields began to get back to normal and repairs had an effect. The Spitfires were, however, only part of Malta's salvation. The island could only be truly saved by a convoy. The already stringent food rationing was tightened yet again.

Malta had won an important battle. Only time would tell whether the island could win the war against starvation; a distinct possibility which concerned Gort greatly. Although *Welshman* made a number of runs, and submarines delivered oil and other essentials, the situation remained bleak. The plight of civilians and servicemen alike was distressing, although most remained cheerful and complaints were largely good-natured. The relatively high morale was down to the success of the Spitfires, which many could see overhead every day. As a result of their dramatic

---

12. *Royal Air Force 1939–1945, Volume 2, The Fight Avails*, Denis Richards and Hilary St George Saunders, page 197.

impact on the Luftwaffe, along with, 'the tonic touch of springtime, the spirits of the islanders rose up and scraped the sky. People began to enjoy themselves again. Letting their hair down to hip-level, they flocked in their thousands to what places of entertainment were still left standing. The whirl of social life was stepped up to a fast and furious tempo, nobody caring a damn about the Italian Air Force.

'Confidence in our defenders was such that when the siren went there was no more scurrying to earth like frightened rabbits and foxes. In the cinemas, audiences sat through the picture they had gone to see without recourse to the "Rock Shelter on Premises" – a tag which had become as much a part of a film advertisement as the names of the stars and times of showing. At home, in the streets, in shops and offices, people got back their nerve and faced up to life with fresh courage.

'Once again *Strada Reale* in Valletta became the promenade of the evening stroller; the happy hunting ground of the lover for his lass. Up and down, between the ancient gates of the city and the Palace Square, the light-hearted crowds surged to and fro, gossiping and laughing – relaxing for the first time in many months. And relaxing with them in their leisure hours were the Spitfire pilots. Attired in an outrageous combination of flying kit uniform and civilian dress, they were a great attraction as they ambled the street – often followed by gangs of small boys eager to get a close-up view of their new-found heroes.

'Not unmindful of the charms that lay beneath the bastions of Lascaris, the air boys displayed a lively interest in the work carried on at Fighter Control. Bunches of off-duty crews could be seen hanging round the entrance to the Ops Room like so many stage-door Johnnies. If they could think up some excuse to get inside, so much the better and, as can be imagined, with the influx of all this manhood-in-flower, the private life of a plotter became a thing of joy.

'A girl didn't need to be pretty to get a date – it was enough just to be feminine … as invitations came in by the conveyor belt: meet me tonight at the Premier; let's roller skate at the Rockyvale; see you at eight in the Monico.

'It is doubtful whether the Union Club in Valletta will witness again such scenes of revelry and wild abandon as were enacted between its stately walls at the Saturday night dances… . On Saturday evenings, the Ladies Lounge, famed far beyond the shores of Malta as the "Snake Pit", was cleared of its furniture and carpets, and a rollicking ragtime band moved in to charm the serpents. You wouldn't have known the place. Rank and position went by the board as stuffed shirts and staid old colonels cavorted with the rest of us in such frivolities as "Boomps-a-Daisy", "Hokey-Kokey" and "Knees up, Mother Brown".'[13] Helen Cuell also described their social life as very hectic with lots of dances organised for every imaginable occasion.[14]

---

13. *Carve Malta on my heart and other wartime stories*, by Frederick Galea, pages 63–4.
14. *The People's War Malta: 1940/43*, by Laurence Mizzi, pages 65–6.

Laddie Lucas considered Lloyd and Woody as principal architects of victory with Woody, 'the Service's outstanding controller of the war.'[15] One squadron commander said his pilots had a fanatical faith in Woody's controlling, a faith that gave them completely unreasonable confidence. Woody was a regular at the Union Club to the dismay of those attempting to gain entrance by impersonating officers. Two sergeant pilots, Australian Paul Brennan and New Zealander Ray Hesselyn, found this out for themselves. Woody described them as a perfect team of two who became very fine fighter leaders. They were inseparable, whether fighting brilliantly in the air, or in trouble on the ground. One evening, they awarded themselves 'commissions' to gain access to the Union Club. Wearing officers' rank tabs, they were horrified to bump into Woody. Impersonating an officer was a court martial offence. Woody greeted them warmly, congratulated them on their 'commissions', bought them a whisky apiece, then told them to drink up and scarper before anyone else recognised them. He neglected to mention he was involved in recommending the two 'cobbers' for the commissions they received a few weeks later.

Godfrey Caruana was proprietor of Captain Caruana's, a small tobacconist's shop and bar on Kingsway. Godfrey also owned a cinema, which he kept open as long as possible in spite of the bombing. He took many of the RAF crews to his heart. With liquor scarce, and profiteering rife, Godfrey always managed to serve the real stuff at less than the controlled price and offered a bottle of precious champagne 'on the house' whenever any of his RAF friends left the island. Woody considered the always-smiling Godfrey a brave, generous and resourceful friend, who always offered a warm welcome in a way few could.

With so much destruction, and many historical buildings gone, rebuilding would take years. Nor was the bombing yet over. Many were killed and many more would carry the scars of what they suffered for the rest of their lives. Others had gone beyond their mental endurance. Tamara was one. Late in the afternoon of 30 May, she received the order to leave Malta at 10.00 pm that evening and, 'two years of the most gruelling experience in my life had drawn to a close. I packed two very meagre suitcases, had a last party at Captain Caruana's bar and, at ten o'clock sharp, we were at Luqa aerodrome where the Lodestar I was to embark on was warming its engines. Christina and my husband had come to see me off. I left with the feeling that I should have been braver and stayed to the end.'[16] Tamara urged Christina to leave but, 'I did not want to be a Ratcliffe deserting a sinking ship and besides, after having gone so far, I wanted to stay and see things through.'[17] Tamara's friend Aida was found and was buried in *Santa Maria Addolorata* cemetery in Paola.

---

15. *Malta, The Thorn in Rommel's Side*, Laddie Lucas, page 38.
16. *Women of Malta*, by Frederick Galea, page 126.
17. *Carve Malta on my Heart and other wartime stories*, by Frederick Galea, page 64.

Malta's situation remained desperate and it was a problem the Spitfires could not alleviate. Starvation date was calculated as mid-August, with the surrender date earlier; these were inescapable facts. Only a convoy could save the island. After the disaster of the March attempt, Hugh Lloyd made it clear he was not prepared to accept another until the air situation improved. Tedder had earlier asked Lloyd whether he would like to be relieved, having been AOC for eleven months, two months longer than the maximum envisaged. Lloyd asked to stay until the anticipated May delivery of Spitfires, which he thought sufficient to safeguard any vessels coming within range of Malta. By mid-May, the continuous fighting had reduced the number of available Spitfires to twenty-five. Lloyd insisted he must have sixty as a minimum. He was again asked whether he wished to be relieved. He requested the privilege of seeing the next convoy safely into Grand Harbour. The planned May convoy became two, delayed until June.

Despite the presence of more Spitfires, what befell the earlier efforts at resupply did not bode well for the clearer days and shorter nights of June. The Luftwaffe and the Regia Aeronautica were ready and waiting in Sardinia and Sicily for merchantmen from the west, and in Crete and Cyrenaica for those from the east. To prepare the way, Malta's Wellingtons renewed their assaults on the Italian fleet. Kesselring's counters against Luqa impacted the Wellington operations, but this time they were not driven away. In the face of the Wellingtons' persistence, the Italian warships in Cagliari and Messina were withdrawn. Those at Palermo and Taranto proved more stubborn. The Wellington bombers were then replaced by torpedo-carrying Wellingtons as it was certain the Italian fleet would put to sea. The new Wellingtons, along with torpedo-carrying Beauforts for day operations, posed a significant threat to the Italians. The Spitfires, which by then were reinforced, planned to maintain a continuous air patrol over the next merchantmen once within 100 miles of the island. Lloyd prepared the airfields well against anticipated attacks. Nearby were 250 soldiers with trucks loaded for rapid-runway repair, and 200 more to help look after the aircraft. With the RN's Swordfish and Albacores at readiness, this was another display of 'jointery' at its best.

Operation Vigorous came from the east, Operation Harpoon from the west, both scheduled to arrive simultaneously to split the Axis response. Admiral Vian sailed with Vigorous, reporting to Admiral Harwood, the new C-in-C Mediterranean. With little adverse weather to hide the vast armada of over fifty ships, Harwood sought Tedder's help to keep the Italians at bay, but rapidly unfolding events in the desert impacted significantly on what the RAF could provide. Command of Vigorous was also remote, exercised jointly by Harwood and Tedder in Alexandria. This resulted in an inflexible structure, removed from the scene, relying on rapid communications.

Part of the RAF contribution came from 39 Squadron's Beauforts in Egypt. Patrick Gibbs was a flight commander and attended a conference to coordinate RAF missions. He recalled his AOC's opening words: 'I need hardly tell you gentlemen that the fate of Malta may depend on the success of this operation.'[18] Gibbs thought the operation bore the stamp of desperation. The plan included a feint, four ships sailing ahead to draw the Italian fleet to sea prematurely. It was bombed soon after setting sail. Worryingly, information was very slow to reach Harwood and Tedder. By the time they realised the inadequacy of their communications Vigorous was at sea. Coinciding with its departure, Rommel attacked, resulting in the loss of many RAF desert strips and much of the convoy's air umbrella. Vigorous was now at the mercy of Axis aircraft from Crete and Cyrenaica.

What followed was a catalogue of confusion compounded by delayed communications. Two slow cargo ships were sent back to Alexandria and two corvettes returned with engine trouble. A merchant ship also went down to enemy bombers. Overnight, Vian was ordered to reverse course as the Italian fleet was said to be closing and in the confusion of turning so many vessels around, a destroyer was lost and a cruiser damaged by E-boats. Dawn saw the ships retracing their route into the area of the greatest air threat. Meanwhile, news about RAF assaults on the Italian fleet was anxiously awaited. No news came. In fact communications were so poor Harwood and Tedder had no hope of making timely, informed judgements. Nevertheless, they ordered all available RAF attack aircraft to launch.

The Malta-based Wellingtons and Beauforts were unsuccessful. American-built Liberators from Egypt were next and claimed twenty-three hits. The reality was a single hit which had no effect. As they departed, they witnessed the final air assault by five 39 Squadron Beauforts, all that remained of twelve decimated by enemy fighters en route. Their torpedoes missed. Gibbs was a member of the lucky five exhausted crews to reach Luqa. All the aircraft were damaged, Gibbs himself crash-landing wheels up; 39 Squadron ceased to exist as a useful striking force. Despite the airmen's bravery, all their attacks failed.

Unaware of the true outcome, Harwood and Tedder ordered Vigorous to turn around, placing it into the path of the Italian fleet. When a report was received the Italians were closing, Vian was again ordered to reverse course. Two hours later, the order was reversed but Vian made a judgement call: he elected to continue to withdraw. He was advised by Admiral Harwood that the threat posed by the Italian fleet had abated and the way to Malta was now clear, but Vian no longer had sufficient anti-aircraft ammunition for the passage.

Vigorous was an abject failure. The Allies lost two merchantmen, three destroyers and one torpedo boat. Many other vessels were damaged. But there were lessons

---

18. *Torpedo Leader on Malta*, by Wg Cdr Patrick Gibbs, page 68.

here about jointery and effective liaison, the need for meticulous planning and timely communication. Command of a Malta convoy by remote control was never again used.

Harpoon, from Gibraltar, was also subject to intense air assaults. A cruiser and merchant ship were disabled at a cost of eighteen enemy aircraft. It faced its greatest challenge in the narrow Sicilian Straits after the withdrawal of the RN's heavy escorts. At dawn on 16 June, the escorts were engaged by Italian warships and suffered heavily. At the same time, one cargo vessel was sunk by dive-bombers. The remainder of Harpoon, under Captain C.C. Hardy, headed for Malta, leaving behind two disabled destroyers and one merchant ship under tow. Another cargo ship was crippled and Hardy then made the brave decision to save what he could. The crews of the two merchantmen were taken off and the ships torpedoed. One was a tanker. The two very badly damaged destroyers were left to their own devices. These were HMS *Bedouin* and HMS *Partridge*. Soon afterwards they fought a distinguished action against two Italian cruisers and Italian torpedo bombers. *Bedouin* succeeded in shooting down her last assailant, but then sank within eight minutes. Her crew were picked up by the Italian cruisers which then withdrew unexpectedly at high speed, pursued by Fleet Air Arm Albacores. *Partridge* eventually reached Gibraltar.

When Harpoon's two remaining battered, damaged merchant ships – *Troilus* and *Orari* – finally entered Grand Harbour, they were greeted by thousands of people in silence, almost in reverence, given what they had endured. That was it – two out of six – but they delivered 20,000 tons of vital supplies. Gort ensured there was no delay in unloading, completed within forty-eight hours by soldiers and sailors working around the clock. It was a great achievement to get even two ships through, and although the quantity of stores was relatively small, it saved Malta from starvation for a further two to three months. Nevertheless, rationing now reached its peak, the hunger of both garrison and population growing worse. Hugh Lloyd later commented: 'Had we taken serious notice of our supply situation in 1941, and had we taken a strong line and brought the Maltese fully into our confidence, we should not have been reduced to our very parlous state in the spring of 1942.'[19] The cost of both operations was the loss of eleven ships and eleven more damaged; the RAF lost at least forty aircraft. But more time, very valuable time, was bought by the lives of Allied sailors and airmen. Meanwhile, Churchill pressed for another resupply run.

Without an aircraft, Patrick Gibbs had time on his hands. He was convinced the way to deal with Axis shipping was to have a strong anti-shipping force permanently based in Malta, rather than Lloyd having to beg, borrow or 'steal' aircraft passing through. His Group HQ in Alexandria hadn't been receptive to

---

19. *Briefed to Attack*, by AM Sir Hugh Lloyd, page 230.

his ideas so he took himself off to Lascaris and gave the SASO (Senior Air Staff Officer) the benefit of his wisdom. He soon found himself in front of Hugh Lloyd. 'I found him not only the personification of aggression, but also the possessor of sufficient sense of humour not to resent my ideas; on the contrary he welcomed them.'[20] Gibbs suggested two Beaufort squadrons be based on the island, with 39 Squadron transferred from Egypt. Neither the failure of Vigorous, nor Rommel's apparently unstoppable advance, 'influenced the decision of this great leader who never thought in terms of retreat; the idea of using Malta as a means of stabbing Rommel in the back and frustrating his plan at this last moment must have been irresistible to him.'[21] Gibbs left Malta on 16 June; six days later he was back with six Beauforts of 39 Squadron. Within three hours he and his crews were in action. Two aircraft were shot down and Gibbs' aircraft was written off because of flak damage. But that didn't put Gibbs or Lloyd off either.

There was a discordant note that month involving Harry Coldbeck's Spitfire recce unit. A bombing mission was planned against an Axis tanker subject to confirmation it was at Benghazi. Harry allocated the mission to a recently-arrived pilot who reported the tanker was not there as expected. Based on the pilot's visual report the strike was cancelled. When the photographs were developed, they showed the tanker was indeed in harbour. By then it was too late to mount the bombing mission.[22] This infuriated the AOC: a tanker, whether empty or laden, was the most prized target of all and to have missed such an opportunity was a major failing. Few could have any doubts about the importance of a tanker to the Afrika Korps pressing forward against a retreating 8th Army. Air HQ, so long accustomed to their recce aircraft always coming back with the goods, would have felt very badly let down.

On 15 June, an investiture to decorate some of Malta's servicemen was held in front of the *Auberge de Castille*. There was some anxiety about the likelihood of an air raid and the risk to the crowd, but everything went without a hitch. Personnel from all three services, and from every part of the Commonwealth, were applauded by colleagues and by thousands of Maltese. High above, friends of those honoured were in action holding off the enemy. But news from North Africa was bleak. Tobruk, which held out so well when isolated in 1941, fell to Rommel on 21 June with over 35,000 taken prisoner. Churchill considered its loss a disgrace. Rommel continued relentlessly into Egypt. Despite German and Italian Army staffs opposing the advance, Hitler backed Rommel to press on, solving his supply problems by capturing Allied dumps. A few days later, the Germans began a new offensive in Russia, aimed at the Caucasus.

---

20. *Torpedo Leader on Malta*, by Wg Cdr Patrick Gibbs, page 86.
21. *Ibid.*
22. *The Maltese Spitfire*, by Sqn Ldr Harry Coldbeck, pages 55–6.

Kesselring renewed his assault on Malta at the beginning of July, timed to coincide with the Afrika Korps' advance. Allied attacks on Axis shipping continued, but preoccupation with the June convoys had allowed Axis supplies to reach North Africa, contributing to Rommel's success. By then 39 Squadron was well established and shared the same building at Luqa as 69 Squadron. Hugh Lloyd often visited Gibbs and his crews prior to their night missions to impress on them how important their attacks were. Invariably he would be waiting on their return. One particular night Lloyd was at Luqa when an air raid occurred. He ordered all onlookers to the shelters, but he remained next to the runway to direct operations. 'His orders kept the beacon of searchlights alight at intervals during the raid to guide our aircraft in, and caused the flare path to be lit when our petrol was running dangerously low. While raiders circled above, interspersed with friendly aircraft, he made the aerodrome a lighted target to help us, and stood on the runway in the open while flares hung overhead and the bombs fell, making every effort to bring his aircraft safely down.'[23] This occurred just after Gibbs landed following a six-hour mission. Having personally debriefed Gibbs, Hugh Lloyd returned to the runway to see the remaining Beauforts in. Lloyd was so inspiring, that if he had asked it of him, Gibbs would have taken off for another six-hour flight.

Luqa was hit time and time again, but repaired quickly. Delayed action bombs were a constant menace and there were many casualties as well as acts of courage from personnel on the ground. One day, Jack Vowles and his friend 'Ginge', an aircraft radio technician, were making their way from the aircraft pens to the dining hall. There was a short cut using a road which crossed the runway, but they usually walked the longer way round the perimeter as there were slit-trenches and sandbagged emplacements every twenty to thirty yards in which to take shelter. Ginge pointed to a storeroom across the airfield; its door was open and he thought cigarettes might be available, but Jack refused to take the direct route. Ginge left Jack, heading to the storeroom alone shouting back as he left, 'chicken, chicken'.

Later, Jack was with a half a dozen others in the dining hall when the siren sounded. Four of his friends leapt up and ran for the nearest shelter shouting for Jack to come with them. Jack was starving and said no; he was determined to get something to eat. Sitting opposite him was a fitter from the transport section; he also stayed, as well as one other, also desperate for food. Soon bombs began to fall and the far end of the dining hall collapsed. Now was the time to make their exit but they had left it late. As the fitter opened the door he was hit, falling backwards into Jack, who fell back into the chap behind him. When they got to their feet it was clear the fitter was dead, killed by shrapnel hitting him in the chest. They picked him up and laid him on a table. With the noise overhead having abated, Jack went in search

---

23. *Torpedo Leader on Malta*, by Wg Cdr Patrick Gibbs, page 134.

of something to eat, pulling open a serving hatch. The small space was occupied by a Maltese cook who shouted: 'My shelter, my shelter!'

Jack left to find his friends. All four had been caught in the open and blown to pieces. On his way back across the airfield to the squadron dispersal, Jack came across a stray dog nosing around something; it was something ginger. He retrieved what the dog had. It was Ginge's scalp; all that remained of his friend. He took it to a gun emplacement and explained what it was before reporting back for duty. 'You couldn't afford to dwell on things,' said Jack. He formed part of the firing party for his friends' funerals. There were four normal coffins and one small box.

Within days Jack was taken ill again and admitted to Mtarfa Hospital which was bombed during his stay, and not for the first time, despite it being clearly marked. The hospital's commanding officer, Lieutenant Colonel William Hamilton, was very seriously injured; sadly, his wife Florence died of her wounds. Following another operation, Jack spent a few days at the St Paul's Bay rest area before reporting back to Luqa. It was work, work, work – days, dates and times meant nothing. They just had to get on with things. Jack still belonged to 69 Squadron, but remained attached to the Wellingtons of 221 Squadron. He never lost his caution when crossing the airfield. They would often walk in pairs carrying a machine gun – loaded with tracer – from a wrecked Wellington. They walked back-to-back watching for marauding German fighters. If one swooped toward them, a burst of tracer fired in front of the enemy fighter was usually enough to put it off.

The air fighting was relentless, but the Spitfires continued to enjoy significant success with superb controlling by Woody. Axis control was heard at one stage to say, 'Look after that 88 in the sea,' to which a German fighter pilot replied, 'which one'.[24] Kesselring kept up the pressure, but he knew he was losing. The RAF suffered losses, but there was a constant stream of Spitfires flown in as reinforcements from the carriers *Eagle* and *Furious*. Squadron Leader Lord David Douglas-Hamilton commanded 603 (City of Edinburgh) Squadron. He considered Woody to be Malta's outstanding fighter controller who, 'was absolutely tireless, and always considered the pilots first. During practically every big raid … he controlled the fighters from the operating room. It was a miracle how he stood up to the strain, but every pilot was extremely grateful that he did; for nothing was better calculated to inspire confidence during a big battle than 'Woody' giving instructions on the R/T in his calm friendly voice.'[25]

Luqa's importance as a staging post was emphasised when it despatched the 901st aircraft on the night of 10 July. Given the situation for much of the last two years, this was a remarkable achievement. It was clear from the reduced attacks, and the unwillingness of Axis aircraft to fully commit, that the air battle of Malta

24. Quoted in *Briefed to Attack*, by AM Sir Hugh Lloyd, page 226.
25. *The Air Battle of Malta*, by James Douglas-Hamilton, page 39.

was almost over. In the first thirteen days of July, Hugh Lloyd put the total of Axis aircraft as definitely destroyed at 102 against the loss of 25 Spitfire pilots killed or missing. He estimated the figure of Axis aircraft shot down the previous year at 693, with a further 191 destroyed on the ground. By mid-July, not surprisingly, 'Smiling Albert' Kesselring was no longer smiling; he had had enough.

The raids may have lessened, but devastation and heartbreak was still being caused by legacies of previous bombing. Guza Bondin, married to a gunner serving in the Royal Malta Artillery, was seven months pregnant when she went with her nine-month-old daughter to collect her milk ration on 23 July. As she turned a corner in St Michael Street Zurrieq, delayed action bombs began to explode. Guza squeezed herself against a door and covered her child as best she could to protect her from stones raining down all around. Despite her efforts, her daughter was struck in the head by a splinter. Her unconscious baby died on the way home. Guza also lost the child she was carrying. Her experience that summer of 1942 contributed to two further miscarriages.

On the island many were exhausted and it was time to relieve key personnel. Keith Park arrived to take over from Hugh Lloyd. He wanted to retain Woody, but Lloyd insisted he be relieved as he was exhausted. Woody left in July after his third successive tour as a senior controller. Park knew Adrian Warburton, still in Egypt, where he'd been for four of Park's six months as AOC Air HQ Cairo. No doubt Hugh Lloyd also briefed him about the man he judged as his premier recce pilot. The critical Benghazi recce failure which had so upset Lloyd may also have been an important factor in determining Adrian's future. Lloyd departed to join Tedder's staff, having served as AOC for fourteen months. An unknown civilian presented him with a cigarette case bearing the letters MTAP. Lloyd discovered the inscription stood for 'Malta thanks air protection.' Two weeks later, Air Vice-Marshal Hugh Pughe Lloyd, CBE, was knighted, his earlier CBE dating from September 1941. Malta had taken a battering and when the Chief of the Imperial General Staff, General Alan Brooke, toured Valletta and the dockyards at the beginning of August, he thought the destruction inconceivable; it reminded him of Ypres and Arras at their worst in the First World War.

Keith Park further developed the forward interception policy often credited with winning Malta's air war, but this was won by Lloyd in the hard-pressed days of April and May. With the RAF growing ever stronger, Malta's offensive roles could now be sharpened and made more deadly. Patrick Gibbs likened Lloyd to a bastion, Park to a rapier. 'Rarely can two such different personalities have been so right in the right place at the right time.'[26] At the end of Gibbs' first meeting with Park he was promoted to wing commander.

---

26. *Torpedo Leader on Malta*, by Wg Cdr Patrick Gibbs, page 145.

Park said only fighter aircraft were to remain within the perimeter of Luqa. Other aircraft continued to operate from there, but were parked in dispersals elsewhere. This ensured the fighters were as close as possible to the runways in order to scramble quickly. As the PR Spitfires were not fighters, Harry Coldbeck was directed to move them to Safi, connected to Luqa by a series of taxiways. From then on, he was required to plan three flying waves each day, the first of which meant getting airborne an hour before dawn, then at midday, and once more at dusk. As the recce Spitfires had no form of cockpit lighting, the pilots used torches attached by rubber bands to various fittings in the cockpit. Harry kept on top of these challenges and led his unit well; he was a planner by instinct and quickly adapted to the requirements of his new AOC.

Adrian's second so-called 'rest period', from March, turned out much like his first. He was determined to get back onto operations, but first took some leave. Having borrowed an old Hawker Hind biplane, he set off to visit his father, Geoffrey, now in Haifa. Somewhere over Gaza, the aircraft's engine failed and he made a forced landing in the desert. The aircraft was a total loss, although Adrian emerged unhurt and made his way out of the desert on foot. On later photographs, he wears the 'flying boot' emblem on his left breast pocket which was awarded unofficially to those who crashed in the desert and 'walked out'.

Adrian and his father were on very good terms by then, both holders of the DSO. Geoffrey was also appointed OBE for gallantry when leading a shore party onto a burning ship and fighting the fire for two days. Adrian wrote to his mother from Haifa, but said nothing about the realities of his work. He spent two weeks there before returning to 2 PRU at Heliopolis in April. For the remainder of the month, he seemed content to undertake routine air tests and delivery flights. Of great significance for him was a short flight in a PR Spitfire, with which 2 PRU was being equipped, although to begin with he mostly flew the Beaufighter, which was further modified with additional cameras. On at least three flights he was accompanied by his father, who spent some time in the Cairo area. From May, Adrian mostly flew PR Spitfires. His flights took him throughout the Middle East, covering Greece and Crete, and many of the Greek Islands. He also became familiar with airfields in Palestine, Lebanon and Syria, and often photographed the coastal road along which Rommel was advancing toward Egypt. Adrian was never daunted by equipment failures, always endeavouring to find a way of bringing back the goods. On one flight operating above 30,000 feet, his oxygen system failed. He simply dropped down to 19,000 feet to complete the task, despite being at risk of interception by enemy fighters and within range of the heavier flak weapons.

Adrian was now much more comfortable in the company of others, and he attended many parties where, according to some, he was idolised by women. This was unsurprising given his looks and array of medal ribbons; he was twenty-three years old. Tony Spooner, who earlier commanded the Wellington Special Duties Flight at Luqa, was in Egypt at the time and later questioned whether Adrian played the field. This may have been the case, although Tony himself acknowledged this may have been what others may have expected. Squadron crewrooms are ideal for discussions about air tactics, but they are also notorious hotbeds of gossip. Whatever the situation, Adrian did not appear to have been involved in any serious relationships away from Malta.

He still had a thirst for ultra-low flying. Apparently he flew his Beaufighter down the Cairo–Suez road, aiming at an army staff car. He was so low the terrified driver swerved into a ditch. Later he did the same thing to a Bedouin on a camel. Both totally ignored him.

By the summer, the Allies were very much on the back foot in North Africa. Had it only been six months since Tedder considered plans for potential landings in Sicily? Rommel's Afrika Korps now appeared unstoppable with Cairo and the Suez Canal within reach. Defeat stared Britain in the face and in the battle for supplies, the Axis was winning. Rommel's advances were evidence of that, whereas Malta was being strangled. It took General Auchinleck to stop Rommel at a little known railway halt only sixty miles from Alexandria. Hitler again postponed the invasion of Malta in favour of Rommel's advance, against the German High Command's advice. Hitler's decision would be judged at that railway halt; it was called El Alamein.

With Rommel so close, Admiral Harwood moved the Mediterranean Fleet and its HQ further east. There were also some hastily arranged evacuations of female personnel and civilians to Israel, and Adrian undertook a number of these flights. He also accompanied the first bombing raid flown by American crews in their Liberator heavy bombers. Much was made about the accuracy of the American technique of precision bombing. Adrian's task was to photograph the results of this first raid flown against no opposition; he was unimpressed and recorded no damage resulted. He was even less impressed when fired at by the American crews.

The relatively comfortable life 2 PRU had enjoyed at Heliopolis came to an end with the looming threat from the west. The unit relocated to desert strips less vulnerable to enemy attack. At one such strip, Adrian talked to Norman Shirley. Afterwards, Norman reflected, Adrian didn't seem to have an aim in life and he wondered whether he had lost the edge. Not long afterwards, on 11 August, Adrian was on his way back to Malta in a PR Spitfire where the situation was in the balance.

A resupply run to Malta in July was impossible given the demands of the Battle of the Atlantic, the Russian convoys, and the situation in the Far East; there were simply insufficient ships available. Operation Pedestal was therefore planned for August. There was little point in secrecy as it was on such a vast scale and, as it was from the west, secrecy was impossible once it passed through the narrow straits at Gibraltar. The armada comprised of fifty-nine warships to support fourteen merchant ships. Three aircraft carriers, carrying a total of seventy-two aircraft, were also included; *Indomitable* from the Indian Ocean, *Victorious* from the Home Fleet and *Eagle*, based in Gibraltar. One other carrier, *Furious*, carried forty Spitfires destined for Malta. After so many 'lessons learnt' on previous deliveries, surely the embarkation authorities would get this one right.

Geoffrey Wellum was 20-years-old and already an experienced Spitfire flight commander. Having joined the RAF at seventeen, he fought throughout the Battle of Britain, earning the nickname 'Boy'. With just twenty-four hours' notice he found himself on *Furious*, detailed to lead ten of forty Spitfires to Malta. As soon as he and his colleagues looked at their aircraft they noticed they were fitted with old De Haviland airscrews which limited the aircraft's thrust. *Furious* also had a ramp two-thirds of the way down her flight deck to throw biplanes into the air and help slow them down on landing. Such a ramp would also throw the Spitfires into the air before they had flying speed. With overload tanks fitted, and reduced power available because of the airscrew, there was little prospect of a safe take-off, especially for those aircraft at the front of the queue. A trial take-off confirmed this: the aircraft just made it, but of course was unable to land back on the carrier and landed elsewhere. That reduced the number of Spitfires to thirty-nine. After much discussion with the ship's captain, the latter signalled the Air Ministry, stating the operation would have to be called off unless hydromatic airscrews were made available. Two days later the airscrews arrived and a further successful trial was carried out, although that reduced the number of Spitfires by one more.[27] Now *Furious* was ready and another lesson was learnt.

Pedestal was commanded by Vice Admiral Edward Neville Syfret, an experienced and determined officer familiar with the Mediterranean. The merchant ships were large and fast, carrying between them 120,000 tons of supplies. Eleven were British and two were American. One was American-built and British-manned. This was the largest, the modern oil tanker *Ohio* of 14,150 tons, the most vital and most vulnerable of all. Full of fuel oil, a single hit could easily turn her into an inferno. She had an all-British crew of fifty-three and her master, Dudley Mason, was a quietly spoken man of thirty-nine. The combined crews of those sailing under the Red Duster and the White Ensign numbered 10,000.

Opposing Admiral Syfret was the Italian fleet, together with eighty E-boats and two dozen submarines, the latter split between the Western Mediterranean and the narrows between Sicily and Tunisia. Available Axis aircraft numbered 420.

---

27. *First Light*, by Geoffrey Wellum, pages 309–24.

The day before the planned Spitfire launch, Geoffrey Wellum gave his allocated aircraft the once over. Armourers arrived at the same time and promptly removed all his aircraft's ammunition, replacing it with cigarettes. This was to save weight they said, although it would also do wonders for Malta's garrison. Geoffrey hoped the Germans and Italians didn't know.[28]

Soon after passing Gibraltar on 11 August, Pedestal was overflown by a Spanish airliner, almost certainly spotting for the Axis. An hour later, *U-73*, one of a wolf-pack of twelve strung out across the flotilla's line of advance, dived under a destroyer screen disrupted by some ships refuelling from oilers. At the time *Furious* was flying off her aircraft. *U-73* launched four torpedoes. All hit HMS *Eagle*. She capsized and sank within eight minutes, taking with her all her aircraft except four which were airborne at the time. Remarkably, given the speed with which *Eagle* sank, 929 of her crew were rescued; 160 perished.

Geoffrey was sitting in his aircraft on *Furious* when *Eagle* was hit and saw the plume of smoke. This added urgency to the aircraft launch and he was soon airborne seconds before an incoming air raid arrived overhead. His three-hour flight to Luqa was uneventful and all nine of Geoffrey's section arrived safely. Only one of thirty-eight Spitfires failed to arrive. A well-rehearsed plan was immediately put into action. Geoffrey was directed to a blast pen, and surrounded by soldiers and airmen who quickly refuelled and rearmed his aircraft for a waiting pilot to fly. Even before he could remove his parachute, an open MG drove up and he recognised Keith Park who told him to stay quiet about the *Eagle*.[29]

Back at sea and for the rest of the day, the U-boats tried their hand, but the destroyer screen held. Nevertheless, tracks of many torpedoes were seen and, in a six-hour period, the vast fleet made seventeen emergency turns to steer away from the submarine threat. No other ships were hit. By evening the submarines were left well astern. Soon after dark, only minutes after the last of the defending fighters landed back on the carriers, the vessels were targeted by thirty-six Ju88s and He111s in a very carefully planned and well-coordinated attack delivered with skill and daring. Somehow, none of the ships were hit, despite Axis claims to have sunk an aircraft carrier, a cruiser and a merchant ship. Four German aircraft were shot down. Throughout the night, Admiral Syfret could do nothing to counter the Italian long-range reconnaissance seaplanes from Sardinia which shadowed the armada keeping just out of range of his guns. The RAF in Malta hit the Italian airbases in Sardinia that night, and early next morning Syfret launched his fighters which successfully engaged and shot down two of the seaplanes; the third escaped into cloud.

The first Axis air raid of 12 August involved twenty-four aircraft; eight were shot down by carrier-borne Martlets and Hurricanes, and only eleven reached the

---

28. *Ibid.*
29. *Ibid.*

merchant ships, where two more were shot down by gunners. The ships suffered no damage. That afternoon came another carefully planned air assault involving seventy bombers with sixty long-range fighter escorts. It was a good plan but, perhaps because of the overnight RAF strikes on their bases, the attackers were ineffective. The Axis mission was disrupted by defending fighters and the bombers achieved only one success. The merchant ship *Deucalion* was hit and had to be abandoned. No sooner was the crew clear of the vessel than it exploded and sank. Thirteen merchant ships remained.

At the end of an afternoon dodging torpedoes, a destroyer sank another Italian submarine. So far, Pedestal was doing well having covered 800 miles; they were now only 300 miles from Malta. They had sunk two submarines, and shot down twenty-six aircraft for the loss of *Eagle* and *Deucalion*. Although there was no longer any risk of being targeted from Sardinia, they were now entering the most dangerous stretch of waters, the narrows between Tunisia and Sicily.

At 6.00 pm that evening, 120 German and Italian aircraft arrived in yet another series of well-coordinated attacks, culminating in all the bombers being overhead the ships within a twenty-minute window. When they left, there were still thirteen merchant ships heading for Malta. But the aircraft carrier *Indomitable* was very badly damaged. Her aircraft landed on the already crowded *Victorious*. On top of that, the destroyer, HMS *Foresight*, was left listing with engines stopped; she was scuttled the following day. Pedestal pressed on; 250 miles to go. An hour later, Admiral Syfret turned back for Gibraltar, taking with him those heavy units unable to risk the narrows. He left four cruisers and twelve destroyers under Admiral Harold Burrough to protect the thirteen remaining merchant ships.

Less than an hour later, Burrough's flagship, HMS *Nigeria*, leading the port column of merchant ships, was hit by a torpedo and came to a sudden halt. Within a minute, HMS *Cairo*, leading the starboard column, was torpedoed and began to sink. The *Ohio* was hit two minutes later and also stopped. Within three minutes, Pedestal's three most important ships were disabled. *Nigeria* and *Cairo*, being column leaders, were the only ships equipped with fighter-direction apparatus. This was essential in order to work with Malta-based Beaufighters, the only aircraft capable of offering any form of air cover at that distance from Malta.

When *Ohio* was hit, a twenty-four foot high by twenty-seven foot wide hole was blown out of her side. A RN signaller said, 'when ours came the shock didn't seem so bad. There wasn't much noise about it. So little in fact, that after I made my way to the bridge, I found the first mate unaware of the fact. It seemed a silly situation and I actually tapped him on the shoulder and said, "Excuse me, Sir, but we've been hit and we are burning badly".'[30] Thankfully the water surging into the ship helped

---

30. *The Air Battle of Malta*, by the Ministry of Information, page 82.

suppress the fires which were brought under control. When the *Ohio* got under way she could barely make seven knots because of difficulty steering.

Time was lost as Burrough transferred his flag to a destroyer and regained effective command. For a time, things were chaotic and confused as individual ships swung wildly to avoid torpedoes, and one another, before moving to starboard away from the perceived U-boat threat. Later, with no fighter direction, Malta's Beaufighters were forced to return to base. Soon afterwards the flotilla was found by torpedo bombers. The hours of darkness were long and hard for Pedestal's sailors, and dawn was a long time coming.

Santa Eliza was damaged by a bomber in the very last minutes of daylight on 12 August. She struggled on at reduced speed, trailing behind the rest as darkness fell at last. *Empire Hope* was the first to go that night, torpedoed by an Italian aircraft and abandoned. Then there were twelve. Next was *Clan Ferguson*, hit twice by torpedo-aircraft about fifteen minutes later. An ammunition ship, she lasted all of thirty seconds before blowing up. Now there were eleven. The same aircraft that torpedoed *Clan Ferguson* then hit *Brisbane Star*. With its bow blown off, taking on water and her engines stopped, only the determination of her master, Captain Neville Riley, kept her afloat. After twenty minutes, she was underway again at very slow speed, heading for Tunisia. Captain Riley was determined to reach Grand Harbour, if necessary on his own.

Then the E-boats came. *Glenorchy* was sunk by an E-boat at 4.00 am, no survivors. Ten left. *Almeria Lykes* was hit fifteen minutes later, and was abandoned by her crew; now nine. Bringing up the rear, *Santa Eliza* was also found by the E-boats and sunk at 5.00 am. Her crew was picked up by the destroyers *Penn* and *Bramham*. Then there were eight. At about the same time *Wairangi* also went down to an E-boat. That left seven. *Rochester Castle* was manoeuvred hard by her captain, Richard Wren, trying to avoid torpedoes launched by E-boats. By skilful handling, he avoided eleven, but not the twelfth. Despite a huge hole through which water flooded her forward holds, Captain Wren was able to steer and maintain a good speed. 'It had been a wild night's work: starshells, tracers, gun flashes; the MTBs came within 50 yards or so of their prey, sweeping the decks of the Allied ships with the fire of their automatic weapons. Torpedoes burst with dull crashes that were heard only too plainly; huge columns of dirty water were thrown up by the explosions as high as the mastheads and seemed to hang, glittering for minutes over the decks of the stricken ships.'[31]

After the E-boats left, the convoy got into some sort of order, two cruisers and seven destroyers escorting *Rochester Castle*, *Wainarama* and the *Melbourne Star*. Meanwhile, *Ohio* and *Port Chalmers* were doing their best to catch up. The cruiser

---

31. *Malta: The Siege is Raised*, by David Woodward, published in *History of the Second World War, Volume 3, No 13* (Purnell, 1967), page 1257.

*Manchest*er, disabled overnight, was scuttled. Another cruiser, HMS *Kenya,* was torpedoed but was able to continue. By dawn *Ohio,* now making thirteen knots, re-joined the group, whose exhausted crews tried to keep their damaged and leaking charges afloat and together. Then the bombers returned.

Without fighter-direction, there was no continuous fighter cover and the bombing was relentless. In less than an hour, *Ohio* suffered six near misses from dive-bombers screaming down to masthead height. *Wainarama* was hit by a dive-bomber, and with petrol stored on her deck, exploded and sank immediately. All that was left was blazing oil on the surface of the sea slowly spreading toward the survivors. Now there were six. The *Melbourne Star,* immediately behind *Wainarama,* was unable to turn quickly enough to clear the flames. In the confusion and chaos of the next few seconds, thirty-four of *Melbourne Star's* crew, thinking their ship was going down, jumped overboard into the burning sea. HMS *Ledbury* rescued thirty. The *Ohio,* passing close by, was set ablaze once more. *Rochester Castle* had also been hit but pressed on. The *Ohio* suffered more near misses and a Ju88 bomber crashed onto her deck. Later, she was perfectly straddled by 500lb bombs which lifted her clean out of the water. A few minutes later, a Ju87 Stuka dive-bomber, damaged by *Ohio's* guns, crashed onto her deck. By now, the ship's engines were vibrating badly and she was listing. Her engines soon stopped; they were never restarted. Slowly, *Ohio* slipped behind. Her chances were slim.

The *Rochester Castle* was damaged at about the same time, her engines stopped and fires broke out. The engines were restarted and eventually the fires brought under control, but she was dangerously low in the water and damage to the steering made it hard to steer a course. *Dorset* was hit by a dive-bomber and disabled. She was damaged again by a later attack and finally sunk that evening. That left five. *Port Chalmers* was hit by a torpedo bomber just before midday, but she struggled on.

They were still many miles from Malta, but now, at last, they were within range of the Spitfires. The bombing slackened off, but they still had a long way to go.

Chapter Fourteen

Deliverance

Christina enjoyed a free morning on Wednesday, 12 August; she was not on watch until that afternoon. She also had a new home, her apartment in her very own leaning tower of Floriana having been declared uninhabitable. Her landlord was Gustav Vincenti, a wealthy architect; he owned many properties and rented Christina another apartment, also known as Vincenti Buildings, but in Valletta itself. This was just up the street from the *Whizz-Bangs* first rehearsal venue, the Victoria. But that particular morning, Christina couldn't settle. She had woken early, before dawn, and as usual her thoughts were full of the man she missed so much. It was five months since he had flown off in his pale blue Beaufighter, not into the sunset, but into the sunrise, east to Egypt and she earnestly hoped to safety, at least for a while. She was glad he had been sent away. The bombing had become truly awful and the air boys had been decimated. These days she never saw a Maryland on the plot. No doubt Warby would be up to his usual tricks in Egypt. Whatever his bosses said, they couldn't keep him on the ground. Surely he would be safer in Egypt than over Sicily or Italy, or even on the ground in Malta. Please keep him safe.

As soon as it got light, things began to happen outside. There was a constant buzz of aircraft overhead. They had to be ours, she thought, these days were blitz-free; well, not quite, the raids were all relative to what had gone before. The arrival of the Spitfires in numbers in May made such a difference, but even they had been thinned out since. This morning sounded different again, with a constant coming and going of Spitfires overhead. They were definitely Spitfires; she was well-capable of recognising the sound of their Merlin engines and there were very few Hurricanes now; they had done their job well. Christina just had to know what was happening. She tried to busy herself and even went up on the roof to see what was going on. That was something she wouldn't have contemplated a few weeks earlier. There was definitely something up, with Spitfires getting airborne and heading north-west out to sea. Maybe a convoy was coming in. Heaven knows they needed one.

Time dragged by. Long before the beginning of her shift at 1.00 pm, Christina set off for the short walk to Lascaris. From her apartment block she turned right, and then left onto Britannia Street, following it across Kingsway and Merchants Street and passing the Victory Kitchens she used so often. By then she was behind the *Auberge de Castille*. She crossed St Paul Street before turning right into St Ursula

Street. Ahead of her was Upper Barracca Gardens, but a few yards short, she turned left into Battery Street making for a very tall doorway. The top entrance to Lascaris, protected by sandbags standing eight feet tall, was guarded by Maltese soldiers. Having shown her pass she headed down the many steps leading to her very secret world. That afternoon she completed the journey in record time.

Christina could foresee a busy time but she didn't care, she knew it would be interesting and she just loved being in the know, being in the centre of things. Once down the steps, she walked quickly down the long, dimly lit corridor. As soon as she opened the 'restricted access' door into the ops room she could sense the atmosphere, the tension in the air, much as it was back in May on the day *Wasp's* Spitfires flew in. Everyone was at their places and totally professional as usual, but there was an evident sense of excitement, an undercurrent of suspense. From the serious expressions on every face it was obvious something very much out of the ordinary was afoot. Even the off-going watch dallied, reluctant to leave. Before signing her name in the register, Christina asked the supervisor what was going on. He pointed to the left of the plotting table and one word said it all – convoy. Apparently there was a hell of a scrap going on.

Christina climbed the narrow stairway to the platform, the shelf, and pushed her way through the crowd of spectators to the front row of benches to take her place amongst the chaps-in-the-gods. Now she had been elevated to the lofty position of assistant controller, did that make her a 'chap'? The thought made her smile, but only on the inside, she had very serious work to do this afternoon.

Her place was next to Guy Westray, Ops B, in a seat of honour near the controller. Her new job involved more than just plotting; she recorded each new track along with its grid position and whether it was friendly or hostile. She then noted the time each plot was removed from the table. It was something of an optical feat, keeping one eye on the plotting table and the other on the hands in front of the blue, yellow and red triangles of the clock face. Somehow she also had to write everything down longhand in the hardbacked logbook. Her job needed total focus.

Having been given the log by her opposite number on C Watch, Christina sat down. She surveyed the scene below to try and take in what was a complicated plot with lots of activity as the girls, all wearing their headsets, moved their long rods to and fro. On the plotting table itself, there was the usual array of red, blue and yellow arrows, most of them on the left-hand side of the M for Monkey square. This covered the area through which any ships approaching Malta from the west, from Gibraltar, would come. Amid the thick of the aircraft plots, Christina noticed the dark blue discs they only used rarely to plot ships. There was also something on the table that looked almost alien, a cigar-shaped yellow indicator which she had never seen on the table before. In answer to her question, Guy explained it was the *Ohio*, an oil tanker, hit many times and in very poor shape. Before she could ask more, Guy drew her attention to a new plot to the north: aircraft, hostile aircraft, thirty plus over Comiso. Christina quickly entered the northerly plot in the log and once again felt something mounting inside her, the pleasure of being on duty on yet another thrilling occasion; it was just like that memorable day in May.

Malta was now providing air cover for the remnants of a once mighty fleet that had fought hard to reach their beleaguered island and right now, right in front of her, a ding-dong battle was being fought out between their Spitfires and the attacking Luftwaffe. The Regia Aeronautica was involved too. The Germans and the Eyeties had turned their attention onto the ships endeavouring to save their agonised island, attacking with a new and strengthened determination to beat them into submission by starvation. Given everything they had lived through, everything they had suffered, Christina was convinced they wouldn't let them win.

She gradually picked up from Guy and from the senior controller, Bill Farnes, something of the drama that had befallen the convoy called Pedestal. Of the fourteen ships that had set sail from Britain, only five had survived a terrific pounding. Only five had survived, so far. The suffering endured by the crews of merchant ships and warships alike was unimaginable. Now it looked as if the American-built tanker *Ohio,* with her precious and desperately needed cargo of oil, was to be beaten even as her goal came into sight. She had been hit many times Guy explained and was making only very slow progress towards them.

Everyone present was aware their lives depended on those remaining ships. Do or die, they just had to reach harbour. The air attacks on the island may have lessened, but they were still at the height of the siege and far from safe. Food stocks were almost non-existent and they were desperately low on fuel and ammunition. Christina thought about the VKs. They weren't at all popular in the beginning, but now everyone recognised how important they were. Even so they could not hold out much longer. The aircraft and guns were using ammunition at an alarming rate. As for fuel, no one knew how much was left, but there couldn't be much, especially with the number of aircraft she knew staged through every night.

Christina watched as one of her girls pushed out another arrow to its grid position in the north-west corner of N for Nuts. She made a sign to the controller and pointed her rod to the plot. 'Another hostile plot, sir; twenty plus,' she said.

'Okay. Scramble Red Section,' said Bill Farnes.

Guy immediately passed the order down the 'blower' to Luqa. As the minute hand on the large ops room clock slowly ticked by, the plots on the table came up thick and fast. When she listened to the loudspeakers and heard the excited 'natter' of the fighter pilots over the radio, Christina often felt she was up there too, high up above the deep blue sea watching the action unfold beneath her. Some of the action had been described to her by Warby, but he only focused on the good bits, or the bits he thought funny. He did have an odd sense of humour sometimes. But Christina knew the reality of what those brave boys were doing up there. She also heard it on the radio as did her girls, some as young as fifteen. It touched them all. But they kept on doing their job, total professionals. It would hit them when they were off-shift, yet it was not something they could ever share with family or friends. What they did down here stayed down here in their own secret world.

Spitfires took off and others landed. They were refuelled and rearmed in a matter of minutes, and were off again with a fresh pilot. There was no respite, not for anyone, pilots, airmen, ops room staff – all were working as if their lives depended on what they did that day. And they did.

The afternoon wore on. It was getting warmer. The ventilation couldn't cope at the best of times, but with so many more people in the ops room it was much worse than usual. After a staff visit earlier in the year, all the hangers-on were banned; now there was a notice on the door saying no unauthorised person was allowed to enter. For the most part it worked, but inevitably, when something special was going on, the numbers on the shelf increased. People from neighbouring sections sometimes vested themselves with authority and bluffed their way in. Bill Farnes could clear the shelf in an instant with one or two well-chosen words which made some of the girls blush, but today he was simply too busy; there was too much going on to notice the hangers-on.

There were 'No Smoking' orders and signs everywhere. That was a laugh, as the atmosphere was heavily charged with the fumes of 'V for Victory' cigarettes. Issued free to troops, they were regarded in the smoker's world as the next best thing to army socks. Like everything else, even they were at a premium as non-smokers bartered their ration of the evil-smelling weed, or sold them to addicts for a princely sum. While the fumes of 'Victory' were usually nauseating, they did have one advantage that hot, stifling afternoon in that crowded place so deep beneath Valletta's protective walls. They disguised, but only now and again, the ever-present smell of sweat and soap-starved khaki drill coming from the bodies all around.

As it approached quarter-to-four, Christina remembered nostalgically, in happier times they would have been sipping a refreshing cup of tea and working through that ever popular product of the NAAFI – a wad. Tea and buns, both alas well up on the list of things that used to be. The heat and the oppressive atmosphere began to get to Christina; she felt faint. The colours of the clock face began to merge one into the other and soon a merry-go-round of colour began to spin in front of her. She felt as if she was beginning to float up into the clouds. Get a grip girl, she said to herself; in her position she could not afford to keel over. She would not allow herself to do that. The haze cleared and the clock resumed its normal position on the wall. She realised it was either the heat or the hunger, or a combination of both. She longed for a draught of cool clear air, a stimulating cup of tea, but it was like wanting the moon. That was not the only thing she longed for. She felt another wave of giddiness begin to wash over her, the clock did a couple of somersaults and Christina felt herself beginning to drift into the clouds once more... .

Then there came a thud as a large brown-paper parcel fell into her lap. She sat bolt upright in shock as a hand gripped her shoulder tightly. Turning round she saw a handsome, bronzed face leaning over close to hers. Christina gazed up into a pair of brilliant blue eyes, laughing at her from beneath the battered peak of an old familiar and much-loved cap. He was back. Sometimes things she longed for in her dreams did come true. She smiled at her beloved Warby, but of all the emotions she experienced within those brief moments, she felt curiously disappointed. After an eternity of waiting, after months of scheming and planning for his homecoming, and after so many dreams of a wonderful reunion, he had pitched up, unheralded, unexpected and bang in the middle of a battle. It was typical Warby. He could be so inconsiderate. Christina had to fight a desire to go on gazing into Warby's blue eyes and return her attention to the plotting table. He understood. 'See you after six – in Captain Caruana's,' he whispered. Then he slipped away.

Despite the drama of a long, exciting afternoon, Christina couldn't wait for her shift to end. She hurried down the long corridor and climbed the many steps up into Valletta. She headed for Godfrey Caruana's bar, a popular drinking den in Kingsway. It was just the sort of cosy place where you could forget your troubles for a little while and put aside all thoughts about a horrid war. But without the war, she wouldn't have been in Malta and she certainly wouldn't have met her Warby.

No one knew quite how dear Godfrey, bless him, could still provide anything in the way of 'genuine' drinks and heavens knows how he was still able to charge pre-war rates, unlike some. Godfrey had some special magic, but whenever he was asked how he did it, he just smiled. He was a very warm human being. Most of the local bars put up their shutters long ago, or charged extortionate rates with many resorting to selling 'Stuka Juice' – as the airmen called the local wine. Yet Godfrey could still produce a very good Scotch and soda, and there was nothing the least bit phoney about his Horse's Neck, Pink Gins, Green Goddesses and White Ladies. Horse's Neck! She smiled broadly at the memory of that frightening ride so long ago. They had laughed so much about it, afterwards. She stopped smiling immediately as she wondered what had become of those horses.

She was nearly there. It was crowded when she arrived and she had to force her way in. She glanced round the bar and immediately spotted her Warby at the far end, completely walled in by a mob of air boys. Christina had to use her elbows to steer a course, treading over a carpet of shoe leather to reach him, but no one seemed to mind in the least. She just smiled and said, 'I am sorry, was that your foot' and, 'Oh dear, please excuse me'. They just smiled back. At last she was alongside him.

'Wotcher, Chris,' he said, as if he hadn't been away.

'Wotcher, Warby,' said Christina.

While Warby was giving his order to the barman, Chris began to untie the knots on the brown-paper parcel she had been nursing since his unexpected appearance in the ops room.

'Open carefully,' Warby said as he turned around.

'Treat me for shock,' Christina gasped, as she gazed at true splendour, fresh from the Middle East. Beneath her eyes were unheard of treasures: a tube of toothpaste, toilet soap, a facecloth, a jar of cold cream, cards of hair grips, several bundles of curlers. There was a comb too. She had a comb of course, more than one, but wonders never cease – this one had a full set of teeth. There was also a box of face powder, a lipstick and a small bottle of Coty's *L'Aimant* perfume. Had Warby really thought of all of this on his own, she thought? Never in a million years! She smiled questioningly at Warby.

'How did you guess?' she asked.

'I met your friend Tamara one day in Heliopolis. She said you were running rather short of these things.'

Rather short, thought Christina! Thank goodness for Tamara; she would have known exactly what Christina needed, what would be impossible to get hold of. What lay in front of her were memories of a bygone age. In place of hair curlers, she had been making do with 'blitzed' telephone wire, salvaged from the ruins. It worked but it was a very rough and ready substitute. She said so.

'Then next time I'll load up my kite with curlers,' Warby said with a laugh. Christina felt her heart miss a beat, was he leaving straight away?

'Next time?' she asked.

Warby just laughed. 'Come on, drink up and let's go to the Monico to see good old Tony. Then we must eat,' he said.

Warby patted his tummy significantly. 'Big eats,' he said.

'Didn't Tamara tell you? We don't eat around here anymore. That was in the good old days.'

She then explained all restaurants had been closed since April. Everyone had to make do with the offerings of the VKs and what they could get from the black market. Big eats were now the lightest of light snacks. Warby put his arm around her waist and helped her down from the bar stool. He held her very close for a second or two, and then ran his hand across her ribs. He gave a low whistle.[1]

Adrian had arrived on 11 August. He called in briefly at the PR Spitfire office where he was seen by Harry Coldbeck; both men were junior officers. Although they had not met before, Harry recognised Adrian and was aware of his reputation. He had also seen Adrian 'holding court', as he called it, in the bar at Luqa a few days

---

1. *A Day of Rejoicing*, by Christina Ratcliffe, published in the *Sunday Times of Malta*, 15 August 1982.

after he himself arrived in Malta on 7 March. That may have coincided with the announcement of Adrian's DSO. If so, it is unsurprising Adrian was the centre of attention. Such a prestigious award to a junior officer was very rare indeed. Adrian left for Egypt a day or two later.

Harry enquired if Adrian was just in; he replied yes. There were no introductions. With Pedestal in full swing, Adrian's expertise was needed in the cockpit and he flew twice on 12 August to Taranto, and twice more the next day covering Messina and Palermo. There was no sign of the main body of the Italian fleet putting to sea. Pedestal's sailors were fighting desperately and were now within sight of their goal. Then they heard the news that some Italian warships were making for what was left of them. In a game of bluff, perhaps learnt from Woody, messages were sent in clear about an air sweep in search of the Italian ships. The Italian ships turned back, but two Italian cruisers were torpedoed by a British submarine. At 6.00 pm, on the evening of 13 August, three damaged merchant ships entered Grand Harbour: *Rochester Castle*, *Melbourne Star* and *Port Chalmers*. The following day, they were joined by *Brisbane Star*, which had slowly made its way through shallow, Vichy French territorial waters bluffing torpedo bombers and shore stations, and outwitting a U-boat trying to get into a position to fire its torpedoes. She was boarded, but the ship's Irish master, Captain Riley, 'politely' refused the French request to sail to the nearest French port. He was later appointed OBE.

Ohio's story was remarkable. The crews of the destroyers *Penn* and *Ledbury*, and the minesweepers *Rye* and *Speedy*, also performed incredibly well. When *Ohio* was disabled, Captain Mason ordered his crew off. Later, it seemed there might be a chance of towing the stricken vessel and every single member of the crew volunteered to go back. Throughout the night they fought desperately to make headway despite further bombing. Progress was painfully slow, the tow wires often parting, with *Ohio* getting lower and lower in the water. By dawn on 14 August, *Ohio's* freeboard was less than three feet. Then the bombers came back. This time, the enemy aircraft were met by Malta's Spitfires. Only three aircraft of twenty-four broke through the fighter screen, but one managed to drop a 1000lb bomb behind the tanker's stern. The *Ohio's* rudder was carried away and water gushed in through a large hole. There was a great risk the tanker would break in half. Even then, Captain Mason was confident he might be able to save the forward portion of the ship. Progress toward Grand Harbour was at a snail's pace, *Bramham* and *Penn* secured on either side of *Ohio*, the *Rye* secured to her bow. That night the U-boats came back to try their luck, but were kept at bay. At 8.00 am, on 15 August, *Ohio* entered Grand Harbour. It was the Feast of *Santa Maria*.

When she came in sight, the loud cheering from everyone slowly subsided until there was absolute silence. Men removed their hats and women removed their black hoods and cloaks. From Fort St Angelo, a bugler sounded *Still*. Not a soul moved.

Of the fourteen merchant ships assembled off the west coast of Scotland two weeks earlier, nine were lost and all the rest arrived damaged. One carrier was sunk and another damaged, two cruisers sunk and one damaged, and one destroyer sunk with four others damaged. For his gallantry, Captain Mason of the *Ohio* was awarded the George Cross. His ship never went to sea again.

Over the next few days, Adrian and others conducted sea searches between Tunisia and Sardinia only to find wreckage; by then the remnants of Pedestal were safely in Grand Harbour. The remnants were enough – just. A total of 55,000 tons of supplies delivered to the beleaguered island at great human cost – the cost of Malta's salvation. From the day of its arrival, Pedestal became known to the Maltese as the *Santa Maria* convoy. Its seamen were deservedly applauded on the island. Soon afterwards the RAF *Fly Gang* put on a special performance in the Manoel Theatre for the Merchant Navy crews.

Lem Palmer was an anti-aircraft gunner on the island and he remembered Pedestal's arrival clearly. 'When the few surviving ships eventually reached the Grand Harbour, the order was, "these ships have to be unloaded at all cost!" As we hung around the guns, waiting for an imminent attack, there was hardly a word spoken. Just a grim silence for the most part, and every man wishing, really wishing, that he could get closer to the Germans and really have a go at them.

'"Take Post!"

'And as we reached for our tin hats, a shout of, "Sixty-nine Spitfires and one Hurricane airborne!" came from the command post. We were all paralysed for several seconds, all movement ceased. We were all absolutely shocked into immobility. We had come a long way since the days of, "Three Gladiators airborne".

'Then, from every throat came a tremendous yell and steel helmets were hurled high in the air. The lads were pounding each other on chests, shoulders, backs, with clenched fists, and really and truly enjoying it. Until that moment, it was undoubtedly the greatest boost to our morale any of us had ever experienced.

'I fired just two rounds at the approaching Stukas while they were still out to sea, and then came the order, "Stop! Fighters engaging!" We scrambled up on the sandbags to get a better view of what we were positive was going to happen. Suddenly, 'Spanky' Williams was pointing skywards and screaming, "Spits! Spits! Spits!", and then again "Spits! Spits! Spits!" He turned appealingly to us all and again screamed, "Spits! Spits! Spits! Look at 'em for God's sake! Look at 'em!"

'I saw the sun flash on the wing of a Spitfire as it banked and went into a dive. A long line of Spitfires followed him down onto the Stukas. Only a few guns had fired and of the few shells that were still bursting, one blew off the tail of the second Spitfire. The pilot baled out safely.

'A second line of Spitfires went down, and then a third. I could see it all happening, but my brain refused to believe what I was seeing. Perhaps five or ten seconds later, everything came right to me, as I saw, for the first time, Spitfire pilots in sufficient strength to give the enemy a damn good hiding. A huge weight seemed to be lifted from the top of my head, and I realised for the first time what a strain we had all been under, and we were just ordinary gunners. As we watched the Stukas running home our morale must have been about a hundred miles higher than it had ever been. My own exultation was tremendous, and at that very moment, without the slightest doubt, I was absolutely convinced that the siege was over. Malta had won through. It was a terrific feeling of absolute certainty. If Winston Churchill himself had appeared in the gun pit at that moment and tried to bring us back to earth by talking sense to us, his words would have been like water off a duck's back. I think we were back on earth a minute or two later, when one man said hopefully, "Now perhaps we'll get a decent meal!"

'It did nothing to cheer him up, nor the rest of the gun crew, when I told him, "The first decent meal you'll get will be on Xmas day!" I was right. '[2]

Pedestal was Keith Park's baptism of fire, although the air situation had changed since May and Malta was now much more secure from an air defence perspective. Park intended to rebuild the bomber force and develop further Hugh Lloyd's approach of taking the attack to the enemy. For that to be successful, he needed to rebuild a decimated 69 Squadron. At one stage, command had fallen to a pilot officer. What Park now required was a capable officer, a proven recce pilot, who would lead from the front as 69 was expanded and re-equipped. Adrian was the obvious choice.

These were still testing days and perhaps the formalities of informing subordinates of changes in command were not followed, Adrian's appointment being a case in point. Word spread by rumour until Adrian arrived in Harry Coldbeck's office wearing squadron leader rank a week after their first brief encounter. There was no notification of any kind, Harry having heard the news on the grapevine. At the time 69 Squadron comprised a few Baltimores and four PR Spitfires, all the Marylands having been lost or destroyed on the ground.

Adrian and Harry were very different and it is clear that Harry, who had been running the Spitfire unit for months, resented Adrian's unexpected arrival as his superior. There was also much for both of them to do in the air and no time for the 'niceties'. Laddie Lucas later described the two men as a fascinating study in opposite personalities. Lucas knew Coldbeck well; they were close friends. He described him as dogged with a capacity for taking infinite pains. He contrasted this with Adrian's flamboyance, saying his performance and lifestyle had prospered under Hugh Lloyd, equally known for individualism and resource. Lucas did not know Adrian well, but who did? Lucas arrived on the island on 18 February and flew from Ta' Qali; Adrian operated from Luqa but left the island about three weeks

---

2. Letter from Lem Palmer to Jack Vowles, 23 February 1994.

later. If they met at all, their acquaintance could only have been very brief as Lucas himself left Malta before Adrian's return in August. Much of what Lucas learnt about Adrian must have come from others, although Lucas said Adrian's character was by far the most difficult to read. He judged him remote, insular and separate, with small regard for convention. But he was brave to the point of being virtually nerveless. At times Adrian was an easily identifiable extrovert; at others he was withdrawn and secretive, and he spent less time on the station than any operational pilot on the island. Lucas considered Adrian's dress as, 'a pose, a prop, maybe for the play actor and a means of appearing to be different'.[3] If that was the case, then Adrian had a lot in common with many notable wartime commanders.

Within days of Pedestal's unloading, rations were increased, not to normal levels as stockpiles were so low, but to a level which provided adequate nutrition. Fuel and ammunition were also delivered, all necessary to renew the offensive on Rommel's supply lines. Malta could now hit out at Axis shipping with renewed vigour from a base under a protective umbrella. The timing of Malta's deliverance was vitally important for the whole Allied strategy in North Africa. Everything depended on supplies and if Rommel's supply lines could now be cut, even temporarily, he would be hard-pressed to hold the line against the 8th Army in the east and what was planned to come from the west.

Over the coming weeks, Park created three separate flights within 69 Squadron, each operating a different type of aircraft. One of Baltimores, one of PR Spitfires, and the third was made up of Wellingtons fitted with radar and modified to carry two torpedoes for night attacks. Such a unique squadron, operating three diverse aircraft types, was a challenging command. Jack Vowles also returned to the fold when 221 Squadron's Wellingtons became C Flight of 69 Squadron.

Adrian's approach to tasking had an immediate impact on Harry, the team-player, communicator and methodical programmer. Harry's irritation may have begun as soon as he heard of Adrian's appointment, but it increased markedly within days. Harry was about to depart on the midday recce flight to Cagliari in Sardinia. As always, his preparation was meticulous and, having spoken to both the meteorological forecaster and air control, he was strapping into his aircraft. At that moment, Adrian climbed onto the Spitfire's wing and told Harry, without explanation, that he was taking the aircraft. Adrian then asked Harry to go to an address in Valletta to meet Christina, whom Harry did not know, and accompany her to lunch with Captain Riley, the Irish master of the Brisbane Star. What Harry felt inside can only be imagined, but he got out of his aircraft, changed out of the heavy flying gear he was wearing for his high-level mission, before cycling to the address given him. On arrival, Christina was immediately apprehensive, fearing the worst.

---

3. *Malta, The Thorn in Rommel's Side*, Laddie Lucas, page 141.

Harry quickly reassured her. She said they were too late for the lunch engagement but instead invited Harry into her apartment for a cup of tea. It was Harry's first ever experience of tea laced with whisky and it was one he enjoyed. But it hardly dampened his feelings toward his commanding officer.

There could be little doubt Adrian intended to put 69 Squadron firmly 'on the map' with Air HQ. Within days of taking command, he adopted the style so successful in the past, communicating directly with the AOC or with the SASO (Senior Air Staff Officer), and debriefing them personally immediately after landing. Such an approach could be portrayed by those who arrived, subsequent to Adrian's earlier tours, as by-passing the normal chain of command; a very different way of doing business than the home RAF. But it was often the 'norm' in Malta. Indeed, it had been Hugh Lloyd's preferred way of doing business and Harry could hardly have been surprised as he himself had often been tasked directly by the SASO.

Adrian played little part in the running of the Spitfire flight, simply deciding which missions he would undertake, leaving the rest of the pilots to do the others. With much broader responsibilities, Adrian increasingly ignored Harry's carefully crafted programme without saying why. Others sometimes found aircraft allocated to them already airborne with Adrian at the controls, having left incomplete paperwork behind. On his return, Adrian occasionally spoke to the AOC or the SASO from his office in what Harry described as 'flamboyant' terms. He also said other pilots pretended to vomit when Adrian was on the telephone to a senior officer. This may seem rather odd, but it is not unusual 'crewroom' behaviour. If done when the officer concerned was present, it was usually meant in jest and as a means of putting off the individual speaking on the telephone. If done behind the squadron commander's back it perhaps took on a different meaning, and if this was the case, it should have been curbed by the senior officer present, in this case Harry Coldbeck. Was Harry the only one not to see such behaviour as light-hearted?

It seems clear Adrian, despite his achievements, irritated Harry no end. Harry was a courageous and capable recce pilot, having completed similar tasks when Adrian was in Egypt; a period which coincided with the RAF's most desperate months on Malta. Did Harry feel he had not received sufficient recognition for his earlier work and Adrian had taken the job that should have been his? The information flow, or lack of it, emphasised the change. But what better way was there to keep information secure? Adrian's habit of spending as much time as possible at Air HQ to gain the best possible picture of the tactical situation was well ingrained, but it also ensured his squadron remained centre stage. There was ground to make up after the Benghazi tanker incident and Adrian would have done whatever was necessary to reassure his new AOC that 69 Squadron would now always deliver the goods.

Harry said Adrian regaled off-duty pilots with his tales. Adrian certainly led his squadron from the front, but there is little evidence he bragged about his achievements. For example, his father had to rely on others to find out what his son was up to. The phrase 'shooting a line', coined long ago on RAF squadrons, meant very few others heard at first hand of anyone's exploits. Within a squadron it was simply not tolerated. 'Talking shop' in front of civilians often resulted in a response from colleagues of 'close the hangar door', usually followed by a shout of 'clang' as those present brought their hands together.

Some of the characteristics Harry recognised lay deep within Adrian. It also seems neither gave the other any leeway. Yet there was much more to the situation than strong personalities clashing, as resentment built up in Adrian's subordinate. Adrian usually stayed with Christina; the other 69 Squadron Spitfire pilots were accommodated together at Siggiewi. Their lives became busier as tasking increased. They flew in accordance with Harry's programme, with Adrian appearing unannounced from time to time, and from they knew not where, to take an aircraft and complete a task others knew little about.

Was there another reason why Adrian did not share information about certain tasks? He would have realised long ago there was another source of intelligence which fed many of their operations. Air HQ were getting more information than ever before from Ultra and individual recce pilots were asking one another questions, questions which Adrian would have pondered long ago. Harry had himself discussed some of the more unusual tasking with Laddie Lucas. Being relatively junior in rank, and at risk of capture, Adrian would not have been told of Ultra, or any other intelligence source, but he certainly would have come to his own conclusion. The SASO, as the AOC's deputy, was privy to the information, if not the source, and he made a point of seeking out Adrian to brief him in the same way he had previously sought out Harry. It was Adrian's responsibility to decide how far information was shared – that's why he was selected for command. By choosing to keep matters closely guarded, the information was even safer since Adrian did not share his pilot's accommodation and picked his missions at very short notice, keeping details to himself. If he was indeed so selfish, so self-centred, why would he have gone flying and stand-up a very worried Christina when she was waiting for him to join her for a planned luncheon on board *Brisbane Star*?

What did others think of Adrian's leadership? The ground crew worshipped him, as did many of his pilots. Lloyd and Park were good judges of the men they placed in command. Harry felt Adrian's reputation was overstated, but this view was not shared by others like Les Colquhoun who worked for both men. Harry recommended Les for a DFM; Adrian recommended him for a commission. Les later confirmed Adrian's completely informal relationship with senior officers in Air HQ who never questioned his comings and goings. According to Les, Adrian set a very high standard of personal performance and expected everyone else to do the same. He thought Adrian an outstanding operational recce pilot. He rarely would stand off from a target at height but would fly much lower, taking far greater risks to get the best possible results. Later, when the Germans landed troops by parachute in North Africa, Les recalled Adrian flew within a formation of German Ju52s. Was this single-minded determination to get the job done, or courage? Even Harry witnessed Adrian calmly standing in the open firing his favoured Luger pistol at a Ju87 Stuka that appeared to be pointing directly at him. Harry characterised this as a complete disregard for personal safety rather than courage.

At one stage Adrian talked to Harry about granting him leave in Cairo before a UK posting and a long-desired conversion to the PR Mosquito. This was an unexpected surprise as Harry assumed he and the others would continue until they were shot down. That Adrian was aware of Harry's ambition indicates he knew what was going on. He also ensured Harry was formally appointed as flight commander of the PR flight with the acting rank of flight lieutenant. Throughout the remainder of Harry's time in Malta, he appears to have continued to resent Adrian's manner. It is sad two such worthy men, individually so courageous in unarmed aircraft in their lonely war, could not have bridged the gulf between them. But there was a war on, and the call on each of them was constant and terribly wearing.

An indication of the lonely war of the photo-recce Spitfire pilots comes from a rhyme they put together:

> When you're seven miles up in the heavens
> That's a hell of a lonely spot
> And its fifty degrees below zero
> Which isn't exactly hot
> When you're frozen blue like your Spitfire
> And you're scared a green shade of pink
> When you're hundreds of miles from nowhere
> And there's nothing below but the drink.

Sandy Johnstone arrived at Luqa in September to take command of a wing of three Spitfire squadrons. Like many before him, his appointment did not work out quite as he anticipated. His flight from Egypt was in an aircraft's bomb bay, cramped between pairs of boots, sacks of dehydrated potatoes, a naval torpedo and the commander of Malta's artillery; such was the reality of wartime air travel. The following morning, Sandy thumbed a lift from the ration wagon and reported his arrival at the RAF administrative HQ. He described how the stone face behind the small concrete offices which served as the HQ was honeycombed with subterranean passages hewn out of the soft, porous rock. This was his first sight of Lascaris, the heart of operational activity on Malta, and immune from air attack.

With his appointment to Spitfires delayed, Sandy became one of two deputy station commanders at Luqa taking turns operating from the only building left standing on the airfield, a small stone tower at one end of the runway. Below the tower was G Shelter, an exceptionally deep air raid shelter. A field telephone was Sandy's link with Lascaris, Malta's heart. One of his tasks was to plot the bombs and issue local air raid warnings. The moment the last bomb fell, he, 'would shin down the ladder, jump into our little Ford car, filled with red flags, and drive to place a flag on every bomb crater which pitted the runways. Six or seven lorries loaded with clinker and gravel were always kept standing by to race out after us and to make for the flag-marked holes into which they dumped their loads. A dilapidated steam roller brought up the rear of this strange caravan.'[4] They called her *Faithful Annie* and she was one of their most treasured possessions with her own shelter. By that autumn, runway repair was a well-rehearsed drill, and it rarely took more than twenty minutes for the teams of airmen and soldiers to make the runways ready to use. After a final check, the RAF fighters circling high above were signalled to land, despite the constant hazard of delayed action bombs. The RAF also made use of the one tank on the island, which dragged crashed aircraft from runways and taxiways. It saw constant use.

Despite having arrived at the beginning of the good times, Sandy long reflected on a great sense of loneliness he felt. Morale was high, but it was impossible not to feel isolated with the odds still stacked against the island's survival. Their nearest friends were over 1,200 miles away. Lack of food was a constant worry and lack of heat in winter made life difficult. Half a small loaf of bread had to last all day, occasionally supplemented by a packet of dehydrated potatoes or vegetables. The few eggs sent across from Gozo rightly found their way into hospitals. If one was found on the black market the price was ten shillings each and, 'one had to make a proper meal out of it, lingering over the golden yolk as one might do with a superb steak.'[5] Supplementary items were sometimes available such as: 'stews made from goat's flesh, although at times we were certain that dog meat was being used... . Hot dishes were liberally speckled with large blobs of soot, as the only means of heating ... worked on the principle of dripping burning salvaged engine oil on to a metal plate.'[6] At one stage there was a serious epidemic of scabies amongst the Lascaris girls, which resulted in a tragedy for Sandy and his friends when they had to give up their very last bottle of whisky to be used to disinfect the ops room telephone.

There was a planning conference on 5 September, prior to an important mission against Axis merchant ships midway between western Greece and Italy. Keith Park presided and participants included Patrick Gibbs, awarded a DSO two weeks earlier.

4. *Where no Angels Dwell*, by AVM Sandy Johnstone, pages 112–9.
5. *Ibid.*
6. *Ibid.*

Adrian bore the responsibility of locating the target. He took off in a PR Spitfire in the dark, early on 6 September, to assess the course and speed of the targets, and identify whether they were escorted by a battleship. Once he got back the attack force would launch, preceded by one 69 Squadron Baltimore with another to photograph the strike. Gibbs was due to be relieved the following day as squadron commander, and was directed to delegate leadership of his Beauforts to his senior flight commander. Adrian landed at 9.00 am after a long trip. Gibbs watched him climb out of his aircraft, stretch himself and then get into the transport to bring him to the control tower. At the foot of the ladder Adrian looked up and shook his head, a gesture which set Gibbs' mind at rest: there was no battleship. Adrian had found two separate forces which, when combined, comprised four merchant ships and eleven destroyers. He also reported on aircraft in considerable strength protecting the convoy. Gibbs thought Adrian brilliant. Despite having flown the earlier long Spitfire mission, he then flew the photographic Baltimore accompanying the strike force. This was Adrian's 242nd mission. Attempts were made by Air HQ to curtail Adrian's operational flying, but he simply ignored them.

Of the twelve Beauforts involved, two were lost, including the leader who flew in Gibbs' place. Every other Beaufort was damaged. Two Beaufighters also failed to return. One Axis cargo ship was sunk.

On 13 September, amidst the ruins of Palace Square Valletta, Viscount Gort attended one of the most memorable ceremonies of the Second World War. Jack Vowles was there as an uninvited guest and filmed the formal presentation of the George Cross to Sir George Borg, Malta's Chief Justice. Over the following days, the case was moved from village to village so all the people might see it.

Throughout the autumn Adrian undertook a series of 'special flights'. These began after one of his visits to Cairo where he may have learnt about plans for the invasion of North Africa and the subsequent invasion of Sicily. Again, when he got back, Adrian played his cards close to his chest. Details of the flights were vague, but on his first mission he photographed sixty miles of the Sicilian coastline at low-level. Most of Adrian's operational flights when in command of 69 Squadron were in Spitfires, although he undertook some in Baltimores and Wellingtons. He flew as second pilot in a Wellington on a night mission against shipping near Corfu. He also flew in Wellingtons a couple of times as a gunner.

In October, to demonstrate life went on despite the siege, Christina was photographed by Sergeant J. Deakin, a War Office photographer, as she went about her daily business when off duty. Fifty photographs were taken in three series: *A Fighter Control Girl, Malta GC, has 24 hrs leave; Wearing the Faldetta* and *Christina rehearses her dance.* They offered a unique glimpse into part of Christina's life and were widely circulated. One taken against a backdrop of ruined buildings in Valletta was published in the *Times of Malta* under the headline, 'Christina of George Cross

Island.' The caption said: 'Bright sunlight lends an added dignity to the bombed streets and squares of Valletta through which Christina is walking. And on her way to the shops she meets an officer friend.' Some photographs were later featured in the magazines *Illustrated* and *Life* on both sides of the Atlantic.

The Axis embarked on its final blitz of Malta over a ten-day period in mid-October after which the bulk of the Luftwaffe units in Sicily were transferred to North Africa to sustain Rommel and his Afrika Korps. From then on, raids on the island tapered off and by the end of the month, daylight bombing had virtually ended. Night raids continued. One night at Luqa, Jack awaited the return of a stream of Wellingtons. When they began to circle prior to landing it was clear there was one too many. One was probably a Ju88, but which one? With the Wellingtons short of fuel, nothing could be done except clear them to land. Halfway through, the lone intruder swooped in, dropping its bombs on Luqa's runway. Such raids continued, but their impact was minimal. Kesselring had met his match and the defeat of the Luftwaffe was now complete. The cost to the Axis was an estimated 1,378 aircraft lost between June 1940 and October 1942.

On 14 October, Adrian flew the post-attack reconnaissance mission with which this story opened. He was in support of three Beaufighters of 227 Squadron. The Italian merchant ship was the *Trapani* and its escort was the large motor torpedo boat the *Giacomo Medici*. The lead aircraft, Q for Queen, crashed into the sea killing 22-year-old Squadron Leader Peter Underwood and 21-year-old Flight Sergeant Ivor Miller. The second was damaged and Y for Yorker ditched, Adrian guiding the Italian warship to Yorker's crew. For Pilot Officer John Bryce and navigator Flight Sergeant Cole the war was over, but without Adrian's intervention they would have died a slow death. This selfless act contributed to a second Bar to Adrian's DFC, gazetted three weeks later.

Tunisian targets were now included regularly in 69 Squadron's tasks, although few in Malta were aware of the planned landings in North Africa. Given the nature of the tasking, it is highly likely Adrian knew either by direct briefings or by putting two-and-two together. This may have been another reason why he often flew the Tunisian sorties personally with his pilots dealing with routine assignments. He also continued to photograph Sicilian beaches. After these trips, Adrian sometimes flew back to Heliopolis in Egypt. Many thought these flights were simply to restock Christina's larder or to obtain alcohol and cigarettes for the airmen. There is no doubt he did this, but the main reason was most likely to deliver photographs and attend intelligence briefings. On his return, the fact his aircraft was invariably packed with items unobtainable in Malta was a huge bonus for the airmen, who remained devoted to him.

The switch of Luftwaffe units to North Africa was provoked by the Battle of El Alamein which lasted from 20 October to 11 November. This was in fact the second battle at that location, the first being in July when Auchinleck successfully halted the Axis advance. Subsequent Allied counter-offensives failed. This allowed Rommel to regroup, but his eye was always on the offensive. In August, Auchinleck was replaced as C-in-C Middle East by Sir Harold Alexander. There was also a new commander for the 8th Army, William Gott. Unfortunately, on his way to Cairo to take command, his aircraft was shot down and Gott was killed. His replacement was Bernard Montgomery, another second choice. Rommel studied his opponents well. He realised Montgomery would plan thoroughly before attacking. On the other hand, Rommel's own options were now limited as his reinforcements were increasingly disrupted by Allied strikes from Malta. Rommel dug in.

Montgomery spent weeks building his forces, resisting prompting from Churchill. On the opening day of the battle, he had a two-to-one superiority over Rommel in both men and tanks. Importantly, Rommel was in Germany and did not return until five days later. He quickly realised he needed to disengage but, having lost a tanker to a torpedo from a Malta-based Wellington, he had insufficient fuel to complete the manoeuvre and had little choice but to fight. On 30 October, two further fuel supply ships were sunk from the air near Tobruk. El Alamein was extremely hard fought, but on 3 November the Allies broke out, and the following day Rommel ordered a full retreat. Four days later, the Allies landed in Algeria and from then on the Axis was squeezed on two fronts.

El Alamein was a major turning point for the Allies. It was the first major offensive against the Germans since the European war began and had an immediate impact on Allied morale. Rommel was now on the run. Montgomery fully recognised Malta's vital role in his victory. At a crucial moment, Axis aircraft were withdrawn from the desert in support of Kesselring's final fling against Malta. They did not return until some days after Montgomery's opening assault. Subsequent attacks by aircraft and submarines on cargo ships destined for the Afrika Korps proved decisive, and Rommel later admitted the Axis lost the battle of supplies by a wide margin, saying Malta had the lives of many Axis soldiers on its conscience. El Alamein could not have taken place without Malta being held, and everyone involved in the island's defence and resupply contributed enormously to the Allied victory. Also, without Malta on the offensive, at great cost, supplies would have reached Rommel virtually unhindered. The Afrika Korps would rapidly have built up its strength, probably seizing all of Egypt. The war in North Africa would have taken a very different course. The threat to the Suez Canal was now over and the Axis was denied Middle Eastern oil once and for all.

On 8 November there was deserved recognition for Harry Coldbeck whose gallantry over a prolonged period was recognised with a DFC, recommended by Adrian. But Harry still resented his squadron commander. 'I had become tired, not only of Warburton's boorish smug behaviour, but the long series of before first-lights and last-lights was taking its toll.'[7] One day Harry traded a sortie for one at last-light to break up three early morning trips in a row. The weather proved particularly difficult, forcing him much lower than planned. When flying at 4,000 feet near Augusta, his aircraft was hit by ground fire and he lost consciousness. He came to clear of the aircraft, although he hadn't baled out. His parachute opened only seconds before he hit the water. After flying more than 150 recce missions from Malta in only six months, Harry spent the remainder of the war in captivity. Adrian later recorded in his own logbook Harry had been shot down.

The squadron's misfortune continued. Another pilot was shot down two days later, and on 15 November, Adrian went missing over Tunisia. Marion Gould, a 16-year-old British plotter, said they were all on edge and many were upset. Christina in particular was in great distress but carried on. At the same time, rumours began to circulate that a higher HQ, probably Tedder's, had suggested Keith Park might consider Adrian for the VC. Park apparently did not agree.

On the day in question, with his mission accomplished, Adrian was heading home. Near Cape Bon he was intercepted by Me109s. Luckily, at the instant a cannon shell hit his cockpit; Adrian had twisted around and was leaning to one side with his head in one of the plastic blisters unique to PR Spitfires. The cannon shell missed Adrian, ripped through the instrument panel and into the engine. Adrian entered cloud to evade the pursuing fighters, but he was in serious trouble: his engine had lost its oil and seizure appeared imminent. But he had height and a remarkable Rolls-Royce Merlin on his side. He converted his height into distance and his engine kept going, although at much reduced power. Adrian glided west toward, he hoped, advancing Allied troops, although he was unsure of the extent of the Allied advance. He was in luck; British paratroops dropped on 12 November had captured the airfield at Bône, which fortuitously was where Adrian was headed. He successfully force-landed, although his faithful Spitfire would never fly again. He was greeted by the recently-arrived Spitfire pilots of 111 Squadron. Their squadron commander was perplexed by the long-haired, flamboyantly dressed, recce pilot, without rank, but wearing medal ribbons which made any pilot stand out in a crowd.

Bône was in Vichy territory and the response of the Vichy French to the landings varied. Some welcomed the Allies with open arms; others were hostile, at least initially. The German response was immediate and they advanced quickly into Tunisia. They were also strongly reinforced from Sicily. Adrian somehow managed to persuade the local Vichy French Governor, Admiral Villeneuve, who was sympathetic to the Allies, to fly to Maison Blanche airfield outside Algiers, taking Adrian with him. Once there, Adrian then persuaded the Czech captain of an RAF Halifax bomber to take him to Gibraltar as an additional crew member. Adrian arrived in Gibraltar dirty and unshaven. His unusual attire, lack of rank, sinister-

---

7. *The Maltese Spitfire*, by Sqn Ldr Harry Coldbeck, page 80.

looking commando knife tucked in one of his flying boots, and German pistol, did not immediately convince his unexpected hosts he was a squadron leader. But his winning smile and persuasive manner did, and AHQ Malta was duly notified their favourite son was alive and well. Bill Farnes, the senior controller, sent a note to Christina: 'I suppose you will have heard that Adrian Warburton is on the map once more – at Gib?' Later he sent another: 'Miss Ratcliffe: S/L Warburton flying in from Gib tomorrow. Farnes.'[8]

Adrian borrowed a Spitfire in Gibraltar that didn't appear to have a ferry pilot, flew to Maison Blanche and then to Bône to retrieve his undamaged camera magazine from his crashed aircraft; he always came back with the goods. He left Bône the following day heading for Malta. His adventures far from over, he spotted two Ju88 bombers which he promptly intercepted. This time he was flying an armed Spitfire and shot one Ju88 down, the other escaped. On arrival back at Luqa on 21 November, where few were aware he was safe, Adrian was met by Group Captain William Le May, Luqa's Station Commander. In answer to Le May's question as to where he had been, Adrian apologised for being late. Le May then told Adrian he had been promoted to wing commander; he was 24-years-old. He took his film to be developed six days after taking off on the original mission.

On the surface, Adrian's promotion from flight lieutenant to wing commander within three months didn't affect him. Previously, when asked by his ground crew when he would replace his old and shabby cap, he would say, 'when I'm a Wingco.' But he couldn't ever bear to part with it. He also continued to fly often and in the remainder of that remarkable week completed a further nine operational missions. On one mission to Tunisia, he was chased by Me109s, eventually landing hundreds of miles to the west in Morocco with some damage to his aircraft. Neither orders, nor his new rank, could keep him on the ground. A posting to a ground appointment within AHQ might have done the trick if Keith Park was concerned about the amount of operational flying Adrian was doing. On the other hand, Adrian was quite obviously doing a very remarkable job both individually and in leading his unusual multi-type squadron. The reality was, despite Adrian biting enormous chunks out of his renowned luck, he was most valuable to the war effort when in the cockpit.

It was discovered that two gunners on one of the Pedestal ships were American naval personnel. This was another opportunity for morale-building publicity, and Adrian and Christina, by then a well-known couple and recognised as part of Malta's story, agreed to be involved. A series of photographs were taken with the Americans on the roof of Christina's Valletta apartment. With Adrian a wing commander, this is a further indication the military hierarchy were still unaware he was a married

---

8. Shown in *Carve Malta on my Heart and other wartime stories*, by Frederick Galea, page 67.

man. Adrian was also involved in a similar way when a senior Soviet officer later visited Malta as an official guest.

Stocktaking indicated Malta could hold out on its meagre stocks until December, but even so the civilian population had been put back on near starvation rations from late September despite Pedestal. Male adults received 1,687 calories per day; everyone else 1,511, only just above the figure necessary to maintain life. There was also an outbreak of infantile paralysis which was kept secret. In Britain rations never fell below 2,800. Aviation stocks were also of concern and needed constant replenishment if Malta's aircraft were to target the much-reinforced Axis army in Tunisia. In October and November, there was still no sign of relief and the beginning of December was the predicted limit of Malta's endurance. There were again discussions about Malta's possible surrender and Keith Park became increasingly concerned about Gort's references to ending up, 'in the bag'.

Sandy Johnstone didn't get his hoped for Spitfire wing, but instead joined Bill Farnes at Lascaris. By November, the Luftwaffe and the Regia Aeronautica were well and truly on the back foot, and Sandy and his colleagues took a leaf out of Woody Woodhall's book in keeping them there, sometimes with false transmissions from non-existent RAF squadrons heading toward Sicily. It was very satisfying plotting Axis fighters flying to and fro over Sicily trying to intercept elusive, but actually non-existent, RAF raiders. There were still bombing raids and following one, Viscount Gort demonstrated something of the personal courage which earned him the VC in 1918. A petrol dump in Hamrun was hit and Gort was quickly on the scene, personally removing petrol cans from a burning building. One he was carrying burst into flames. Despite being badly burned he refused to be hospitalised, continuing with his duties despite great pain. The burns took weeks to heal and a cancerous growth, treated some twenty years earlier, reoccurred, and he was forced to return to London for treatment before flying back to Malta. The disease would kill him in 1946 at the age of sixty.

The siege of Malta was effectively raised by a convoy which left Alexandria in mid-November. On its five-day voyage, it benefitted enormously from the lightning advance of the 8th Army along the Libyan coast. Sadly, HMS *Arethusa* was torpedoed by an Axis aircraft and 155 of her crew were killed. For the last few miles, the ships sailed under a protective fighter umbrella. Before entering harbour, the flotilla formed line ahead and bands played on the decks of the escorting warships, so reminiscent of the 1930s when the Mediterranean Fleet was in Grand Harbour. The ships were welcomed by thousands of Maltese lining the bastions of Valletta, the Barracca Gardens and the Three Cities. They were joined by many members of Malta's garrison and everyone cheered and waved flags as each ship entered harbour. Sandy Johnstone was there to witness the, 'frenzied outburst of tears, laughter, and loud unrestrained cheering. Young boys and girls leaped and screamed, while their parents roared themselves hoarse as they watched the long-awaited convoy gliding in to safety. Old and young hugged and kissed each other; a few people just stood quietly, the tears of relief rolling unashamedly down their cheeks.... I have never seen such a heartfelt welcome being given to any force as was given to that small band of mariners who had ... given Malta the chance to breathe more easily.'[9]

The four merchantmen delivered 35,000 tons of supplies at dusk on 20 November, the same day Benghazi fell to the British. The Germans sent a small force of Ju88s to disrupt unloading and every one was shot down; there was no damage. This was the island's deliverance.

It had taken a valiant defence and a resilient people to see Malta through incessant bombing, the most prolonged, the most severe, endured anywhere throughout the Second World War. The skies above the besieged island also saw the most ferocious air combat of the war. The more famous Battle of Britain officially lasted four months, whereas the air battle of Malta lasted almost two and a half years. Throughout those long hard years, the Maltese people, and the defenders of the island who lived among them, faced near starvation. Yet the Maltese demonstrated resilience even greater than was shown against the Turks almost 400 years earlier, reinforcing their island home's place in history.

'Blue water lapped against the wreckage of many gallant ships in Grand Harbour. Great mounds of broken masonry disfigured the streets of stairs and the alleys in towns and villages. The airfields were unlovely with thousands of old wounds. Upon the steep hill of Bighi, overlooking the harbour, the churches and the streets, a shapely tree flowered magenta against the cypresses and firs shading the resting place of the airmen who fought and died upon this battlefield of rock and sky and sea.'[10]

After the war, Tedder expressed the hope the lessons of Malta would not be forgotten saying, in those vital months the human spirit overcame odds which on any rational basis were overwhelming. 'There is, however, a limit beyond which even the unquenchable spirit cannot prevail, and I trust that never again shall our unpreparedness lead to our men having to face such odds or be stretched so near to the ultimate limit of endurance.'[11]

9. *Where no Angels Dwell*, by AVM Sandy Johnstone, pages 119–120.
10. *The Air Battle of Malta*, by the Ministry of Information, page 95.
11. *Briefed to Attack*, by AM Sir Hugh Lloyd, page 6.

Chapter Fifteen

Springboard

In December 1942, five more merchantmen delivered 55,000 tons of supplies. The comparatively light escort of sixteen warships reflected the very different tactical situation which now existed. With hunger receding, the issue of four candles and eight nightlights to every family before Christmas demonstrates the shortage of everyday items. Later the same month, fourteen merchantmen, again with only a light destroyer escort, delivered 120,000 tons of cargo. From that moment on, the task of the British authorities in Malta changed and the island became a springboard for the invasion of southern Europe.

Lascaris became busier than ever. A secure combined services HQ was excavated further down the tunnel. The engineers went to great lengths to disguise the construction by distributing excavated stone amongst ruined buildings. The new war rooms were expected to be ready to start operations early in 1943 for use as the Advanced HQ for the invasion of Sicily, scheduled for July.

December also brought Warby a dose of influenza, but that didn't slow him down much. In the first nineteen days of the month he flew seventeen missions covering airfields in Sicily and Italy. He also photographed targets in Tunisia, frequently returning to his older hunting ground of Tripoli. To many admirers of his operational talent, he was the 'King of the Mediterranean'. On 19 December, Adrian was granted ten days hard-earned, local leave. But again he was up to something, planning a rather special totally unofficial flight, one completely in character and completely against the rules.

From the moment Adrian joined his first squadron in 1939, he was conscious of the work of the airmen and made every effort to learn about their tasks. He struck up close working relationships with many, including Jack Vowles. In Malta he was well aware the majority of airmen, unlike the aircrew, did not get the benefit of rest tours in quieter locations. Many simply carried on under immense pressure and dreadful living conditions until the war was won. The concentrated bombing on Malta's airbases often resulted in almost intolerable stress for the ground staff. Adrian went much further than most, always endeavouring to maintain a close, often informal, relationship with his men. His reputation amongst them grew far beyond what was seen in those days as the normal pilot-ground crew association. Most crews signed over their aircraft to the engineers immediately after landing and left them to it; Adrian often helped clean out his own aircraft.

With 69 Squadron's aircraft relegated to Safi Strip, largely a graveyard of damaged and written-off aircraft, Adrian conceived an almost unbelievable plan. With over 100 aircraft wrecks spread around Safi's various corners, he persuaded some of his airmen to rebuild a damaged Wellington, which had been struck off charge many months earlier. One night within his December leave, he took off in the 'non-existent' Wellington and flew to Cairo, where it was filled with food and 'goodies', as well as Christmas booze. He returned, also at night, the cargo being quickly squirreled away. Adrian's reputation amongst the airmen peaked. There is little doubt senior officers on the island knew, or quickly learnt about this escapade, but they continued to give Adrian free rein. And he continued to pay back well. Before Christmas dinner for the airmen, traditionally served by their officers, Adrian invited some to his office for a glass of champagne, first introducing them to the various group captains present.

By the end of 1942, a new Warby had emerged, very much more mature in relation to his duties, and well aware of his responsibilities. Adrian's longer than regulation haircut was gone and his flamboyant dress, at least on the ground, was a thing of the past. Inevitably, some changes impacted on his relationship with Christina. They were both living and working under great pressure and, although Adrian benefitted from two rest periods in Egypt, Christina had been on the island since March 1940. She worked tirelessly through the harshest period of Malta's long siege, a period when Adrian was in Egypt, and she saw the area surrounding her home devastated by bombing; even her own flat becoming uninhabitable. Now Adrian was back, she suffered yet more stress, ever fearful the man she loved was putting himself at tremendous risk every time he took off. When he went missing in November, the strain and worry must have been unbearable, but she carried on doing her duty. Now the siege was over, the bombing greatly diminished, and everyone realised the war in North Africa was drawing to a close. This was the moment when pressure on Christina should have eased. Instead she saw her precious Warby taking on more and more. By then, maybe Christina knew the pressure came from within. Inevitably this led to tension. Adrian knew no other way and even his love for Christina could not diminish his determination to lead his squadron in the only way he knew: from the front.

Lem Palmer was quite right about the next decent meal being on Christmas Day. 'We were really looking forward to having a really good meal, the first in a really long time. The good news from the cooks was that Christmas dinner would consist of a whole steak and kidney pudding to each man, plus real potatoes. The fact that the pudding was to come from a tin bothered us not at all, and it would have been enthusiastically received had it been served from a wheelbarrow. We sat around the table with knives and forks at the ready. Volunteers helping the cooks brought the food. I was ravenously hungry and wasted no time. I think I had eaten just a few fork-laden items of food when, astonishingly, I no longer felt hungry. Impatiently, I thrust the feeling to one side.

'I tried to eat a little more, but try as I might, I could not eat another morsel. It was the one and only occasion of my life when I was too ashamed to look other men in the face. Bent over my food, I looked slyly out of the sides of my eyes at the other chaps. To my relief, I found everybody was doing the same thing, looking from the sides of their eyes at everybody else. We all realised almost at the same moment that we were all in the same boat. We could not eat because, as we were told later, our stomachs had shrunk. Plates of good, almost untouched food were placed on the floor for our two dogs. Just a few mouthfuls and they too were unable to eat any more. I can never forget all those men who died getting food through to us. We wasted it, not through any fault of ours, but that is poor consolation when I think of those men.'[1]

In January, another of 69 Squadron's pilots went missing over the sea. There was a widespread search involving air-sea rescue launches, aircraft, and Adrian personally, but the pilot was never found. Adrian was well-known throughout the island and visited schools in his spare time talking to pupils about the valuable role played by air-sea rescue. He continually warned of the risks of picking up souvenirs which could easily be deadly anti-personnel bombs. Most children were excited by their gas masks and the long hours of the blackout, and no doubt welcomed the talks given by Adrian and others they regarded as heroes. They also enjoyed interruptions to their schooling and moves from school buildings to private houses. Joseph Camilleri often came across debris and shrapnel fallen from the skies as he walked to school. One pupil in his class was in the habit of collecting small explosive devices from the fields and terrifying his friends by rolling them down the stairs for a bit of fun. His short life ended one day when he tampered with one device too many. The same fate befell Edwin Gatt, and brothers Francis and Albino Bezzina from Mosta.[2]

Adrian's leadership was seen by many as inspirational. Some ground crew particularly close to Adrian would 'bully' or 'berate' him if he brought back a damaged aircraft. The airmen worried about Adrian, perhaps far more so than he worried about himself, and they never gave up trying to persuade him to do up the shoulder straps of his seat harness; he rarely bothered. His habit of pushing the remains of his cigarettes underneath his parachute was constantly remarked upon, but to no avail. Eventually, an ashtray was fitted to the Spitfire he flew most often.

Ken Rogers was a pre-war regular who got to know Adrian well. He thought Malta the ideal place for Adrian; it allowed him to express his individuality, which would have been smothered in the UK. He said Adrian needed both Christina and the informal atmosphere of Malta. He also said if Adrian returned from a flight early

1. Letter from Lem Palmer to Jack Vowles, 23 February 1994.
2. *The People's War Malta: 1940/43*, by Laurence Mizzi, pages 10–11.

he would often fly on a fighter patrol with a Ta' Qali based Spitfire squadron. Adrian did not include these flights in his logbook, as this would reveal to his superiors the true amount of Adrian's flying. That almost certainly would have resulted in further efforts to curtail his flying.

Two Canadians, 'Mac' Brown and Ed Maloney, joined 69 Squadron, although in slightly unusual circumstances. Both were PR Spitfire pilots and Adrian very thoughtfully found bunks for them when they landed at Luqa en route to Egypt. The following day, he announced he was keeping their aircraft; they could continue in two of 69's rather 'tired' aircraft. Having heard about Mac and Ed's ability and keenness, Adrian spoke to each of them separately, saying the other wished to stay but only if his friend would do the same. For Mac and Ed, this was their introduction to one of the greatest men they ever met. They judged Adrian as a total professional and a superb example to his pilots. Yet he was sympathetic to those not up to the task, quietly posting them away without any stigma attached to their names. If a pilot returned without the necessary pictures, then another was immediately sent off to complete the job. Adrian's squadron always came back with the goods. Both Canadians became close to Adrian. They were mature and serious men, older than Adrian, and they had a positive effect on him, especially with regard to his dress. More and more he looked the part of a conventional squadron commander. Ed and Mac became Adrian's deputies and two of his greatest admirers.

Adrian had by now moved into a Mess acquired for all of 69 Squadron's aircrew. It was the former Meadowbank Hotel on Tower Road in Sliema. Given the nature of the squadron's task, it was sensible for all sorts of reasons to have the aircrew accommodated together. Adrian shared a room with the two Canadians. Mac often accompanied Adrian socially and soon found himself seconded as a dance partner to Christina. 'Warby claimed that he could only dance to the tune *Jealously* and for his sake orchestras would play it when he appeared, but even then he danced it poorly: with Christina, of course.'[3] Both Mac and Ed described how glamorous Christina was and how envious they were of Adrian's monopoly of her.

There were still elements of irresponsibility associated with Adrian such as his frequent use of his Luger pistol when in the Mess. Once, when trying to get a lift back from Tripoli soon after it was taken by the Allies, Adrian persuaded Mac to accompany him in a barely flyable Blenheim, a type with which Warby insisted he was familiar; he was, but not as a pilot. One engine failed before take-off so Mac never got to see at first hand the extent of Adrian's Blenheim 'experience'.

Adrian became very close to Mac, probably closer to him than with anyone he met in the RAF, and they often spoke at length about personal matters. Adrian admitted to Mac he married hastily in 1939. He said the marriage was to ensure

3. *Warburton's War*, by Tony Spooner, page 146.

someone would benefit from his death by receiving a widow's pension. This suggests that only days after war commenced, with no knowledge of what direction it would take or how long it would last, Adrian did not anticipate surviving. It is an extraordinary comment to make considering Adrian never informed the RAF of his marriage and he could easily have been killed early on, with little publicity marking his passing. His wife may never have known and she would have received nothing. His admission to Mac may have been an attempt to explain away his marriage in a manner which would not lessen Mac's obvious regard for Adrian. It is also possible Adrian may have admitted his marriage to Christina, although that is by no means certain. Regardless, like the few others before him who knew Adrian's secret, Mac wouldn't have 'queered Warby's pitch' with Christina given the high regard in which he held his young squadron commander. Maybe Mac had already concluded Adrian was unlikely to survive the war.

When Mac and Ed came to the end of their tour, Adrian helped arrange for them to return to North America on a publicity tour to lecture at photo-reconnaissance schools in the United States. Mac later described Adrian as a wonderful man who did not know what fear was. He also said nothing ever seemed to upset him, and he was able to react to every emergency skilfully and decisively. He thought Adrian, with his typically dry English sense of humour, well-disciplined and considered him to be highly regarded by everyone. Ed said there was nothing in the least bit phoney about Adrian, who treated everyone as gentlemen. Clearly by early 1943, Adrian was no longer the loner of his early days in Malta.

Sandy Johnstone was at last given command of a Spitfire Wing, his being based on the newly completed strip at Qrendi. There were still very few vehicles on the island and all were reserved for operational use. Sandy's wing was supplied with an old Chevrolet with one side of its bodywork completely missing. Up to twelve pilots would squeeze inside. They would often meet Lord Gort on his bicycle: 'What should have been a succession of smart salutes normally developed into something more reminiscent of the waving of arms in good natured greetings on both sides. But no one minded – least of all the Governor.'[4] They had the greatest admiration for Gort, and he and his ADC would often be found on the airfields before dawn talking to pilots and ground crew as they prepared for the first flights of the day. He proved to be a popular figure leading a community under siege. Sandy later succumbed to undulant fever and was evacuated to England. When he left the island, he did so with a lasting memory of the marvellous spirit of a people who had stood defiantly, even when they were alone and isolated. Their determination had been an example to all.

---

4. *Where no Angels Dwell*, by AVM Sandy Johnstone, page 116.

By February, 69 Squadron was enormous and the decision was taken to split it into three separate squadrons. The Wellingtons became part of 458 Squadron and the PR Spitfire flight became 683 Squadron, with Adrian its first commanding officer. He was granted UK leave in March. He attended many parties in Piccadilly at the Wings' Club, a favourite venue for RAF personnel. Adrian also sought out his old friend Tich at RAF Cranage in Cheshire. Adrian stayed for a time with Tich in the Officers' Mess; by then he looked immaculate in a brand-new uniform. It was Tich who, back in 1940, took on the task of sorting out Adrian's finances by having a proportion of Adrian's pay deducted to go toward paying off his debts. Adrian took no interest in the deductions, but now learnt there was a significant credit balance. Having paid all his debts, Adrian attempted to leave half of the remainder in an envelope for Tich to open after he left. No sooner had Adrian departed than Tich deposited the money back into Adrian's bank account. Tich later said he was very proud to have Adrian in the Mess. This was a very different Adrian to the youngster foisted upon him by Jos Braithwaite at North Coates in 1940.

The strategic situation in North Africa was changing rapidly when Adrian arrived back in Malta. What was left of the Afrika Korps was being squeezed between Montgomery's 8th Army, advancing from the east, and the Americans and British advancing from the west. With Tripoli having fallen to the 8th Army on 23 January 1943, the combined German and Italian troops were now contained within a shrinking perimeter around Tunis.

The Americans were keen to learn more about photo-reconnaissance and despatched a small section of a PR unit to Malta to liaise directly with the RAF. They arrived in six Lightning P-38s at the end of March but got off to a bad start; one aircraft was wrecked by taxiing too fast on Luqa's difficult perimeter track, and soon afterwards their American commander crashed in Sicily and was taken prisoner. A planned joint beer call was about to be called off by the Americans because of the loss of their commanding officer. Adrian insisted it go ahead and this did a great deal to break the ice

To begin with, the American approach to photo-recce was very conservative and their results were unimpressive. Adrian demanded to fly the P-38, despite some initial local American resistance. Typically, he won the day and did what he always did best: lead by example. He even wore a US uniform for his first operational mission in a P-38 over Sicily, although he took the sensible precaution of practicing some take-offs and landings first. In the past, Adrian struggled on take-off to counter the torque and slipstream produced in twin-engine aircraft; this resulted in the curved take-off runs which so often horrified onlookers. The P-38 was ideal for him as each of its propellers rotated in opposite directions resulting in no swing. The Americans responded well to Adrian's example and to his no-nonsense, get-the-photographs approach, and they listened carefully to what he had to say. From then on Wing Commander War*burt*on, as they pronounced his surname, was one of the good guys, and his laid-back attitude and involvement with American aircrew and ground crew alike was warmly welcomed. They responded well to his very broad interpretation of rules and regulations.

When a new sergeant pilot, Keith Durbridge, joined 683 Squadron, he impressed Adrian, who suggested he apply for a commission. Durbridge said he would think about it. Adrian gave him thirty minutes, then advised him he had a commissioning interview with the AOC later that day. When his commission was announced, Adrian was the first to buy Keith a celebratory drink in the Mess. He then accused Keith of drinking before ops and promptly flew the sortie himself. Keith soon realised Adrian demanded operational efficiency above all things. When Keith later reported back about a prize target, a tanker proceeding south, an attack force was quickly despatched from Malta and duly consigned the 'tanker' to the deep. The oil pipes on the ship's deck were in fact tree trunks. Keith was duly reprimanded by Adrian for faulty ship recognition. Durbridge thought Adrian looked after his men very well and he could not have had a better commanding officer.

At some stage Adrian met Elliot Roosevelt, son of the American President, Franklin D. Roosevelt. Elliot was in command of all US photo-recce units in North West Africa and a close friendship developed between the two. Elliot was an unconventional character and he had 'clout'; he soon developed a deep admiration for the equally unconventional War*burt*on. The Americans primarily used the twin-engine P-38, but Elliot was not a pilot and retained a B-17 Flying Fortress as his personal transport. It was often used to bring supplies to his units, not all of which were official. He brought Adrian a jeep, which he subsequently used throughout the remainder of his time in Malta.

Tedder now commanded all Allied Air Forces from Gibraltar to Egypt. Hugh Lloyd was promoted to Air Marshal in command of all North West African Coastal Air Forces. With the African campaign coming to a close, and Tunis on the brink of capture, Adrian frequently visited Algiers, and it is likely he was involved in the planning for the next stage of the war in the Mediterranean: the Allied landings in Sicily. The end came for the Axis in North Africa on 12 May 1943, when General Alexander reported all enemy resistance had ceased; over 240,000 prisoners were taken. Once again, Malta's air and naval forces were vitally important, sinking fifty-seven ships between Italy and Tunisia, almost half of the Axis losses on that route. The Italians described the route as the *rotta del morte*.

Adrian played a key role in a task that preceded the main event in Sicily: the capture of the small, heavily-defended island of Pantelleria. Of strategic importance because of its location between Tunisia and Sicily, he flew the photographic missions personally. He was provided with a fighter escort for each of the four trips required, often flown below the 400-foot high cliffs. Keith Durbridge later remarked Adrian was the only pilot he ever heard of who was fired at by anti-aircraft guns from *above*. Adrian, of course, delivered the goods once more, photographing the complete shoreline, as well as all the defences and coastal batteries. The photography exceeded all expectations and allowed the Allied planners to pinpoint every defensive location, all of which were then subjected to a merciless bombardment. As soon as the invading force was sighted, the defending garrison surrendered. The Americans freely acknowledged Adrian's work saved many lives.

King George VI's Birthday Honours were published on 4 June. Christina was awarded the British Empire Medal (BEM). From the day Italy declared war, through and beyond the island's most trying days, she had shared the risk and the rations, and worked tirelessly to entertain troops. For six months, she combined her work with the *Whizz-Bangs* with duties as a plotter, before becoming captain of her watch at the height of the air battle, and then assistant controller. Like many other civilians, she could have opted for evacuation. Her award was richly deserved and entirely on her own merit. The following day, she received a telegram of congratulation from Adrian's mother, Muriel, saying how glad and proud she was to hear of Christina's decoration. This confirms Muriel was still unaware of her son's earlier marriage; she would hardly have sent such a message to someone she would regard as the 'other woman', regardless of the circumstances of her son's hasty action.

Six 'Lascaris ladies' were recognised for their contribution, including Phyllis Frederick, who trained Christina, Marigold 'Pickles' Fletcher, another founder member of the *Whizz-Bangs*, and Irene Cameron, also of the *Raffians* concert party. Carmel Galea, who wouldn't let bombs, bullets or injury stop her from reporting for duty, was also awarded the BEM. Bill Farnes, D Watch's very able controller, was appointed OBE. As in any Honours' List, there were others who merited recognition who were not included, but there is no doubt the awards to the ladies of Lascaris were hard-earned and well-deserved.

At dawn on 20 June, the cruiser *Aurora*, with a destroyer escort, made her way into Grand Harbour. A large fighter escort provided protection for the last few miles and the channel into Grand Harbour was carefully swept for mines. On board the cruiser was the former C-in-C Mediterranean Fleet, Admiral Cunningham, upon whom so much depended throughout Malta's early days. On this trip he too was an escort, but to a far more important visitor, so important the visit was kept secret until 5.00 am that morning. The visitor was King George VI.

Every vantage point around Grand Harbour was thick with cheering people as *Aurora*, flying the Royal Standard, passed the breakwater at 8.00 am. The King stood on a special platform built in front of the bridge so people could see him. Everyone went wild with enthusiasm. When the King stepped onto Maltese soil, all the bells in Malta's many churches began ringing. The King made an extensive tour of the island and later lunched at Verdala Palace with the recently promoted

Field Marshal Viscount Gort. This was the first visit of a reigning Sovereign to Malta since 1911. Admiral Cunningham later said the visit produced the most spontaneous and genuine demonstration of loyalty and affection he had ever seen.

By the summer, 683 Squadron had re-equipped with Spitfire Mark IXs. Surprisingly, not all were fitted with cockpit mirrors, vital for such unarmed aircraft. Adrian refused to have one fitted prior to one flight, insisting instead it was fitted to an aircraft allocated to a less experienced pilot. Adrian later remonstrated with one young pilot for taking photographs lower than the assigned height, having done so to stay below cloud, although this exposed him to ground fire. Adrian told the pilot, aged twenty-three, he was too young to die and Adrian had no wish to inform his wife she was now a widow. The pilot concerned was utterly deflated. A few minutes later Adrian congratulated him for producing excellent photographs which delighted the interpreters. Adrian was two years older than the 'young pilot' and he had been doing exactly the same, taking risks to bring back the goods, for the best part of three years.

A further example of Adrian's sense of responsibility occurred when he flew to La Marsa in Tunisia to personally inform a flight sergeant pilot a very close friend of his, a sergeant pilot, had lost his life in a mid-air collision. Adrian continued to note in his flying logbook the number of pilot friends and colleagues lost on reconnaissance missions; by 1943 the number had reached forty.

Another newcomer was Canadian, William Keir Carr, known as Bill. He delivered a brand-new PR Spitfire Mark XI and had high hopes of joining Adrian's squadron, hopes he thought dashed when the adjutant said he would not be staying long. 'The intelligence officer advised that if I wanted to see the CO about staying with 683, I had better go down to dispersal where I would most likely find him "shooting the breeze with the erks (airmen)." I did so and in a revetment shack, found a person without rank badges stretched out on a table surrounded by airmen drinking tea. This was the CO. He asked me about the Spit and why I had come to the airfield that day when I could have stayed in the sack.' Whatever answer Bill offered was sufficient; he could stay.

'I later discovered that all that I had heard about this fabulous character was true. Wing Commander Warburton with all his medals was already a legend. 683 was Warby's squadron and everyone was there only because he accepted them. His groundcrew worshipped him. Individuals who didn't impress him, and there were many, were sent packing. I can recall that this practice, and others such as Warby's disdain for rank badges, spit and polish, ID cards and "dog tags", on occasion greatly annoyed the RAF Station Commander, Group Captain Willy Merton. The poor man, try as he might, couldn't do much about it. Warby was far too valuable – a one-man air force – to be disciplined in the normal way for such prosaic violations. Air Vice-Marshal Park, too, had his troubles with Wing Commander Warburton, not the least of which was Warby's habit of taking off into the blue without even bothering to tell people where he was going.

'Cairo, for example, had its attractions for him and on one ... flight in a borrowed Mark IX Spitfire, Warby was attacked by a group of Me109s. He shot down two of them, but neglected to report the incident until five days later when he returned from Cairo and was asked to explain the bullet holes in the rear of the borrowed aircraft.

'The ladies saw Warby as a charming handsome man and were universally attracted to him. His obvious unique talent in the air against the enemy seems to add to his success in dealing with this problem. He was greatly envied by us, his young pilots, and not just in the air.

'On one occasion, Warby's father, a salty naval commander, visited his Air Force son in the Sliema mess. I remember that he, too, wore the ribbons of the DSO and other decorations. On this occasion, it was interesting to see the Senior Service representative was not only a great story teller, but could also handle his grog better than most. The evening ended with the famous son and father happily weaving their way out of the mess arm in arm, and arguing simultaneously about who had drunk too much to drive the vehicle.' It must have been a fascinating sight, father and son of equal rank, arm in arm, sporting a remarkable array of decorations between them.

Planning was well underway for the Sicily landings and 683 Squadron was called upon to play its part. Despite his rank, wide responsibilities, and discouragement from Air HQ, Adrian undertook the task of photographing the beaches personally. This caused some irritation amongst his pilots. He worked closely with two US Army intelligence officers attached to 683 whose presence was a mystery to many. A number of flights were needed to obtain the necessary coverage and, as Sicily was defended by Me109F units, a fighter escort was again provided for Adrian's missions. He covered the area from Gela to Syracuse from a height of 200 feet on four missions. Hugh O'Neill flew the fighter escort and commented that Adrian was undeterred by the flak, simply smoking a large cigar as he went about his task. Once again Adrian's photographs exceeded expectations and he received numerous letters of congratulation. The C-in-C Middle East, General Harold Alexander, signalled Malta asking that Adrian be personally thanked. He said the pictures were as technically perfect as if taken on a peacetime exercise.

Operation Husky, the invasion of Sicily, saw Lascaris also occupied by Eisenhower and Alexander, Cunningham and Tedder overseeing the largest scale amphibious and airborne landings ever attempted. The atmosphere in Malta changed again. The few air raids were of little consequence. The airfields were all expanded. Soon, there were seven Spitfire squadrons at Luqa, four at Hal Far and five more at Ta' Qali. With Qrendi also an operational fighter base, and a newly-constructed US base on Gozo, there were nearly 500 Spitfires and twenty-two fighter squadrons on the islands. This was a far cry from the days of *Faith*, *Hope* and *Charity*.

Adrian flew to North Africa often, cementing further his relationship with the influential Elliot Roosevelt. At the many meetings and conferences, Adrian always looked the part as a neatly uniformed wing commander. He was invited to join the American independence celebrations at La Marsa, near Tunis, on 4 July. Attempting to return two days later, his Spitfire was unserviceable and he was given a P-38 Lightning instead. This particular aircraft had one or two known idiosyncrasies and was never flown operationally. He was warned about problems with the engine superchargers and advised to make sure both engines were stabilised before releasing the brakes. If they were not, the consequences could be dire. Perhaps in his anxiety to get airborne, Adrian simply did what he usually did, applied full power and released the brakes. Not long afterwards, one supercharger ran away and the aircraft veered onto rough ground, the undercarriage collapsed and the aircraft came to a halt on fire. When crash crews arrived, Adrian was not in the cockpit; he was sitting not far from the blazing wreck having a cigarette. He escaped injury by being thrown clear, having not fully strapped in. He was completely unperturbed and calmly walked back to dispersal. To the consternation of many, he was soon airborne heading for Malta in another borrowed P-38, leaving his first aircraft still burning.

Others were noting changes in Adrian. He still flew far more than a normal squadron commander and continued to select the most dangerous missions, but he exercised his responsibility over his subordinates well. He was, however, long overdue a genuine rest tour. There were also signs he was becoming weary and edgy. He was less of a loner and drank more than before, being more inclined to party. He may have been more conscious of his increased attractiveness to ladies, many of whom were drawn toward him. Adrian and Christina were still very much a couple, but she was aware of what was going on and had concerns. She would have known better than anyone that Adrian was in desperate need of a prolonged rest. She must have been torn by such thoughts, as a rest tour would likely take him away from Malta. Nevertheless, Christina was always more concerned about Adrian's welfare, which she put above all things. She too was under immense strain.

The Allied invasion of Sicily began on 9 July and achieved all of its strategic goals. By the date of the assault, 'a complete picture of the enemy's dispositions and movements had been obtained by photographic interpretation. The vertical and low oblique photographs of the coastline, which General Patton considered, "essential to the success of the operation", were of the highest value to the whole force. Operation Torch had shown how necessary such photographs were to Force Commanders and staffs in the assault phase, and arrangements were made to supply all HQ ships with copies of the assault beaches.'[5] All the photographs of the assault

---

5. *RAF Narrative Photographic Reconnaissance Volume II, May 1941 to August 1943*, written by the Air Historical Branch, page 123.

beaches were taken by Adrian. The invasion launched the Italian campaign, marking the beginning of the end for Mussolini, who was imprisoned by the Italians on 24 July. Later rescued by German forces, he was subsequently captured by Italian partisans and summarily executed, along with his mistress.

On the first day of the invasion, Adrian was tasked with taking photographs of the beach landings as they took place. He was particularly concerned about the American tendency to shoot at any aircraft near their ships and took pains to ensure they were well briefed about his mission. Nevertheless, his PR Spitfire was hit repeatedly by friendly fire and he was only just able to get it back to Malta. Warby's luck held. His engineers were horrified at the damage. As Adrian climbed down from the aircraft, ignoring a large hole in his wing, he said laconically to the waiting airmen the radio didn't work. Later the same day, Adrian borrowed a fighter Spitfire and accompanied three experienced Spitfire flight commanders on a fighter sweep over Syracuse to vent his frustration on the enemy. By then, he had officially flown 379 operational sorties totalling 1,300 flying hours. He also had confirmation of nine aircraft shot down, one probably shot down and two others damaged.

More and more photo-reconnaissance tasks were now being conducted by increasing numbers of Americans and this impacted on the RAF recce pilots. Those who served within the often unique, relatively informal, operational arrangements existing on Malta, were being drawn back into the greater military fold and they were perhaps losing the independence of operation they had enjoyed for so long. Rules and regulations were also becoming more apparent as the situation took on a normality not previously seen in wartime Malta.

By late July, Adrian's squadron was operating in and out of captured airfields in Sicily. In the same month, he was awarded a bar to his DSO. There was more work for Christina's needle. The honours were important to Adrian, although to others he appeared casual, almost indifferent, about them. By then he was wearing the DSO and bar, and the DFC and two bars; the bars being shown as a rosette on the medal ribbon. One pilot said it looked as if his medal ribbons were riveted onto his tunic. Mac Brown later said Adrian had aspirations of equalling, or exceeding, his father's rank before the war was over. He actually reached his father's rank in November 1942, only four years after being commissioned, and now had a second DSO. On 26 July he flew to Cairo and spent a few days in Haifa celebrating with his father.

Adrian knew better than anyone the glory days of independent operations from Malta were over. He still flew operationally as often as possible, but given the nature of the drive within him he was looking for more. An RAF North African photo-recce wing was about to be formed and Adrian wanted to be considered for command. This involved even more trips to Tunisia. Christina knew this was a difficult time for Adrian. There were quarrels and Adrian's more outgoing behaviour was bound to have been a factor. The quarrels always ended with reconciliations, but Christina was becoming increasingly worried she might be losing her man. They both must have been near the end of their tether. They needed time together, but there was none. Others commented Adrian appeared to be war-weary, but he always seemed to be ready for another mission or another party. Others saw Adrian as warm and caring about people, but also serious, even sad.

Having lost his two Canadian friends and roommates, Adrian now shared a room with an engineering officer, 'Tich' Iddon. Tich said Adrian kept very irregular hours, no doubt continuing to spend a lot of time with Christina. Luqa's adjutant was Syd Collins, and Adrian confided in him more and more. Syd became aware Adrian was married. He also knew Adrian arrived in Malta in debt and Tich Whiteley dealt with this on Adrian's behalf. As adjutant he would have been aware that some of Adrian's pay was withheld and he also knew about Adrian's relationship with Christina. Syd considered Adrian to be remarkable, without conceit in relation to what he did, and the bravest pilot he ever met in his service career.

With at least two of his closest confidants aware of his marriage, Adrian must have revealed it to Christina. By then, she was completely in love with him and if she knew, it is unlikely to have made a great deal of difference to her feelings, especially as the marriage was so short-lived. Rumours Adrian was married may have reached Air HQ. Despite the official attitude, the ignorance of Adrian's marriage amongst the majority of his colleagues and his undoubted worth may have caused Keith Park to stay his hand. The fact Adrian was now officially accommodated with his squadron may also have been a factor. Some thought Park thought the world of Adrian; others felt Park didn't know how to handle him. Whatever the situation, the AOC might also have been aware Adrian's time in Malta was coming to an end, so if there were any concerns they would soon go away.

During the summer of 1943, the war artist Leslie Cole undertook a series of paintings of scenes of devastation, as well as portraits of Maltese children, housewives and some of the island's personalities. One portrait was of the AOC, Air Vice-Marshal Keith Park; another was of Christina. The war photographer R. Deakin (now a lieutenant), who completed the series of images of Christina the previous year, was again on hand for publicity purposes and photographed Christina in early August at Leslie Cole's studio.

On 3 September there was a ceremony in which Air Vice-Marshal Park presented *Faith* to the Maltese people. He said: 'The defence of Malta can justifiably be included amongst the epics of this war, and *Faith* has earned a place of honour in the armour of Malta.'[6] By then Adrian had stopped entering his flights in his logbook. There were no further entries after August, although he took part in some routine

---

6. *The Air Battle of Malta*, by the Ministry of Information, page 12.

mapping tasks over the Adriatic, flying one on 6 September. Italy surrendered to the Allies two days later. At long last, everyone had something to celebrate.

Church bells rang out and in no time at all the streets were festooned with bunting and flags as the whole island went wild with joy. Crowds not seen since June 1940 gathered everywhere, with people singing and dancing; all except Christina. The one person she wanted to share the victory with wasn't there and she had had no word. She walked the streets they had walked together many times – *Porta Reale* up to and along Merchants Street, then left down Britannia Street back to Kingsway. She continued down the steepening slope to Strait Street, but instead of going home she turned left to meander back to the city walls. After all she and Adrian had gone through together, it seemed she was destined to celebrate Malta's victory on her own, miserable and feeling more alone than she had done before. After an hour she turned into South Street and headed for the Monico; perhaps she should just go and get sloshed.

'And then suddenly I saw him coming towards me, running down the street, with his arms outstretched:

'"Chris, I've been looking all over the bloody place for you."

'It was the first time I'd heard him swear and I loved it. Right there in the middle of South Street he went down on his knees and pleaded forgiveness. I wept buckets of tears. Passers-by must have thought we were nuts.'[7]

On 10 September 1943, the Italian fleet arrived within sight of Malta to formally surrender. Adrian paraded with 683 Squadron for the final time a week later. He left Malta on posting in October having been in continuous command of an operational Spitfire squadron operating within the heart of an intense war zone for fourteen months.

On 1 October 1943, 683 Squadron's ORB records Adrian was posted to the UK via North Africa.

---

7. Quoted in *Warburton's War*, by Tony Spooner, page 174.

Chapter Sixteen

Loss

'April is the cruellest month'

From *The Waste Land* by T.S. Elliot

Adrian spent a few days in Tunisia and three weeks in England. Although 683 Squadron's ORB made no reference to Adrian's next appointment, it is inconceivable he left Malta without that knowledge. Before going on leave, he flew to Tunisia, as he was to become the commanding officer of the newly-formed 336 (PR) Wing at La Marsa, near the capital Tunis. The wing was to be declared operational on 1 November 1943. It comprised of Adrian's former squadron, 683 Squadron, still at Luqa, 682 Squadron, also with PR Spitfires, and 60 (South African Air Force) Squadron which operated PR Mosquitos.

In England, Adrian spent some time at home. His mother recalled travelling on a bus with him when the bus conductor refused to take Adrian's fare, saying they didn't take money from 'you people'. Adrian was acutely embarrassed. He again caught up with Tich and later they met to ferry two aircraft to Gibraltar, Tich flying a Beaufighter and Adrian a Spitfire. In talking to Tich's navigator, Adrian said he had found his wife living with someone else. There is no evidence to support this and Adrian's motive in saying it to a stranger is unclear. He had still not advised the RAF he was married and his parents remained in ignorance. Years later, Betty said she had no contact with Adrian after their brief meeting in Blackpool in 1940. To the Beaufighter navigator, Adrian seemed unconcerned about his safety and the outcome of the ferry flight. But this could easily have been Adrian's 'way', which may have appeared odd to anyone who did not know him.

Tich's Beaufighter had ample fuel to skirt Spanish airspace, but Adrian had to fly a direct route, jettisoning a long-range fuel tank over neutral Spain. Even so, he had no margin, no fuel reserve. With very poor weather grounding all aircraft, Adrian insisted in getting airborne and was only allowed to take off at his own risk. In the event he cut things too fine, running out of fuel over forty miles from Gibraltar. He only just made it gliding the rest of the way. When Tich arrived, Adrian was already airborne, heading for La Marsa and a new challenge.

Despite his leave, after so many operational missions under the most trying of circumstances, Adrian must have been affected by stress. Many pilots ended up physical or nervous wrecks after less than six months of ops from Malta. Denis Barnham was one: 'I'm burnt out. I seem cut off from my excited companions, yet there's only one thing to be done: I must build on the ashes of myself some kind of intense enthusiasm by which I can pretend to lead and inspire them.'[1] Dennis only spent ten weeks in Malta, but there was little left of the enthusiasm and *joie de vivre* his wife Diana had known well: 'He was thin, ill and distraught; physically intact but wounded in spirit.'[2] Dennis was invalided out of the RAF before the war's end. Yet Adrian flew on operations for over three years with only very short breaks between his three tours in Malta. His final tour in command – fourteen months – was unusually long in wartime. Nor could his rest tours be described as such and attempts by senior officers to curb his flying were cursory. Should more have been done to give him a longer break? No doubt he would have fiercely resisted, but selecting him for yet another demanding command appointment was hardly likely to reduce the pressure on him. It must have been obvious to all concerned he would drive himself hard. Tedder and Lloyd, as well as Park, would have been instrumental in agreeing Adrian's appointment to 336 Wing.

By late 1943, the Americans were asserting their majority holding on the war in Europe. They expanded their photo-reconnaissance activities dramatically and the RAF was inevitably being pushed sideways. How better to reassert the British position than by establishing an RAF reconnaissance wing, the first of its kind in the Mediterranean, commanded by someone well regarded by the Americans and by the influential Elliot Roosevelt? From an RAF perspective, perhaps it was a case of needs must and having the best man for the job, regardless of the cost to the individual.

Adrian hit the ground running at La Marsa and set about getting his new wing into shape. His impact on the South Africans of 60 Squadron was immediate and positive, and he spent much of his spare time in their Mess, where he was popular with officers and NCOs alike. He was also said to party well. His former squadron, 683 Squadron, arrived from Malta in mid-November making the wing complete. Soon afterwards, as a result of his exceptional work prior to the Pantelleria and Sicily landings, Adrian was awarded the American DFC, although it was not gazetted until mid-January 1944.

On the evening of 26 November, Adrian was involved in a road accident. He was the only occupant in a vehicle thought to have been hit by an American truck which failed to stop. He crawled out of the overturned vehicle seriously injured, and was taken to hospital in Carthage with a broken pelvis and other injuries; he was expected to be hospitalised for at least three months with the lower part of his body encased in plaster. He was soon transferred to No 2 RAF General Hospital at Maison Carée

---

1. *Malta Spitfire Pilot*, by Denis Barnham, page 196.
2. *Malta Spitfire Pilot*, by Denis Barnham, page 3.

Algiers. The accident could not have occurred at a worse time for Adrian. He had worked tirelessly to bring the wing together. Now his hopes were cruelly dashed. To make matters worse, 336 Wing moved to San Severo on the Foggia Plain in southern Italy, with 683 Squadron the last to complete the journey on 20 December. Adrian had high hopes of defying the doctors' timetable for recovery so he could rejoin his wing, but, on 27 December, he was relieved of command. Gordon Hughes was posted out from England and appointed in his place. Adrian would have been devastated. There was little for him to celebrate on New Year's Eve 1943. He wrote to Christina from Maison Carée and in mid-January also wrote to his father. By then he had been in bed for seven weeks, with another three or four to go.

Adrian was a consummate planner and now had little else to do but think about his future. Could he could get back in the air and perhaps regain command of 'his' wing? Once discharged from hospital, he would have to prove his fitness to fly, probably back in England. But there he would most likely be swallowed up within the mainstream RAF. He had few influential connections in Britain. Could he get himself back amongst friends? What about Elliot Roosevelt? Could he help? In his letter to his father, Adrian said Elliott was moving on and he hoped to accompany him. For obvious security reasons, he said nothing about Elliot's destination, but Elliot was in command of the 90th Reconnaissance Wing which had already moved to San Severo. Adrian's former wing, 336, formed part of the 90th which was the equivalent of an RAF group. Adrian told his father that if he was able to follow Elliot, he might be able to settle with his friend once and for all. It is almost certain he meant Christina who was only thirty minutes flying time from San Severo.

Canadian Bill Carr, one of Adrian's pilots on 683 Squadron, takes up the story: 'Growing tired of being bed-ridden he climbed out of the window, "borrowed" a vehicle and made his way to the airport. There, he located some old friends who helped him cut off his cast. He borrowed shorts and a shirt, and a Mark IX Spit from a friendly squadron commander, and flew to see us of his old squadron, now located in Italy. While he had a parachute he had no maps and the aircraft had no oxygen. In due course he found us, and among other things en route had flown over a weather front that topped out at 25,000 feet. Lesser mortals in the best of health would not have survived such a flight, yet, the following day, he visited us at dispersal in San Severo and allowed that he must be getting old because he felt too tired to share a few noggins with us that evening.'

Not long afterwards, General Eisenhower requested Elliot Roosevelt's transfer to England along with key personnel from 90th Wing, with the assigned purpose of studying the European theatre of operations prior to setting up a new reconnaissance wing. On the list of personnel named by Eisenhower was Adrian Warburton, who came back to the UK with Elliot later in January. The new wing was the 8th Reconnaissance Wing (Provisional) which was later renamed the 325th

Reconnaissance Wing, located at the 8th Air Force HQ at High Wycombe. The new wing was to include two RAF wings alongside three American groups, a US group being of similar size to an RAF wing. Elliot wanted Adrian as his deputy, but officially Adrian was still listed as 'sick'. With no airfield at High Wycombe, Adrian gravitated to a unit subordinate to the 325th, and where the action was: the 7th Photo-Recce Group (PRG) at RAF Mount Farm near Oxford. Lieutenant Colonel George Lawson commanded Mount Farm and confirmed Adrian, his, 'friend and confidant in fighting the reconnaissance war',[3] arrived there in January or February, many weeks before his official RAF posting to Mount Farm.

There are uncertainties about what exactly Adrian got up to over the next few weeks. He had never been part of the UK recce establishment centred on nearby RAF Benson and it is unlikely he was needed or wanted there. Word of his unorthodoxy would have reached the Benson hierarchy long before. But at Mount Farm, Adrian was amongst friends. In George Lawson's opinion, Adrian was 'a fine fellow' who liked the way the Americans operated. Tedder subsequently said Warby was the most valuable pilot in the RAF in North Africa, but in Lawson's view, 'the RAF kind of threw him out in the cold because he was one who did not conform to what the RAF thought he should. He was pro-enlisted man (airmen), he wore whatever uniform he wanted to, he said and did what he wanted to, and that did not sit well with the RAF brass even though he was a hero and one of the best pilots of the RAF... . Warby lived at Mount Farm ... and he lived there until his last flight. He would come and go as he pleased, drank with us, and tried to gamble with us (he did not last long because he did not have any money to speak of).'[4]

Ron Foster was a young New Zealander serving on 544 Squadron at RAF Benson. In February or March 1944, when having lunch in the Officers' Mess, he recalled the Spitfire squadron commanders and flight commanders bursting into the dining room, clutching pints of beer, all in a rowdy mood even though it was only midday. They were celebrating the unexpected arrival of someone Ron described as the most dashing and exuberant character he ever saw throughout the war: Adrian Warburton. Ron said Adrian's presence created an electric atmosphere and the impression he made on Ron lasted a lifetime. 'A bowl of vitamin pills was on his table, and he scooped up a small handful and chucked them into his mashed potato; with huge laughter all around, he then gobbled the lot, washing it down with his pint of bitter.'[5] Years later, Ron recalled it was a rare experience to see Benson's elite paying such homage to a man whose life read like exaggerated fiction.

---

3. Letter from Lt Col Lawson to Frank Dorber dated Sep 1994, published in the 7th *Photo Recon Association Journal* 1994.
4. *Ibid*.
5. *Focus on Europe*, by Ronald H. Foster, pages 28–9.

Some later suggested Adrian was depressed, others said this was nonsense. He would have been desperately disappointed at having lost his wing and probably yearned to get back into the air again. To feel fulfilled he needed to hold another command and he had no chance of one in England. He may have felt he was marking time when others were getting on with the war. He needed to be on ops and struggled when out of his element, relegated to the side lines as a supporting player. Like Christina, he needed the limelight. Yet it does appear as if Adrian was flying regularly from Mount Farm, although not on operational missions. Sometime in March, he was seen in Gibraltar in an American P-38 and heading for Britain. To one pilot he met there, whom he knew, he seemed physically fit, and his conversation was rational and normal. This is in contrast to those who hinted at depression.

Adrian continued to make no entries in his flying logbook. The previous summer it was probably to avoid his superiors finding out about how much flying he was doing. This time it may have been because he was still officially unfit to fly; one look at his logbook would have revealed all. How much did the US authorities know of his medical category? Or had Adrian simply omitted the word 'sick' when he arrived at Mount Farm on 'leave'? Adrian's formal posting to Mount Farm, on 1 April 1944, as Liaison Officer to the US 7th PRG, probably marked from an RAF perspective he was now fit for duty.

In the ten weeks or so Adrian spent at Mount Farm, he became friendly with two young American recce pilots: Carl Chapman flew the P-38 Lightning and John Blyth, a former P-38 pilot, flew American PR Spitfires. John initially shared a room with Carl and later witnessed him trying to teach Adrian baseball. Adrian seemed incapable of catching the ball and was hit on the head a number of times to the great amusement of everyone, including Adrian. John thought it very odd that Adrian apparently had such poor hand-eye coordination. John liked Adrian very much and they got on extremely well despite their difference in rank, which meant little to Adrian. John's nickname was 'Limey' because of his British background. They talked often and Adrian told John about a trip he made to London. He visited an American-style bar with stools at the counter. Adrian said he noticed his mother sitting at the bar with a friend. Their exchange was brief and to John it seemed unemotional, involving simply 'hello', 'how are you?' and 'fine', before they said their goodbyes. John wondered whether such a lack of emotion and apparent aloofness had anything to do with Adrian's boarding school education. This was almost certainly the last occasion Adrian and his mother met.

Adrian's former command, 336 Wing, was now part of an Anglo-American unit at San Severo called the Mediterranean Photographic Intelligence Centre. One of Adrian's South African friends there said Adrian visited San Severo after taking up his US appointment and let it be known he would be back on about 12 April. He asked for a party to be laid on. Others on 60 (SAAF) Squadron also said Adrian was expected on that date.

The sortie Adrian had in mind for 12 April was, therefore, far from being impromptu. What he intended was carefully thought through and discussed with Carl Chapman, although it appears he did not bring Carl fully into his confidence. As the 7th PRG's Operations Officer, Carl had access to any aircraft; he would also lead the planned mission and carry out any necessary coordination. George Lawson, in overall command of the unit, opposed Adrian flying on a combat mission in a P 38 when there were fifteen or sixteen American PR Spitfires with which Adrian was much more familiar. The Spitfires also had a similar range. Why was Adrian insistent on a P-38? Carl, a favourite of Elliot Roosevelt, went over Lawson's head and gained approval directly from Roosevelt for Adrian to accompany Carl in a second P-38 on a programmed recce flight to Germany. Elliot may also have known more than he let on to Carl.

The plan was to fly to southern Germany escorted by eight long-range P-51 fighters for part of their route. The recce aircraft would then proceed to separate targets, then rendezvous before flying to Alghero in Sardinia, returning later to Mount Farm. That was the plan according to Carl Chapman. George Lawson knew differently: 'Warby told me he was going to San Severo in Italy and had no intention of going to Sardinia. Many of his old buddies from North Africa were stationed at San Severo and they told me later they were expecting him. He may have had in mind going back to Malta from San Severo to see his old girlfriend.'[6]

On 12 April, both aircraft took off with Adrian flying Lightning P-38F5b serial number 42-67325. For at least part of the way, they were escorted by two P-51s; not eight as originally planned. The aircraft stayed together until about 100 miles north of Munich where they split up to proceed to their separate targets. After completing his tasks, Carl flew to the rendezvous arriving at the scheduled time. Adrian did not show up. Carl waited a while, repeatedly calling Adrian on the radio. He heard nothing.

George Lawson didn't initially report Adrian missing because he was sure he was in Italy or Malta. It was almost two weeks later, on 25 April, that the Air Ministry was formally notified Adrian was missing on what Lawson later described as an, 'ill-fated, ill-advised and strange mission.'[7] The notification was in the form of a signal from Elliot Roosevelt quoting Lawson. It said Adrian went missing in action on 12 April 1944 when on an operational shuttle run mission to Italy and was last contacted by a P-51 pilot near Lake Constance. The P51 pilot reported all was well as Adrian headed south. The signal said Adrian's destination was either Alghero

---

6. Letter from Lt Col Lawson to Frank Dorber dated Sep 1994, published in the 7th *Photo Recon Association Journal* 1994.

7. *Ibid.*

or San Severo. So there was admitted official uncertainty about the ultimate destination.

The news Adrian was missing was met with disbelief. Signals were sent to various RAF bases, including Malta, asking if he had landed there. It took the RAF until 1 May before they notified Adrian's mother. Even then the dreaded telegram raised doubts as the Air Ministry asked to be advised if she heard news of Adrian from any other source. Evidently there were some who believed he would still turn up. Adrian's wife was not informed, the RAF still unaware of her existence. Christina found out in April when, 'an airman at Regional Control where I was then working said to me quite casually: "I suppose you've heard about your old friend Wing Commander Warburton?"

'He brought me a copy from the filing cabinet. It was a request for news of Warby, missing on a flight from England. To begin with I was not unduly worried. Nor was anyone else. He had been missing before and, anyway, nothing could ever happen to Warby. But each time I went on duty my first question was: "Any news about Warby?" There was none. All sorts of rumours began to run around. Warby had been shot down. Then from another source: No, Warby had crashed into the Alps. I wrote to his mother and she told me that Warby was missing, and had last been heard of over Lake Constance. My belief is that he had an engine failure while actually over the lake.'[8]

Christina's belief about Adrian going down into a lake was pure speculation as she shared the view held by many that he would not have been shot down. Many questions were asked about Adrian's last flight to try and determine where he might have been lost, with the focus very much on the 7th PRG, its parent HQ and Elliot Roosevelt. Despite Lawson being against Adrian's involvement in a P-38, he was nevertheless operationally responsible for the mission. He later said: 'He was one of the greatest and had no business deep inside Germany in early 1944 in the airplane he flew. This was a sad loss for the RAF (who never wanted him) and his American friends. I collected all of his belongings and delivered them to his mother. These only filled a RAF flying scarf.'[9] So where was the rest of Adrian's kit? Where was his immaculate service dress uniform? George Lawson believed Adrian was wearing a standard American flying suit over his well-worn RAF uniform. Had he taken everything else with him?

Chapman insisted Adrian's destination was Alghero. Lawson and Roosevelt said it was San Severo. Some suggested Adrian may have been heading for Malta to see Christina, others that he deliberately crashed in Switzerland. Where was his aircraft likely to be? Most thought it had come down in the sea or into a lake, but there

---

8. *One Woman Goes to War*, by Christina Ratcliffe, published in *The Star* newspaper, April 1958.

9. Letter from Lt Col Lawson to Frank Dorber dated Sep 1994, published in the 7th *Photo Recon Association Journal* 1994.

was no evidence either way. No other information was ever uncovered about the apparent last contact with Adrian by a P-51 pilot near Lake Constance. Could this have been erroneous, referring to an earlier sighting of Adrian's aircraft?

Others questioned Adrian's state of mind. Although increasingly fatalistic as the war continued, there were no indications he harboured a death wish. Lawson had no truck with the stories of depression saying, 'there are many rumours, lies, tales about him by some people who wanted to play on his name and probably did not know him. I saw him every day he was at Mount Farm, as he hung around the operations building and all the pilots wanted to talk to him. He was well thought of by all American pilots, and they respected what he had accomplished in North Africa and on Malta. I never found him depressed, down on his luck, or anything like that; another unfounded rumour that is put to rest.'[10]

Jack Vowles summed up many people's thoughts about Warby the legend: 'We never thought that he would not come back.' Many of the risks Adrian took were extraordinary, almost as if he was happy to leave his fate in another's hands. Perhaps George Lawson summed up Adrian better than anyone: 'He was without fear. Ice flowed through his veins when in combat.'[11]

Whatever had happened on 12 April 1944, there wasn't much of a trail to follow, and what little there was soon went cold. The speculation about his destination no doubt contributed to no serious attempt being made to find out where 42-67325 had come down. In fact the evidence was out there; there were witnesses.

10. *Ibid.*
11. *Ibid.*

Chapter Seventeen

Waiting

'Tout mon amour, pour que tu me n'oublie pas completement.'

From a note from Adrian to Christina

With Sicily and southern Italy in Allied hands, 69 Squadron moved to Italy having served in Malta longer than any other RAF squadron; the risks associated with air reconnaissance from the island demonstrated by the loss of ninety of its aircrew killed. Corporal Jack Vowles was shipped back to England and granted three weeks well-deserved leave. When he arrived in Halifax, he was met by his wife Barbara whom he had not seen since 1941. She gasped when she saw how thin he was.

Jack was an engineer; an engine and airframe fitter. But he was no ordinary engineer and had lived through extraordinary times. He also grabbed every possible opportunity to fly, mostly on air tests. He made a forced landing at Hendon in a Blenheim, had engine trouble over the Irish Sea in a Harrow, was almost air sick in a Boston, and dodged around Manchester's balloon barrage. In total he flew in twenty-five different types, including the Battle, Beaufighter, Beaufort, Maryland, Wellington and Whitley. No, Jack Vowles was no ordinary engineer.

He was later posted to RAF Hutton Cranswick, in the East Riding of Yorkshire, where he saw out the rest of his war in much calmer conditions than those he experienced in Malta. Now he had an attachment to a small island in the sun that drew him back many times to visit friends left behind. In his mind, he could hear them talking as they did all those years ago. 'Then I would tell them *sahha* until next year,' he said. Adrian had a telling impact on Jack and he would often reflect on their unique friendship, and wonder what became of the 'King of the Mediterranean'.

In Malta, Christina kept her emotions hidden, as she had when Adrian went missing in November 1942. Part of her still hoped he would somehow turn up. Soon after being invested with her BEM in Malta, her former headmistress at Manchester High School for Girls wrote to congratulate her. Christina's reply was published in the school magazine in May 1945:

'It is extremely nice of you to send both your own and the school's congratulations on my award of the BEM. There are possibilities of my being able to visit before the autumn, though everything depends on the course of the war, for I am still working at RAF headquarters here and cannot get away for leave in England until the war in Europe is over. I have been in Malta for almost five years – the most eventful five years of my life – so you can well imagine how I am longing to get back home. Your invitation to come and tell the school of my experience would be accepted with pleasure. I think I should really enjoy telling the girls about the adventures I have had in Malta.'

After the war, Malta became partially self-governing, with Britain responsible for defence. The island was an active staging post for air routes to the east, but the task of clearing debris and rebuilding was immense. Christina's landlord was well off and an architect, and it wasn't long before the partially damaged Vincenti Buildings in Floriana were repaired and Christina moved back into her original apartment with the amazing views. She continued to work for the RAF, becoming a civilian secretary to successive station commanders at Luqa and she stayed in this role for many years. Through her connections, she heard various rumours about Adrian, but there was no certainty, no real closure. She continued to hope that, as in the past, he would simply turn up unannounced, even though she would have been certain he had 'bought it'. A light went out of her life. She never did visit her old school.

In 1946, Eileen 'Betty' Warburton came forward and was invited to Buckingham Palace to be presented with Adrian's medals. There was much publicity after the investiture and a headline of 'Medals but no Bread' referring to the lack of any allowance for Betty until that point. Christina would have seen the headlines; if she hadn't known the truth before, she certainly knew it then. At some stage Betty passed on Adrian's decorations to his parents. As Adrian forecast to some, Betty now received a war widows' pension which she claimed until 1966 when she re-married; she later moved to Australia.

Christina was in touch with Tamara, who had earlier urged her to join her in Egypt, but Christina always said her place was on the island. Tamara never returned to Malta despite invitations to do so. Maybe there were too many unhappy memories: the horrors of the bombing, the tragic loss of her friend Aida Kelly and of course her own attempted suicide. If Christina fell in love with Jacques Méhauas before she met Adrian, Tamara may also have fallen a little in love with René Duvauchelle. As Christina later reflected, 'they never lived to see the liberation of their country, the victory for which they had risked so much to attain.'[1] Jacques, René and their British navigator, George Taylor, were buried near Catania in Sicily. René and Jacques were later reburied in the French military cemetery in Rome. In 1949, René

---

1. *Carve Malta on my heart and other wartime stories,* by Frederick Galea, page 47.

was appointed as a Knight of the Legion of Honour, a Companion of the Liberation and awarded the Croix de Guerre with Palm. In 1950, he was brought home to France and buried at Vaux-le-Penil in Saint-et-Maine.

Soon after the war Christina opened a small café in Valletta – The Café Christina – which she ran when off-duty. It was at 66a Britannia Street, on the left-hand corner just beyond Old Mint Street, and around the corner from the Valletta apartment she shared with Adrian and close to many of the bars and restaurants they had known well. Maybe she dreamt Adrian might find her there one day. How long she kept the café is not known, although in April 1952 it was advertised in the *Luqa Lens*, the RAF station magazine:

FALL IN. DOWN KINGSWAY TO BLACKLEY'S – MARCH
HALT. LEFT TURN. 250 PACES DOWN THE SIDE STREET
QUICK MARCH. YOU'RE THERE! WHERE?
THE CAFE CHRISTINA
66a, Britannia Street, Valletta
AN ENGLISH BAR WITH A CONTINENTAL
ATMOSPHERE
SOFT LIGHTS – SWEET MUSIC – PALM TREES

Sir Hugh Lloyd continued a successful career in the RAF. In 1949, he wrote of his Malta experience in *Briefed to Attack*. Promoted air chief marshal in 1951, his final tour prior to retirement in 1953 was as C-in-C Bomber Command. By then, the Rank Organisation was making a film about wartime Malta for which Lloyd was a screenwriter. Christina also provided material for the film which was partly shot in Malta in autumn 1952. It was called *Malta Story* and went a long way in capturing the impact of war on Malta, and the people who lived and served there. Although the film makers exercised artistic licence concerning the personal storylines and timescales, the Jack Hawkins character is based on Hugh Lloyd. The main theme is a touching love story between a photo-recce Spitfire pilot, played by Alec Guinness, and a Maltese civilian plotter working at Lascaris, played by Muriel Pavlov. There are many parallels with a man they called Warby and a girl he called Chris. The film's success resulted in more interest in Adrian.

Miriam Farrugia knew Christina from when she was a little girl. Her family had property in Bugibba in the north of the island, and they spent their Easter and summer vacations in a house on the promenade close to what was Angelo's Restaurant on Islet Promenade. Christina rented the house next door from Miriam's family and spent her summers there. She retained this summer house for the rest of her life. At the time Bugibba was a very small community of about twenty families, many of whom only came to stay for their holidays. Christina was approaching her fortieth birthday when Miriam first met her; she looked much younger and Miriam remembers her well:

'She was always a very friendly person, friendly with everyone; she would come to our place as if she was one of the family and join in with everyone in all the various activities. *Fenkatas* [rabbit stew] were often organised and, with so little traffic, long tables were placed outside across the road and everyone was invited; it was like one big family.

'We were quite a big family; I was the eldest of five children. I remember Mum used to put my two brothers and two sisters to sleep in the afternoon, but I never slept. From when I was about six or seven years old, Christina would come for me every day in summer at around two in the afternoon and ask my Mum if she could take "Mimi" with her to swim. We went to a place right opposite where we lived. I was always fascinated by her; she was so beautiful. I can still picture her lovely face. She would wear a two-piece bathing costume and her blonde hair was shoulder length with hanging curls. She was stunning. I used to go to her place with her and she showed me pictures of herself and her friends. Once I did hear her say to my aunt who visited that she loved a man called Adrian very much and now she would never get married. At the time I didn't know who Adrian was. She was a very lonely person, even though she had quite a few friends coming over to stay during the summer months. I admired her a great deal, a vibrant and vivacious lady, and she liked me, always wanting me to be with her. Christina longed for company.'

From the late 1950s, Miriam's family didn't stay at Bugibba quite so often. Miriam began to return there as a teenager, but never saw Christina, whose door was always shut. It would be a long time before Miriam saw her again in Bugibba. By then Christina had changed a great deal.

Roy Nash, a journalist, wrote a fifteen-part series entitled *The Unknown Air Ace*, published in *The Star* in 1958. Christina also wrote a five-part series entitled *One Woman Goes to War*, published in the same newspaper soon afterwards. The well-written articles describe her childhood, early dancing career, and then Malta and fighter control. She also talks about her friend, Adrian Warburton. She doesn't hint at any relationship between them other than friendship. Christina confirmed she was still working as a secretary for the RAF in Malta where Adrian had become a legend. 'But for me he still lives. He could come walking in tomorrow and I don't think I should be a bit surprised.'[2] But he didn't come walking in tomorrow or the next day, or the day after that. Missing, believed killed, nothing more.

By then, Adrian had been missing for fourteen years. Some photographs of Christina are included with the articles, one of which looked recent. It showed an older and still very slim Christina, very smartly dressed with her blonde hair

---

2. *One Woman Goes to War*, by Christina Ratcliffe, published in *The Star*, April 1958.

curled to the shoulder. She is smiling and wearing her BEM, complete with bow, with great pride. She also kept a scrapbook and increasingly pursued her hobby of writing, even making a start on her own story which she never completed. Christina was approached to tell her tale, but declined all offers and tried to avoid attempts by authors to seek her out.

Christina was an attractive, outgoing, and charismatic lady who enjoyed the company of others. She would have come into contact with lots of people in Malta after the war as well as RAF personnel through her work at Luqa. But she never met anyone to match her Warby. She also had many Maltese friends, especially those from her Lascaris days. By the war's end Christina was thirty-one, and many of her 'girls' were a lot younger. Inevitably, they married and had families of their own, and her contacts with them gradually diminished. She also had a soft-top Austin Seven. At one stage she owned a Scottie dog, adorned with a tartan ribbon; Christina's mother was a Scot.

There were strong voices in Malta for closer links with Britain and others for independence. The idea of political union foundered in the 1950s and more strident voices were then heard for independence. Relations between the RAF and the Maltese people were generally good, strengthened by the formation in 1948 of the RAF Malta Force whose Maltese airmen were part of the RAF establishment. As Britain reduced commitments east of Suez, the strategic importance of Malta declined and, with Britain the largest employer on the island, the impact on the Maltese economy was immediate. The pressure for independence grew and Malta became independent in 1964. This was linked with a ten-year agreement on the stationing of British forces.

In 1965, Tony Spooner's autobiography was published. Tony ended the war highly decorated, his few months in Malta having coincided in part with one of Adrian's periods there. Included in the book is a photograph labelled 'Christina', but with no surname, the caption simply saying she served the RAF so well, she was decorated for her work. There are no direct references within the text to her by name although Spooner says Adrian lived in a flat in Valletta with a charming cabaret artiste; he makes no link with the girl in the photograph. Was Tony holding a veil over her identity yet somehow felt compelled to include a photograph knowing how important she was in Adrian's life? Perhaps he was aware she wanted a degree of anonymity over the true nature of her relationship with Adrian.

Christina used the National Bank of Malta, later the Bank of Valletta, on Kingsway, where she was often seen by George Darmanin, the chief cashier. George retired in 1968 and often spoke of Christina to his daughter Valerie and her husband Frederick Galea, who developed an increasing interest in Malta's air war. Over the years, Frederick endeavoured to find out more about Christina's story. How long she worked for the RAF is uncertain, but it was long enough for her to become entitled to a pension. She would have been fully involved in the comings and goings at Luqa where the inevitable accidents would have been poignant reminders of her former life. She may have been affected more than many by the fatal accidents involving Luqa-based recce aircraft. Two such accidents occurred early in 1969, one of which saw a PR Canberra crash into *Santa Maria Addolorata* cemetery in Paola.

In 1971, a Labour Government under Dom Mintoff was elected, and there were immediate and increased demands on Britain to offset the loss of income caused by the reduction in British forces. Britain opted to withdraw, which began in 1974. Christina had retired from the RAF by then and she would also have become entitled to an old-age pension that year. At the last moment, the Maltese Government, mindful of the effect of British departure on the economy, offered a basing agreement until 1979 in exchange for increased aid. The withdrawal went into reverse, but the situation remained unsatisfactory for Britain, with further pressure for more concessions as Malta forged closer links with Libya, now under the control of Colonel Gaddafi following a military coup.

In 1974, Christina expanded on her earlier writings and a fifteen-part series was published in a Maltese newspaper. She wrote with great fluency, her memory of her wartime days assisted no doubt by her notes and scrapbooks. Adrian had been missing for thirty years. Yet she again avoided any reference to the true nature of her feelings, or their relationship, simply referring to Adrian as a good friend. She was also an occasional contributor to the *Times of Malta*. She wrote a one-page article entitled *Food for Thought* in which she compared the varied menus available in hotels and restaurants in 1974 with the situation in 1942. She described how rationing affected everyone and also talked about the Victory Kitchens. Her article *Three Pence Charity*, published the following year, is an uplifting story based on her experiences running Café Christina.

There was a tragedy for the RAF and for Malta in 1975 with the crash of an RAF Vulcan following a catastrophic fire. Five of the crew of seven were killed, along with a Maltese lady in the town of Zabbar, on which the wreckage fell. Later, and only weeks before Britain withdrew from Malta, there was another tragedy when a XIII Squadron recce Canberra crashed on take-off from Luqa. One of the crew of three was killed. It was a sad precursor to Britain's formal withdrawal on 1 April 1979.

Christina, of course, stayed on and continued writing as she approached her seventieth birthday. In 1982, *The Merry Tenth of May* was published to coincide with the fortieth anniversary of 10 May 1942, the day many felt marked the turning point in the air battle of Malta. She expressed disbelief that it was almost forty years since that day. With time passing more quickly the older she grew, she wondered what its speed would be like when she was a centenarian. Later the same year, on 15 August, another of Christina's articles was published. It was entitled *A Day of*

Rejoicing and coincided with the fortieth anniversary of the arrival of the *Santa Maria* convoy. In this article, Christina offers the first and only glimpse into the true nature of her relationship with Adrian. She refers to her emotions on his unexpected return to the island in August 1942, her dreams of a wonderful reunion and how, in the middle of a battle, she had to fight a desire to go on gazing into Warby's blue eyes. This was Christina at her most heartfelt. Was the time now right to reveal something of her feelings, almost thirty-nine years after Adrian went missing? Did she feel she could now open her heart and tell her story?

The same year saw a number of Malta veterans return to the island, including Jack Vowles. Another was Tony Spooner, who had been working on a biography of Adrian for twenty-five years. He met Christina, whom he may have been in contact with prior to the publication of his earlier book. Then, she would have welcomed his discretion about her involvement with Adrian. In 1982 she would no doubt have enjoyed talking about their common experiences and mutual friends. They may have speculated about her Warby and the mystery surrounding his disappearance. Given the amount of personal information Tony included in his book, Christina must have cooperated fully. Did he mention to her the letter Adrian wrote to his father in which he expressed the hope he would be able to settle with his friend once and for all? Tony was sure Adrian meant Christina and if he mentioned this reference, then she is likely to have grasped it as confirmation her Warby was planning to get back to her. It would have meant a great deal.

With Tony writing a positive story about a man he admired, and a man Christina loved, this may have led Christina to reveal even more. Was she aware she had a heart condition? Did she suspect this might be her last opportunity to talk freely of her love for Warby? Or did she simply feel the time was now right to put the record straight, say a little more about a deeply moving and ultimately tragic love story in those desperate days in Malta?

In all of her own writings, why did Christina say so little about her involvement with Adrian and nothing about her feelings toward him until 1982? Were they still too personal, too private? Or had there been other factors at play? When did she learn Adrian was married? Did he tell her, or did she find out from someone else? Or did she first find out in 1946 when Betty Warburton came forward?

When Adrian introduced himself to Christina in the ERA Club in Floriana in January 1941, she would have been as unaware as everyone else he was married. Nor at that stage would she have cared a great deal. As far as she was concerned 'a Greek God' had walked into her life only days after the devastating loss of her young Frenchman Jacques. Would Adrian have revealed his secretive marriage to the attractive blonde he had just met? No way.

Adrian's closest confidant at the time was Tich and we can be certain he knew nothing of the marriage when in Malta. Tich was an honourable man and if he knew

Adrian had a wife in England he would have ensured an appropriate allowance went to her. He knew about Christina and, even as late as 1978, he was discreet about her relationship with Adrian. In writing about the understandable inaccuracies in 69 Squadron's ORB, Tich said the most reliable historical records of the period when he was in command were the logbooks of the aircrew, six of the original nine members of 431 Flight having survived the war. 'Presumably someone still has Warby's logbooks – perhaps a lady whose name begins with C – perhaps his family. I hope they will in due course present them to the RAF Museum.'[3] Tich had retired from the RAF soon after the war, returning to Australia, where he eventually became chairman of the Australian Broadcasting Corporation.

Adrian's relationship with Christina probably started soon after they met. Given the precarious nature of his job, it is unlikely he would have revealed his marriage then. For both of them, it was probably a case of *carpe diem*. Many had the same attitude and even though one or two became aware of Adrian's marriage over time, they were hardly likely to say anything. He was a popular hero. Live and let live and most would have wished them both well, to enjoy what they had for as long as they could. Another important factor was the attitude of the British military to any hint of scandal involving officers. There were two notable examples of RAF officers being posted within twenty-four hours when talk of social misconduct reached the ears of the military hierarchy. With Christina working for the RAF at Lascaris, little wonder Adrian guarded his secret well.

Who in Malta knew of the marriage? His close friend Paddy Moran was probably the first when Adrian said toward the end of their tour in 1941 that he married in haste. It is most unlikely Adrian shared this with anyone else at the time, perhaps not even Christina; he may have been unsure whether he would ever return to the island. Return he did and their relationship intensified immediately. He may have told her in early 1942 or when he came back later that August. By then he would have been in no doubt about her feelings toward him. During this third longer spell, lasting fifteen months, he confided in the Canadian Mac Brown, and Syd Collins, Luqa's adjutant. With three people aware of the marriage, Adrian probably explained things to Christina. By then she was in too deep, very much in love with Adrian, and any admission by him is unlikely to have made any difference to how she felt. She herself was no shrinking violet and was certainly not naïve about relationships. She was engaged once before and was very close to it a second time. Also, her theatrical career from a young age would have broadened her perspective and her mind. Christina would have forgiven Adrian many things and is unlikely to have held his rash decision in 1939 against him, given the circumstances.

---

3. *Warburton and PR from Malta*, by E.A. Whiteley, published in *The Royal Air Forces Quarterly*, Spring 1978, page 30.

Regardless of whether Adrian told Christina or not, it would be wrong to make a judgement from this distance about the attitudes and emotional responses of people living under the conditions existing on an island under siege when death, serious injury or separation was around every corner. There were different rules and expectations in those days. And love is a most powerful human emotion, as well as being the most enduring.

When Betty appeared in 1946, if Christina had not known about her, she would have been shocked at Adrian's deceit, perhaps even heartbroken, especially if she did not know the circumstances of the hasty marriage. If that was the case, surely she would have closed that chapter on an exciting, very romantic, but ultimately sad part of her life and moved on. She certainly had the strength of character and resilience to do so, and could easily have made another life for herself with someone else. That she did not move on suggests she was not taken by surprise and chose to harbour what had long been in her heart, and to protect it.

The publicity involving Betty would have focused on Malta's very own hero and some of this may have reflected on Christina. Many who knew her well also knew of her involvement with Adrian. Now was the opportunity for her to reveal all, to tell her story, but instead she chose to keep it to herself, refusing to be drawn, refusing to reveal her side of a story about one of the Second World War's most highly decorated airmen. When she did write, she described Adrian as a friend. It is easy to understand why.

Roman Catholic Malta has a clear attitude to marriage; it is for life and divorce was illegal until 2011. Adrian's name and reputation were well known. If Christina revealed she had a love affair with Adrian, a married man, this would have been terribly damaging to his reputation on the island which made him. She would wish to avoid this, knowing those friends of hers who knew the truth would respect her discretion. She chose to do nothing to tarnish the memory of the man she had loved and lost, and who was applauded, almost revered, in Malta. She kept her memories to herself.

There was another factor. Christina made her home in Malta and worked for many years for the RAF. She would have been conscious of her position and would, if at all possible, avoid what some might consider a scandal which could impact on her standing within her community. Only in her final article in 1982 did she offer a brief, almost tantalising glimpse of something more than friendship. By then she was entering her twilight years, and she probably knew it. Maybe she realised the time was right to hint at their story. And it is a beautiful story.

Adrian's disappearance hit Christina very hard. To begin with she would have covered her feelings, but she felt his loss very deeply and over time it had a devastating effect on her life. She never married, admitting she never found anyone who even came close to Adrian. Perhaps part of what she was doing was trying to hold on to the memory of their happy times, maybe hoping someone who had known her Warby, or had news of what happened to him, might get in touch.

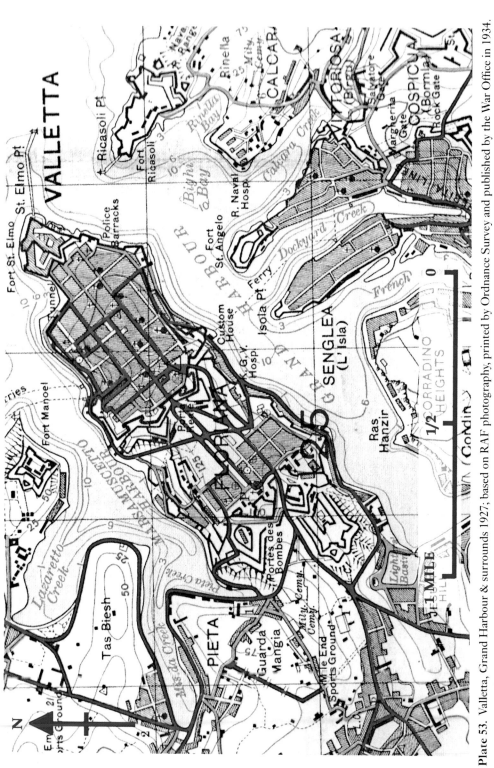

Plate 53. Valletta, Grand Harbour & surrounds 1927; based on RAF photography, printed by Ordnance Survey and published by the War Office in 1934.

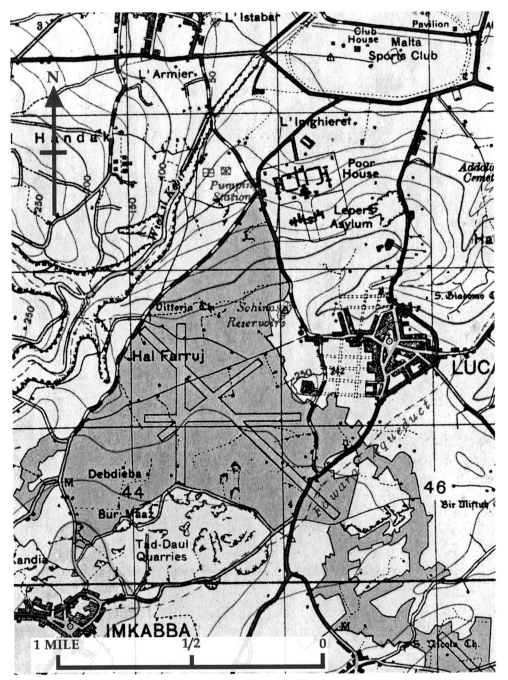

Plate 54. RAF Luqa & surrounds 1942; based on the 1934 original with roads, buildings, airfields and dispersal areas revised in 1942. It was published by the War Office and the Air Ministry in 1958. The area shaded yellow indicates the extent of taxiways and dispersal areas extended into the surrounding countryside. To the south-east, they link with RAF Safi; they also extend further to RAF Hal Far.

Plate 55. '*Prelude to Taranto*' by Ivan Berryman. Adrian is flying a Maryland over Italian battleships of the Regio Marina moored in Mar Grande Taranto before the Fleet Air Arm's successful night attack on 11 November 1940. From right to left, the battleships are *Vittorio Veneto, Littorio* and *Caio Dulio; Giulio Cesare* is in the background. In the attack, *Littorio* was hit by three torpedoes and suffered extensive damage, only being saved by being run aground; by the next morning, the ship's bow was totally submerged. *Caio Dulio* was hit by a single torpedo; repairs took seven months.

Plate 56. '*Tribute to Wg Cdr Adrian Warburton*' by Ivan Berryman. Adrian in a Maryland attacking a Cant Z.506B seaplane of Italy's Regia Aeronautica. He was credited with shooting down a number of these reconnaissance aircraft.

Plate 57. Memorial Service for Wing Commander Adrian Warburton at *Pfarrkirche St Agidius*, Gmund-am-Tergensee, on 14 May 2003.

Plate 58. '*Their names liveth for evermore.*' Durnbach Commonwealth War Graves Cemetery.

Plate 59. The coffin arrives at Durnbach. In a moving gesture, confirming the high regard in which Adrian Warburton was held by the Americans, the Honour Guard, both saluting, are US military personnel.

Plate 60. Entering the Commonwealth War Graves cemetery at Durnbach; Adrian's widow, Betty, is behind Ramstein's chaplain, Squadron Leader the Reverend Alan Coates.

Plate 61. Adrian's headstone.

Plate 62. Adrian is lowered into his final resting place. Betty is on the right holding the Union Flag which had draped the coffin.

Plate 63. Jack Vowles lays a flower on behalf of Christina. '*She'd been gone a while by then bless her.... No one else thought about doing such a thing. She never came back to Britain. She waited for him there.*' (Jack Vowles).

Plate 64. Jack Vowles, proudly wearing his George Cross Island Association tie, paid a separate visit to Adrian's grave. He 'now knew where his friend was and if he wished to pay his respects to him, he could go and do it.'

Plate 65. Open for opera lovers once more: The Royal Opera House, Valletta.

Plate 66. The Saluting Battery, Valletta, 2014, looking toward Fort St Angelo.

Plate 67. *Auberge de Castille*, 2014. Upper Barracca Gardens, with Lascaris beneath, and the Saluting Battery are to the right.

Plate 68. A quiet corner of Herbert Ganado Gardens, Floriana. The tunnel entrance in the background leads to the Lascaris War Rooms.

Plate 69. Manoel Theatre, Valletta, 2014. This was the venue for the *Whizz-Bangs'* performance of Cinderella, Christmas 1940.

Plate 70. The corner of Strait Street and Old Theatre Street, Valletta. A faded advertisement for the Old Vic is still visible. The Victoria was the *Whizz-Bangs'* first rehearsal venue.

Plate 71. The Phoenicia Hotel, Floriana, with the Malta Memorial in the foreground.

Plate 72. St Publius' Church, Floriana, 2014.

Plate 73. A distant view of Christina's Floriana apartment; directly beneath the Maltese flag.

Plate 74. Valletta's skyline from the roof of Christina's apartment in 2014; it has changed little since she described the view in the autumn of 1940. On the left is the memorial erected to the dead of the First World War, in the centre is the *Auberge de Castille*, while on the right on the horizon are the Upper Barracca Gardens and the Barracca Lift

Plate 75. Adrian in the National War Museum of Malta.

Plate 76. Adrian at the Malta Aviation Museum, Ta' Qali, 2014. From left to right his decorations are: Distinguished Service Order & Bar, Distinguished Flying Cross & two Bars, 1939-1945 Star, Atlantic Star, Africa Star & Clasp, Italy Star, Defence Medal, War Medal, Distinguished Flying Cross (USA).

Plate 77. Christina in the National War Museum of Malta.

Plate 78. Christina's final resting place, with *Santa Maria Addolorata* Church in the background.

Plate 79. '*Christina of George Cross Island*'.

Plate 80. The Malta Memorial, Floriana. It commemorates those Commonwealth airmen who were lost, flying from bases in the Mediterranean theatre in the Second World War, and who have no known grave. On the column's circular base are bronze panels showing the names of 2,301 airmen. There is also the following inscription:

PROPOSITI INSULA TENAX TENACES VIROS COMMEMORAT
An island resolute of purpose remembers resolute men.

By the 1960s, Christina was committed to living out the rest of her life alone, in the apartment she shared with her memories of her lost love. She was never ever likely to leave there through choice. As she grew older and became lonelier she sought company by visiting the places where she had experienced laughter and good company all those years ago: the small corner cafés which are such a feature of Malta's towns and villages. She became a regular in two in particular where she had her own seat, one in Floriana and the other in Bugibba. The Green Shutters was on St Thomas Street in Floriana, just across the road from what was the Queen's Store, owned by the Mallia family, who had looked after Christina and the Roches in their hour of need in 1940. The other was in Bugibba between Summer Street and Winter Street. Christina no doubt tried to relive happy memories of her earlier years. But, with alcohol becoming her only solace, she spent far too much time in the two cafés and became increasingly withdrawn from her friends. She carried her BEM in her pocket and often showed it to others interested in her story. She was not well-off, although she had two pensions and some shares she later sold. Christina later donated her medal, so richly deserved, as well as photographs, her scrapbook and notes, to the National War Museum in Valletta. By then, there was very little remaining of the decoration's red bow with the white edges on which her BEM was mounted. No doubt, she often held it in her hands over the years, one of few links with the life she had and the love she lost.

How much of Adrian's life when he was away from Malta did Christina know? There were certainly some letters between them. Because of her job, Christina would also have been aware of his movements, and their many mutual friends and acquaintances would have passed on information, but whether Adrian wrote to her from England is unknown. What is clear is that Adrian was sustained by Christina, and he, in his turn, gave her his love. There is no doubt Christina loved Adrian very deeply, but she would have known other women were attracted to him; she may have suspected he was flirtatious, but there is no indication of any serious involvement with anyone else. His remark in the letter to his father about being with his friend once more would probably have reassured Christina her love was reciprocated and Adrian had hopes and plans for a future with her. In the same letter Adrian refers to a 'Cairo BINT' with whom his father saw Adrian in Cairo. Adrian referred to the lady in question as relaxation. Tony Spooner quoted the letter in *Warburton's War*. Did Tony show Christina the letter?

Tony had heard suggestions about Adrian's social life away from Malta. Was the information accurate? It could have been hearsay based on crewroom gossip. Christina may have heard rumours too and may not have been surprised. Adrian had grown more comfortable with and enjoyed female company. She may have harboured doubts, wondered over the years whether he was faithful to her, whether she was just one of many love interests. Tony Spooner questioned whether Christina smoothed the raw edges of Adrian's character to, 'later pay the penalty by having him casually play the field as in Cairo and Tunisia.'[4] Did he reveal any of this to Christina when they met in 1982? If she had no inkling, then her cherished memories would have been shattered when *Warburton's War* hit the shelves in 1987. It would have been a popular read in Malta. If it was the first indication of Adrian's possible infidelity, it would have come as a crushing blow to Christina. How would she then have reacted having kept a candle burning for Warby for over forty-three years? She was now terribly lonely and was probably an alcoholic. Did she now have to cope with a broken heart?

Miriam Farrugia saw Christina in Bugibba in about 1981. It was a Saturday afternoon and Christina was coming out of her Bugibba home. She had changed a great deal, perhaps already showing signs of heart disease exacerbated by alcohol. Her condition had probably been deteriorating for some time. 'I went over to speak to her and as soon as I told her that I was Miriam, she gave me a big hug and called me little Miriam.' Later that evening Miriam saw her again; Christina needed help getting home and going to bed. That was the last time Miriam saw Christina.

The bank teller was concerned. He only knew her as 'Miss Christina' a customer, not someone to talk to except over the counter. She only ever came into the Bank of Valletta on Republic Street on the first of every month to cash her pension. She had done so for years, regular as clockwork, apart from the summer months which she must have spent elsewhere. Yet she had missed September, October and November which was very unusual and now, with only minutes to go before closing, she was again overdue. This was most unlike Miss Christina and he was increasingly worried on her behalf.

He could tell by looking at her she was not very well-off and the pension amounts were small. Yet she always raised a smile for him from beneath her wide-brimmed, straw hat. He hadn't seen her small Scottie dog with the tartan ribbon for a long time; it must have died.

Miss Christina was always polite and her Maltese was good, which was rare for an English lady. He thought her use of his language was a huge compliment to his small country, the country she made her home. He knew she lived in Floriana and had done since the war but wasn't sure exactly where. Other than that he knew little except what George Darmanin, the chief cashier when he first began work at the bank over twenty years earlier, had told him. Apparently, in the small bars and cafés, old men spoke about Miss Christina and a dashing RAF pilot. They said they were symbols of Maltese resistance and of suffering too. He always thought it slightly odd how an English lady and a pilot could be held in such adulation, especially as a

---

4. *Warburton's War*, by Tony Spooner, page 207.

lot of pilots served on the island in the Second World War. What was special about him? And what happened to him? No one seemed to know.

He knew he had to do something; he owed it to her. He mentioned it to his manager who suggested he telephone the British High Commission, which was responsible for paying one of Miss Christina's pensions. He phoned immediately and the Maltese clerk within the Pension Branch shared his concern. The clerk contacted the Divisional police at 7 pm on Friday, 2 December 1988, saying Miss Ratcliffe had not been seen since August and he was concerned there may have been foul play. The Maltese police acted immediately and an inspector, two sergeants and two constables went to Vilhena Terrace that evening. Everyone hoped all was well. But of course it wasn't.

After knocking on the door several times without success, the police pushed the door open and entered the apartment. They soon found a lady's body in bed, apparently dead. A Floriana doctor was immediately called and he said because of the advanced state of decomposition he couldn't exclude violence. At this stage the cause of death was unknown.

The following day a magisterial enquiry was held and the body was moved to the mortuary at St Luke's Hospital in nearby Pietà where Miss Christina was formally identified by two local policemen. They had sometimes seen her safely home down *Triq San Frangisk* when it was dark and she was struggling on her own. A post mortem was carried at 1 pm on the same day. The cause of death was established as natural causes, probably ischemic heart disease. A death certificate was then issued and Miss Christina was released for burial.

She had died alone and unnoticed in her bed in the cold apartment high above Grand Harbour with a chill wind blowing through some broken windows. She had been dead for two or three months. She was seventy-four years old and had lived alone in the same apartment for over forty years. There were lots of tins of cat food in the flat; she must have been in the habit of feeding the many strays that frequented the gardens below the large apartment block facing Valletta. There were always so many strays, living out their solitary existence, just like Miss Christina must have done in her final years. The cats would miss her kindness and understanding of their lives. Would anyone miss Christina?

She was buried at 10.00 am on Sunday, 4 December, in shared grave No 161 in Section A of the East Division of the Government Section of *Santa Maria Addolorata* Cemetery in Paola. She was the second occupant in the shared grave which was then sealed; the third space was not used. There were few to say farewell.

Mary Christina Ratcliffe, Chris, as Adrian called her, died sometime between September and October 1988, a year after *Warburton's War* was published. The apartment was sealed and the Maltese authorities worked with the British High Commission who contacted her next-of-kin Jack Downs, a Scottish uncle on her mother's side. He advertised through Manchester newspapers seeking relatives and was contacted by Martin Ratcliffe, a nephew of Christina's. Tony Spooner heard of Christina's passing and wrote a moving obituary published on 22 January 1990 in the *Sunday Times of Malta*. Later that year, and about two years after Christina died, Martin Ratcliffe, who had met Christina around the time of her mother's funeral, travelled to Malta to settle Christina's affairs. The apartment was still sealed having been left almost untouched, everything covered in a layer of fumigation dust. Christina's bed still bore the indentation of where she had lain for so long.

Martin later wrote to the *Times of Malta* to see if Christina could be reburied in a grave of her own. His enquiry was passed to Frederick Galea, by now well-known as a historian and author, and an active member of Malta's National War Museum. Frederick and his wife Valerie took up the request, contacting various agencies to have Christina reburied. This was not a straightforward task given the shortage of burial plots on the rocky island and the waiting list of over 4,000 whose families sought individual graves for their loved ones. Frederick persisted and his efforts were successful. It was through Valerie's father that Frederick had heard of Christina and he was happy to do what he could. And it was Valerie Galea who kept company with Christina when she was disinterred.

With money available from Christina's account, a marble headstone was obtained and Frederick arranged to have a photograph mounted with a suitable inscription beneath. The *Sunday Times of Malta* ran a short article announcing Christina's re-interment, which took place on 28 April 1993. The short service, taken by a Capuchin friar, was attended by her uncle, Jack Downs, her nephew Martin Ratcliffe and his family, and by Frederick and Valerie, a few well-wishers and a representative of the British High Commission.

Thanks largely to Frederick and Valerie Galea, Christina now rests in Grave No 4, Section MA-D East Division of *Santa Maria Addolorata* cemetery, only a few miles from where she lived and died. The cemetery is well named – Our Lady of Sorrows.

Miriam Farrugia, the young Maltese girl Christina befriended in the 1950s, summed up the situation movingly and well: 'I think it was a very sad story, loving someone and waiting for him to come back, and for him never to return. I think it is a very sad story to love somebody and you can't be with him. And then as she grew older she started drinking a lot. I think that people that drink, they are sad when they drink a lot. Christina Ratcliffe didn't deserve to die this way because she died all alone and with no one to take care of her.'

Chapter Eighteen

Finding Warby

The trail of Lightning P-38F5b, serial number 42-67325, had long gone cold. Then in 1992, Frank Dorber, a British aviation enthusiast, read *Warburton's War*. Frank had long been interested in what became of a number of missing airmen and over the years his interest became a passion. He was intrigued about what became of Adrian and, as no serious attempt had been made to solve the mystery for nearly fifty years, he was determined to investigate.

Frank established seven P-38s were lost on 12 April 1944, two of which were recce variants. He consulted US archives and various organisations and individuals in Europe and the US, including Lieutenant Colonel George Lawson at the 7th PRG Association, painstakingly matching records for those aircraft lost, against anti-aircraft and crash reports. He obtained details about six of the losses.

In 1999, Frank came across a report on a P-38 crash near the village of Egling-an-der-Paar, ten miles north-east of Landsberg-am-Lech in Bavaria. This was the seventh aircraft, Adrian's aircraft. It seemed he had not come down into a lake or the sea after all. Frank contacted Augsberg University and the Landsberg Heritage Centre, which resulted in eyewitnesses being traced, although there were contradictions about how the P-38 was brought down. With no air combat reports in the area, it was probably brought down by ground fire, but there were multiple claims from different flak units. One unit in the Ramersdorf suburb of Munich claimed hits on a P-38 at 11.26 am. Another, near Regensburg some sixty-five miles north of Munich, claimed to have shot down a P-38 at 14.45 pm. This location was near one of Carl Chapman's targets, but the timing is three hours too late.

The Luftwaffe credited the Egling P-38 to a third unit, *Heimatflakbatterie* 211/ VII, a home flak battery at Lochausen on the western outskirts of Munich. Part of Flak Regiment 130, parented by Flak Brigade 4, the unit was equipped with 75mm guns which had a maximum effective height of 30,000 feet. Home batteries were usually manned by teenagers, elderly men and Soviet prisoners turned conscripts. They may have fired at the lone P-38, but these local guns were notoriously inaccurate and only capable of firing box barrages rather than carefully tracking a single aircraft. Also, the battery was located well to the east of Egling, but the eyewitness evidence indicated the P-38 came from the west. So how was it brought down? The answer must have been west of Egling.

On the morning of 12 April, two Egling schoolboys heard gunfire to the west from the direction of the Luftwaffe base at Lechfeld. Not long afterwards – *Der*

Gabelschwanz Teufel – a fork-tailed devil – came from that direction, on fire, trailing smoke and rapidly losing height. The aircraft bored itself into a field just south of Egling. When the boys got to the scene about 400 yards south of the village, it was already cordoned off by the Luftwaffe and the *Feldgendarmerie* (Field Police). They saw medics remove some human remains. The impact area was relatively small, indicating the P-38 was largely intact when it hit the ground. The crater was about ten feet deep. The twin tail plane was on the surface. The surface wreckage was removed and the crater filled in. The Luftwaffe noted the pilot as *unbekannt* (unknown) and the aircraft was correctly recorded as American.

No record of human remains being removed ever came to light, nor was there any record of the crash in the Egling archives. Nevertheless, rumours persisted locally that the remains were buried in a grave at *St Johannes* Baptist Church in Kaufering, which already contained seven airmen from an RAF Halifax shot down the previous year. A grave report in 1946 recorded there were approximately seven airmen in the plot, all subsequently reburied at Durnbach.

With this almost certainly the site of Adrian's crash, Frank wrote to the American Embassy in London in March 2001. The US authorities then requested the assistance of the German War Graves Commission in recovering the pilot. A recovery operation began on 19 August, although the results were largely a forgone conclusion.

Evidence was soon found of a superficial excavation in 1944 and of a subsequent investigation conducted by a US graves registration unit not long after the war. Little excavation was carried out as the wreckage was too deep. The 2002 team found an engine and about fifteen per cent of the pilot's remains. Other material confirmed the wreck as a Lightning P-38F5b. Two propeller blades damaged by flak splinters were also found. The cockpit was burnt out and the canopy had either been torn off or jettisoned. Signal flares in the cockpit had caught fire, although it was impossible to tell whether this occurred before or after impact. Eyewitnesses unanimously agreed the aircraft was on fire before it hit the ground and the fire continued afterwards for some time. One witness reported hearing explosions from the wreckage, which could have been the exploding signal flares.

The human remains were passed to US authorities although DNA analysis was impossible due to their carbonised condition. On 21 November, the British Air Attaché in Berlin was contacted and advised there was sufficient evidence to conclude the human remains were those of Warburton. They were then sent to RAF Innsworth in Gloucester and, on 16 December, the UK MOD formally announced Adrian Warburton had been found.

Sue Raftree was the case officer at the Joint Compassionate and Casualty Centre at Innsworth, responsible for tracing next-of-kin and arranging burial. Frank Dorber was already in touch with Adrian's nearest blood relatives, three children of Adrian's older sister Alison who had married Dr Robert Gethen, a former RN surgeon. Soon afterwards 93-year-old Betty Westcott, formerly Warburton, came forward. She and Adrian never divorced, so she was the official next-of-kin.

Glyn Strong, Head of External Communications at RAF Innsworth, was appointed as the RAF media lead with a team to liaise with the press, and with Adrian's family and friends. The BBC was also involved making *The Missing Airman, Adrian Warburton*. It was transmitted in 2003, part of the *Timewatch* series. The RAF team included a young RAF photographer, Heidi Cox, now Burton, assigned to take the official photographs. Over the months leading up to the funeral, Heidi considered herself fortunate to meet some of the people who had known Adrian. One was Betty, whom Heidi thought was a wonderful lady. Another was 81-year-old Jack Vowles. He was relieved when Adrian was discovered as it meant speculation about the nature of his demise would end. His greatest difficulty before the funeral was his concern about meeting Betty as he knew she was bound to ask about Christina. Her opening words were: 'Were there any children?'

'No, none at all,' said Jack.

'That's alright then,' said Betty.

After that Jack and Betty became friends. As far as her marriage to Adrian was concerned, she said it was a wartime thing. Adrian was incredibly young and Betty was simply bowled over by him. In a way they were never really married, she said, as they never lived together. He was a nice man, Betty said, but too young.

The funeral service, with full military honours, took place at *Pfarrkirche St Agidius*, Gmund-am-Tergensee, on 14 May 2003. Betty was supported by her daughter, Sheila, and about 100 others attended including Jack Vowles and Frank Dorber, the man responsible more than any other for solving the mystery of the missing airman. Heidi found the experience quite emotional, having learnt so much about Adrian, and she reflected on the years he never experienced and the future he never had. The day had begun sunny and remained so throughout the service. At 11.45 am the cortege left the church, but when it arrived at Durnbach, the weather turned bitterly cold, the heavens opened and it began to hail. The RAF Regiment pall-bearers had hailstones on their heads and shoulders. Shortly after Adrian was lowered into the grave, the Last Post was sounded and a lone piper played *Lament*. As if on cue, the weather cleared and the sun came out. Jack insisted Warby arranged the weather to have the last laugh on everyone.

That was the final chapter of *Warburton's War*, a fitting if belated farewell to an RAF recce pilot who would never be forgotten in Malta, yet was not well known in Britain despite his exploits. Sadly, Tony Spooner went to his grave a year earlier without knowing how or where Adrian met his end.

Adrian's funeral impacted on many of the attendees. Jack was particularly moved when he realised there were a dozen or so Luftwaffe veterans present. In a beautiful gesture, he placed a single rose on Adrian's coffin from Christina, whom he described as having 'sagged' in her last years.

'She'd been gone a while by then bless her,' Jack said. 'No one else thought about doing such a thing. She never came back to Britain. She waited for him there. Warby was never a swaggerer. There was some jealousy about his awards, but he never cared about medals. He was driven by an absolute determination to get the job done. If he did a job badly – and that was extremely rare – he would refuel and go back straight away and do it again. He was one of those who everyone assumed would survive the war. Warby was the man who always came back.'

Reflecting on his death, Jack thought had Adrian survived and been demobbed, as a rebel with no qualifications, he may have found life difficult. Jack now knew where his friend was and if he wished to pay his respects to him, he could go and do it.

Over ten years after the funeral, Tim Callaway, a military historian and editor of *Aviation Classics,* was able to recall it clearly, such was the impact on him: 'I remember feeling terribly sad. What a bloody miserable lonely way to die. The weather was grey, sleet and rain adding to the general air of gloom. But there was also something else. I was looking across the grave, and watching Jack's face. He knew where his mate, a man he clearly loved, was lying at last. That this meant the world to him was written on his craggy features. I for one was suddenly glad that the work of all these people had allowed this to come about, not just for Jack, but for Adrian as well. Lying forgotten in a field is no place for anyone.

'Hearing about Warburton's character first hand, seeing Jack's reaction to the burial at last, I think I finally understand something about many of the people who fly combat aircraft quite clearly, something the poem captures far better than I ever could. I took away a lot from that burial, but most of all I have gained something that has affected the way I write history ever since. After the ceremony, as the sun lit the snow-capped mountains behind the town, there was a sense of homecoming, of peace. This may be just the way it affected me, but I think others felt it as well. There is a strange satisfaction in bringing the missing home, even when you play a very small part in it.'

The poem Tim referred to is *An Irish Airman Foresees His Death* by W.B. Yeats.

> 'Nor law, nor duty bade me fight,
> Nor public men, nor cheering crowds,
> A lonely impulse of delight
> Drove to this tumult in the skies.'

Two years after Adrian's funeral, on 12 April 2004, sixty years to the day after Adrian took off on his last flight, another memorial service took place, this time in England. It was at the burial ground at Berinsfield, near Oxford, on part of what was RAF Mount Farm. The old airfield is slowly returning to farmland, but the runways and dispersals are visible, and there is still much atmosphere there, even now. The service involved representatives of the RAF, the USAF, local dignitaries, as well as friends and colleagues of Adrian, and many who came to admire him after his death. Betty was there, as were Paddy Moren's two brothers, Paddy himself having died a few years earlier. Jack was there too, as was Tony Spooner's widow. The service and dedication came about through the efforts of the Ridgeway Military and Aviation Group, a small band of volunteers based at the USAF facility at RAF Welford. They had been conducting research about Adrian for some years and were successful in bringing parts of the wreckage of his aircraft to their museum. There has been a service at Berinsfield each year on the anniversary of Adrian's last flight. The group, under its president Alan Bovingdon Cox, also donated items of the wreckage of Adrian's aircraft to the Malta Aviation Museum at Ta' Qali in Malta.

In 2004, Frederick Galea published *Carve Malta on my heart and other wartime stories*. It contains Christina's story and two others: *The Unknown Airman* by Roy Nash and *A Woman of Malta* by Tamara Marks, published in Egypt in November 1943. In 2006 Frederick re-published Christina and Tamara's stories in *Women of Malta*.

On 15 April 2008, sixty-six years after the award of the George Cross to Malta, Jack was back in exactly the same place in Valletta to film the re-enactment. He was eighty-seven years old by then and a widower. Although he was not meant to have been at the original ceremony, he had used a notebook to mark everyone's position. His original footage was also used by the Malta Tourism Authority to ensure the 2008 ceremony was as close as possible to the original.

The speculation about what happened to Adrian was now over. But had the mystery been solved? What exactly was he doing on that fateful day? Was his simply an 'operational shuttle run mission to Italy', or was there more to it? Information was out there, but time and fading memories contributed to confusion. Years afterwards, Carl Chapman said his personal target on 12 April was the Regensburg ball-bearing plant. He suggested Adrian was going to the other ball-bearing plant at Schweinfurt. This was repeated in many subsequent accounts. With most recce missions involving multiple targets, Carl could be forgiven for getting one small detail wrong. One of his targets was indeed Regensburg, but it was not the ball-bearing plant but the Luftwaffe airfield at Regensburg-Obertrauling.

The late Roy Conyers Nesbit, highly regarded as an RAF historian and writer, discovered from official US records that Carl was allocated five targets on 12 April; they were all airfields. All were associated with the production and testing of the Me262 jet fighter, soon to make a dramatic appearance over Europe. Four of Carl's targets were east of Munich, one of which was Regensburg-Obertrauling. With Regensburg's ball-bearing plant being a target of some prominence, perhaps that is why the name of the town stuck in Carl's mind. This may have led him to erroneously suggest Adrian was tasked against the other well-known ball-bearing factory at Schweinfurt. But with the latter being the target of the day for a B-17 bombing mission on 12 April, it is unlikely Adrian would have been tasked against it, and certainly not a few hours before it was scheduled to be hit.

At the time, the Allies were most concerned about the development of the Me262, a revolutionary German jet fighter, and recce aircraft were regularly tasked against the factories and test airfields involved to determine when the new aircraft might become operational. Testing was well advanced and the first Me262s were operational within days of Carl and Adrian's mission. If these facilities were an intelligence priority for Carl, could Adrian's targets have been similar, perhaps west of Munich and close to where he crashed? Although there is nothing within American records to indicate Adrian's targets, a valuable clue comes from Constance Babington Smith. She was a highly acclaimed WAAF photo interpreter and headed the aircraft section of the Central Interpretation Unit based at Medmenham in Buckinghamshire. She said Adrian's targets on 12 April were German airfields. She also said Adrian intended to land at San Severo.[1]

Lechfeld had long been used to test the Me262 and General Adolf Galland flew the fourth prototype from there as early as April 1942. The first operational Me262 squadron was formed at Lechfeld within a week of Adrian's flight and there would have been evidence of the Me262 on the ground. Allied intelligence was aware of activity around Landsberg, centred on the two major airfields of Kaufering and Lechfeld. Nearby, five other facilities were being built using slave labour from eleven local concentration camps. The new structures were thought to be command posts, aircraft production and assembly plants, and hangars for the new generation of aircraft. Lechfeld airfield itself was also scheduled to be bombed on 13 April, so Adrian's sortie could easily have been the final pre-strike reconnaissance mission.

Another Luftwaffe airfield was Fürstenfeldbruck on the outskirts of Munich. It was near Lochausen, the location of *Heimatflakbatterie* 211/VI which was credited with having shot down Adrian's P-38. If Adrian was fired at by this battery, and the other in the southern suburbs of Munich, and was then seen to make off to the west where he later crashed, this may have supported both batteries' claims.

All of this suggests Adrian was tasked with obtaining imagery of targets near Munich and to the west, including Lechfeld, with Chapman concentrating on similar targets to the east. Schweinfurt was a red herring, but an understandable one.

The evidence of what happened seems clear. Shortly before 11.45 am on 12 April, Adrian overflew Lechfeld and its flak defences immediately opened fire. The airfield was equipped with the well-named *Jaboschrek* 'fighter-blaster'. These quadruple

---

1. *Evidence in Camera*, by Constance Babington Smith, page 218.

guns fired explosive shells, were fully automatic and fitted with sophisticated sighting, and they could traverse quickly through 360 degrees with a very fast rate of fire. They were particularly effective against aircraft below 7,000 feet. The battery commander was so convinced his unit hit the lone P-38, he despatched troops in the direction of the flight path of the obviously damaged aircraft. This explains why Luftwaffe personnel were on the scene so quickly.

The only unanswered question is why was Adrian so low, below 7,000 feet, to be hit by a *Jaboschrek*? Was he 'doing a Warby', intending to come back with the goods regardless of risk, or had he been higher when his keen eye spotted something to arouse his interest? The Me262 left telltale evidence of its passing either burnt into the grass or long black scorch marks on concrete runways. These would have been visible from a considerable height. If Adrian saw this evidence, did he come down to have a look, to get better photographs, flying straight into the path of the 'fighter-blaster'?

Adrian was well-known for keeping his cards close to his chest and, despite some occasional 'wildness' in his early flying days, whatever he got up to always seemed to be based on a carefully considered plan. There will never be any *certainty* about his intentions on 12 April after he had photographed his targets, but there are pointers to what he may have been up to.

Adrian would never fit into the RAF establishment in England; he would be stifled with little chance of operational flying. Even an appointment as a 'liaison officer' would do little to satisfy him. He was *the* Mediterranean specialist, and that's where he wanted to be. But it is simply not credible that Adrian, despite the consummate planner he was, would have mapped out his future in his hospital bed in Maison Carée. He may, however, have decided to follow Elliot Roosevelt as a first move. Adrian was also very much an opportunist. Gordon Hughes replaced Adrian in command of 336 Wing on 27 December 1943. Wartime command appointments tended to be of short duration, so a replacement for Hughes between April and June would have been entirely normal. The brief time Adrian spent at San Severo before moving to England with Elliot may have been enough for him to learn that Hughes was earmarked to return to Britain before the long-expected invasion of France. The choice of Hughes' successor may also have been in the gift of Hugh Lloyd, very much a key figure in the Mediterranean theatre. But even Lloyd might not have the 'pull' to get Adrian back from England. But if Adrian just happened to be available, medically fit, and actually at San Severo, would he not be perfectly placed to retake command of 336 Wing on Hughes's departure? Why would Hugh Lloyd, Adrian's long-term mentor, consider anyone else?

Adrian's appointment to Mount Farm on 1 April could easily have been the successful outcome, not of a single plan, but of a series of opportunities Adrian grasped. By then he was officially fit. With frequent visits to RAF Benson, the home of RAF reconnaissance, Adrian would have picked up a lot of information about what was going on. Did he find out his old squadron, 69 Squadron, would soon arrive at RAF Northolt where it was to form part of 34 Wing, a photo-reconnaissance wing formed the previous year? The wing moved to Northolt on 7 April, five days before Adrian's final flight. Finally, and most importantly, did Adrian learn the name of 34 Wing's next commanding officer? It was Gordon Hughes. Now was the time for Adrian to act. The 12 April flight was therefore far from being a spur of the moment affair; it was the final step in something very typically 'Warby'. But why did Adrian want a P-38 when Mount Farm had a number of PR Spitfires with which Adrian was more familiar? Both types had similar range.

Adrian probably did not reveal his full intent as he had no intention of rejoining Carl knowing he wouldn't hang about near heavily-defended Munich. In later years, Elliot Roosevelt always said Adrian's planned destination was San Severo. Others put this down to fading memory, but George Lawson also confirmed Adrian's destination. If the plan had worked, Adrian would have been less than thirty minutes flying time from 'his friend' in Malta.

At Mount Farm, on the morning in question, Staff Sergeant Wallace 'Moe' Arnold, an American camera technician, and a colleague, was told to install film magazines in two P-38s and check out the pilots. 'Check-out' is the term used by American ground crew and is the same as 'see-off' used by the RAF. It involves strapping in the pilot and assisting with engine start. Moe remembered the RAF wing commander wearing American coveralls over his uniform. When Moe came down off the port wing after having strapped Adrian into the cockpit, he remarked to his colleague that the wing commander said he did not intend to come back to Mount Farm after the mission.[2]

The suggestion Adrian had a plan fits the known facts and would have been entirely in character. Perhaps Adrian still planned a future with a girl from Cheshire whom he left behind on an island in the sun – a girl he called Chris. But he did not count on a *Jaboschrek*.

No one will ever know the truth of what happened that day, or why, but there can be no doubt Adrian had a plan. It may have been a very simple one, conceived in outline in a hospital bed in Maison Carée. It is only sad Christina never knew her Warby was trying to get back to her with hopes of a life together on the island carved on both of their hearts.

Whatever his personal idiosyncrasies may have been, Adrian Warburton was a true hero and should be remembered – and not just in Malta. Within a service renowned for remarkable people, his achievements were as remarkable as those of the RAF's most illustrious pilots such as Douglas Bader and Guy Gibson. All three

---

2. From information contained within a letter about Staff Sgt Arnold provided by Lt Col John Blyth USAF Ret'd.

were pupils at the same preparatory school in Oxford. Adrian's reputation as a recce pilot was well-known within the closeted and highly secret world of photographic interpretation. Constance Babington Smith said: 'He had already been jokingly called "King of the Mediterranean", but the legend of his infallibility that was growing was serious. He always did get his photographs. He always did fly straight through enemy defences. He always did get back. Admittedly, the circumstances at Malta were unique, and Warburton's personal achievements, both legendary and factual, put him in an unorthodox class by himself. Nevertheless, he can be said to stand for the pilots of British photographic reconnaissance in more ways than one.

'The photographic pilot has to have all the accuracy of the bomber pilot, as well as the alertness and tactical skill of the fighter pilot. In addition, he must be an individualist who can make quick responsible decisions entirely on his own. And he must have the persistent purpose and the endurance not only to reach his target, but to bring back the photographs to his base. In all these things Warburton excelled.... . The names of Bader and Gibson are rightly famous, but the name of Adrian Warburton has hardly been heard outside the circle of those who actually knew him, and there is no single mention of him in the official RAF history of the Second World War.'[3]

At a time when operational flying tours for RAF bomber crews were measured in multiples of twenty-five, and RAF fighter pilots were rested usually after six months, Adrian's achievement of more than 390 missions is staggering. That so many were flown from Malta, under siege, and in the most hazardous of circumstances, is remarkable. He also flew many unrecorded operational sorties in Spitfires on fighter sweeps, as a gunner in Wellingtons, and in various crew positions on other types. Even when he was supposedly enjoying a rest, he found his way back into the cockpit and into action. He also shot down nine enemy aircraft, a highly unusual achievement for a reconnaissance pilot. From being an obscure, below average pilot who achieved virtually nothing in the first year of the war, Adrian developed in the opinion of many into the most daring and valuable pilot of the entire RAF. Having left Malta, he moved out of the spotlight, but personally, I am convinced he would have recaptured it. If he had done so, perhaps he would have been afforded the decoration he richly deserved, the VC. Even without it, Adrian Warburton remains the most highly decorated photo-reconnaissance pilot ever to serve in the RAF. He should be well remembered.

In 1958, at the beginning of Tony Spooner's research about Adrian, he offered his personal views in a letter to Hugh Lloyd. Tony said he did not support the popular theories that Adrian lacked imagination and was foolishly brave, or was determined to cover himself in glory even at the cost of his own life. In Tony's

---

3. *Evidence in Camera*, by Constance Babington Smith, pages 133–4.

view, Adrian simply set his own operational standards and lived up to them. Those standards were so high the standard way of doing things had little value. Adrian's acute mathematical mind also gave him an ability to calculate risks incredibly well. He proved beyond doubt he could live up to the ideal standards he envisaged and that individualism had a place in warfare.[4]

Bill Carr, the young Canadian who joined Adrian's 683 Squadron in 1943, and on whom Adrian made a lasting impression, went on to become a Lieutenant General in the Royal Canadian Air Force (RCAF). He has been described as the father of the modern CAF. He said Adrian's, 'charisma was unlike any I ever experienced. While none of us ever hoped to achieve his level of competence as a pilot or his prowess against the enemy, we sincerely hoped for his approval. And this he was wont to give generously when it was justified. How hard we young pilots tried to achieve this may be reflected in the unique achievements of 683 during his tenure as CO. The ground crew too worked like slaves; indeed I believe they loved the man.

'Warby was a unique officer in a great many ways. Not only was he a very brave person, braver than any I have ever met, but also he was a warm and sensitive human being who tried to hide these facets in his make-up.

'He had the mark of a great leader. He inspired his colleagues and his subordinates to achieve goals most would not have thought themselves capable of achieving. His disappearance brought disbelief and sadness, and generated such a sense of loss and regret in wartime as to be remembered. We lost a great leader; the RAF and the allies: one of the very best.'

Perhaps, like many others in wartime, Adrian was like a flame that burns brightly before being snuffed out. How many more were like that? Countless others never made the headlines. How many tales are left untold, only known by a few members of their families and a small number of their friends? How many, if they had survived, would have been able to adjust to peace after such intensity so early in their lives? *Carpe diem;* seize the day, take no thought of the morrow may well have been their motto. For many thousands, there was no morrow. For others who were touched by them, the morrow proved to be as long and lingering as it was for a girl he called Chris.

---

4. From a letter to AM Sir Hugh Lloyd dated 10 April 1958, held by the RAF Museum.

Chapter Nineteen

Finding Christina

I t was dark when we touched down at Luqa. There was little I recognised. The terminal bore no resemblance to the one I looked at many times from XIII Squadron's HQ. The drive to Valletta didn't ring any bells either, so much had changed, so much redevelopment and new roads since Malta joined the EU.

I thought about the stories of the air battle of Malta and the people who endured it. I had met many characters through their own words and those of others – Adrian, Christina, Tamara, Hugh Lloyd, Michael Longyear and many more. I had also become good friends with a survivor of those days, one on whom Adrian made an impression that lasted a lifetime. Jack Vowles was no longer 'young Jack' but, at ninety-three, his stories often retold remain vibrant, although as he often reminded me, days and dates meant little to him back then, although events stayed with him. He spoke with much warmth about Malta and the Maltese. He journeyed back often, always with his cameras, sometimes for ceremonies, sometimes just to say hello to friends he left behind and relax amongst memories. Jack's travelling days are over now; it was up to me to say '*sahha*' on his behalf. Nearly all the other main players in my tale are long gone.

I hoped to uncover more on a visit. There were also two ghosts I felt could only be found there. Would I be able to match old images to present-day locations? Would wartime buildings be recognisable? What about the apartments Christina and Adrian shared? And, of course, having visited Adrian's grave at Durnbach, I simply must find Christina's final resting place on the island carved on her heart. Perhaps I could also pass on a message. What started for me as accidental interest following a chance phone call was now a quest I was determined to see through.

I didn't recognise where we were until we approached *Porte des Bombes*, the scene of Malta's very first civilian death on Tuesday, 11 June 1940. The dual carriageway of the former *Strada Sant' Anna* was also familiar, as was the circular bus terminus in front of Valletta's curtain walls. Sadly, the famous old buses are gone. We then entered the grounds of the Phoenicia Hotel.

Gazing across from her apartment roof in 1940, Christina described the Phoenicia as unfinished. Today it is a magnificent hotel built by the Stricklands, well known on the island and within its politics. Mabel Strickland was the editor of the *Times of Malta* which, despite its offices being in heavily-bombed Valletta, didn't miss a single edition throughout the Second World War. Afterwards, the newspaper offered occasional glimpses into Christina's world. The hotel is charming and elegant, and as welcoming as the island itself. And so are the Maltese who work there. It was touching to recognise the fondness they have for the British, not just as guests, but as old friends. It takes a long time to grow an old friend. Many spoke with genuine affection about the RAF when it was based on the island thirty-five years previously. I wondered if Christina ever visited. Did she sit on the balcony overlooking the gardens; perhaps smiling at a particular memory as she sipped a Horse's Neck, watching the sunset over Marsamxett Harbour and dreaming of a long-overdue Warby returning with a fantastic tale to tell? As I discovered later, Christina is certainly in the Phoenicia now.

Great Siege Road leads from Floriana down to Marsamxett Harbour; from there, a harbour side road heads to Fort St Elmo. It is an ideal route from which to take in the scale of the fortress walls with bastion following bastion. Within the harbour is Manoel Island, one of Michael Longyear's goals when learning to swim. Fort Manoel is probably little different from when it was built in the eighteenth century, although there is nothing to indicate its role as a haven for submariners as they lay submerged alongside at the height of the siege.

The majesty of Valletta can only be grasped from within Grand Harbour. For a first-time visitor arriving by sea, the impression must have been awe inspiring. So it was for Christina and her friend, Sheila, when they arrived on the *Knight of Malta* that spring evening in 1937. How different it must have looked to the sailors who fought their way to a bombed and battered island a few years later.

Dockyard Creek and Parlatorio Wharf are where a badly injured *Illustrious*, such a symbol of survival, spent a few crucial days being made ready for a rush to safety. Directly opposite is the old Customs House on Barrier Wharf, Christina's last stepping stone on her journey to the island. The ground rises steeply behind the wharf with Valetta on the right and the Phoenicia on the horizon. To the left are apartment blocks commanding magnificent views. Were these Floriana's Vincenti Buildings from which Christina painted a fascinating panorama with her words? She looked in shock from there at what was left of the Three Cities – Senglea, Vittoriosa and Cospicua – after devastating bombing by the Luftwaffe trying to seek out *Illustrious*. Directly below her apartment Christina spotted the beached wreck of the appropriately named HMS *Gallant*, minus its bow, as it lay below Crucifix Hill. It was the *Gallant* which delivered Christina and the *Rodney Hudson Girls* to safety in France, away from the Spanish Civil War.

Christina crossed the harbour often. There were sad times, as on 17 January 1941, when she and Tamara caught the ferry to a scene of unutterable destruction in Senglea. But there were lots of good times too, and Christina would have been captivated by the magic of the capital. In the late afternoon Valletta is an unforgettable site, its limestone buildings almost luminous as the light fades, with the many churches cresting high above the houses and immense walls as the city begins to fall quiet. After the war there would have been much to remind Christina of good times and sad times. Wherever she went she was never far away from the resting places of many she and Warby knew – friends with whom they laughed and danced, now resting amongst other friends in well-kept places.

One of the more poignant is tucked away in a corner, not far from Rinella. It is Capuccini Commonwealth War Graves Cemetery, which takes its name from the nearby Capuchin monastery. It is planted with cypresses and pines, and the paths around the hundreds of graves are lined with low, silvery-green hedgerows. Four of Jack's friends share the same resting place, killed together near the dining hall on the day Jack used up two of his lives. What little was left of Ginge is there too. Nearby is Peter Keeble, who flew *Faith, Hope* and *Charity*, but who died in a Hurricane, the first of many. He is close to John Dowland, who almost made it back to Luqa. Next to John is 'Willie' Williams, the 431 Flight pilot Jack met at Bircham Newton and who welcomed Jack to Luqa in 1941. The inscription on Willie's tomb applies to many:

> '…that it is well with you,
> Among the chosen few,
> Among the brave,
> the very true.'[1]

All the characters in my story passed through *Porta Reale*, City Gate, beyond the great ditch between Valletta's limestone walls. To the right is the entrance to the railway tunnel in which hundreds of Maltese, as well as Christina and the Roches, found protection. Time, neglect and bombing took their toll on Valletta, yet the cobbled streets are still a haunting reminder of the Knights of St John. On Republic Street, formerly Kingsway and the *Strada Reale*, is the Royal Opera House. Famous for decades until the evening of 7 April 1942, for over seventy years since, it has served as a memorial to fascist aggression. There is much to remind the islanders of their Greater Siege, so a few years ago it was judged time to give the Maltese people back their Opera House. It is now complete, though not rebuilt. The auditorium has rows of chairs and there is a covered stage. The entrance is beneath the original imposing steps, but the walls and pillars have only been partially restored, leaving most of the building open to the elements. It is a telling reminder of darker days.

The Wembley Store, a shop Christina favoured, is on the junction of Republic Street with South Street. The outer façade has changed little since the 1930s, apart from the addition of cash machines. The cavernous interior is a delight to explore,

---

1. From *In Memoriam A.H.*, by Maurice Baring.

a reminder of the old general stores and bazaars. The Monico bar was on South Street but is long gone, as is Cilia's, its former premises now housing a gent's outfitters. It was on South Street on the evening of 8 September 1943, the day of Italy's surrender, that a brooding Christina walked. Despite the bells and the bunting, she felt miserable and alone until she saw Adrian running toward her with arms outstretched. Oblivious to the stares of passers-by, he got down on his knees to plead forgiveness. Christina wept buckets. Midst the many tourists and passers-by in 2014, I found it difficult to picture the scene.

On the left on Republic Street is the National Museum of Archaeology, formerly the *Auberge de Provence*. The 'Snake Pit' was now full of exhibits. As the 'officers-only' Union Club, it was the scene of parties and many a fond farewell. Now there is no sense of what it was. Did Adrian and Christina spend their last evening together here in October 1943 or did they, like Tamara, prefer the more relaxed atmosphere of Captain Caruana's Bar? It too is long gone. Republic Square was Queen's Square and the Grand Master's Palace is now the seat of the Maltese Government. On its wall are three plaques: The first contains Malta's George Cross citation, the second a message from President Roosevelt on 7 December 1943. The third, in Maltese, commemorates independence on 21 September 1964.

A gradually steepening hill drops down toward Fort St Elmo. The former *Strada San Nicola* crosses at right angles, but there is no door labelled '105', nothing to show the location of the Morning Star in another life. The Morning Star closed to Jolly Jack in the 1950s and was replaced by modern apartments. I could gain no sense of what this place must have been like seventy years earlier. Maybe something of the atmosphere still existed at night.

I knew the old Drill Hall of Lower Fort St Elmo housed Malta's National War Museum which was full of links with my story. Once there, maybe I would feel a connection. The museum focuses on the contribution of the Maltese in both World Wars and especially under the appalling conditions of 1942. Close to the entrance there are displays devoted to Adrian and Christina. They include a piece of wreckage from the P-38 Lightning in which Adrian was found and items donated by Christina, including her BEM, so well earned in 1943. It is mounted in a frame along with a photograph of Christina at Lascaris. To my eye, the ribbon looked slightly odd; this could have been due to age. It was the civilian version without the light-coloured stripe in the centre of the ribbon, but without a bow. Like exhibits in any museum, it felt cold; it was impossible to get a feel for the lady in the photograph. I needed to find something else. I wasn't sure exactly what.

The museum describes Malta's war well. There is the last remaining Gladiator of the famous three. There is the jeep named *Husky* used by Eisenhower, no doubt identical to the one Elliot Roosevelt gave to Adrian. There is the wreckage of a Spitfire and an Me109 recovered from the seabed, and a surviving black-painted boat the Italian Navy used in their ill-fated assault on Grand Harbour. In pride of place is the replica George Cross famously awarded to the Maltese people in 1942 and still proudly emblazoned on the Maltese flag. The museum is an easy place to lose track of time. The photographs of bomb damage have great impact and give an indication of the extent of rebuilding needed after the war. Toward the exit I paused to look at a display dedicated to many Maltese who gave their lives fighting valiantly on the island and elsewhere. Many were in the Royal Malta Artillery, so resolute in defence; many more served and died in the dockyards, and on board ships sailing under the White Ensign or the 'Red Duster'. I left for the Lascaris War Rooms hoping to find a connection with my characters on the way.

I headed for the infamous Gut. It was daylight and deserted. Even by night I suspect it would be the same. No faded charm here; just faded. Boarded up windows and long-locked doors. There were one or two signs of its past, but few passers-by by would look closely. For most of its length there was no activity, commercial or otherwise, a dusty run-down forgotten street. When I got up the hill toward Old Theatre Street, the 'officers and civilians only' part, it was different, with smart cafés, up-market restaurants and shops. I hoped to find my connection a little further on, where Strait Street widened. When I got there I stopped, facing Valletta's Vincenti Buildings, also owned by Christina's Floriana landlord. I was looking directly at the apartment block Christina moved into in 1942, and where a number of photographs of her and Adrian were taken on the roof. It was mostly office accommodation, but on a whim, I entered and climbed the many steps until I faced the top-floor apartment Christina occupied; it was still a private residence. I went through a nearby open door onto the roof. It was here that she and many of the Lascaris girls practiced dancing against an amazing skyline. And it was here in the late autumn of 1942 that the only photograph of Adrian and Christina together was taken.

On leaving, I followed the footsteps Christina would have taken on her way to Lascaris. I turned right out of her front door then left onto Melita Street. Having crossed Republic Street I continued across Merchants Street. Nearby is the last reminder of Victory Kitchens, a small sign beneath a specially placed street light on the left just beyond Clarks Shoes. Christina was photographed here in October 1942 having collected her midday meal. I then passed directly behind the block which contained the *Auberge de Castille,* crossing St Paul Street before turning right into St Ursula Street. Ahead of me was Upper Barracca Gardens, but a few yards short, I turned left into Battery Street, making for what would have been the sandbagged and guarded entrance to No 8 Sector Operations Centre. The very high walls are still there, but without the eight-foot tall sandbags; but I could imagine the efficient Maltese soldiers standing guard. Here, Christina would have shown her pass before hurrying down the many steps as she had done on 12 August 1942. On that day she completed the route in record time anxious to find out what was going on. Seventy-two years later, I hurried too, and, as I stepped into the tunnel, I entered her world.

After the war, Lascaris was used as a NATO HQ until NATO withdrew at the request of the newly-elected Dom Mintoff in 1971. The UK then continued to lease facilities for a further eight years. With the departure of British forces, Lascaris, disused for some time, was simply locked up. There were attempts to open it as a tourist attraction, but none were long-lasting. Christina is unlikely ever to have returned there. In 2009, the property was passed to Heritage Malta. When access was gained to the combined operations room, a large map of the Mediterranean showing Soviet buoys and moorings of the 1970s covered an entire wall. The map had not weathered well and fell apart when touched, revealing an astonishing oil painting dating back to 1943. The painting's condition is superb, and it shows the map used for the Allied invasion of Sicily. Overlooking the room are offices used by Eisenhower and his three single-service commanders, Cunningham, Alexander and Tedder. Each had a single telephone, the main method of communication outside of coded signals and despatch riders. It is difficult to imagine how they kept control of their forces, including 160,000 troops in North Africa, from the tiny offices.

The war rooms were finally opened to the public in 2010, and my Maltese guide told the story of Lascaris and the air battle very well. He brought the place alive. The fighter control room is fascinating and I could visualise Hugh Lloyd's girls, British and Maltese alike, surrounding the plotting table. Looking down on them from the shelf were the chaps-in-the-gods, Bill Farnes, sitting centre stage, with Guy Westray, Ops B, in the next chair. Next to him was the assistant controller, a totally professional Christina Ratcliffe. Where would Woodie have been, wearing his monocle? What about Lloyd? Maybe he was lurking unobtrusively, holding his cigarette holder, keeping his eye on things, or even orchestrating events from time to time. Yes, this was better; there was a real feel about this place despite the passage of time, an atmosphere kept alive by enthusiastic staff. Within minutes I could imagine the atmosphere, if not the noise, the oppressively hot working conditions and the smell, for those who served long hours here between 1940 and 1943.

I paused to look at the many photographs adorning the walls. In a corner is one of Christina. It shows her and a young Maltese girl called Lisa, the daughter of a Valletta neighbour, carrying a large container of their daily supply of water, collected from a nearby street tap. The caption simply says 'Street in Valletta, corner with Law Courts.' There is nothing to identify the blonde lady with the apron over her dress as Christina, but I had seen the photograph before. She would have been thrilled to be back at Lascaris.

On leaving the war rooms, I turned left, exiting the tunnel into the ditch with Valletta's inner and outer walls high above. Hugh Lloyd's office, with its corrugated iron roof, was located here. There is a long-disused single-storey stone building with a corrugated iron roof beneath one arch of the viaduct, but there was nothing to indicate whether it had served as Lloyd's office. Another left turn took me into a short tunnel which exits beneath Upper Barracca Gardens into Herbert Ganado Gardens, overlooking Grand Harbour. Before Christina was forced to move from Floriana, she would have followed a similar path after an arduous shift, perhaps in an air raid, or hurrying to get home in advance of the curfew, picking her way carefully through the rubble in the blackout. Maybe she had a *Whizz-Bangs'* rehearsal to go to or a date with Adrian. No doubt they walked this path many times together, with ruins all around, to them unseen. It felt very real.

The gardens' exit is opposite the war memorial, and next to one devoted to the Royal Malta Artillery, so much admired by King George VI. An extract from the letter he sent to General Dobbie in April 1942, assuming the Colonelcy-in-Chief of the regiment, is now engraved on the memorial. Vilhena Terrace is on the left and the apartment blocks facing me must be Floriana's Vincenti Buildings. I couldn't help wondering about the twists and turns that brought Christina to a siege and a life she never could have imagined, to a love she barely had, and couldn't live without nor truly hold. It was the war, the bloody war.

Vilhena Terrace faces Valletta and the apartment blocks were indeed those I had seen from Grand Harbour. Christina's flat from autumn 1940 was on the top floor of one; she said there were eighty-eight steps to climb from the entrance. From her description, her balcony must have looked, at least partially, toward the former George V Gardens, facing directly across Grand Harbour toward the Three Cities. Adrian spent much of his off-duty time there. She was forced to leave in 1942 because of bomb damage, but returned immediately her flat became habitable. She lived there for over forty years until she died.

Vilhena Terrace and *Pietro Floriani* Street are parallel streets running at right angles from the former *Strada Sant' Anna* toward Grand Harbour. The large apartment blocks on both streets form squares with entrance doors on each of the four sides, but there is nothing to identify any of them as Vincenti Buildings. This area was badly damaged and much rebuilding had taken place. In *Pietro Floriani* Street I asked an elderly Maltese gentleman if he knew of Vincenti Buildings. He pointed to both of the blocks facing me. The opposite side of them was on Vilhena Terrace, also the wartime location of the ERA Club, the scene of many a dance, with its very own air raid shelter. The gentleman then asked who I was looking for and I said an English lady who lived there after the war until she died over twenty-five years earlier. 'What was her name?' he asked.

'Ratcliffe,' I replied. The name meant nothing to him. I then said: 'Christina.'

'Oh, yes, Christina,' he said. 'I often saw her on this street. She lived up there,' he said, pointing to a top floor corner balcony.

I was dumbfounded. So this was where Christina lived and where she died all those years ago. I hadn't even needed to find her address. The first Maltese man of whom I had enquired actually knew Christina by sight.

'It is the flat with the darker coloured balcony,' he said.

He indicated a balcony on a street connecting *Pietro Floriani* Street to Vilhena Terrace. The entrance was round the corner. She always opted for top-floor apartments despite the many steps. Of course she was young and fit in those days and the roofs commanded the views she loved. They were also great places to rehearse in the open air. They were cheaper too of course. It is understandable why she would have wished to move back here as it was the first home she shared with Adrian. But the stairs must have become increasingly difficult as she grew older. They must have been a terrible struggle during her last few years.

The Maltese gentleman went on to say the enclosed wooden balconies, so typical of Maltese homes, were replaced after Christina's death. When access was gained to her apartment, there were lots of tins of cat food, he said. Christina was obviously in the habit of feeding the strays always around the streets or perhaps in the gardens across from her front door. Maybe she felt an affinity with their lonely lives. I found myself visualising a desperately sad situation. In a touch of irony, an apartment in the building immediately next to Christina's was now the home of the Italian Ambassador, representing the very country whose action caused Christina to be stranded in the first place.

As I made my way back to the Phoenicia, I reflected on a remarkable coincidence: the very first person I had spoken to in Malta about Christina remembered her from twenty-five years earlier. I was already aware that, in her last years, Christina suffered from terrible loneliness and became withdrawn. Just as she considered doing on the evening of Italy's surrender when she found herself alone, perhaps the only thing to do was to go and get sloshed. Had that been her solace, her only comfort in those final years? Was that how she tried to ease the pain in her heart, the pain of the loss she had always felt intensely, perhaps made worse in her last years because of uncertainty over whether her Warby had truly felt the same as she?

For over forty-four years she lived with no closure. Perhaps she then faced uncertainty. And then she died. It was difficult to correlate the picture of Christina in the 1940s, a vivacious, outgoing, intelligent girl who took such pride in her appearance, with the image emerging of a desperately sad and unhappy recluse. Hopefully, her spirit was now in a happier place.

The following day I drove to Ta' Qali. Only the old Nissen huts seemed to point to the airfield's wartime past until I found what I was looking for in a quiet corner: the Malta Aviation Museum, set up and maintained by dedicated Maltese enthusiasts. As if to demonstrate the unbreakable link which tied two peoples together at a critical part of their histories, the majority of exhibits are about the RAF and the

Fleet Air Arm. There is a display about Adrian which includes a photograph of his decorations and pieces of wreckage of the aircraft in which he was found. Elsewhere there are examples of aircraft that operated from Malta, including the Swordfish of Taranto fame. In a new hangar, built following an appeal for donations I heard in far-away Ramstein, is a Spitfire, and also a Hurricane recovered from the seabed near the Blue Grotto after fifty-four years underwater.

On leaving the museum, I recognised a Maltese gentleman coming in, although we had never met. I was slightly shocked. If I was right, this was another remarkable coincidence. He looked embarrassed, aware I was staring as he approached. 'Mr Galea?' I asked.

'Yes.' He said.

'Frederick?'

He again said yes, although he was clearly taken aback by the unexpected approach from a complete stranger. I recognised Frederick from his photograph on the cover of his books. Our conversation soon turned to Christina and I queried her BEM medal ribbon. Frederick said when she donated it only a few threads remained. He recovered what he could, matching it locally so the medal could be displayed mounted on a single ribbon. I later found out more about Frederick and his wife Valerie's involvement in Christina's re-burial in 1993. On their regular visits to *Santa Maria Addolorata* cemetery to visit family graves, they always walk further to pay their respects to Christina and were often pleasantly surprised to find flowers on her grave. She hadn't been completely forgotten.

As I left the museum, I again reflected on the remarkable coincidence of meeting the man who knew more about Christina than anyone. Without his work in publishing her story, it is unlikely I would ever have begun my quest. Frederick also has a vast knowledge of the air battle of Malta, through detailed research and writing. Still, I was very much saddened by what he told me: it seemed as if Christina's life ended very badly after years of loneliness. I began to question whether my quest was likely to uncover anything positive, but I endeavoured to try and find out more.

It is only a short drive from Ta' Qali up the steep incline to Rabat and the ancient capital Mdina. A clockwise route then brought us to the courtyard of the Xara Palace. This was the Officers' Mess for RAF Ta' Qali and it was from the roof that many wartime officers, including Tedder, watched Luftwaffe aircraft strafing and bombing the airfield below. A ricochet badly wounded one Spitfire pilot as he ran up the stairs to get a better view. For many of those involved, this was their final home. For sheer drama, nothing can beat the views from the terrace of the hotel's restaurant or from the battlemented walls at the northern end of the citadel. These vantage points take in much to the north and east. Little wonder early conquerors chose this spot for their capital with so much of the island laid out in front of them. The view also emphasised just how exposed were Malta's airfields.

I was familiar with the route to Luqa forty years earlier. Back then they were the same roads the *Whizz-Bangs* old bus often followed, but much had changed with villages merging one into another. Christina would have driven past the Malta Sports Club at Marsa many times in her old soft-top Austin Seven on her way to Luqa. It is easy to imagine her with shoulder-length blonde hair, probably beneath her characteristic straw hat. She may have laughed in the open-topped car as she passed the racecourse where she had hung on to a horse's neck for dear life. As the road climbs the hill to Luqa, on the left is the former Poor House where Jack Vowles was accommodated as a young airman and where he lost one of his nine lives.

I was saddened when we got to what had been RAF Luqa. The sprawling industrial estate seemed haphazard and uncontrolled. It looked nothing like the pristine RAF station I remembered. Even the guardroom, where Jack bumped into Willie Williams, was gone. On the main administrative site, I couldn't identify a single building from the 1970s, yet incongruously there were some recognisable wartime Nissen huts. Some were still in use, yet others were relics of war, untouched for decades. It was as if all traces of the post-war RAF had been deliberately rubbed-out. Only when I drove toward the airfield were the hangars recognisable, but access was controlled and we could not get near them. We left the main site behind and stopped on the road opposite the former Officers' Mess. That at least was how we remembered it, with the main building separated from the accommodation blocks by a car park and the 'bull-ring', the scene of many RAF social functions. But these buildings were post-war, built on the ruins of what had gone before. There was nothing I saw at Luqa that touched my tale.

Later I visited Upper Barracca Gardens to look down at Grand Harbour. Next to the gardens is the Saluting Battery, which still resonates twice daily at midday and at 4.00 pm. The fountains and flowers frame magnificent views of the harbour. Looking south-west, the ground slopes down toward Floriana and I could easily make out what I now knew was Christina's top-floor apartment with the dark green, enclosed balcony. In fact the apartment is visible from almost anywhere on the city walls. It reminded me of the painting of *The Laughing Cavalier*, whose eyes are said to follow the viewer from every angle. I was beginning to think that about Christina: everywhere I went there seemed to be something to remind me, something to draw me back to her story. Did she want it told? I followed again the route she would have used from Lascaris back to her Floriana home. Despite the daylight, the traffic and the tourists, it felt real.

Wherever we went we seemed to stumble across links that drew me back to my quest. When the *Whizz-Bangs* concert party was formed, a rehearsal room was needed. By then Strait Street, or 'The Gut', famous and popular amongst British servicemen for decades, was declared 'off limits', but many still found their way there. It is now home to a branch of Marks and Spencer. As we exited the store, we faced an old theatre with a public convenience on its left. Surely not, I thought, not after seventy-four years? I walked to the corner and there, high up on the wall next to the public convenience sign, was a faded notice, 'The Old Vic – Cabaret every evening'. This was the very place where the *Whizz-Bangs* had their origin. Was there no escape from Christina's story? We then turned left, walking down Old Theatre Street. Soon we came to the Manoel Theatre where Christina played *Cinderella* in the *Whizz-Bangs'* Christmas pantomime in 1940. Belying the dusty, faded exterior, the interior has been tastefully restored and is quite magnificent. It was easy to imagine the concert party playing to a packed house full of laughter.

The walls of the Phoenicia's Club Bar are adorned with black and white photographs from the 1930s and 1940s. One evening, I sat near the French doors that open onto the balcony overlooking the gardens with Marsamxett Harbour beyond. As I looked up, on the wall opposite was a photograph of Christina which I immediately recognised. I walked across to look more closely. It was taken in October 1942 and shows her sitting in bed in her Valletta apartment, already wearing make-up, reading the *Times of Malta*. Could I not get away from this lady?

Turning round, I got another shock. There was yet another photograph of Christina immediately above my chair. It showed her sitting on the Valletta-Sliema ferry holding a straw hat and wearing gold bangles on her right forearm. Underneath, it is signed, 'Christina, Fighter Control, RAF'. Was there no escape from her, dead for over twenty-five years? Were these simply coincidences or was a hidden hand guiding me, pushing me toward finding Christina? I had certainly felt her presence many times, a haunting ageless presence, but not haunting in any negative way.

Later I called at the Malta Memorial, which is directly opposite the Phoenicia. It commemorates those Commonwealth airmen who have no known grave, lost flying from bases in the Mediterranean theatre in the Second World War. On top of the tall marble column is a magnificent gilded eagle, and on the column's circular base are bronze panels showing the names of 2,301 airmen. It includes many names I recognised, including Bob Gridley, Adrian's navigator on his flight from Thorney Island to Malta on 6 September 1940, and tragically lost with John Dowland in January 1942. The central panel reads:

OVER THESE AND NEIGHBOURING
LANDS AND SEAS THE AIRMEN
WHOSE NAMES ARE RECORDED HERE
FELL IN RAID OR SORTIE
AND HAVE NO KNOWN GRAVE
MALTA GIBRALTAR
MEDITERRANEAN ADRIATIC

TUNISIA SICILY ITALY
YUGOSLAVIA AUSTRIA

PROPOSITI INSULA TENAX
TENACES VIROS COMMEMORAT

The Latin translates to, 'an island resolute of purpose remembers resolute men'.

I was determined to revisit Floriana and find out as much as I could about the district and the home in which Christina spent most of her life. I also had made contact with Ingrid Scerri, a Maltese lady now living in Christina's former home; in fact Ingrid was the very next occupant after Christina and she very kindly agreed to allow me access to the apartment block.

With some time to spare, I first walked toward *Porte des Bombes*. These days Floriana is a town of faded Baroque beauty, dominated by the church of St Publius, the patron saint of Floriana and the Roman governor of Malta when St Paul was shipwrecked. I asked a local man if he knew of the Green Shutters. He confirmed it existed and pointed me in the right direction. It was on the corner of *Triq San Tumas* (St Thomas Street) and *Triq San Franġisk* (St Francis Street), but was closed, with tables and chairs stacked inside ready to be placed on the pavement. It was only a few hundred yards from Vilhena Terrace.

When Christina first came to Malta in 1937, and when she returned in 1940, she shared a large house in Floriana. On the evening of 10 June, after Mussolini had declared war on Britain and France, Christina described how she walked home on that beautiful warm evening along *Strada Capuccini* at the top of which a huge wooden cross mounted on a ten-foot plinth stood silhouetted against the sky. I walked the same route. The plinth is still there, but the wooden cross has now been replaced by another marking the entrance road to the Capuchin Monastery. After the first bombing raid, Christina looked from her balcony toward St Francis Barracks and talked to a soldier there. I knew the barracks from the 1970s as the NAAFI and a medical centre. The plaza overlooking the old barracks is called *Pietro Paulo Floriani* and one house there was Christina's home in those early days, although it was impossible to determine which. This is where she sat on a deckchair on her balcony with Cecil and Babs Roche, watching as the sun disappeared behind the high ground around Mdina.

I headed back to the Green Shutters. It is a pleasant corner café, typical of many throughout the towns and villages of Malta. I could well imagine old men sitting in similar bars some years earlier talking about Miss Christina and a dashing RAF pilot, symbols of Maltese resistance and of suffering. But the Green Shutters' new owner knew nothing of a lady called Christina.

On the other side of the road was the location of the former Queen's Store, owned by the Mallia family who looked after Christina and the Roches when they found themselves without food in the opening days of the war. I then walked slowly down St Francis Street, before turning right into *Pietro Floriani* Street, then left into the short cross-street leading to Vilhena Terrace. Christina would have done the same. She would of course have been on her own, walking in the dark to an empty apartment and a lonely life with only the stray cats in the gardens over the road for company, and memories of a short, intense period in her life and her lost love. I didn't feel alone; I felt I was walking in the footsteps of her ghost.

Christina said there were eighty-eight steps up to her top-floor apartment. There are two more immediately off the street. They were quite a climb, perhaps easy for a young fit dancer, but I found them a real challenge. There are another two flights of steps up from her apartment to the roof, but the views were worth the climb and exactly as she described in the autumn of 1940. The Phoenicia Hotel could just be glimpsed to the left and then an amazing panorama took in Valletta and its approaches, with the imposing *Auberge de Castille* in the centre. The Barracca Lift, now in use once more, and the Upper Barracca Gardens are clearly visible atop Lascaris Bastion. And to the right are magnificent views of Grand Harbour and the Three Cities, now recovered from the devastation wreaked upon them in 1941 and 1942. It was a privilege to take in the views Christina loved.

Ingrid had clear memories of the quiet English lady who lived just around the corner from where she grew up and she knew something of the English officer, the 'English colonel' she called him, with whom Christina was involved. Ingrid said Christina invariably wore a straw hat and smiled at everyone. She would often see her with her Scottie dog. As I slowly made my way down those many stairs, down which Christina had often run helter-skelter, I needed to find my quiet, ever-smiling ghost and say hello in person.

It was only a short drive to Paola and the cemetery of *Santa Maria Addolorata*. The high spire of the church is visible from some distance. The large car park was almost empty with cars outnumbered by flower sellers' vans and trailers. The cemetery is large, built in a fan-shape with the point beginning at the car park and the fan opens up across the steep hill toward the church. There are thousands of graves in the stony ground. Many have ornate headstones, some have photographs. In the absence of soil, and for the impossibility of keeping grass alive through Malta's long hot summer, the graves are covered with stone or concrete slabs. There are also many shared plots; originally Christina rested in one of those.

Thinking it would be straightforward to find the grave, I walked up the left-hand side, East Division, trying to locate the letters identifying each section. I was looking for MA-D. There are some single letters on the kerbstones and on adjacent walls, but many are missing or not visible from the footpath. Toward the church I found a row designated M. I walked up and down looking at each grave, but to no avail. Many rows are confusing and after about forty-five minutes of fruitless searching, I was hot and tired and getting nowhere. I then skirted the church to the left to find it is only halfway up the cemetery, not at the top as I first thought. The cemetery continued far beyond, less steeply, but widening left and right. This was proving difficult and a much longer task than I anticipated. I also could find no indication of rows or sections beginning with double letters. I headed back to the office, which is where I should have called in the first place. There I met a young man called Eman Bonnici. I said I was trying to locate the grave of an English lady who died over twenty-five years earlier.

'Ratcliffe?' he asked.

I was again lost for words, finding someone who instantly thought of Christina. Eman was the cemetery's archivist and knew much of Christina and Adrian's story. He was very helpful. Apparently a number of visitors sought out Christina's grave which is at the very top of the hill in the far left corner near the boundary.

I bought some red silk roses which I hoped would last through the coming Maltese winter and into the following summer. I also wrote a message on a small card, but not from me. I figured not many people who called to pay their respects would also have had the opportunity as I had done to visit the grave of her lost love in Bavaria. I climbed the slope once more, passing the church heading for the far left corner of the graveyard. Once there, it wasn't difficult to find what I was looking for, almost at the highest point in the cemetery and within a few yards of the boundary. The marble headstone had withstood the rigours of the twenty-one years well. It includes a lovely enamelled photograph of Christina looking directly at the camera. It could have been taken yesterday.

MARY CHRISTINA RATCLIFFE
BEM
'CHRISTINA OF GEORGE
CROSS ISLAND'
1914–1988
RIP

In front of the headstone were some faded flowers; she was remembered. I spent a few minutes paying my respects. A few words from Christina Rossetti's *Remember* came to mind:

> 'Better by far you should forget and smile
> Than that you should remember and be sad.'

I couldn't help wondering about her later life and the circumstances to which she was reduced as she grew older. Although she had a few friends, she became more and more of a recluse, and of course decades went by without her ever knowing what had befallen the love of her life. After she died, Adrian lay undiscovered in a field for another fifteen years.

Christina was a very worldly-wise lady when she arrived back in Malta in 1940. She was then twenty-six and four years older than Adrian. I am sure she, like many others in those years, lived for the moment, not knowing what the future held. She was only thirty-one when the war ended and by then she must have realised Adrian wasn't coming back. Yet she was still the same intelligent, well-educated, outgoing and confident lady she had always been, well capable of handling herself and making her own choices and decisions. She chose to remain in Malta which meant so much to her. Her life with Warby was terribly short, totalling two years, accounting for three separate periods he spent on the island. By saying nothing in public about their relationship, and by avoiding journalists who wished to write about her story, Christina chose to protect Adrian's name and reputation on the island on which he was revered. I wondered if she found out in the 1980s about Adrian's alleged relationships. How would this have impacted on her and her memory of the man to whom she was devoted? Did it contribute to her death soon afterwards? Regardless, Christina Ratcliffe was a very genuine hero, and she did not deserve so many lonely years and a tragic death. She should be well-remembered on the island whose suffering she shared and to whose victory she contributed.

I rearranged the flowers before I left her grave on the hillside in the sun. Christina now rests in a place of honour thanks largely to Frederick and Valerie Galea. In the background, to the right of Christina's headstone, is the beautiful church of *Santa Maria Addolorata* with its unusual spire which looks almost English. I slowly walked down the long hill through an empty cemetery in the sunlight, leaving behind a bunch of silk roses and a note sent on behalf of someone far away. I thanked Eman and the flower seller; perhaps they thought me rather odd. Maybe I was, allowing myself to get caught up in an old story, the main players in which had left the stage a long time ago.

In her August 1982 article, Christina hinted more than ever before at the true nature of her relationship with Adrian. That was the year she met Tony Spooner and opened up about her past life in a way she had never done before. Did Adrian's and her story come out in the way she hoped? Or was the time now right to try and offer another perspective and the balance only the passage of time can bring? Christina faithfully guarded the reputation of the man she loved and lost, and continued to do so long after he was presumed dead. She was an honourable lady and, for her work in the long years of the air battle of Malta, she was very much a hero too.

Christina described herself as a 'back-room girl', but she was very much more than that. Although she never, 'hit the headlines as a prima ballerina',[2] or enthralled,

---

2. *Carve Malta on my heart and other wartime stories*, by Frederick Galea, page 6.

'an audience at Covent Garden or even the Manchester Opera House',[3] she danced beneath the spotlights in some of Europe's capitals, lights soon dimmed as Europe marched blindly toward the catastrophe of another war. She saw some of the latter days of French Colonial Africa and found herself on the steps of Valletta's Customs House. Arguably her many dozens of performances with the *Whizz-Bangs* were worth far more to her audiences than any in Covent Garden, while their shows outran many staged in the West End. Christina had a string of adventures, dancing across Europe and North Africa and down to Dakar, waltzing 'in and out of the Spanish Civil War and, finally, to take a last curtain call in the battle and siege of Malta. All of which was not bad going on a pair of wooden legs.'[4]

Yet Christina did hit the headlines, although not in the manner she could ever have imagined. As 'Christina of George Cross Island', Mary Christina Ratcliffe, from Dukinfield in Cheshire, was a symbol of heroic resistance and resilience. She too should be remembered, and not just in Malta.

I had found Christina.

---

3. *Ibid.*
4. *Ibid.*

The Last Flight

'He laughed at death,
Pursued him with a kiss
Climbed to the skies
Pursued him to a star
But death, who never had
Been wooed like this
Remained aloof, afar.

With spurt and gleam and
Brightness like the sun's
He circled death as with a
Wheel of flame
But death, capricious,
Sought those other ones
Who had not called his name.

He mocked at death
Pursued him into hell
Mocked him afresh, then
Crashed to burning space
But death, grown gentle
Caught him as he fell
Nor let him see his face.'

The Airman – author unknown[1]

12 April 1944

He woke up early as usual these days. His pelvis still gave him discomfort which often disturbed him. But he could live with it. It was still dark outside and he dressed quickly. There was much to do before people stirred. There was rarely much

---

1. Quoted in *Wings of War*, by Laddie Lucas, pages 248–9.

activity at Mount Farm overnight. They hadn't started doing night photography using photoflash flares yet, but would soon, 69 Squadron was coming back to do just that. Although England didn't suit him, it meant he could keep his ear close to the ground and find out what was going on. So far, things were working out just fine, far better than he ever imagined, and today was the final stage of the plan he conceived in outline in those tedious hours in a hospital bed in Maison Carée.

He glanced out of the Nissen hut window; it was cold overnight, but at least the Americans heated their huts rather better than the RAF. It looked like being a clear, spring day. He told Carl he would go to the Met Office to get the 'gen' before meeting in the ops room later to brief, but there wouldn't be much to say; it was all covered yesterday. The current intelligence focus was on Luftwaffe airfields near Munich. A 'milk-run' was how Carl described it. Elliot called it a shuttle run, but there was more to it than that. Adrian needed to be on his own at the Met Office as he wanted a little more info than Carl expected. George Lawson knew where he was going but didn't know Adrian wasn't planning on coming back. That's why Adrian needed a P-38 despite George's objections.

It was good to see Elliot last night in the Officers' Mess at RAF Benson. He was a good friend. Without him he would not be flying a P-38 today; his plan wouldn't have worked, not entirely anyway. If Elliot had guessed Adrian's intentions he had said nothing. John Spires, one of Adrian's Maryland navigators in Malta, was also at the same party at Benson, which finished up with the adjutant being rolled in a carpet and stood in a corner. Adrian said goodnight early.

He was soon ready and most of his gear went into a small kit bag, with just a few bits and pieces left in his room. With his uniform beneath American coveralls, no one would suspect he was not coming back until he was long gone.

His allocated aircraft was 42-67325, the last three numbers coincidental with 7th PRG's parent wing, the 325th. Maybe that was a good sign. He thought the American system of numbering their aircraft a bit too clinical. At least the RAF included a couple of letters. He thought back to his favourite Maryland – AR 733; Terry Channon's wheels-up landing at Luqa marked the end for her, not even Jack could fix her again. Why were aircraft always talked about as female? He liked the Maryland, and the faster Beaufighter, but he was always conscious of his crew, his responsibility. With the Spitfire and the P-38 he only had himself to look after. He hoped Frank and Paddy would see out the war. They were the ones who really saved him as a pilot. Was it only three years ago? As for him, he would see Malta again, and Chris. He didn't believe in fate, you needed to make your own luck in this game. He'd made quite a bit in the past. He just needed a little more today.

The ever security conscious American guards stopped him as he approached the aircraft. They recognised him soon enough – Wing Commander War*bur*ton. The trans-Atlantic pronunciation of his surname always made him smile. On this occasion Adrian was grateful for the vagaries of RAF ranks. Most Americans thought him more senior than he was. RAF squadrons formed wings which were placed into groups. Within the RAF, the rank of wing commander, commanding two or three squadrons, fitted perfectly within the organisation. Within the US system, things were the other way round, squadrons placed into groups which formed part of a wing. Many Americans confused Adrian's RAF rank with an appointment as commanding a group. This often worked in his favour, as it did this morning. With smart salutes from the guards, he was soon on his way to his aircraft. He enjoyed working with the Americans. With them there was no pretentiousness. He got on well with the Canadians and South Africans too; they had the same relaxed attitude on the ground, but were total professionals in the air. He did play up to his image as a 'true Brit' though.

As he approached the earth revetments he could see her in the coming dawn. The P-38 was such a sleek machine and he could just make out the pale blue colour of the recce variant, the P-38F5b. The Lightning's twin-tailed design was unique. *Der Gabelschwanz Teufel* – the Fork-Tailed Devil – was certainly an impressive aircraft, although it was outperformed by the latest marks of PR Spitfires which he actually preferred. But he needed a P-38 for this trip, not because of its range, which was pretty similar, but for one essential reason: he could fit his kit bag into a P-38; in a Spitfire he was as snug as a bug in a rug, only carrying what he was wearing. If he had taken Elliot or George fully into his confidence, it might place them in a difficult position if things didn't work out. He accepted the possibility things might go wrong. Elliot would understand; he seemed to know what drove Adrian.

With his bag safely stowed, Adrian went to the Met Office. The duty forecaster – the met man as they called him – would have been up for hours, poring over the charts and observations. Adrian hoped he would handle Adrian's slightly 'off the cuff' questions. He listened carefully. With high pressure over southern Germany it was going to be a good day for flying once the sun was up. Winds were light and there was about five-tenths cloud at 2,500 feet. The early morning stratus would soon burn off and shouldn't affect them at the height they were planning to fly. The only cloud expected was some altostratus and cirrus above 18,000 feet. That might affect the bomber boys, but where Adrian and Carl were going only about half-cover was forecast, clear enough for photography but only in the gaps. The high-level winds were westerly. The high cloud might affect their photography. Even though you could sometimes see through thin wispy cirrus, it didn't make for good images. They would have to wait and see. The cirrus cloud also meant contrails were much more likely, forming at about 28,000 feet. That was important. If their aircraft formed contrails, the Germans wouldn't need radar. As usual the forecaster asked if Adrian had questions.

'Will my old base on Malta be enjoying a beautiful spring day?' Adrian asked. The met man was not fazed by Adrian's question; he was well prepared. He said there was an upper trough over the Adriatic which would result in some early morning cumulonimbus clouds down that way.

'So my old wing at San Severo might be getting wet,' said Adrian with a laugh. The forecaster laughed too, saying by the time they got out of bed, they would enjoy a nice day with their vino. They both laughed. There was nothing else Adrian needed to know. As he left he could already see some quite extensive high altocumulus and cirrus overhead.

Back at the 7th PRG's HQ in the farmhouse, the briefing with Carl was pleasingly short. Adrian would take-off after Carl and they would climb together to the north-east before turning south for Manston in Kent to meet with eight P-51 Mustangs acting as escort for most of the outbound part of the flight.

John Spires was there as he walked to his aircraft. 'I'll see you,' said Adrian with a wave. Although it might be a while, Adrian thought. Then he was in the hands of two American staff sergeants who strapped him in and 'saw him off' from the revetment.

Take-off went as planned and in the climb they encountered thick haze which was taking its time to burn off. There was also some altostratus about at 14,000 feet and cirrus high above. The moment they hit 28,000 feet, contrails began to form behind them, so it was just as well their routing was not direct to the Channel. No doubt the Germans would identify them soon enough on radar, but there was no need to make their job easier. The Luftwaffe might not take a great deal of interest; they had far bigger fish to fry these days in the shape of groups of Flying Fortresses and Liberators already forming up over East Anglia. Adrian knew the ball-bearing plant at Schweinfurt, north of Munich, was due to be hit today, so hopefully, enemy attention would be firmly focused on the bomber stream. Soon they were joined by two P-51s. Where were the others, he wondered? There was no R/T, no need for any chit-chat as they all knew their game.

The first couple of hours of these high-level trips were always quiet. How had someone once described their work? Hours of intense boredom interspersed with a few seconds of sheer terror. Thankfully, he had been spared the terror, although his mind had been concentrated once or twice. He had had a lot of time to think about his future and he had needed patience, not a virtue he was noted for. He was certain if he could present himself at San Severo, fully fit, and ready to go, Hugh Pughe would look no further for a new boss for 336 Wing.

He thought about Chris, ever-faithful, ever-loving Chris. He had to sort out things with Betty and get a divorce. He had been so stupid back then. He knew Betty would agree to divorce; why hadn't he sorted that out long ago? Now others looked up to him. They wouldn't when they realised he had apparently abandoned his wife, although they didn't know the circumstances. Lots of blokes had received 'Dear John' letters; lots of marriages had fallen apart under the strain of separation.

It was the war, the bloody war, many said. Adrian's situation was different, but he had still dropped a few hints here and there that the same thing had happened to him, so maybe people wouldn't think the worse of him when he got a divorce. But he felt guilty about hinting he was a totally innocent party. It had not been an honourable thing to do and he would say no more about his marriage to anyone. He had simply made one huge mistake when he was young. Now he had to face the consequences and that was that. He had to sort it out, for Chris.

What had happened to their rear guard? There was now no sign of the P-51s. Had they been unable to keep up in the long turns to stay clear of the Ruhr? Still, they were a bonus, very much an experiment on recce missions. They would need closer liaison before they became truly effective. And anyway, this trip was a milk-run. Soon they were approaching their split point. It was clear enough at 35,000 feet, but the cirrus below was quite extensive. Certainly in this area it was not good enough for decent photography. But there was no way he intended to pitch up at San Severo without the goods. After all, he had a reputation.

He gave Carl a wave and they went their separate ways, Adrian south toward Munich, whereas Carl had one target not far from their split point. Carl's were then east of Munich. The weather – the haze – looked troublesome for Adrian, but it looked a lot better where Carl would end up. He felt bad about not telling Carl what was going on but he had no choice. They had agreed on a rendezvous time plus one minute to avoid lingering over enemy territory. He had emphasised to Carl not to hang about. He could do no more.

As Adrian continued south, he could see the haze and cloud below him toward Munich precluded decent photography. It looked no better to the west. He couldn't afford to waste time, he needed to get the photos then head south to see his boys. He had no choice, he had to descend. The conditions up here were just rubbish. As he passed 30,000 feet, contrails began to form behind his aircraft, but there was nothing he could do other than get down below the minimum height at which they would form as fast as possible. It was all about temperature. The met man had said 28,000 feet was the minimum trail level and so it was. But even as he left his contrails behind to slowly dissipate, Adrian was still above hazy cirrus. He kept descending. There was probably activity on the ground now, maybe alarms, alerts to the guns; perhaps people pointing at the contrail left high above. But they might not bother about a single aircraft when there would have been so much going on further north. He got down to just below 17,000 feet. Conditions were now ideal for photos.

His first target was Fürstenfeldbruck on the western outskirts of Munich. A run from east or west would have meant overflying the city, so he had chosen a simple run from the north; one run would do it with his vertical cameras seeing all. He would then head west for the other targets. Almost on cue, Adrian spotted some of those dirty white and grey smudges just off to the left; someone was awake down there. He eased right a little. At this distance they looked like pretty clusters of mini-cumulus clouds. But he knew they weren't harmless up close.

It would take a very lucky shot to get him. This wouldn't take long. OK, camera on, keep the wings level, a gentle tweak on the rudders to adjust his tracking, but he must keep the wings level for decent photos. Just a few seconds more. Done; camera off, hard turn right. Get the hell away from Munich, some of those mini-cumulus clouds were getting damnably close.

All the other targets – Lechfeld, Kaufering, and a few others around Landsberg – were all close together and a couple of straight runs would cover them all. He couldn't climb because of the cloud above, but all was quiet now, no flak. First run from the south, camera on, hold her steady, camera off, extend to the north, but turn well short of Augsburg. One done; one more should do it.

'What's that down there?' Adrian said to himself. Even from this height something stood out. They looked like black parallel stripes on the concrete of Lechfeld's runway. How odd. Could that be what the intelligence boys were interested in? Steady, he had to hold the aircraft nice and level for a few seconds longer to get good images with the required overlap. OK, done, camera off.

Maybe he could present intelligence with a little more than they expected; he was known for that. Adrian swung to the west and descended at high speed before turning east. One fast run from west to east should do it. With 'Warby's luck' they wouldn't see him coming.

Thwack! The P-38 lurched, yawing markedly to the left. Even as he instinctively pushed his right foot forward, he knew his aircraft was hurt, badly. He was in trouble. Thwack again! Another hit. He felt a severe impact to his right arm and the canopy shattered. This time he knew it wasn't just his aircraft that was hurt.

He fought to keep the aircraft on an even keel but he couldn't keep the left wing up; the engine on that side must have taken most of the first impact from the sharp, penetrating shrapnel. Some had also reached the cockpit, and him. He closed the throttle on the left engine instantly as he went through the drills, but it was harder than normal, he was slower. The pressure on his right leg was enormous as he pushed hard against the rudder pedal, trying to hold the asymmetric load. He glanced at the engine instruments. The oil pressure on the left engine had dropped like a stone. He looked at the engine; she was done for. He could see jagged holes on the cowling. The engine began to smoke – it was on fire.

'Fly the aircraft first Adrian,' he said to himself, 'try and keep the nose up, keep heading east away from those bloody guns, shut the engine down, feather the prop, see what performance you can get out of your *Gabelschwanz Teufel*'. It might be a devil but it was a badly wounded devil. And so was Adrian. He still couldn't hold the left wing up, so he closed the throttle on the right-hand engine too. That was a little better, but he was still going down very fast. Not that he had much choice. The smoke lessened immediately he cut the fuel to the damaged engine, but he knew his aircraft was done for. He tried to increase power on the good engine to stay level, but the yaw to the left quickly became too much. He ran out of rudder control and the aircraft lurched again to the left. 'That shouldn't be happening,' he thought. 'What else is wrong?'

As he looked again at the wreck of his left engine he could see the problem. The feathering mechanism must have been damaged, and now the blades of the propeller were stationary, with the flat part of the blades meeting the airflow and creating enormous drag. Where was Jack when he needed him? If anyone could, young Jack would have been able to feather the propeller. He smiled at the thought. But this time he was on his own. There were bits of metal sticking out into the airflow of his once slick machine, increasing the drag on that side. He had to put her down. There was no way he was going to step over the side; he hadn't so far in this bloody war and he wasn't going to now. He could hack it.

He kept the nose down and the speed high to maintain lateral stability. He was doing over 200 knots, not a good speed for a belly landing, much too high. But when he tried to raise the nose to slow down, the rudder load increased enormously and he couldn't hold it. What was wrong with his right leg?

'Going down,' Adrian said out loud. He was already down to 3,000 feet and still coming down fast. There was a village slightly off to the left, but open fields ahead and to the right. He could put her down there. Now he was down to 2,000 feet, falling at a hell of a rate. The wispy black smoke coming from the left engine was thickening now, she was burning again. Keep going, maybe this speed might stop the fire from taking hold. Now at 1,000 feet, every man and his dog would be able to see him, and anyone with a gun would be pointing it in his direction. He was going to make it. Just a few seconds more. If he could just slow down a fraction a belly landing should be easy enough in a Lightning; he'd landed wheels-up before. It was looking good; but there was more smoke now and flames too, but he was nearly there; just a few hundred feet to go now, a few more seconds. He gently tried to move the Lightning's large control yoke back toward him, but he felt so weak, he had to use both hands; what was wrong with him, his right leg was shaking on the rudder pedal. He shut down the right-hand engine as well. 'Come on my beauty, come up, come up.'

But the nose didn't come up; it dropped.

Gallantry Awards And Citations

Adrian – Distinguished Flying Cross 1940

Awarded 27 December 1940; gazetted in the *London Gazette*, 11 February 1941.

This officer has carried out numerous long distance reconnaissance flights and has taken part in night [author's note: this was a typing error, it should have read eight] air combats. In October, 1940, he destroyed an aircraft and again, in December, he shot down an enemy bomber in flames. Flying Officer Warburton has at all times displayed a fine sense of devotion to duty.

Adrian – Bar to Distinguished Flying Cross 1941

Awarded 9 August 1941; gazetted in the *London Gazette*, 9 September 1941.

This officer is a most determined and skilful pilot and has carried out 125 operational missions. Flying Officer Warburton has never failed to complete the missions he has undertaken, and in the actions fought, he has destroyed at least three hostile aircraft in combat and another three on the ground.

Adrian – Distinguished Service Order 1942

Gazetted in the *London Gazette*, 20 March 1942.

This officer has carried out many missions each of which has demanded the highest degree of courage and skill: On one occasion whilst carrying out a reconnaissance of Taranto, Flight Lieutenant Warburton made 2 attempts to penetrate the harbour, although as there was much low cloud this entailed flying at a height of 50 feet over an enemy battleship. In spite of the failure of his port engine and repeated attacks from enemy aircraft he completed his mission and made a safe return. On another occasion he obtained photographs of Tripoli in spite of enemy fighter patrols over the harbour. In March 1942 Flight Lieutenant Warburton carried out a reconnaissance of Palermo and obtained photographs revealing the damage caused by our attacks. This officer has never failed to obtain photographs from a very low altitude, regardless of enemy opposition. His work has been most valuable and he has displayed great skill and tenacity.

Adrian – Second Bar to Distinguished Flying Cross 1942

Awarded October 1942; gazetted in the *London Gazette*, 3 November 1942.

Since August 1942, this officer has completed numerous operational photographic sorties, many of them at low altitudes and often in the face of opposition from enemy fighters. His work has been of the utmost value. In October 1942, his gallantry was well illustrated when he directed an enemy destroyer to a dinghy in which were the crew of one of our aircraft, which had been shot down. Although he was fired upon by the destroyer and engaged by Italian aircraft, he remained over the area until he observed the drifting crew were picked up by the destroyer.

Adrian – Bar to Distinguished Service Order 1943

Gazetted in the *London Gazette*, 6 August 1943.

Wing Commander Warburton has commanded No. 683 Photographic Reconnaissance Squadron since its formation on 8th February, 1943 and prior to the formation of this squadron he commanded No. 69 Squadron.

This officer has flown a total of 375 operational sorties involving 1300 hours flying. From Malta he has completed 360 sorties with a total of 1240 hours. During his tour of duty in Malta, he covered all the Italian and Sicilian targets continuously, invariably obtaining 100% cover with his photography.

In recent months, since he commanded No 683 Squadron, he has continued to operate on all the routine sorties required from pilots of the squadron, selecting for himself the sorties which have been considered of a most dangerous nature.

On a recent operation, one camera became unserviceable. In order to ensure that full photographic coverage would be obtained, he covered every target, including Taranto, three times being continuously chased by M.E.109s.

On 15th November, 1942, Wing Commander Warburton was despatched on a photographic reconnaissance of Bizerta. He was attacked by M.E.109s and his aircraft being damaged he force landed at Bone. From there he went to Gibraltar, returning to Malta a few days later in a fighter aircraft. He encountered two J.U. 88s on his return journey which he engaged, destroying one and damaging the other.

On December 5th, this officer carried out a photographic reconnaissance of Naples. In spite of intense flak and enemy fighter opposition he covered the whole of the target area at 4,000 feet.

On May 18th, he took low level obliques of the whole of the Pantellaria coastline from a height of 200 feet. He was fired on continuously by the A.A. coastal batteries but succeeded in obtaining results which proved extremely valuable in the eventual invasion of the island.

Wing Commander Warburton has destroyed a total of nine enemy aircraft when flying armed reconnaissance aircraft and three on the ground.

The importance of the results obtained by this officer in spite of intense enemy opposition and in all weathers cannot be too highly estimated. The success of operations carried out from this Island, the safe arrival and departures of convoys are largely dependent on the accuracy of photographic reconnaissance.

Wing Commander Warburton is to a great extent responsible for this successful reconnaissance. His personal enthusiasm for operations, his courage and devotion to duty have set the highest example to all with whom he has associated.

Adrian – United States Distinguished Flying Cross 1944

Conferred by the President of the United States of America and gazetted in the *London Gazette,* 18 January 1944.

While on a mission to obtain urgently needed photographs of the coast-line of Pantellaria on Jun 3rd, he distinguished himself through his resolute courage and calm efficiency under fire. Flying over the island at two hundred feet, within easy range of every type of anti-aircraft battery and drawing fire of even large coastal guns, Warburton photographed virtually the entire shore line, gaining information of inestimable value to the allied Force which later invaded the island. His proficiency as pilot and photographer, and his selfless devotion to duty reflect great credit upon him and the armed forces of the United Nations.

Christina – British Empire Medal 1943

Awarded in King George VI's Birthday Honours, June 1943.

Miss Christina Ratcliffe has been employed as a plotter in the operations room at Air Headquarters, Malta, since 15 June 1941. She was in charge of her watch and throughout the heavy air attacks on the island, never once failed to report to duty on time. She lived a considerable distance from the headquarters. When raids were in progress there was no transport, but she walked to work regardless of bombs and shrapnel. During one raid her home was destroyed, but she carried on her work with her customary coolness and efficiency. Throughout, her work was of a high standard and her brave and cheerful demeanour were an inspiration to those who served under her.

Bibliography & Sources

Books:

Agius, John, and Galea, Frederick, *Lest We Forget*, (Progress Press, Malta, 1999)
Austin, Douglas, *Churchill and Malta's War 1939–1943*, (Amberley, Stroud, 2010)
Babington Smith, Constance, *Evidence in Camera*, (Penguin, London, 1957)
Barnham, Denis, *Malta Spitfire Pilot*, (Pen & Sword, Barnsley, 2011)
Bradford, Ernle, *Siege Malta 1940–1943*, (Pen & Sword, Barnsley, 2003)
Brookes, Andrew J., *Photo Reconnaissance*, (Ian Allan Ltd, Shepperton, Surrey, 1975)
Cameron, Ian, *Red Duster, White Ensign*, (Futura, 1959)
Caruana, Richard J., *Victory in the Air*, (Modelaid International Publications, 1996)
Coldbeck, Harry, *The Maltese Spitfire*, (Airlife, 1997)
Cull, Brian, and Galea, Frederick
    Gladiators over Malta, (Wise Owl, Malta, 2008)
    Hurricanes over Malta, (Grub Street, London, 2001)
    Marylands over Malta, (Wise Owl, Malta, 2014)
    Spitfires over Malta, (Grub Street, London, 2005)
Dobbie, Sir William, *A Very Present Help*, (Marshal, Morgan & Scott, London, 1944)
Dobbie, Sybil, *Grace under Malta*, (Lindsay Drummond, London, 1944)
Douglas-Hamilton, James, *The Air Battle for Malta*, (Mainstream Publishing, Edinburgh, 1981)
Dowling, Taylor, *Spies in the Skies*, (Abacus, 2011)
Embry, Sir Basil, *Mission Completed*, (Methuen & Co Ltd, London, 1957)
Foster, Ronald, *Focus on Europe*, (Crowood Press, Marlborough, 2004)
Galea, Frederick R.,
    Call-Out, (Frederick R. Galea, Malta, 2002)
    Carve Malta on my heart and other wartime stories, (Frederick R. Galea, Malta, 2004)
    Mines over Malta, Wartime Exploits of Commander Edward D. Wooley, GM & Bar, RNVR,
        (Wise Owl, Malta, 2008)
    Women of Malta, (Wise Owl, Malta, 2006)
Gibbs, Patrick, *Torpedo Leader on Malta*, (Grub Street, London, 2002)
Holland, James, *Fortress Malta*, (Hyperion, 2003)
Johnson, Brian, *The Secret War*, (BBC, London, 1975)
Johnstone, Sandy, *Where No Angels Dwell*, (Cedric Chivers Limited, Bath, 1974)
Lloyd, Sir Hugh, *Briefed to Attack*, (Hodder & Stoughton, London, 1949)
Longyear, Michael, *Malta 1937–1942*, (2006)
Lucas, Laddie,
    Malta: The Thorn in Rommel's Side, (Penguin, London, 1993)
    Wings of War, (Hutchinson & Co, London, 1983)
Mercieca, Simon, *The Knights of St John in Malta*, (Casa Editrice Boncchi, Florence, 2010)
Mizzi, Laurence, *The People's War*, (Progress Press, Valletta, 2002)
Nesbit, Roy Conyers, *Reported Missing*, (Pen & Sword, 2009)
Parkinson, Roger, *The War in the Desert*, (Book Club Associates, 1976)
Richards, Denis, *Royal Air Force 1939–1945 Volume 1, The Fight at Odds*, (HMSO, London,
    1974)

Richards, Denis, and Saunders, Hilary St George, *Royal Air Force 1939–1945 Volume 2, The Fight Avails*, (HMSO, London, 1974)

Schofield, John and Morrisey, Emily, *Strait Street Malta's 'Red-Light District' Revealed*, (Midsea Books Ltd, Valletta, Malta, 2013)

Shores, Christopher and Cull, Brian with Malizia, Nicola,
Malta: The Hurricane Years 1940–41, (Grub Street, London, 1987)
Malta: The Spitfire Year 1942, (Grub Street, London, 1991)

Spooner, Tony,
In Full Flight, (Wingham Press, Kent, 1991)
Supreme Gallantry, (John Murray, London, 1996)
Warburton's War, (Crécy, 1994)

Tedder, Lord, *With Prejudice*, (Cassell, London, 1966)

Terraine, John, *The Right of the Line*, (Hodder and Stoughton, Great Britain, 1985)

Wellum, Geoffrey, *First Light*, (Viking, 2002)

Williamson, David, *The Siege of Malta 1940–1942*, (Pen & Sword, Barnsley, 2007)

Woodhall, Woody, *Soldier, Sailor & Airman Too*, (Grub Street, London, 2008)

Documents, Magazines, Newspapers & Periodicals:

After the Battle No 121, (Battle of Britain International Ltd, 2003):
Adrian Warburton: RAF Photo-Recce Ace, by Robin J. Brooks
Adrian Warburton – The Mystery Solved, by Hermann Laage and Norbert Rödel

Air Power Review, Volume 16, No 1, 2013: Air Power and the British Anti-Shipping Campaign in the Mediterranean, 1940–1944, by Richard Hammond

Canadian Military Journal Volume 15, No.2 (March 2015):
Leadership by Example: What makes a good (or bad) squadron commander? by Bill Carr

History of the Second World War (Purnell, 1967):
Volume 1 No 11, Operation Catapult, Britain Attacks the Vichy Fleet, by Malcolm Saunders
Volume 1 No 13, Italian Fiasco: The Attack on Greece, by Edwin Packer
Volume 1 No 13, Malta Digs In, by Malcolm Saunders
Volume 1 No 16, Naval War in the Mediterranean, by J.C.E. Smith
Volume 2 No 7, Malta under Fire, by Malcolm Saunders
Volume 2 No 11, The Royal Navy's Time of Trial: Mediterranean, March/December 1941, by David Woodward
Volume 3 No 4, Desperate Venture: The Malta Convoys, Mediterranean, January/June 1942, by Captain Donald Macintyre
Volume 3 No 5, George Cross Island: Malta, September 1941/May 1942, by Charles Maclean
Volume 3 No 13, Malta: The Siege is Raised, by David Woodward

Love in Time of War, by Fiona Vella (2014)

Malta Aviation Museum Ta' Qali, by Anthony Spiteri (2005)

RAF Quarterly, Volume 18, No 1 (1978): *Warburton and PR from Malta, 1940–41*, by Earnest Whiteley

The Air Battle of Malta, (HMSO, 1944)

The Star:
One Woman goes to War, by Christina Ratcliffe (14–18 April 1958)
The Unknown Air Ace, by Roy Nash (3–18 March 1958)

The Sunday Times of Malta:
A Day of Rejoicing, by Christina Ratcliffe (15 August 1982)
A Tribute to a Wartime Heroine, by Tony Spooner, DSO, DFC (ex Sqn Ldr RAFVR) (22 January 1989)
Food for Thought, by Christina Ratcliffe (22 December 1974)

The Merry Tenth of May, by Christina Ratcliffe (18 May 1980)
Three Pence Charity, by Christina Ratcliffe (26 October 1975)
The Times (of Malta):
New Resting Place for War Heroine (19 April 1993)

Unpublished Sources:

Fleet Air Arm flying logbook of Cdr G.A.L. Woods, DSO, RN (courtesy of his son, Wg Cdr P. Woods, RAF Ret'd)
Memoirs of Air Cdre Robert Carter Jonas (RAF Museum)
National Archives, Kew, London:
AIR/20/4302 – *Review of Fighter Defences*, by Gp Capt Basil Embry
AIR 20/4877 – Letters associated with *The Air Battle of Malta* pamphlet
AIR 20/7866 – *Luqa Lens* – Copies of RAF Luqa magazine
AIR 23/5556-5575 – No 8 Sector Operations Room Ops B logs 1942 and 1943
AIR 27/278 – 22 Squadron Operational Readiness Book (ORB)
AIR 27/606-611 – 431 Flight/69 Squadron ORB
AIR 27/2209 – 683 Squadron ORB
AIR 41/7 – RAF narrative, *Photographic Reconnaissance Volume II*
PREM 3/266/1 – Replacement of Sir William Dobbie with Lord Gort
RAF flying logbook of Frank Bastard, DFM, RAF (courtesy of his son Keith Bastard)

Interviews/Personal Recollections/Other Sources:

Mark Beswick, Archive Information Officer Met Office, National Meteorological Archive, Exeter, Devon
Lt Col (Ret'd) John S. Blyth USAF, pilot of PR Spitfire 944 at RAF Mount Farm, near Oxford (through his son Scott Blyth), and friend of Adrian Warburton
Eman Bonnici, archivist, *Santa Maria Addolorata* cemetery
Major Joseph Q. Borg, Malta Police Force
Heidi Burton (née Cox), photographer
Tim Calloway, aviation historian and Editor *Aviation Classics*
Lt Gen (Ret'd) William Keir 'Bill' Carr, CMM, DFC, CD, former PR Spitfire pilot 683 Squadron, RAF Luqa, and colleague of Adrian Warburton
Frank Dorber, aviation historian
Peter Elliot, senior researcher, RAF Museum, Hendon, London
Miriam Farrugia, Maltese citizen and friend of Christina Ratcliffe
Frederick R. Galea, historian and author
Valerie Galea (née Darmanin), Maltese citizen
Imperial War Museum
Dr Chris Joy, archivist, Manchester High School for Girls
John Miles, Forecaster, Met Office, RAF Linton-on-Ouse
Sue Raftree, Service Personnel and Veterans' Agency
Martin Ratcliffe, Christina Ratcliffe's nephew
Ingrid Scerri, Maltese citizen
Spitfire 944, a short documentary film produced by Jason R. Savage and directed by William Lorton (2006)
Glyn Strong, Media Aid, Veterans' Agency
Jack Vowles, a former 69 Squadron airman and friend of Adrian Warburton

Index